Journal of the American Revolution

JOURNAL
OF THE
AMERICAN REVOLUTION

Annual Volume 2025

WESTHOLME
Yardley

Westholme Publishing, LLC
904 Edgewood Road
Yardley, Pennsylvania 19067
Visit our Web site at www.westholmepublishing.com

ISBN: 978–1–59416–444-6
Also available as an eBook.

Printed in the United States of America.

CONTENTS

EDITOR'S INTRODUCTION

One of the submission guidelines for *Journal of the American Revolution* is that articles must not comment on current events—especially not politics. Our goal is to tell history as it actually happened, using first-hand accounts, and let readers decide why it matters. But current events often influence the topics our contributors choose, because understanding the origins of the United States Constitution, in the context of the times in which it was created, is often a crucial part of understanding today's government. So it is that during the turbulent American political year of 2024, JAR published articles on Benjamin Franklin's fear of "kingly" government, the trial and conviction of a state governor, John Adams' perspective on the "pillars" that united the colonies into states, and the assertions of founders on the importance of the rule of law. The American Revolution was, after all, a revolution in government.

Fully acknowledging that this revolution in government was brought about by a long and difficult war, the majority of JAR articles focused on battles, campaigns, and, most important of all, people. For those who are famous, we have different perspectives, such as John Warren's reaction to the tragic death of his firebrand brother Joseph Warren, renowned General Nathanael Greene's struggles with physical ailments, John Adams' inclinations towards athletics, the influence of a pastor on poet Phillis Wheatley, and an untried plan to end the war penned by General Henry Clinton.

And stories of names seldom heard: two British soldiers who succumbed to the allure of alcohol; a company of Connecticut soldiers suffering as prisoners of war; soldier-sailors who ably manned whaleboats on Long Island Sound; a young German soldier who moved from army to army; a man's journey from slavery to freedom; the machinations of a Spanish diplomat; and more.

An important mission of JAR is to unravel misconceptions and present accurate stories that are often more interesting than popular but inaccurate retellings. Did Patrick Ferguson really threaten to lay the Carolina backcountry to waste "with fire and sword"? Was the play *Cato* staged at Valley Forge? Who really provided Joseph Warren with secret information about British plans? Did Benedict Arnold act without orders at the Battle of Bemis Heights? These and other questions are investigated and answered with primary sources.

This is just a sample of what awaits in this, JAR's 2025 Annual Volume, containing thirty-five articles selected from some 150 posted on our web site at http://allthingsliberty.com. Enjoy them, and be sure to watch the web for more articles, reviews, podcasts and videos about America's most important history.

Parliament and the American Revolution: The British Perspective

DAVID OTERSEN

James III of England, although born as the rightful and lawful heir to the English throne, never became King of England. In early 1689, while he was still an infant, Parliament, after having declared that his father, James II, had abdicated the throne, proceeded to inaugurate William of Orange and his wife Mary as the King and Queen of England. Parliament, exercising its immense and illimitable sovereign authority, had altered the line of succession for the British Crown. History records these events as the "Glorious Revolution," and one of its primary effects was to cement the doctrine of parliamentary sovereignty as the first principle of the British Constitution.

During the British Imperial Crisis, however, American colonists would, remarkably, entirely disavow the doctrine of parliamentary sovereignty, and they did so by introducing and adhering to a series of radical innovations and interpretations that had no basis in British constitutional law. As Lord Mansfield, Chief Justice of the King's Bench, trenchantly remarked in 1766, "It is now settled that there is no Restriction to the Legislative Authority of Great Britain. The Americans have adopted on this fatal occasion a new principle that they are not subject to the Legislative Authority of Great Britain. They have refused the law."[1]

Indeed, during the Revolution, American colonists responded to the various legislative initiatives of Parliament with a deluge of hyperbolic complaints and logorrheic protests, countering that they had established a confederated union among themselves with interests separate and distinct from the British Empire and demanding the right to be

1. *Debates on the Declaratory Act and Repeal of the Stamp Act* (London, 1766; Forgotten Books, 2016), 584.

treated accordingly. Hans Stanley, a Member of the House of Commons since 1743, was genuinely stunned by the blatant illegality of these acts and, on the floor of Parliament, exclaimed, "They have exceeded what this House has ever done, meeting in a federal Union not to be dissolved by the Crown ... All their petitions are insults on your authority."[2] In fact, when the colonists rejected the doctrine of parliamentary sovereignty and then declared themselves a de facto state within a state (as early as 1765), they flagrantly violated two fundamental maxims of their historic Constitution: parliamentary sovereignty itself and the unitary nature of the British Empire.

THE HIGH COURT OF PARLIAMENT: SOVEREIGNTY

Parliamentary sovereignty was an incontrovertible, bedrock principle of eighteenth-century British constitutionalism. Accordingly, Parliament was irrefutably the supreme legal authority of the British Empire, and its legislative acts were, by definition, inherently lawful and necessarily constitutional. No court, or any other legal or political institution other than Parliament itself, could abrogate or reverse an Act of Parliament. William Blackstone, a peerless British jurist and Member of Parliament, in his illustrious work *Commentaries on the Laws of England*, gave the quintessential statement describing and defining parliamentary sovereignty under the British Constitution. Regarding Parliament and its constitutional preeminence, Blackstone wrote:

> It has sovereign and uncontrollable authority in making, confirming, enlarging, restraining, abrogating, repealing, reviving, and expounding of laws, concerning matters of all possible denominations, ecclesiastical, or temporal, civil, military, maritime, or criminal: this being the place where that absolute despotic power, which must in all governments reside somewhere, is entrusted by the constitution of these kingdoms. All mischiefs and grievances, operations and remedies, that transcend the ordinary course of the laws, are within the reach of this extraordinary tribunal. It can regulate or new model the succession to the crown; as was done in the reign of Henry VIII. and William III. It can alter the established religion of the land; as was done in a variety of instances, in the reigns of king Henry VIII. and his three children. It can change and create afresh even the constitution of the kingdom and of parliaments themselves; as was done by the act of union, and the several statutes for triennial and septennial elections. It can, in short, do everything that is not naturally impossible; and therefore some have not scrupled to call

2. *Debates on the Declaratory Act*, 566.

> its power, by a figure rather too bold, the omnipotence of parliament. True it is, that what they do, no authority upon earth can undo.[3]

Parliamentary sovereignty did not originate with Blackstone, of course, and he was far from the only distinguished British jurist and constitutional scholar to observe and acknowledge the unique and extraordinary constitutional authority of Parliament. In 1644, Sir Edward Coke wrote of the supremacy of parliament: "it is so transcendent and absolute, as it cannot be confined either for causes or persons, within any bounds."[4] And Sir Matthew Hale, still another esteemed British jurist and scholar, proclaimed, "The Parliament, being the highest and greatest court, over which none other can have Jurisdiction in the Kingdom. If by any means a Misgovernment should any ways fall upon it, the Subjects of this Kingdom are left without all manner of Remedy."[5] Later, in 1766, a distinguished Member of Parliament, Alexander Wedderburn, emphasized the point during a debate in the House of Commons on the Declaratory Act: "The Sovereignty of this Nation resides in the King, Lords, and Commons who represent the whole State of the Kingdom and must be Sovereign in taxes as well as others."[6]

Therefore, if Parliament, acting in the best interest of the British Commonwealth, imposed a tax on either Virginia, Antigua, Barbados, Massachusetts, or any other British polity, then the tax was fundamentally and intrinsically lawful. And whether those subject to the tax disapproved and regarded the measure as an innovation, a departure from customary practice, or a violation of certain claimed rights was utterly irrelevant, because it was well within the authority of Parliament to initiate constitutional innovations, alter existing customs, and both judge and deny the claimed rights in question. The renowned literary genius and autodidactic constitutionalist Samuel Johnson remarked upon this indispensable characteristic of sovereignty in his pamphlet *Taxation, no Tyranny:* "But an English individual may by the supreme authority be deprived of liberty, and a Colony divested of its powers, for reasons of which that authority is the only judge."[7]

3. Sir William Blackstone, *Commentaries on the Laws of England*, Wilfrid Prest ed. (New York: Oxford University Press, 2016), 1:107.
4. Sir Edward Coke, *The Fourth Part of the Institutes of the Laws of England* (London, 1644), 36, https://lawlibrary.wm.edu/wythepedia/library/CokeFourthPartOfTheInstitutesOfTheLawsOfEngland1644.pdf.
5. Sir Matthew Hale, *The Original Institution, Power and Jurisdiction of Parliaments* (London, 1707), 49.
6. *Debates on the Declaratory Act*, 570.
7. Samuel Johnson, *Taxation no Tyranny; an Answer to the Resolutions and Addresses of the American Congress* (London, 1775), 24.

To the same end, in 1765, Soame Jenyns, an author and Member of Parliament since 1742, also considered the American arguments denying the right of Parliament to tax the colonies in a brief twenty-page pamphlet entitled *The Objections to the Taxation of Our American Colonies by the Legislature of Great Britain.* Jenyns opened his paper with a simple, matter-of-fact statement:

> The right of the Legislature of Great-Britain to impose taxes on her American Colonies, and the expediency of exerting that right in the present conjuncture, are propositions so indisputably clear, that I should never have thought it necessary to have undertaken their defence had not many arguments been lately flung out, both in papers and conversation, which with insolence equal to their absurdity deny them both.[8]

As a Member of Parliament, Jenyns, like Mansfield, Wedderburn, and the overwhelming majority of Parliament, understood perfectly well that when it convened in 1765 and passed the Stamp Act, constituted as it was by the King, Lords Spiritual and Temporal, and Commons, it was the highest power in the British Empire, and it acknowledged no superior authority on earth. And certainly, no subordinate component of that empire, whether it was the colony of Virginia, Maryland, Massachusetts, or Jamaica, had the legal authority to resist or defy it.

THE HIGH COURT OF PARLIAMENT: COMMONWEALTH AND REPRESENTATION

Under the British Constitution, there was no legal or constitutional relationship between the American colonies other than the fact that they were all citizens of the British Empire and that they all owed allegiance and obedience to the same King and, of course, Parliament. Other than those commonalities, which they shared with every other British colony, whether in North America or the West Indies, the American colonies were no more connected to each other than they were to Antigua or Newfoundland, and they were certainly not, in any way, a lawful, independent, confederated political body.

Indeed, within the British Empire, the only political interest to be represented was that of the empire, and members of Parliament faithfully represented the whole of the Commonwealth and not an individual county, city, town, borough, province, colony, district, or any other geographic entity. To that end, Sir William Blackstone carefully ex-

8. Soame Jenyns, *The Objections to the Taxation of our American Colonies by the Legislature of Great Britain Briefly Considered* (London, 1765), 3-4.

plained the solemn obligations of individual members of Parliament in the *Commentaries*: "And every member, though chosen by one district, when elected and returned serves for the whole realm. For the end of his coming thither is not particular, but general; not barely to advantage his constituents, but the commonwealth."[9]

Consequently, it was repugnant to the Constitution for the American colonists to assert that they were a separate and distinct people entitled to legislative independence and representation in the Empire on such a basis (i.e., *imperium in imperio*). Legislative representation, as the colonists advocated, was inexpugnably unconstitutional precisely because they were demanding a scheme of representation that was based on their falsely claimed right to advance and protect their own interests independent of the interests of the whole of the Commonwealth. In 1774, Whig statesman Edmund Burke, a Member of Parliament since 1765, emphasized the point in a speech to the citizens of Bristol:

> Parliament is not a *congress* of ambassadors from different and hostile interests; which interests each must maintain, as an agent and advocate, against other agents and advocates; but parliament is a *deliberative* assembly of *one* nation, with *one* interest, that of the whole; where, not local purposes, not local prejudices, ought to guide, but the general good, resulting from the general reason of the whole. You choose a member indeed; but when you have chosen him, he is not a member of Bristol, but he is a member of *parliament*. If the local constituent should have an interest, or should form an hasty opinion, evidently opposite to the real good of the rest of the community, the member for that place ought to be as far, as any other, from any endeavour to give it effect.[10]

In 1776, Thomas Hutchinson, a loyalist and former Governor of Massachusetts, also emphasized the unitary nature of the British Empire in his published response to the Declaration of Independence. In a lengthy essay entitled *Strictures upon the Declaration of the Congress at Philadelphia*, Hutchinson meticulously and exhaustively refuted the Declaration, and when he considered Jefferson's claim that it had become "necessary for one people to dissolve the political bands which have connected them with another," Hutchinson answered:

> They begin my Lord, with a false hypothesis, that the colonies are one *distinct people*, and the kingdom another, connected by *political*

9. Blackstone, *Commentaries*, 106.
10. Edmund Burke, "Speech to the Electors of Bristol, November 3, 1774," https://press-pubs.uchicago.edu/founders/documents/v1ch13s7.html.

> bands. The Colonies, *politically* considered, never were a *distinct* people from the kingdom. There never has been but one *political* band, and that was just the same before the first Colonists emigrated as it has been ever since, the Supreme Legislative Authority.[11]

Because representation is general and extends to the entire Commonwealth, it is important to understand and stress that under the British Constitution, it is the orders, or estates, of civil society that are represented in Parliament and not, again, any geographic entity. Specifically, the constituent elements of Parliament are the King "sitting in his royal and political capacity," the Lords Spiritual and Temporal, and the Commons. While the King's constitutional role in Parliament was perhaps more complex, the Lords Spiritual and Temporal represented the nobility (those identified and distinguished by title, rank, and honor, i.e., dukes, marquises, earls, viscounts, or barons), and the Commons represented the democratic order, or the whole body of the people (principally the property and commercial order).

It is also crucial to reiterate that general representation did not apply to the American colonies in an aggregate capacity because, under the British Constitution, there was no confederation or union of American colonies. The constitutional question pertaining to colonial representation, therefore, was not whether 2.5 million American colonists in thirteen unified colonies were represented in Parliament, but whether the citizens in each individual colony, as constituent members of the Commonwealth, were represented.

Accordingly, it was spurious for any British colony to complain that its citizens were unrepresented in Parliament. As citizens of the British Empire, whether in Nova Scotia, Bermuda, or New York, they were as well represented, pursuant to their respective class or order, in the House of Commons as the citizens of London were. In his pamphlet, *Objections to the Taxation*, Soame Jenyns, while contemplating the doctrine of general representation, pointedly noted that several populous commercial cities in England had no direct representation in Parliament but were nevertheless constitutionally represented. Jenyns wrote, "If the Towns of Manchester and Birmingham sending no Representatives to Parliament are notwithstanding there represented, why are not the Cities of Albany and Boston equally represented in that Assembly?"[12]

11. Thomas Hutchinson, *Strictures Upon The Declaration Of The Congress At Philadelphia* (London, 1776).
12. Jenyns, *The Objections to the Taxation*, 9.

Under the British Constitution, the colonists, whether in Canada, America, or the Caribbean, were all constitutionally represented as a function of their civil order; accordingly, the American complaint of "taxation without representation" was unfounded.

THE HIGH COURT OF PARLIAMENT: TAXATION

An Act of Parliament, said Blackstone:

> Is the exercise of the highest authority that this kingdom acknowledges upon earth. It has power to bind every subject in the land, and the dominions thereunto belonging; nay, even the king himself, if particularly named therein. And it cannot be altered, amended, dispensed with, suspended, or repealed, but in the same forms and by the same authority of parliament.[13]

Accordingly, the Stamp Act of 1765, lawfully passed by the King, Lords, and Commons in Parliament, was the supreme law of the land. It was also an eminently fair and reasonable parliamentary initiative, and the American colonists had neither cause for complaint nor the authority to refuse it. The taxes, in fact, were intended to reduce and defray the costs of maintaining a necessary postwar military presence in North America. It is also an ineluctable truth that, by the revolutionary logic of the American colonists, the French and Indian War was fought for their benefit and funded, ironically, largely by the English Stamp Act.

As of 1765, Stamp Act taxes, as applied in England, had been a feature of British fiscal policy for over seventy years. The taxes were originally implemented in 1694 to fund the war effort against France in the Nine Years War and then remained a source of the king's perpetual revenue thereafter. Consequently, during the French and Indian War, the English Stamp Act taxes, imposed on the English citizenry and from which the American colonists were exempt, were a critical source of wartime funding. Such facts prompted Samuel Johnson to remark in his pamphlet *Taxation, No Tyranny*, "I should gladly see America return half of what England has expended in her defence."[14]

In his pamphlet *Objections to the Taxation*, MP Soame Jenyns made a similar observation, noting that the American colonists did not protest or complain on constitutional grounds when Parliament legislated money for their defense, and he said of the colonists, "Are they

13. Blackstone, *Commentaries*, 121.
14. Johnson, *Taxation no Tyranny*, 64.

not Englishmen, or are they only Englishmen when they solicit for protection but not Englishmen when taxes are required to enable this country to protect them?"[15]

More persuasive still on the topic was the speech of Prime Minister George Grenville in the House of Commons in January of 1766. Grenville, like Johnson and Jenyns, directly referenced the political, moral, and ethical responsibilities of the colonists to contribute to the defense of themselves and their country, while also restating the legal obligations necessarily following from the sovereign authority of Parliament. He remarked:

> That this kingdom has the sovereign, the supreme legislative power over America, is granted. It cannot be denied; and taxation is a part of that sovereign power ... Protection and obedience are reciprocal ... When they want the protection of this kingdom, they are always very ready to ask it. That protection has always been afforded them in the most full and ample manner. The nation has run itself into an immense debt to give them this protection; and now they are called upon to contribute a small share towards the public expense.[16]

Given the historical context of the Stamp Act, the relevant question would seem to be not why Parliament taxed the American colonies for the purpose of revenue in 1765, but why they waited so long to do it.

CONCLUSION

By 1776, American colonists had been indefatigably arguing for over a decade that they were unrepresented in Parliament and, accordingly, were being subjected to the tyranny of taxation without representation. The claims, of course, were untrue. The colonists were not being tyrannized; they were only being asked to pay the necessary and proper taxes to generate revenue and fund the expenses of the Commonwealth. And the American colonists were indeed represented in Parliament; they simply disapproved of the system of representation. Additionally, their grievances had been fairly heard, extensively considered, and thoroughly debated in Parliament. But, in the final analysis, their arguments were also decisively rejected by Parliament.

In part, this was because the arguments advanced by American colonists were not new to the English, and the theoretical limits of Parliament's imperial authority had been challenged well before Americans

15. Jenyns, *The Objections to the Taxation*, 9.
16. John L. Bullion, *A Great and Necessary Measure: George Grenville and the Genesis of the Stamp Act, 1763-1765* (Columbia: University of Missouri Press, 1982).

rose in opposition to it. In 1698, esteemed Irish scientist and philosopher William Molyneux published a historical and political treatise entitled *The Case of Ireland being bound by Acts of Parliament in England, Stated*, in which he disputed, at length and with great specificity and scholarship, the right of the British Parliament to exercise legislative hegemony over Ireland. Molyneux's *Case of Ireland* was explicitly addressed to Parliament, and, predictably, it was received by that august body with intense enmity and acrimony.

Indeed, Parliament eventually responded to Molyneux and the Irish controversies twenty years later, authoritatively, with the Irish Declaratory Act of 1720, which would later serve as the legislative model for the Declaratory Act of 1766. And with the Declaratory Act of 1766, Parliament reaffirmed its constitutional sovereignty and legislative authority over the British colonies and subjects in America "in all cases whatsoever."[17]

Ultimately, of course, the American colonists would reject the Declaratory Act and default to the natural rights philosophy of the Declaration as the intellectual and moral foundation of the Revolution, specifically because their constitutional arguments were unpersuasive. The legal and constitutional arguments were, in fact, firmly in favor of Parliament and the British majoritarian position.

17. "Great Britain : Parliament – The Declaratory Act; March 18, 1766," https://avalon.law.yale.edu/18th_century/declaratory_act_1766.asp.

Champions of Liberty: Phillis Wheatley, Joseph Sewall, and the Old South Church

JOSEPH MANCA

Poet Phillis Wheatley (c. 1753-1784) was a consistent and passionate advocate for liberty in every form: she called for an end to slavery, championed political and religious freedoms, and considered a sinful life to be a kind of servitude. She consistently opposed British infringements on American rights and saw political oppression as a form of slavery. Wheatley was surrounded by other proponents of liberty and human rights, but here we will see her penchant for freedom through the prism of her attendance at the radical Old South Church (at a building now called the Old South Meeting House) and her self-proclaimed, special devotion to Reverend Joseph Sewall (1688-1769), who was her mentor and who passionately backed American freedoms.

Wheatley's life was remarkable. Born in about 1753 on the west coast of Africa, she was enslaved there as a child, transported to the New World, and sold to the family of Boston tailor and merchant John Wheatley (1703-1778). The Wheatleys recognized young Phillis's facility with language and helped her to develop her literary talents. Wheatley was the first African-American to publish a book and was one of the earliest women in the thirteen colonies to publish a book on any subject. After a successful literary trip to London and the publication of her verses in 1773, Wheatley garnered considerable attention. John Wheatley granted Phillis freedom from bondage in September or October of 1773, but times were difficult in Boston for the next decade, even after the British evacuation of the city. Wheatley went on to marry (1778, to a John Peters) and have children, but never published another book of verses, and she died at the age of thirty-one, having recently been working as a seamstress and a maid in a boarding house.

Phillis, like members of the Wheatley family, attended Congregational meetings. In particular, she received significant tutelage from Rev. Joseph Sewall, who was a pastor of the Old South Church for fifty-six years beginning in 1713.[1] Phillis would have known him at the end of his time as minister, between her ages of nine and sixteen or so. Phillis had extensive contact with Sewall, and in a poem of homage upon his death described how she heard his "warnings and advice." She called him "my monitor," a spiritual guardian and mentor who gave her ideas and watched over her moral development. Wheatley was particularly learned, and Sewall may well have offered her access to the substantial library at the church. We have no records of their personal conversations, prayers together, or which sermons she heard, but we know that she heeded his advice that her "monitor" was a consistent and passionate advocate of civil and religious freedoms. After his death in 1769, the congregation became ever more openly rebellious as troubles intensified with Britain.

Sewall was part of a distinguished Massachusetts family. He was the son of Samuel Sewall (1652-1730), perhaps most famous to us for his role as a judge at the Salem Witch Trials. In light of Joseph's later interactions with Miss Wheatley, it is noteworthy that Samuel Sewall wrote the first known treatise in America supporting abolition, in 1700: *The Selling of Joseph.* He argued that "it is most certain that all Men, as they are the Sons of Adam, are Coheirs; and have equal Right unto Liberty." Addressing the Old Testament account of how Joseph's brothers sold him into slavery in Egypt, Samuel wrote:

> Yet through the Indulgence of GOD to our First Parents after the Fall, the outward Estate of all and every of the Children, remains the same, as to one another. So that Originally, and Naturally, there is no such thing as Slavery. Joseph was rightfully no more a Slave to his Brethren, then [*sic*] they were to him.[2]

The judge wrote in his diary that he named his son Joseph "in hopes of the accomplishment of the Prophecy, Ezek. 37th and such like: and not out of respect to any Relation, or other person, except the first

1. There is extensive information on Joseph Sewall's activities and leadership at the Old South Church in Benjamin Wisner, *The History of the Old South Church in Boston, in Four Sermons* (Boston: Crocker & Brewster, 1830). See also Hamilton Andrew Hill, *The Reverend Joseph Sewall: His Youth and Early Manhood* (Boston: David Clapp & Son, 1892); and Clifford K. Shipton, *Sibley's Harvard Graduates, Volume V – 1701-1712* (Boston: Massachusetts Historical Society, 1937), 376-393.
2. Samuel Sewall, *The Selling of Joseph* (Boston: Bartholomew Green and John Allen, 1700), 1.

Joseph." Thus, he named him after the Joseph in Genesis who was sold into slavery, rose to become a political leader in Egypt, and under whose name Ezekiel was prophesied to revive Israel.[3] There is no explicit record about Joseph Sewall's attitude toward abolition, and the minister might not have wanted to take a public stance on a controversial topic, but it is likely that he was sympathetic to the idea, as were some other Congregational ministers and churchgoers in Boston. Noteworthy is his father's abolitionist stance and Joseph Sewall's awareness that his very name was a reminder of the illegitimacy of slavery.

Joseph Sewall favored the downtrodden, and a contemporary noted that Sewall felt deeply for the plight of Native Americans: according to the published obituary of 1769 by Congregational minister Charles Chauncy (1705-1787), Sewall's "heart was strongly touched with pity towards" the "INDIAN natives."[4] To be sure, Joseph Sewall was well-prepared to interact in a sympathetic way with Wheatley. And it is a fitting capstone to the family's anti-slavery history that Joseph Sewall's great-grandsons Samuel Edmund Sewall (1799-1888) and Samuel Joseph May (1797-1871), both Bostonians and Harvard graduates, became fervent abolitionists and collaborators of William Lloyd Garrison (1805-1879).

As Phillis Wheatley would have known well, Joseph Sewall was a champion of both religious and political freedoms. The Congregational Sewall especially deplored the longstanding and continuing infringements by the British upon religious rights, such as the proposals to appoint an Anglican bishop over the colonies, and he opposed their political impositions such as taxation and the stationing of troops in Boston. His last years comprised the distressing time of the Stamp Act (1765), Declaratory Act (1766), and the Townshend Acts (1767-1768). Chauncy again on Sewall:

> He was a strenuous asserter of our civil and ecclesiastical CHARTER-RIGHTS and PRIVILEDGES. He knew the value of them.—He knew they were the purchase of our fore-fathers at the expence of much labor, blood, and treasure.—He could not bear the thought of their being wrested out of our hands.[5]

3. *The Diary of Samuel Sewall, 1674-1729*, 2 vols, M. Halsey Thomas, ed. (New York: Farrar, Straus and Giroux), 1973), vol. 1:175, August 19, 1688.
4. Charles Chauncy, *Discourse Occasioned by the Death of the Reverend Dr. Joseph Sewall* (Boston: Kneeland and Adams, 1769), n. p.
5. Ibid., n. p.

Joseph Sewall, left, and Phillis Wheatley. (*Yale University Art Gallery/Library of Congress*)

An anonymous obituary echoed Chauncy, also stressing Sewall's abhorrence of British infringements both religious and civil and noting how the reverend spoke passionately about such issues:

> He was greatly alarmed with every motion to introduce the Hierarchy into these Colonies, whose predecessors had, at the peril of every earthly comfort, fled from the face of ecclesiastical tyranny. Nor was he less jealous of the attempts made to deprive us of our civil liberties . . . These things lay with weight on his mind as long as he lived, he spake with freedom, and some degree of warmth, on this interesting topic.[6]

Chauncy accurately summarized Sewall's belief in American exceptionalism and his opposition to British curtailment of religious liberties, which he saw as linked to civil liberty. In a sermon of 1724, and quoting Increase Mather (1639-1723), Sewall thundered before the "Lieutenant Governor and the Council of Representatives of the Province of Massachusetts Bay" that "the Principal Design upon which these Colonies were at first Planted, was *to Profess, & Practice & Enjoy*, with undisturbed Liberty, *the Holy Religion of GOD our Saviour*."[7] Phillis Wheat-

6. From an Appendix in the *Boston Evening-Post*, July 3, 1769.

7. Joseph Sewall, *Rulers must be Just, Ruling in the Fear of GOD* (Boston: Printed by B. Green, 1724), 27.

ley's pastor would speak with "some degree of warmth" on such topics, and she was schooled in the ideology that the colonies needed "undisturbed liberty" to establish the right, holy kind of government that was not possible in the Old World.

When Sewall died in 1769 of a paralytic stroke at the age of eighty-one, Wheatley joined the widespread celebrations of his life by writing a poem, which exists in several manuscript variants in addition to the version (cited here) that she published in 1773 in her book of verses. The first lines include a reminiscence of his sermons and conversations ringing in her ears: "Hail, holy man, arriv'd th' immortal shore, / Though we shall hear they warning voice no more."[8]

Sewall seemed to have a special interest in addressing youth like Wheatley:

> Mourn him ye youth, to whom he oft has told
> God's gracious wonder from the times of old.
> I, too have cause this mighty loss to mourn,
> For he my monitor will not return.[9]

Rightly sensing the religious foundation for the thought and poetry of Wheatley, whose poems are indeed infused with theological ideas, Thomas Jefferson (1740-1826) said of her (misspelling her first and last names) that "religion has indeed made a Phyllis Whately."[10] Others have noticed that her poems, which were, after all, subtitled in 1773 as "religious and moral," are often exhortations like sermons.[11] Wheatley did not attend any formal schooling, and she seemed to get many of her ideas and sense of things from the fiery Calvinist preaching that she heard from the likes of her "monitor" Joseph Sewall, among others. She often managed to insert lines into her poems that touched on freedom, and in her poem to Sewall she inserted the Calvinist statement that the kind of "grace divine" that Sewall felt in his life is what "rescues sinners from the chains of guilt," a line that suggestively equates living in sin with chattel slavery.

8. "On The Death of The Rev. Dr. Sewell. 1769," in Phillis Wheatley, *Poems on Various Subjects, Religious and Moral* (London: A. Bell, 1773), 19. Modern editions of her poems include Julian D. Mason Jr, ed., *The Poems of Phillis Wheatley* (Chapel Hill, NC: The University of North Carolina Press, 1989); and William H. Robinson, ed., *Phillis Wheatley and her Writings* (New York and London: Garland Publishing, 1984).

9. Wheatley, *Poems*, 21.

10. Thomas Jefferson, *Notes on the State of Virginia* (London: Printed for John Stockdale, 1787), 234. His observations about Wheatley are not found in earlier editions of his book.

11. See, for example, Paula Loscocco, *Phillis Wheatley's Miltonic Poetics* (New York: Palgrave Macmillan, 2014), 58-59.

Following her early exposure to Sewall and other ministers and congregants there, Phillis Wheatley became an official member of the church upon reaching adulthood (August 1771). Sewall's and Wheatley's house of worship remained a well-known hotbed of the American Revolution through the 1770s, the place later nicknamed the "Sanctuary of Freedom." The firebrand politician and brilliant agitator Samuel Adams (1722-1803) was a notable member of the congregation of Old South Church. Crowded meetings happened there in 1770, a year of tumult over taxation and the large-scale British military occupation of the city. For a meeting on the day after the Boston Massacre (March 5, 1770), of a group too numerous to gather in Faneuil Hall, people were still, a year after Sewall's death, associating the building with him: on March 6, 1770, members "Voted that this Meeting be adjourned to Dr. Sewalls Meeting House."[12] Most famously, patriots convened at the Old South Meeting House at various meetings from November 29 until December 16, 1773, with the tumultuous gathering on this last day occurring just before the Boston Tea Party.[13] Phillis Wheatley, by then a free woman, must certainly have been interested in the dramatic events at her church. The Sons of Liberty, ready for action and further stirred up by the words of Samuel Adams, dressed as Indians and emerged from "Sewall's Meeting House" with war whoops and headed to Boston Harbor to deal with the unwanted tea.

Other Congregational churches in Boston gave strong support to the American cause, including the vigorously pro-patriot First Church, under Charles Chauncy, and the New South Church, where Phillis's owners, John and Susanna Wheatley (1709-1774), attended. Knowing the political positions of the congregation and the leaders of the Old South Church, in October 1775 the occupying British troops cleared out most of the woodwork inside and turned the large interior of the Old South Meeting House into an open space for equestrian and other military training (the pews and other woodwork there now date from the mid-nineteenth century and later).

Wheatley was schooled in freedom by her monitor, Joseph Sewall, and came to see that civic and religious freedoms are desirable and linked. Sewall was hardly promoting religious pluralism, and was most concerned that the British, with their established state religion, would

12. Unsigned, *Freedom and the Old South Meeting-House* (Boston: Directors of the Old South work, 1910), 12.
13. "Minutes of the Tea Meetings, 1773," *Massachusetts Historical Society Proceedings*, vol. 20 (1882): 10-17.

refrain from suppressing American Congregational churches in any way. Still, his way of thinking intersected well with the wider calls for political and personal liberty that were the foundation of the American Revolution. At any rate, Wheatley's idea of freedom was broader than Sewall's. A special focus of her love of liberty, going beyond ideas that Sewall might have shared but not expressed, centered on abolition. Numerous poems and letters from Wheatley's hand decried chattel servitude, and she linked opposition to slavery with the struggle against all political oppressions, including British tyranny over the thirteen colonies. Calling political oppression slavery or bondage was widespread among other American revolutionary writers, but the linkage is especially compelling coming from Wheatley, who experienced enslavement first hand and who (unlike many American agitators) was an actual and open abolitionist.

Wheatley published her book of verses in London in 1773 with the support of William Legge, Earl of Dartmouth (1731-1801), and she dedicated verses to her patron in which she described tyranny over America as like bondage in irons:

> No more, *America*, in mournful strain
> Of wrongs, and grievance unredress'd complain,
> No longer shall thou dread the iron chain,
> Which wanton *Tyranny* with lawless hand
> Had made, and with it meant t' enslave the land.[14]

Wheatley added that her own enslavement gave her a keen sense of the burdens of slavery, and she wanted others never to feel the oppressions of bondage:

> Should you, my lord, while you peruse my song,
> Wonder from whence my love of *Freedom* sprung,
> Whence flow these wishes for the common good,
> By feeling hearts alone best understood,
> I, young in life, by seeming cruel fate
> Was snatch'd from *Afric's* fancy'd happy seat:
> What pangs excruciating must molest,
> What sorrows labour in my parent's breast?
> Steel'd was that soul and by no misery mov'd
> That from a father seiz'd his babe belov'd:

14. Wheatley, *Poems*, "To the Right Honourable WILLIAM, Earl of Dartmouth," 74. She also received support for the publication from Selina Hastings, Countess of Huntingdon (1707-1791).

Such, such my case. And can I then but pray
Others may never feel tyrannic sway?

Another remarkable document indicating Wheatley's holistic idea of liberty—freedom from slavery, from religious persecution, and from political oppression and violation of one's natural rights—is a letter she wrote to Rev. Samson Occom (1723-1792), a Native American, Presbyterian preacher in Connecticut. This important missive of February 11, 1774 was shared with the world, being published in the next few months in a number of American newspapers, including *The Massachusetts Spy*, the *Connecticut Gazette*, and (cited here) *The Connecticut Journal.* She declared that God has implanted in us a love of freedom. As a preacher might do, she linked this important idea with a biblical story, saying that we pant for deliverance from oppression as the Israelites had done during their captivity in Egypt:

> I have this Day received your obliging kind Epistle, and am greatly satisfied with your Reasons respecting the Negroes, and think highly reasonable what you offer in Vindication of their natural Rights: Those that invade them cannot be insensible that the divine Light is chasing away the thick Darkness which broods over the Land of Africa; and the Chaos which has reign'd so long, is converting into beautiful Order, and reveals more and more clearly, the glorious Dispensation of civil and religious Liberty, which are so inseparably Limited, that there is little or no Enjoyment of one Without the other: Otherwise, perhaps, the Israelites had been less solicitous for their Freedom from Egyptian slavery; I do not say they would have been contented without it, by no means, for in every human Breast, God has implanted a Principle, which we call Love of Freedom; it is impatient of Oppression, and pants for Deliverance; and by the Leave of our modern Egyptians I will assert, that the same Principle lives in us . . . How well the Cry for Liberty, and the reverse Disposition for the exercise of oppressive Power over others agree, I humbly think it does not require the Penetration of a Philosopher to determine.[15]

She interpolated here the challenging and extraordinary statement that slaveholders in America were now the "modern Egyptians."

Wheatley, like many others in Boston, had the gratification of seeing the armed struggle for independence underway. She supported that ef-

15. Phillis Wheatley to Samson Occom, *The Connecticut Journal and the New-Haven Post-Boy*, April 1, 1774, front page. See also Robinson, ed., *Phillis Wheatley*, 332.

fort, and, at the same time, was savvy and needed a hit poem, and she found the perfect subject in George Washington, the hero of the day in Massachusetts. Typical of her background and thinking, in her "To His Excellency General Washington" she highlighted the moral essence of Washington's virtues, describing him as "fam'd for thy valour, for thy virtues more," and noting that he led the hopes of a nation:

> Proceed, great chief, with virtue on thy side,
> Thy ev'ry action let the goddess guide.
> A crown, a mansion, and a throne that shine,
> With gold unfading, WASHINGTON! be thine.[16]

She wrote a poem about him in the Fall of 1775 and sent it to him in the hopes that it would find its way to publication. Wheatley wrote to him in a respectful way:

> SIR, I Have taken the freedom to address your Excellency in the enclosed poem, and entreat your acceptance, though I am not insensible of its inaccuracies. Your being appointed by the Grand Continental Congress to be Generalissimo of the armies of North America, together with the fame of your virtues, excite sensations not easy to suppress . . . Wishing your Excellency all possible success in the great cause you are so generously engaged in. I am, Your Excellency's most obedient humble servant, Phillis Wheatley.[17]

Washington had misplaced her letter, and wrote to her on February 28, 1776. It is noteworthy that he took the time to write while anxiously awaiting arrival of the cannons from Fort Ticonderoga and writing just one day after a false alarm that the British were attacking Dorchester Heights, as he alluded to in his letter to her. On March 4 he triumphantly installed the cannons there.[18]

16. Phillis Wheatley to George Washington, October 26, 1775, *The Papers of George Washington Digital Edition, Revolutionary War Series*, vol. 2 (Charlottesville: University of Virginia Press, 2008), 242.
17. Ibid, 242. See also *The Writings of Phillis Wheatley*, Vincent Carretta, ed. (New York and Oxford: Oxford University Press, 2019), 131.
18. Washington to Artemas Ward, February 27, 1776, ibid., 3:384: "We were falsely Alarmed a while ago with an Acct of the Regulars coming over from the Castle to Dorchester . . . w[oul]d it not be prudent to keep Six or Eight trusty men by way of Lookouts or Patrols to Night on the point next the Castle as well as on Nuke Hill. At the same time ordering particular Regimts to be ready to March at a Moments warning to the Heights of Dorchester; For should the Enemy get Possession of those Hills before us they would render it a difficult task to dispossess them—better it is therefore to prevent than remedy an evil."

Washington's letter to Wheatley was genteel and personal. He praised her "genius" as a poet and, in a personal touch, he even confessed his fears to her that the public might consider him self-promoting if he openly arranged to publish the letter:

> Mrs Phillis,
>
> Your favour of the 26th of October did not reach my hands 'till the middle of December. Time enough, you will say, to have given an answer ere this. Granted. But a variety of important occurrences, continually interposing to distract the mind and withdraw the attention, I hope will apologize for the delay, and plead my excuse for the seeming, but not real, neglect.
>
> I thank you most sincerely for your polite notice of me, in the elegant Lines you enclosed; and however undeserving I may be of such encomium and panegyrick, the style and manner exhibit a striking proof of your great poetical Talents. In honour of which, and as a tribute justly due to you, I would have published the Poem, had I not been apprehensive, that, while I only meant to give the World this new instance of your genius, I might have incurred the imputation of Vanity. This, and nothing else, determined me not to give it place in the public Prints.
>
> If you should ever come to Cambridge, or near Head Quarters, I shall be happy to see a person so favour by the Muses, and to whom nature has been so liberal and beneficent in her dispensations. I am, with great Respect, Your obedt humble servant, G. Washington.[19]

That Wheatley visited Washington at headquarters is attested to by one late source: Benson J. Lossing (1813-1891), who was perhaps passing along oral information, and who put a the time of her visit as mid-March 1776:

> Washington invited her to visit him at Cambridge, which she did a few days before the British evacuated Boston; her master, among others, having left the city by permission, and retired, with his family, to Chelsea. She passed half an hour with the commander-in-chief, from whom and his officers she received marked attention.[20]

As he stated, Washington did not want to appear vainglorious by arranging for its publication of the poem, but others, like his aide-de-camp Joseph Reed (1741-1785) did the job for him: the poem appeared

19. George Washington to Phillis Wheatley, February 28, 1776, ibid., 3:387.

20. Benson J. Lossing, *The Pictorial Field-Book of the Revolution*, 2 vols. (New York: Harper & Brothers, 1860), 1:556.

on the front page of the *Virginia Gazette* on March 30, 1776 and again, in the next month, in *The Pennsylvania Magazine* in Philadelphia, a publication headed by editor Thomas Paine (1737-1809).[21]

Wheatley's dealings with Washington were extraordinary, but so was her whole life. She lived as a slave and a colonial subject, but finished her years as a free citizen in an independent republic. All along, Phillis Wheatley's writings and life were deeply enmeshed in the world of revolutionary Boston. As emphasized here, she was brought up in the world of Joseph Sewall, and, as Jefferson rightly noted, religion shaped her thought. Wheatley wrote about liberty from her teenage years onward, but she did not have long to experience peace time and the fruits of American independence. She died on December 5, 1784, less than a year after Washington resigned his commission in Annapolis. Two years after her death, the first American edition of her poetry came out.[22] Her name has never been forgotten, and a vast field of literary and historical scholarship about her life and works flourishes today.[23]

21. Published in the "Poetical Essays" section of *The Pennsylvania Magazine, or American Monthly Museum*, vol. 2 (April 1776), 193.
22. Phillis Wheatley, *Poems on Various Subjects, Religious and Moral* (Philadelphia: Joseph Cruikshank, 1786).
23. Recent studies, with further bibliography, include Vincent Carretta, *Phillis Wheatley Peters: Biography of a Genius in Bondage* (Athens, GA: University of Georgia Press, 2011, and a new, updated edition of 2023); and David Waldstreicher, *The Odyssey of Phillis Wheatley: A Poet's Journeys through American Slavery and Independence* (New York: Farrar, Straus and Giroux, 2023).

Dr. Warren's Crucial Informant

J. L. BELL

On April 18, 1775, Dr. Joseph Warren, leader of the Patriots still inside Boston, gathered information about a possible British army march from many sources. Nineteenth-century accounts spoke of hints coming in from a groom in the governor's stable, a boy who held horses for redcoat officers, a woman who employed a soldier's wife as a maid, sailors gossiping about boats being prepared.[1] But an early chronicler said that Warren turned to one source of intelligence in particular. This article proposes to identify that person by tracing two statements back to the same Patriot insider and by searching newspaper and vital records.

Warren's crucial informant was first described by the Rev. Jeremy Belknap (1744–1798), minister of Dover, New Hampshire. Already collecting information for his *History of New-Hampshire* (published 1784–1792), Belknap kept notes on the events unfolding around him. In the fall of 1775 he visited the Continental Army camps surrounding Boston to check on the New Hampshire troops and observe the siege. He wrote a diary during that trip, published in 1860 by the Massachusetts Historical Society.[2]

A few days after returning to Dover, on October 25, Belknap added an entry to his travel diary:

> Mr. Waters informed me, that the design of the regular troops, when they marched out of Boston the night of April 18, was discovered to Dr. Warren by a person kept in pay for that purpose. . . .

1. Nineteenth-century accounts: Mary Caroline Crawford, *Old Boston Days and Ways* (Boston: Little, Brown, 1913), 118–21. Samuel A. Drake, *Old Landmarks and Historic Personages of Boston* (Boston: J. R. Osgood, 1873), 243, and *Historic Fields and Mansions of Middlesex* (Boston: James R. Osgood, 1874), 354. David Hackett Fischer, *Paul Revere's Ride* (New York: Oxford University Press, 1994), 93–4.

2. Belknap diary: *Massachusetts Historical Society Proceedings* (hereafter *MHSP)*, 4 (1860), 77–86. Belknap was the principal founder of the M.H.S. after he moved to Boston.

> These circumstances [a long list of clues that the British army was about to march] being communicated to Dr. Warren, he applied to the person who had been retained, and got intelligence of their whole design; which was to seize [Samuel] Adams and [John] Hancock, who were at Lexington, and burn the stores at Concord. Two expresses were immediately despatched thither, who passed by the guards on the Neck just before a sergeant arrived with orders to stop passengers. Another messenger went over Charlestown Ferry; so that the alarm was given several hours before the troops arrived at Lexington.[3]

The express rider who left Boston by the Neck was William Dawes, Jr. The rider who crossed the Charles River to Charlestown was Paul Revere.[4] Gen. Thomas Gage had indeed ordered his troops to destroy "the stores at Concord." (Those orders said nothing about Adams and Hancock in Lexington, though.[5])

Despite the account in Belknap's diary being largely accurate, historians have tended to treat it with skepticism. By October, after all, everyone in New England already knew how riders had carried the alarm out of Boston and where the British march ended. Although the minister's journal has been available in print since before the Civil War, almost no book has discussed the "person kept in pay" by Dr. Warren and his colleagues.

David Hackett Fischer used Belknap's statement in *Paul Revere's Ride*, but only partially. He accepted that Dr. Warren "applied to" his best-placed source late on April 18 after hearing from other sources. But Fischer set aside the detail about "a person kept in pay" as "merely a rumor he heard in the American camp" and instead focused on the possibility that that source was the British commander's wife. That theory, while very dramatic, is untenable.[6] Walter R. Borneman's analysis in *American Spring* works through Fischer's analysis skeptically but does not attempt to identify the informant.[7] In his 2014 article for

3. "Mr. Waters informed": *MHSP*, 4:85–6.

4. Dawes and Revere: "Letter from Paul Revere to Jeremy Belknap, circa 1798," www.masshist.org/database/99.

5. Allen French, *General Gage's Informers: New Material Upon Lexington and Concord, Benjamin Thompson as Loyalist and the Treachery of Benjamin Church, Jr.* (Ann Arbor, MI University of Michigan Press, 1932), 29–30.

6. Fischer's analysis: *Paul Revere's Ride*, 96–7, 387. This argument rested on equating Warren's source with a woman who had contacted Samuel Adams days earlier with different information and presenting the Gages' marriage as irreparably damaged even though they remained together and had two more children.

7. Borneman's analysis: *American Spring: Lexington, Concord, and the Road to Revolution* (Boston: Little, Brown, 2014), 124–9.

this website, Derek W. Beck discussed Belknap's journal entry and concluded, "Mr. Waters's statement sounds like an American concoction."[8]

Earlier American authors may have been reluctant to explore the Belknap source because of distaste for the idea of the Patriots bribing an informant. It was more reassuring to stress the unity and perspicacity of Bostonians watching the soldiers prepare. Anyone who wanted reasons to be skeptical about the October 1775 account could easily find gaping questions. Who was this otherwise unidentified "Mr. Waters" who spoke to Belknap? How could the minister have come across inside information about the Boston Patriots' intelligence effort when he was seventy miles away in New Hampshire? Was this statement anything more than well-traveled camp gossip festooned with claims that could never be confirmed?

To make this source into useful evidence, we need to answer these questions: Who was Belknap's acquaintance, the mysterious "Mr. Waters"? Did this man really have connections in Boston's Patriot leadership? And do those answers move us any closer to identifying the "person who had been retained"?

The search for "Mr. Waters" leads to Josiah Waters (1721–1784), a painter by training who became a respected merchant in pre-Revolutionary Boston. He joined the congregation of the Old South Meeting House at age twenty. He was elected to several town offices, including constable, fence viewer, clerk of the market, and finally warden, one of the most respected jobs—in charge of enforcing the Sabbath laws. In 1747 Waters joined the Ancient & Honorable Artillery Company, an old private club for men aspiring to be militia officers, and filled many roles in that organization.[9]

Also in 1747, Josiah and his wife Abigail had a son. Josiah, Jr. (1747-1805), grew up to work with his father in the firm of "Josiah Waters and Son" on Ann Street. In fact, the two men worked so closely together that it is often hard to distinguish the two. Josiah, Jr., also became a member of Old South and the Ancient & Honorable

8. Beck's analysis: "Dr. Joseph Warren's Informant," allthingsliberty.com/2014/04/dr-joseph-warrens-informant/. This article was valuable in gathering sources and pointing to holes in the theory about General Gage's wife. In the end Beck decided that Warren gathered crucial information from his own first-hand observations. See also Beck, *Igniting the American Revolution: 1773–1775* (Naperville, IL: Sourcebooks, 2015), 113.

9. Josiah Waters, Sr.: Oliver Ayer Roberts, *History of the Military Company of the Massachusetts, Now Called The Ancient and Honorable Artillery Company of Massachusetts, 1637-1888* (Boston: Alfred Mudge & Son, 1897), 2:47–8.

Artillery Company, and in 1770 he joined the St. Andrew's Lodge of Freemasons.[10]

In 1768, Josiah Waters, Sr., invested in land in Maine, buying out partners to become the main proprietor of the Massabesick Plantation. That area included the modern towns of Alfred, Sanford, and what the family would modestly name Waterboro.[11]

As of 1770, Josiah Waters, Sr., was a captain in the Boston militia regiment. By 1772, Josiah, Jr., was his lieutenant. According to *Mills and Hicks's British and American Register for the Year 1775*, as war approached the regiment's major was the senior Waters's brother-in-law Thomas Dawes. The adjutant, or administrative officer, was his nephew William Dawes, Jr., who was also Thomas Dawes's nephew. In 1773 both Captain Waters and Adjutant Dawes were asking the Boston selectmen if they could use Faneuil Hall for militia training.[12]

When war broke out on April 19, 1775, the elder Waters sent his "wife, children & maids" out of Boston the next day. Briefly "shut in" the town, he got out as soon as he could.[13] Working as a gentleman volunteer, Waters took on the job of laying out a fort in Roxbury to keep the British army from marching south over the Neck. In his memoirs, Gen. William Heath listed "Capt. Josiah Waters of Boston" among the men "very serviceable in this line."[14] In September, Samuel Adams wrote of hearing about "the ingenuity of [Henry] Knox and Waters in planning the celebrated works at Roxbury."[15] Eventually Josiah, Jr., helped his father with those fortifications.

That October, Gen. George Washington and the Continental Congress started organizing an army for the coming year. Strengthening the artillery regiment with more engineers was a major priority. John Adams was another fan of the Waters family, and on

10. Josiah Waters, Jr.: Roberts, *Ancient and Honorable Artillery Company*, 2:161–2.

11. Waters land in Maine: The Maine Historical Society has digitized the Waters account book and map, digitalmaine.com/hist_docs/13/.

12. Using Faneuil Hall: *Records Relating to the Early History of Boston* (also known as *Boston Town Records)*, volume 23, "Selectmen's Minutes" (Boston: Rockwell and Churchill, 1893), 167.

13. Waters leaving Boston: "Sarah Winslow Deming journal, 1775," www.masshist.org/database/1898. Waters's sister Abigail married James Thompson, matching this source's mention of "Mr. Waters" having a "brother Thomson."

14. "very serviceable": *Heath's Memoirs of the American War* (New York: A. Wessels Company, 1904), 30.

15. "the ingenuity": Samuel Adams to Elbridge Gerry, September 26, 1775, in *The Writings of Samuel Adams*, Harry Alonzo Cushing, editor (New York: G. P. Putnam's Sons, 1908), 3:227.

October 21 he sent his friend and colleague James Warren a letter introducing a couple of Pennsylvanians visiting Massachusetts:

> I could wish them as well as other Strangers introduced to H. Knox and young Josiah Waters, if they are any where about the Camp. These young Fellows if I am not mistaken would give strangers no contemptible Idea of the military Knowledge of Massachusetts in the sublimest Chapters of the Art of War.[16]

Earlier in the same month Adams wrote to Gen. John Thomas asking about Josiah, Sr.'s work as a military engineer, among other men. But Thomas wrote back: "I Apprehend [Waters] has no great Understanding, in Either [gunnery or fortifications], any further than Executing or overseeing works, when Trased out, and by my Observations, we have Several Officers that are Equal or exceed him."[17]

Likewise, by November 2 General Washington was writing candidly to Gov. Jonathan Trumbull of Connecticut, "I sincerely wish this Camp could furnish a good Engineer." The only man Washington named as worthy in that field was "Mr Knox a Gentleman of Worcester."[18] He was not impressed by Josiah Waters, father or son.

In that fall of 1775 it probably became clear to the Waterses that they had not won over the commander-in-chief. They were unlikely to gain appointments in the reorganized army, at least at the ranks they wanted. But they still had the respect of New Englanders like Heath and the Adams cousins. They took a new assignment helping to fortify New London. As shown by how Connecticut calculated the older man's pay, he started that work on November 25. Josiah, Jr., was his assistant, naturally.[19]

Before heading south to New London, I posit, Josiah, Jr., traveled north in October to take stock of the family property. The Massabesick Plantation sat on the western edge of the district of Maine. Just over the border in New Hampshire was the town of Dover, home of the

16. "I could wish them": John Adams to James Warren, October 21, 1775, in *The Papers of John Adams*, vol. 3 (Cambridge, MA: Harvard University Press, 1979), 224–5.

17. "I Apprehend": John Thomas to John Adams, October 24, 1775, *Papers of John Adams*, 3:239–41.

18. "I sincerely wish": George Washington to Jonathan Trumbull, Sr., November 2, 1775, in *The Papers of George Washington*, Revolutionary War Series, vol. 2 (Charlottesville: University Press of Virginia, 1987), 289–90.

19. Waters fortifying New London: Frances Manwaring Caulkins, *History of New London, Connecticut* (New London: n.p., 1852), 520. *American Archives*, Peter Force, editor, 4th series (Washington, DC: U.S. Congress, 1837-53), 4:971.

Rev. Jeremy Belknap. The minister's later correspondence shows that he exchanged letters with Boston clergymen through Josiah Waters, Jr., who became a friend and collected orders for the history of New Hampshire.[20]

Belknap was too smart a man to spend time writing down a story of what had happened in Boston on April 18 unless he had good reason to believe his source was reliable. He must have known that "Mr. Waters" was from Boston and had links to the Patriot movement. That description is a match for Josiah Waters, Jr.—a Boston militia officer; cousin to Dawes, key figure in smuggling artillery out of occupied Boston and Dr. Warren's first alarm rider; respected by Adams and other leaders of the movement; entrusted with designing fortifications.

Furthermore, Josiah Waters, Jr., remained active in local self-defense. By the mid-1780s he was colonel of the Boston militia regiment. People who knew him in the decades after the Revolutionary War recalled that he was particularly interested in preserving military lore. One of the first books about the Ancient and Honorable Artillery Company, which he served as treasurer, stated:

> He collected many facts, for a history, but never published them. The manuscript is lost. The older members used to speak of it as containing important facts, as well as anecdotes of members, now preserved in the imperfect recollection of survivors.[21]

More specifically, a witness recalled hearing Waters tell stories about how Dr. Warren learned about the British army mission and sent off messengers. The militia colonel spoke to a young man from Roxbury named Joseph Curtis (1772–1858), who passed those stories to his daughter Catherine Parker Curtis (1801–1878), who saw them published in the *New England Historic and Genealogical Register* in 1853.

The Curtis account described a particularly useful informant about the British march on April 18:

> The Americans obtained this news, through an individual by the name of Jasper, an Englishman, a gunsmith by trade, whose shop was

20. Waters and Belknap: "Belknap Papers" in *Collections of the Massachusetts Historical Society*, series 6, volume 4 (1891), 199, 210, 232, 263, 268, 272–3, and so on; and series 5, volume 2 (1877), 103, 199, 239, 488, and so on. Hamilton Andrews Hill, *History of the Old South Church* (Boston: Houghton Mifflin, 1890), 2:254. It is also possible that the *senior* Waters was Belknap's informant in Dover in 1775, but that does not affect this essay's argument, given the closeness of father and son.

21. "He collected": Roberts, *Ancient and Honorable Artillery Company,* 2:161.

> in Hatter's Square; he worked for the British, but was friendly to the rebels; a sergeant major quartered in his family and made a confidant of him, telling him all their plans. Jasper repeated the same to Col. Waters, who made it known to the Committee of Safety.[22]

Is this story about a sergeant major credible? The British army did not formalize the duties of a sergeant major until the late 1790s, but it was already the designation of a unit's senior sergeant. No non-commissioned officer would have been privy to General Gage's whole plan, but by late on the afternoon of April 18 a senior sergeant may well have known about some crucial variables. The expedition would leave Boston by water instead of by marching over the Neck, indicating a destination to the northwest rather than Worcester. Those troops were preparing to travel farther and stay out longer than the training marches of previous weeks.

Significantly, a sergeant would not have known about the ultimate goal of the march, which General Gage's orders specified was to destroy provincial military stores in Concord, including artillery pieces and gunpowder. Dr. Warren evidently did not gain that knowledge on April 18. Instead, he sent Dawes and Revere only as far as Lexington to warn Hancock and Adams. Those riders decided on their own to proceed further west toward what would turn out to be the expedition's real goal.

In one important respect, the 1853 source deviates from what we know about the Lexington alarm. The Curtis account stated:

> The intelligence, that the British intended to go out to Lexington, was conveyed over Boston Neck to Roxbury by Ebenezer Dorr, of Boston, a leather dresser, by trade, who was mounted on a slow jogging horse, with saddle bags behind him, and a large flapped hat upon his head, to resemble a countryman on a journey. Col. Josiah Waters . . . followed on foot, on the sidewalk at a short distance from him, until he saw him safely past all the sentinels.

As stated earlier, eighteenth-century sources are clear that the Patriot express rider over the Boston Neck was William Dawes, Jr. The Curtis family tradition may well have muddled that man's surname with Ebenezer Dorr, who came from their town of Roxbury and became prominent in the early China trade; the Yankee pronunciations of "Dawes" and "Dorr" are similar. The other details of this account hold

22. "The Americans": C.C. [Catherine Parker Curtis], "Revolutionary Incidents," *New England Historical and Genealogical Register* (hereafter *NEHGR*), 7 (1853), 139.

up. Dawes was indeed a tanner, or leather dresser, before the war. His horse was slower than Revere's. The younger Waters, as a first cousin to Dawes, might well have watched anxiously to see him "safely past all the sentinels."

Combining these two reports traceable to Josiah Waters suggests that the Patriots' paid informant on April 18, the man Dr. Warren consulted to be certain about the British plan, was this man Jasper. Waters may have overstated Jasper's importance because he himself was involved in collecting that information and conveying it to "the Committee of Safety," headed by Warren. However, Belknap's notes from 1775 do not suggest that Waters portrayed himself at the center of events, simply as someone in the know—and he certainly was close to the Patriot leadership.

Accepting the Waters sources as largely reliable brings on another question: Who was the "individual by the name of Jasper"? That man was almost certainly William Jasper, a maker of cutlery and surgical instruments born in Britain—not a "gunsmith," but someone who might well have made and repaired weapons for the royal army in 1775.

Jasper moved from Britain to North America soon after the French and Indian War, advertising in the August 29, 1763, *New-York Gazette.*

> William Jasper, *Cutler,*
>
> *Just arrived from* England, *is now settled in New-York, near the Fly, Queen-Street, near Burling's and Beekman's Slips, next Door to Mr. Murray's, takes this Method to acquaint the Publick,*
>
> THAT he makes all Kinds of Surgeons Instruments, and grinds and cleans them; makes Razors, Penknives, Scissars, and all Kind of Edge Tools, which he also grinds; and makes Cutlery in general; makes Buckles of the best Block-Tin, wrought and plain Men's Gold and Silver Ware; Pinking-Irons of all Sorts; Sadlers Tools; Fret-Saws; Hatters Knives; likewise draws Teeth with great Ease and Safety, being accustomed to it for many Years. He likewise has brought over a Quantity of Copper and Tin Hard-Ware. All Persons that please to favour him with their Custom, may depend upon being served in the best and cheapest Manner.

William Jasper moved to Boston, where he married Ann Newman on June 29, 1768.[23] This couple appears on the list of marriage intentions read from all the pulpits, but it is not clear where they

23. William Jasper marriage: *Records Relating to the Early History of Boston* (also known as *Boston Town Records),* volume 30, "Boston Marriages from 1752 to 1809" (Boston: Municipal Printing Office, 1903), 428.

actually wed. Likewise, there is no record of the baptism of their children, though later records say they had some. One possible explanation is that the Jasper family worshipped in one of Boston's Baptist Meeting-Houses, whose records have not been published.[24]

The Curtis story said Jasper the gunsmith had a shop "in Hatter's Square," now known as Creek Square. That was near the center of Boston, on the Mill Creek that defined the edge of the North End. Most likely Jasper rented a home and workshop because he does not show up in recorded deeds. Weapons collectors have found William Jasper's name on a couple of blades possibly made in the late 1700s, such as a spontoon in the collection of the Worcester Art Museum.[25]

As a native of Britain, renting space to a British soldier's family, perhaps doing business with the British military, William Jasper could well have appeared reliable enough to an army sergeant to be a confidant. But the cutler did not become a Loyalist, leaving town in the evacuation of March 1776.[26] Instead, the next time William Jasper appeared in a newspaper was this notice in the August 8, 1782, *Continental Journal*:

> TO THE PUBLIC.
> JASPER, Surgeon Instrument Maker in Boston, has lately invented and compleated an Instrument for drawing Teeth perpendicular, which was never done before, for which if he can have a patentee from Congress, it shall be universally known, if not, let it die in oblivion.

24. Later records: On April 10, 1791, Nancy Jasper married Joseph Jones in the Rev. Thomas Baldwin's Second Baptist Meeting-house. The next year, on March 25, 1792, another Baptist minister, the Rev. Samuel Stillman, married Mary Jasper to John Dumaresque Dyer. Those women might have been the daughters or the widow and daughter of the cutler William Jasper. *Boston Town Records*, 30: 115, 117.

25. spontoon: worcester.emuseum.com/objects/48713/spontoon. See also Al Benting, *For Liberty I Live* (New York: Page Publishing, 2019), 76–7.

26. Jasper during the war: No one with the surname Jasper is listed in the comprehensive *Massachusetts Soldiers and Sailors of the Revolutionary War*, indicating how rare that name was in colonial New England. A William Jasper was among the Americans taken prisoner on the Boston-based privateer *Rising States* on April 15, 1777, and held in Forton Prison in Britain that December. *NEHGR*, 33:36; "List of American Prisoners Confined in Forton Prison Decr: 29th: 1777," January 8, 1778, *Naval Documents of the American Revolution*, 11:888-91. There is no indication this is the same man, however. A different William Jasper is remembered for his military service in South Carolina before dying in 1779.

27. Jasper probate file: Suffolk County Probate file 18795, Suffolk County, MA: Probate File Papers database at AmericanAncestors.org, New England Historic Genealogical Society, 2017–2019.

There was no statutory process for the American government to grant patents in 1782, and the Confederation Congress had a lot of other business to handle.

The *Continental Journal* of November 23, 1786, reported that "Mr. William Jasper, Cutler," had died in Boston. Anna Jasper administered William's estate, relying on two men to complete the paperwork since she could not sign her name. William Jasper's property, evaluated at only £24.6.6, included metal-working tools, some old books and pictures, and household utensils, but no real estate. Probate judge Oliver Wendell signed off on the administration, which mentioned children without specifying their names and ages.[27]

While the sparse record of William Jasper's life in America is far from decisive, it shows that he could have been the Patriots' crucial source on British army preparations in April 1775, as Josiah Waters described to different people, first as early that October and then decades later. More importantly, it lends credence to Belknap's statement in 1775 that the Boston Patriots relied not just on volunteers but on a paid informant—just like other groups gathering intelligence throughout history.

Top Ten Battle of Bunker Hill Quotes

KATIE TURNER GETTY

On the blazing afternoon of June 17, 1775, two forces met on the Charlestown peninsula just outside Boston, Massachusetts.

An unstoppable force of red-clad British troops swept ashore and broke upon the immovable walls of the provincial fortifications atop Breed's Hill, crashing across the Charlestown peninsula like a blood-red wave. Flood waters of British soldiery climbed higher and higher up the slopes of the hill, rising until repulsed by heavy fire from the provincial muskets that bristled from the walls of the earthen fort, only to surge again.

Provincial soldiers defended the redoubt atop Breed's Hill, their simple homemade clothing streaked with dirt from digging the walls of the earthen fort that surrounded and sheltered them. New England soil shoveled and shaped overnight for the protection of New England men.

Blood met earth, hundreds of times that afternoon, as men in blood-red coats and men in dirt-dusted homespun, fell to the ground, bone shattered by musket ball, and flesh torn by bayonet.

The smoke from burning Charlestown has long since dissipated. The crack and blaze of musket fire has long since faded. The walls of the redoubt have long since returned to the earth—as have the soldiers who scaled and defended them.

All that remains of the Battle of Bunker Hill are the words of the men who were there.

Cpl. Peter Brown

> "We work'd there undiscoverd till about five in the Morning, then we saw our danger, being against Ships of the Line, and all Boston fortified against Us."[1]

1. Peter Brown to Sarah Brown, June 25, 1775, in *Massachusetts Historical Society Collections Online*, https://www.masshist.org/database/viewer.php?item_id=725&pid=2.

Twenty-two-year-old Peter Brown numbered among the approximately 1,200 provincial soldiers ordered to march from Cambridge and entrench on a hill in Charlestown on the night of June 16, 1775. The troops dug through the darkness, throwing up a fortification on Breed's Hill that would shock British senses when daylight broke on June 17.

Col. William Prescott

> "There was a party of Hampshire in conjunction with some other Forces Lined a Fence at the distance of three score Rods back of the Fort partly to the North."[2]

Colonel Prescott commanded the provincial troops in the redoubt atop Breed's Hill, but American lines expanded beyond Breed's Hill and reached all the way to the shore of Mystic River. As provincial soldiers arrived on the Charlestown peninsula to provide reinforcement, many men from New Hampshire, Connecticut, and Massachusetts took position along an improvised rail fence line. The soldiers at the rail fence ably repelled an assault from the British right wing, which if successful, would have enabled British forces to envelop the men in the redoubt and cut them off from the main army at Cambridge.

Isaac Glynney

> "We Did as before Reservd our fire till they Came within About six or seven Rods then we Shoed. them yankey Play & Drove them Back again But soon they Renud. the attact & Came agin But we Being Destetute of aminition we made use aminition calld. cabel stones."[3]

Isaac Glynney was not yet fourteen years old when he served with the provincial forces at the Battle of Bunker Hill in the stead of his sick father.[4] The British twice attempted to breach the walls of the redoubt but were driven back each time by heavy provincial fire. Finally, as provincial ammunition ran low and fire slackened, the British succeeded in breaching the redoubt in a final surge. Provincial troops

2. William Prescott to John Adams, August 25, 1775, Founders Online, National Archives, https://founders.archives.gov/documents/Adams/06-03-02-0070.

3. Isaac Glynney, "Diary of Isaac Glynney", digital reproduction of original manuscript, Harlan Crow Library, Dallas, TX.

4. *Massachusetts Soldiers and Sailors of the Revolutionary War* (Boston: Wright & Potter Printing Company, 1899), 499. Isaac Glynney's father was John Glenne/Glynney, who enlisted in Captain Bancroft's company, Colonel Bridge's regiment.

wielded their muskets as clubs while others hurled stones as their only defense against British bayonets.

Maj. Gen. John Burgoyne

> "And now ensued one of the greatest scenes of war that can be conceived: if we look to the height, Howe's corps ascending the hill in the face of entrenchments . . . a large and a noble town in one great blaze . . . the roar of cannon, mortars, and musketry . . . to fill the ear; the storm of the redoubts . . . to fill the eye; and the reflection that perhaps a defeat was a final loss to the British empire in America, to fill the mind."[5]

British General John Burgoyne watched the battle from his position at the Copp's Hill battery in the north end of Boston, just across the Charles River from the Charlestown peninsula. With dramatic flair, he captured the overwhelming sensory experience of the battle.

Lt. Francis, Lord Rawdon

> "They rose up and poured in so heavy a fire upon us that the oldest officers say they never saw a sharper action. They kept up the fire till we were within ten yards of them; nay, they even knocked down my captain, close by side me, after we got into the ditch of the entrenchment."[6]

Francis, Lord Rawdon participated in the battle as a lieutenant under Capt. George Harris in the 5th Regiment of Foot grenadier company. Both Lord Rawdon and Captain Harris ascended Breed's Hill in the face of heavy provincial fire in the attempt to storm the redoubt.

Captain Harris was shot in the head and fell to the ground. Lord Rawdon, believing Captain Harris to be dead, attempted to move him to prevent his body from being trampled by surging troops. But upon moving the captain, Rawdon realized that Harris was still alive and ordered four soldiers to carry Harris off the field.

5. John Burgoyne to Lord Stanley, June 25, 1775, *American Archives*, ed. Peter Force (Washington, D.C., 1843), Ser. 4, 2:1095, https://digital.lib.niu.edu/islandora/object/niu-amarch%3A87089.

6. Francis, Lord Rawdon to Francis, tenth Earl of Huntingdon, June 20, 1775 in *The Spirit of 'Seventy-Six: The Story of the American Revolution as Told by Participants*, eds. Henry Steele Commager and Richard B. Morris (New York: Harper & Row, 1975), 130-131.

Capt. George Harris

> "They still every day peep at my brain, which, all things considered, is not an unlucky circumstance, as it may convince you and the rest of the world that I have such a thing."[7]

Captain Harris was ferried back to Boston where he underwent emergency cranial surgery. Surgeons trepanned his skull to relieve the pressure of the blood that was building inside his head due to his wound. Trephination involved boring a hole in the skull to relieve the pressure, and in Captain Harris's case, removing bits of "matter" from inside his head which were causing excruciating pain.

During the procedure, physicians held a mirror up to the back of Captain Harris's head which granted him the dubious opportunity to view his own brain.

Defying all odds, Captain Harris recovered quickly from both the wound and the trephination. A mere five weeks later, in a letter to his cousin, he demonstrated that not only had his body and brain survived the Battle of Bunker Hill intact, but so did his sense of humor.

Lt. John Waller, British Marines

> "I cannot pretend to describe the Horror of the Scene within the Redoubt, when we enter'd it, 'twas streaming with Blood & strew'd with dead & dying Men, the Soldiers stabbing some and dashing out the Brains of others was a sight too dreadful for me to dwell any longer on."[8]

Lt. John Waller of the Marines was among the British troops who stormed the provincial redoubt, dropping over the earthen walls of the fort, and "driving bayonets into all whom opposed them."[9] A final desperate struggle ensued between the defending provincial stalwarts and the furious British troops.

Cpl. Amos Farnsworth

> "I did not leave the entrenchment until the enemy got in. I then retreated ten or fifteen rods. Then I received a wound in my right arm, the ball going through a little below my elbow, breaking the

7. George Harris to cousin, in S.R. Lushington, *The Life and Services of General Lord Harris During His Campaigns in America the West Indies and India* (London: John W. Parker, 1840), 57.
8. John Waller to unidentified recipient, June 21, 1775 in *Massachusetts Historical Society Collections Online*, https://www.masshist.org/database/viewer.php?item_id=726.
9. John Waller to his brother, June 22, 1775, in Samuel Adams Drake, *Bunker Hill: The Story Told in Letters from the Battle Field by British Officers Engaged* (Boston: Nichols and Hall, 1875), 28.

little shell bone. Another ball struck my back, taking a piece of skin about as big as a Penny. But I got to Cambridge that night."[10]

As hand-to-hand combat broke out inside the dirt walls of the redoubt, Col. William Prescott ordered a retreat. Provincial troops like Cpl. Amos Farnsworth of Groton, Massachusetts, fought their way out of the redoubt and retreated toward Bunker Hill and Charlestown Neck, under the cover of other provincial troops who had been positioned elsewhere on the Charlestown peninsula, at the rail fence.

Lt. Samuel Blachley Webb

"But alas how Dismal was the Sight to see the Beautiful & Valuable town of Charlestown all in Flames—and now behold it a heap of Ruins—with nothing Standing but a heap of Chimneys,—which by the by remains an Everlasting Monument of British Cruelty and Barbarity."[11]

Lieutenant Webb served in the company of Capt. John Chester of Connecticut which was ordered to march to Charlestown from Cambridge that afternoon. At the outset of the battle, provincial marksmen had been positioned in the buildings of Charlestown village to harass the British left as it staged its attack on the redoubt. In retaliation, the British reduced the village to a heap of ashes—lobbing exploding shells into the town from the Copp's Hill Battery. Nothing remained of Charlestown village except old stone foundations and the skeletal outlines of chimneys.

General Sir William Howe

"The General's returns will give you the particulars of what I call this unhappy day—I freely confess to you, when I look to the consequences of it, in the loss of so many brave Officers, I do it with horror—The success is too dearly bought."[12]

10. Amos Farnsworth, Diary, June 17, 1775, in *Three Military Diaries Kept by Groton Soldiers in Different Wars*, ed. Samuel A. Green (Cambridge: John Wilson and Son, 1901), 90. Amos Farnsworth's original diary entry is, "I Did not leave the Intrenchment until the Enemy got in I then Retreated ten or Fifteen rods, then I received a wound in my right arm the bawl gowing through a little below my elbow breaking the little shel bone Another bawl struck my back taking a piece of Skin about as big as a Penny but I got to Cambridge that night."

11. Samuel Blachley Webb to Joseph Webb, June 19, 1775, in *Correspondence and Journals of Samuel Blachley Webb*, Volume 1 (Lancaster: Wickersham Press, 1893), 65-66.

12. William Howe to unidentified recipient, June 22 and 24, 1775, in *The Correspondence of King George the Third from 1760 to December 1783*, ed. Hon. Sir John Fortescue, Volume 3 (London: MacMillian & Co., 1928), 223.

General Sir William Howe served as the commanding British officer on the ground in Charlestown during the Battle of Bunker Hill. The battle raged not just on Breed's Hill but across the entire Charlestown peninsula—from Charlestown village on the southwestern tip, to the shore of the Mystic River, over and across both Breed's and Bunker Hills, to Charlestown Neck, that narrow strip of land that connected Charlestown to the mainland. The British drove the Americans across that neck and out of Charlestown within a couple short hours. However, the provincials extracted a heavy price for British possession of the peninsula. Comprising a combined force of Massachusetts, Connecticut, and New Hampshire men, the provincials inflicted over twice as many casualties as the British. Over 1,000 British soldiers were killed, wounded or captured, compared to about 450 provincial troops.

The British encamped in Charlestown on the night of June 17 and fortified Bunker Hill. But they launched no incursions into the Massachusetts countryside for the remainder of the Siege of Boston.

The British evacuated Boston exactly nine months later, on March 17, 1776.

John Warren's Loss of His Brother Joseph Warren

SALINA B. BAKER

On Saturday, June 17, 1775, Abigail Adams and her seven-year-old son, John Quincy, stood on Penn's Hill near her home in Braintree, Massachusetts. They watched sulfuric smoke cloud the sky and heard cannon thunder across Boston Harbor from British ships in the Mystic and Charles Rivers bombarding colonial forces who had built a redoubt on Breed's Hill on the Charlestown peninsula overnight. The fighting continued throughout the day, and the village of Charlestown erupted in flames. From her view in Braintree fifteen miles south of Charlestown, she must have wondered who she knew and loved was dying in the battle that history calls the Battle of Bunker Hill. She soon found out.

Reports of the battle began to come in and filter to towns and villages throughout colonial America. Abigail wrote to her husband, John Adams, who was in Philadelphia serving as a delegate to the Second Continental Congress:

> Dearest Friend
> Sunday June 18 1775
> The Day; perhaps the decisive Day is come on which the fate of America depends. My bursting Heart must find vent at my pen. I have just heard that our dear Friend Dr. Warren is no more but fell gloriously fighting for his Country—saying better to die honourably in the field than ignominiously hang upon the Gallows. Great is our Loss. He has distinguished himself in every engagement, by his courage and fortitude, by animating the Soldiers and leading them on by his own example.[1]

1. "Adams Family Correspondence, volume 1" https://www.masshist.org/publications/adams-papers/index.php/view/ADMS-04-01-02-0150.

On June 17, twenty-two-year-old Dr. John Warren also heard the sounds of battle from his home in Salem, twenty-three miles north of Charlestown. John's oldest brother, Dr. Joseph Warren, was the man Abigail referred to as "our dear Friend" in her letter. John and Joseph, both Harvard graduates, were closely united by family, religion, the premature death of their father, Freemasonry, and by professional and patriotic sympathies.[2] Joseph fondly referred to his adoring younger brother as "Jack." After his 1771 graduation, John served his medical apprenticeship under his brother in Boston and then moved Salem to begin a new medical practice.[3]

Twelve years John's senior, Joseph was deeply involved in the ten-year colonial America political rebellion that began in the mid-1760s, fueled by the British Parliament. Britain's attempt to control colonial autonomy through taxes and acts that strangled trade and interfered in colonial government had turned to force by stationing troops in Boston. Aside from maintaining a successful medical practice, Joseph Warren presided over the Massachusetts Provincial Congress and its Committee of Safety, a colonial body of government illegal under the 1774 Massachusetts Government Act, which limited colonial power and outlawed freely-called town meetings and elected positions.

In June 1775, the Provincial Congress and New England militia were holding the British army under siege in Boston following the outbreak of hostilities on April 19, 1775, when shots were fired between colonists and British regulars in Massachusetts. For several years, Joseph had been preparing himself by study and observation to take a conspicuous rank in military arrangements which he knew must ensue.[4] The Massachusetts Provincial Congress bestowed a major generalship upon him on June 14, 1775, the same day the Second Continental Congress formed the Continental Army and appointed George Washington the commander-in-chief.

John knew of his brother's military interests and political activities which included his participation in the well-organized Sons of Liberty,

2. Edwin Bradford Homes, M.W. Grand Master and Sereno D. Nickerson, R.W. Recording Grand Secretary, *Proceedings of the Most Worshipful Grand Lodge of Ancient Free and Accepted Masons of the Commonwealth of Massachusetts* (Boston: Press of Rockwell and Churchill, 1869), lxvi, 45. Both Joseph and John Warren served as Grand Masters for this lodge. Edward Warren, M.D., *The Life of John Warren, M.D.* (Boston: Noyes, Holmes, and Company, 1874), 261-262.

3. John Cary, *Joseph Warren Physician, Politician, Patriot* (Urbana: University of Illinois Press, 1964), 31.

4. Samuel Lorenzo Knapp, *Biographical Sketches of Eminent Lawyers, Statesmen, and Men of Letters* (Boston: Richardson and Lord, 1821), 116.

an organization founded to advance the rights of the colonists. In 1774, the first of the Coercive Acts, the Boston Port Act, closed the port of Boston. The only imports allowed were provisions for the British Army and necessary goods such as fuel and wheat. The act mandated that the port remain shuttered until Bostonians made restitution to the East India Company for destroying their tea during the Boston Tea Party in December 1773.[5] Joseph worked on a Committee of Donations that asked the other colonies to support the "suffering population" and "to champion the nationalistic policy which he and Samuel Adams had urged" for years. Joseph "recruited his brother into the ranks of propagandists."[6]

When the Boston Committee of Correspondence warned mechanics against working on barracks and other structures for the occupying British army, John wrote a letter to a committee of the mechanics of New York on behalf of the mechanics of Boston dated September 8, 1774:

> Gentlemen,—General Gage being determined to cut off the communication of this town with the country, by fortifying the sole pass between them and the land, has applied to several tradesmen in this town, and found none base enough to engage in so villainous an enterprise, and it is now said he intends to apply to New York for workmen to complete his designs . . . We are, gentlemen, your friends and fellow countrymen. By order of the Committee, John Warren, Chairman[7]

On that decisive day of June 17, Dr. John Warren was "called from Salem," both "by the sound of firing of cannon and, by the flames of Charlestown." John's journal entry demonstrates his distress over conflicting reports:

> June 17, 1775.—This day,—a day ever to be remembered by the United American Colonies,—at four o'clock in the afternoon, I was alarmed with the incessant report of cannon, which appeared to be at, or near Boston. Towards sunsetting, a very great fire was discovered nearly in a direction from Salem to Boston. At the beginning of the evening, news arrived that a smart engagement had happened in the afternoon, on Bunker Hill, in Charlestown, between the King's regular troops and the Provincials. Soon after, we received intelligence that our troops were repulsed with great loss, and the enemy had taken possession of the ground, which we had broke the night before. I was very

5. "The Coercive Acts," https://www.masshist.org/revolution/coercive.php.
6. Cary, *Joseph Warren Physician, Politician, Patriot,* 139.
7. Warren. *The Life of John Warren, M.D.*, 31-32.

anxious, as I was informed that great numbers had fallen on both sides, and that my brother was in all probability in the engagement. I however went home with the determination to take a few hours' sleep, and then go immediately to Cambridge, with my arms.

Accordingly, in the morning about two o'clock, I prepared myself, and went off on horseback, and when I arrived at Medford, received the melancholy and distressing tidings that my brother was missing. Upon this dreadful intelligence I went immediately to Cambridge, and inquired of almost every person I saw whether they could give me any information of him. Some told me he was undoubtedly alive and well, others, that he was wounded; and others, that he fell on the field.

This perplexed me almost to distraction. I went on inquiring, with a solicitude which was such a mixture of hope and fear, as none but one who has felt it can form any conception of. In this manner I passed several days, every day's information diminishing the probability of his safety.[8]

We can imagine John trying to find his brother amid the confusion and news "that the English had obtained possession of the ground, was all that could be known." Further, "while endeavoring on this occasion, to pass a sentinel, in his overwhelming anxiety to ascertain his brother's fate, Dr. [John] Warren received a thrust from a bayonet, the scar of which he bore through life."[9]

At the time of the Battle of Bunker Hill, Joseph Warren was a thirty-four-year-old widower with four children ages ten through two. This added to John's distress as his son, Dr. Edward Warren, wrote:

It was several days before my father could ascertain the fact of his brother's death. He as ever accustomed to feel more for others than for himself. The affliction of his mother, the condition of his brother's children, now completely orphaned and destitute, the loss of so many of his countrymen, not only produced the severest grief, but excited the utmost indignation.[10]

In an undated entry in John's journal he wrote of his indignation toward the British ministry. The entry is long and worth our extended attention to understand John's anxiety, susceptibility and belief in the Patriot cause:

O ye blood-thirsty wretches, who planned this dreadful scene, which you are now forcing your blood-hounds to execute, did you but feel the

8. Warren. *The Life of John Warren, M.D.*, 44-45.
9. Ibid., 46.
10. Ibid., 47.

pangs of heartfelt pungent grief for the cruel wounds you inflicted upon the tenderest part of the public, as well as individuals, you would have execrated those diabolical measures, which by your counsels have been adopted, and precipitated us into all the horrors of civil war.

Unfeeling wretches! Reflect a moment, if you have still one feature of humanity which is unobliterated from your minds, and view the helpless orphan bereft of its fond and only parent, stript of every comfort of life, driven into an inhospitable wild, and exposed to all the misery which is the result of your brutal violence, and forbear to weep if you can; but I defy you to show yourselves so refined in your darling acts of cruelty, as to be capable of supporting the shocking reflection.[11]

John then accused them of "pretensions to honor, justice, and humanity" and being "British cowards." He went on to say what was in the minds of so many other revolutionaries:

Cover your heads with shame, ye guilty wretches. Go home and tell your blood-thirsty master your pitiful tale, and tell him that the laurel which once decorated the soldier has withered on his brow upon the American shore. Tell him that the British honor and fame have received a mortal stab from the brave conduct of the Americans; tell him that even your congress have but served to inspire the sufferers with fresh courage and determined revolution, and let him know that since that accursed day when first the hostile troops of Great Britain put their foot on the American shore, your conduct has been such as has operated in a continued series of disgraceful incidents, weak counsels, and operations replete with ignorance and folly. Tell him this, ye contemptible cowards; hide yourselves like menial slaves in your master's kitchens, nor dare approach the happy asylum of once extinct liberty, for if ye dare, ye die.[12]

John wrote at the end of his rant, "Ye die." He had a choice. Take up a musket or take up his scalpel. Which would serve the cause more? But those who knew him understood that the cause would be served best by his excellent medical qualifications. He was appointed senior surgeon of the military hospital in Cambridge, Massachusetts. After Gen. George Washington arrived in July 1775 to take command of the army, the Continental Congress established an "Army Hospital" to coordinate the medical care required by the Continental Army. John advised John Hancock, Joseph's close friend and president of the

11. Ibid., 48.
12. Ibid., 49.

Continental Congress, about necessities and best practices for hospitals and medical care.

When the siege of Boston ended in March 1776 and the British evacuated, the city was in disarray. John Warren's journal contains descriptions of the condition of the city and inhabitants. The Charlestown peninsula, which the British had been holding since the Battle of Bunker Hill, was also evacuated. This cleared the way for him to look for the remains of his brother Joseph on Breed's Hill where the battle had taken place. On March 21, 1776, he wrote:

> This day I visit Charlestown, and a most melancholy heap of ruins it is. Scarcely the vestiges of those beautiful buildings remain to distinguish them from the mean cottages. The hill, which was the theatre upon which the bloody tragedy of the 17th of June was acted, commands the most affecting view I ever saw in my life. The walls of magnificent buildings tottering to the earth below; above, a great number of rude hillocks, under which are deposited the remains, in clusters, of those deathless heroes, who fell in the field of battle. The scene was inexpressibly solemn, when I considered myself as walking over the bones of the many of my worthy fellow-countrymen, who jeoparded and sacrificed their lives in these high places. When I considered that, perhaps, whilst I was musing on the objects around me, I might be standing over the remains of a dear brother, whose blood had stained these hallowed walks, with what veneration did inspire me![13]

Sometime after, an Englishman who had witnessed the burial informed John and his brother, Eben, of the location of Joseph's grave. Governor Christopher Gore, a Mason with the St. Andrews Lodge, said in an oration, "The rosemary and cassia adorned and discovered his hallowed grave."[14] John and Eben did not discover the body of their brother until April 4, covered with about three feet of ground and much disfigured, "yet it was sufficiently known by two artificial teeth, which were set for him a short time before his glorious exit."[15] The artificial teeth, made for Joseph by Paul Revere, were held in his mouth with a wire. The remains were disinterred and brought to the State House on State Street.

13. Warren. *The Life of John Warren, M.D.*, 72-73.

14. *Lodge of Saint Andrew, and the Massachusetts Grand Lodge* (Boston: Printed by vote of the Lodge of St. Andrew, 1870), 203.

15. Richard Frothingham, *Life and Times of Joseph Warren* (Boston: Little, Brown, & Company, 1856), 522. Frothingham quoted the entry about Joseph's artificial teeth from the *New-England Chronicle*, April 1776.

On Monday, April 8, 1776, an article was submitted to the *Boston Gazette*:

> Notice is hereby given to all brethren of the Ancient and Honorable Society of Freemasons, that this day will be re-interred the remains of the late Most Worshipful Joseph Warren, Esq., Grand Master of Ancient Masonry for North America, who was slain in the Battle of Bunker Hill, June 17, 1775. The procession will be from the State House in Boston at four o'clock, p.m., at which time the brethren are requested to attend with their clothing and jewels. By order of the Right Worshipful Joseph Webb, Esq., Deputy Grand Master.[16]

The call for Masons, and John Warren's presence in Boston to take stock of medicines and hospital stores left behind by the British, indicate he had opportunity to attend the funeral, held at King's Chapel. Because the Warrens did not have a family burial plot in Boston, Joseph's remains were interred in Granary Burying Ground in the tomb of George Richards Minot, a family friend.

At the time of Joseph's death, his four children were in Worcester under the roof of his friend Dr. Elijah Dix, and in the care of their nanny and Joseph's alleged betrothed, Mercy Scollay. He had sent them there for their safety before hostilities erupted on April 19, 1775. John's son Edward wrote of Mercy Scollay:

> The children appear to have been objects of great interest, as it was natural they should be. There seems to have been some jealousy on the part of their friends, as to who should have charge of them. The Miss Scollay, who is here spoken of, was the daughter of John Scollay, and the intimate and dear friend of General Warren. She is said to have been betrothed to him, at the time of his death. She was a woman of great energy and depth of character, and her zeal in behalf of these children, if nothing else, would seem to have given claim to the charge of them.[17]

Mercy Scollay and John Warren did not see eye to eye on who should have custody of the children. She contended that shortly before his death Joseph had asked her to care of them if something should happen to him. Mercy was put out with John Warren. On August 17, 1775, from Watertown where she brought Joseph's two daughters with her and went looking for John Hancock, she wrote to Mrs. Elisha Dix:

16. "The Annotated Newspapers of Harbottle Dorr, Jr. The Boston-Gazette, and Country Journal, 8 April 1776," https://www.masshist.org/dorr/volume/4/sequence/1002.
17. Warren, *The Life of John Warren, M.D.*, 87.

> My first enquiry was for Mr Hancock whom I was lucky eno' to find—I told him that I had learnt since I came down what was doing with the few effects my poor friend was possesst of out of Boston—that John W—-n had sold every feather bed to General Washinton and for ought I know every thing else—that his picture so valuable to those who esteemd the original was somewhere near Roxbury the looking glasses that was brought out of town with it were (through carelessness) broke to pieces and I supposed all that was in their hands would share the same fate—Mr H—k appeared much affected at my relation, said his brother had no right to doo those things without proper authority and would certainly be calld to account for those proceedings.[18]

In the same letter she wrote that she had seen John and Samuel Adams and John Hancock and that "nothing can be done respecting the children till a Judge is appointed and I cannot hold them one moment after the relations claim their right—I have likewise seen their uncle John." She also wrote that his mother, Mary, wanted them removed from Worcester. What John Hancock immediately did for Mercy, if anything, is unknown.

On May 10, 1776, she wrote to Mrs. Elisha Dix about a misunderstanding she had with John—that apparently assumptions between Mercy and Joseph as to who would have the children surprised John, or John was not willing to admit the assumptions:

> I had a visit yesterday from John W—-n and I receiv'd, and treated him with all that tenderness which I shall ever feel for the Brother of my Friend—I tho't he seemd reservd and expected he would say something on former subjects, which he at last did by telling me he understood I had said I tho't myself very ungenerously treated by him, and the rest of the Family that I had a prior claim to the children and some of my family had reported there was a connexion between this Brother and me which he was ignorant of, and was much surpriz'd that his brother should never mention such a design to him—I was a little nettled at his manner of speaking and told him twas an affair of too much delicacy for me to converse upon but had his Brother continued here, he might have been better inform'd perhaps by this time . . . but we parted good friends, I promised to see the children frequently, and begd I might be imployd in any thing, wherein I might be servicable to the dear little creatures—Thus ended a conversation in which I sufferd many pangs.[19]

18. https://historycambridge.org/wp-content/uploads/2021/11/Mercy-Scollay-Transcripts.pdf, 1.
19. Ibid., 11.

After John left the Continental Army field hospitals in 1777 and returned to Boston and married, he legally adopted Joseph's children.[20] The subject of the children's welfare and education arose in the coming years. In a letter written by Samuel Adams on December 20, 1779, to John Hancock and Elbridge Gerry, he conveyed that he had spoken to John Warren on the matter:

> Gentlemen—Since my last letter to you, I have had an opportunity to converse with Dr. John Warren, brother of our deceased friend, concerning the situation of his children. He tells me that the eldest son was, as early as it could be done, put under the care and tuition of the Rev. Mr. Payson of Chelsea . . . The eldest daughter, a miss of about thirteen is with the doctor . . . The two younger children, a boy of about seven years, and a girl somewhat older, are in the family of John Scollay, Esq., under the particular care of his daughter at her most earnest request . . . Miss Scollay deserves the greatest praise for her attention to them.[21]

Reading the entirety of the letter, it is unclear whether Adams was praising Mercy Scollay or whether the praise had come from John. Nevertheless, it appears that John was willing to allow the children to be with her because not only had she loved their father, but she also loved them and provided stability.

John Warren became a distinguished Harvard professor of anatomy and surgery, performed one of the first abdominal operations in the country, and was a founder of the Boston and Massachusetts Medical Societies and Harvard School of Medicine. He was also involved in founding what became the Massachusetts General Hospital in Boston. Through his son, Dr. John Collins Warren, and his blood line, the Warren name became a medical dynasty whose achievements included the first use of ether anesthesia.

John Warren fathered seventeen children. He died on April 4, 1815, at age sixty-one from heart disease; he suffered symptoms of his illness for thirty years. He outlived three of Joseph's children, who died without issue—Betsey died in 1804, Joseph 1790, and Richard 1797. The youngest child, Mary, had one son who survived to adulthood. She died in 1826.

John was reunited with Joseph in death. In the mid-1800s, after previous reburials, the brothers' remains were moved to the Warren family

20. "Orphans of the Revolution: caring for the children of Dr. Joseph Warren," https://www.masshist.org/object-of-the-month/objects/orphans-of-the-revolution-2006-06-01.
21. Frothingham, *Life and Times of Joseph Warren*, 543.

plot in Forest Hills Cemetery in Jamaica Plain, Massachusetts. They were reinterred under a Roxbury pudding stone on which a statue of Joseph Warren was erected on October 22, 2016, by the 6th Masonic District. The district hosted a ceremony in which their Grand Master dedicated a new memorial to "the namesake of our Distinguished Service Medal, M.W. [Most Worshipful] Joseph Warren" in conjunction with members of the Warren family. John and son John Collins Warren share a tombstone with brother and uncle respectively. If John bore the millstone of grief and idolatry for his brother around his neck for the rest of his life as he bore the scar inflicted by a British bayonet, he is quiescent now.

Construing Congress's Ill-Fated 1775 Decision to Invade Canada

GENE PROCKNOW

Just sixty days after the start of armed hostilities at Lexington Green, the Continental Congress's decision to invade Canada resulted in one of the worst defeats in the War for Independence.[1] While exact casualty figures are difficult to discern, likely half of the American forces sent north were killed in battle, wounded, captured, or died of disease.[2] The attacking Rebel Army retreated disease-ridden and in disarray, resulting in the Northern Army's combat ineffectiveness. Before the invasion, the Canadians did not firmly commit to open hostilities against British rule or even send delegates to the First or Second Continental Congresses. Why did a newly formed Congress authorize an invasion of the rebellion-reticent Canada?

Historians posit several explanations for the Rebel offensive, such as the initial expression of manifest destiny,[3] the first in a long line of

1. Canada refers more properly to the British-controlled Quebec Province. Canada did not become a country until after the American Revolution. However, as the Continental Congress and many other primary sources refer to the Province of Quebec as Canada, this article will use them interchangeably.
2. An argument can be made that the Canadian invasion was the deadliest campaign. Mark Mayo Boater estimated that the Rebels left 5,000 casualties in Canada, of which 3,000 were hospital cases. He estimates losses at the 1780 surrender of Charleston to be killed 90, wounded 140, and captured 3,300. Mark Mayo Boatner, *Encyclopedia of the American Revolution*, Bicentennial ed. (New York: D. McKay Co, 1974), 178. Howard H. Peckham offers similar casualty estimates for the fall of Charleston but also identifies additional losses in preparatory and naval battles fought in the lead-up to the Patriot surrender. Howard H. Peckham, *The Toll of Independence: Engagements & Battle Casualties of the American Revolution* (Chicago: University of Chicago Press, 1974), 68-70. Peckham does not offer an estimate of the number of soldiers who died of disease in Canada, so his estimates of the Canadian invasion are lower than Boatner's.
3. Don Higginbotham, *The War of American Independence Military Attitudes, Policies and Practice, 1763-1789* (Norwalk, CT: The Easton Press, 1971), 108.

American wars of liberation,[4] or a *rage militaire* overcoming sagacious Congressional judgment.[5] While these reasons place the Canadian incursion decision in an insightful historical context, they look backward using information from subsequent eras and perspectives. A forward look at the period's events, from the outbreak of combat to Congress's invasion order, reveals a series of misjudgments based upon faulty intelligence, overestimating threats, a lack of strategic military foresight, and insufficient Congressional control over the military.

The decision to invade Canada occurred in June 1775 during the initial formation of the Continental Army and the selection of George Washington as its commander-in-chief. Initially, a cautious Congress appeared to act defensively. Alarmed by the news that a motley amalgamation of unsanctioned rebels took offensive actions to capture Fort Ticonderoga and other British military installations on Lake Champlain, the Second Continental Congress ordered on June 1, 1775: "that no expedition or incursion ought to be undertaken or made by any Colony or body of Colonists against or into Canada."[6] However, just twenty-six days later, the momentous decision-making Congress reversed its position and ordered the just-formed Continental Army to invade peaceful, non-rebelling Canada. Congress authorized Maj. Gen. Philip Schuyler, the newly appointed Continental Army's Northern commander, to invade Quebec if "it would not be disagreeable to the Canadians."[7] Congress was so hurried to have its wishes executed that John Hancock, its President, bypassed commander-in-chief George Washington, issuing the discretionary invasion orders directly to Schuyler. Most historians characterize the subsequent Canadian invasion as a debacle and one of the worst decisions made by the Continental Congress.[8] What caused Congress to reverse itself and quickly make a decisive and disastrous decision?

4. Mark R. Anderson, *The Battle for the Fourteenth Colony: America's War of Liberation in Canada, 1774–1776* (Hanover, NH: University Press of New England, 2013), 1–2.

5. Kevin Phillips, *1775: A Good Year for Revolution* (New York: Viking, 2012), 244.

6. Charles Thomson, "Resolve," Northern Illinois University, *American Archives*, June 1, 1775, https://digital.lib.niu.edu/islandora/object/niu-amarch%3A79871.

7. John Hancock to Philip Schuyler, June 28, 1775, *Letters of Delegates to Congress: Volume I August 1774 to August 1775*, https://memory.loc.gov/cgi-bin/query/r?ammem/hlaw:@field(DOCID+@lit(dg001497)).

8. Mark R. Anderson represents the views of many historians by asserting, "The Continental Congress launched a juggernaut that it was unprepared to control, adequately guide, or properly support." Anderson, *The Battle for the Fourteenth Colony*, 348. A minority opinion that the Canadian invasion served useful purposes, worthy of the great expenditure of

The same day the Second Continental Congress convened, May 10, 1775, a force of less than one hundred militia led by Ethan Allen and Benedict Arnold assaulted and seized Fort Ticonderoga, a post that guarded a strategic position on Lake Champlain. A small detachment under the command of Seth Warner traveled sixteen miles down the lake and captured the small Crown Point garrison the following day. Congress received Massachusetts Militia Col. John Brown's letter describing the daring early morning capture eight days later. In addition, Brown's report raised the specter that the British "planned an attack led by St. Luc le Corne, the notorious villain who let loose the Indians on the prisoners at Fort William Henry, and one of his associates."[9]

There was a divergence of opinions as to the best course of action. Some Congressional members, afraid of taking offensive action, wanted to give the posts back to the British; others sought to move the captured arms and ammunition southward to guard against a British counterattack, while several members wished to reinforce the Lake Champlain forts as a bulwark against British attack. A timid Congress ordered cannon and ammunition moved south to Albany for safekeeping.[10]

While deliberating the next steps, Congress sent a letter to the Canadians stating, "We are your friends, not your enemies."[11] The New York Provincial Congress agreed, ordering a committee to draft a letter to the Canadians "to convince them that nothing hostile is intended against their persons, liberty, or property."[12] On May 31, Congress received a letter from Col. Benedict Arnold describing his version of the military situation in the Champlain Valley. Arnold informed Congress that "he had certain intelligence, that on the 19th last there were then four hundred regulars at St. Johns, making all possible preparations to cross the lake, and expected to be joined by a number of Indians, with

soldiers and resources, is averred by Kevin Phillips: "The invasion accomplished goals of thwarting and delaying Canada as a base for the invasion of New England, stalling Native American support of the British, minimizing British raids from Canada, keeping New England militia in Boston, and seizing British arms and gunpowder. The Canadian invasion caused Britain to overcommit military resources in Canada." Phillips, *1775*, 462.

9. John Brown, "Philadelphia, May 22," *Pennsylvania Packet*, May 22, 1775.

10. Continental Congress, "Thursday, May 18, 1775," https://memory.loc.gov/cgi-bin/query/r?ammem/hlaw:@field(DOCID+@lit(jc00212)).

11. John Dickinson and Thomas Mifflin, trans., "To the Oppressed Inhabitants of Canada," Journals of the Continental Congress, https://memory.loc.gov/cgi-bin/query/r?ammem/hlaw:@field(DOCID+@lit(jc00221)).

12. New York Congress, "Committee of Correspondence Appointed, and Instructed to Inform the People of Canada That Nothing Hostile Is Intended against Them" (New York, May 26, 1775), https://digital.lib.niu.edu/islandora/object/niu-amarch%3A77951.

a design of retaking Crown Point and Ticonderoga and earnestly calling for a reinforcement and supplies."[13] Arnold succeeded in seizing the seventy-ton British sloop at St. Johns, ending the immediate threat to Fort Ticonderoga. As a result, Congress rescinded its order to move all cannon and ammunition south, only transferring those deemed surplus to Albany. As the New York Provincial Congress was slow to dispatch troops to reinforce the Champlain Valley, Congress ordered Connecticut to send one thousand men to reinforce Ft. Ticonderoga's garrison. Also, Congress ordered New York to prepare vessels to defend the lake against British attack from Canada.[14]

As Congress moved to defend Fort Ticonderoga and Crown Point, the delegates voted to make it clear to the Canadians that they had no intention of invading their province. "Resolved, That no expedition or incursion ought to be undertaken or made by any Colony or body of Colonists against or into Canada; and that his Resolve be immediately transmitted to the Commander of the Forces at Ticonderoga."[15] While the resolution was unequivocal, the debate continued on the question of invading Canada to thwart British or Native American threats to Northern New York and New England. In a June 7 letter to James Warren, John Adams reported, "But whether we should march into Canada with an Army Sufficient to break the Power of Governor Carlton, to overawe the Indians, and to protect the French has been a great Question."[16] Demonstrating concern, the Massachusetts assembly wrote to Congress expressing anti-invasion views: "There never has been any intention to give the least disturbance to our brethren of Canada, to whom we most sincerely wish the full and free enjoyment of their civil and religious rights." Massachusetts asked other New England colonies and New York to express sentiments like those voiced by Congress.[17]

Based upon the provincial congresses' input, the Continental Congress drafted and sent a letter "to the oppressed inhabitants of Canada,"

13. "A Letter from Col. Benedict Arnold, May 23, 1775" (Philadelphia, PA, May 31, 1775), Journals of the Continental Congress, https://memory.loc.gov/cgi-bin/query/r?ammem/hlaw:@field(DOCID+@lit(jc00223)).

14. "Connecticut Delegates to William Williams" (Philadelphia, PA, May 31, 1775), https://memory.loc.gov/cgi-bin/query/r?ammem/hlaw:@field(DOCID+@lit(dg001354)).

15. "Resolve, In Congress, June 1, 1775" (Philadelphia, PA, June 1, 1775), https://digital.lib.niu.edu/islandora/object/niu-amarch%3A79871.

16. John Adams to James Warren, June 7, 1775," https://founders.archives.gov/documents/Adams/06-03-02-0012.

17. "The Massachusetts Congress to the Continental Congress, June 12, 1775" (Watertown, MA, June 12, 1775), https://digital.lib.niu.edu/islandora/object/niu-amarch%3A79557.

referring to its residents as "friends and countrymen." The correspondence stressed that "we are your friends, not your enemies" and that to bridge the religious gap, we professed "the fate of the Protestant and Catholic Colonies to be strongly linked together." The communication also contained a threat that if Canadians did injury to the rebelling colonies, it would "reduce us to the disagreeable necessity of treating you as enemies." It concluded, "We entertain hopes of your uniting with us."[18] In addition to the threat, Canadians would recognize that the Americans did not back up their amity statements with actions, as Congress prohibited commercial exports to Quebec, which was not an act of friendship.[19]

During June, Congress received military and political intelligence from leaders in the Champlain Valley, indicating receptive Canadians and weak British garrisons. Ethan Allen, informal leader of the Green Mountain Boys, wrote from Crown Point to the Continental Congress that the conquest of Canada would be an easy military operation. "Should the Colonies forthwith send an army of two or three thousand men and attack Montreal, we should have but little fear from the Canadians or Indians and would easily make a conquest of the place." Further, Allen stated that "advancing an army into Canada will be agreeable to our friends."[20] Col. Benedict Arnold sent a letter to Congress with similar recommendations. As support, Arnold offered that "a great number of the Canadians have expected a visit from us for some time, and are very impatient of our delay, as they are determined to join us whenever we appear in the country with any force to support them." Arnold supported Allen's assertion that a small American force would overpower Gov. Guy Carleton's small garrisons. He concluded with a two-prong invasion plan, which his courier would describe in detail.[21]

On June 25, the newly named commander-in-chief, George Washington, sent a letter to Maj. Gen. Philip Schuyler with orders that he had been named Commander of all New York Department forces, including the Hudson Highlands, Albany, Fort Ticonderoga, and the Champlain Valley. His instructions were strictly defensive: strengthen fortifications, assemble supplies, and gather intelligence. Congress as-

18. "A True Copy, Charles Thomson, Secretary, to the Oppressed Inhabitants of Canada," *Pennsylvania Packet*, June 19, 1775.
19. Continental Congress, "Wednesday, May 17, 1775" (Philadelphia, PA, May 17, 1775), https://memory.loc.gov/cgi-bin/query/r?ammem/hlaw:@field(DOCID+@lit(jc00211)).
20. Ethan Allen and John J. Duffy, *Ethan Allen and His Kin: Correspondence, 1772–1819* (Hanover, NH: University Press of New England, 1998), 1:32.
21. "Benedict Arnold to the Continental Congress" (Crown Point, NY, June 13, 1775), https://digital.lib.niu.edu/islandora/object/niu-amarch%3A86445.

signed the Connecticut militia garrisoning Fort Ticonderoga and the unofficial New Hampshire Grants militia recently sanctioned as the Green Mountain Boys to Schuyler's command. The next day, Congress received a June 21st letter from the Albany Committee containing fresh intelligence gathered by Dirck Swart, one of its members. Swart reported disturbing information from a Scottish Canadian timber merchant, Udney Hay.[22] Swart reported that Hay averred that the influential Caughnawagas Indians "have taken up the hatchet" to support the British. Further, Governor Carlton intimidated English merchants in Montreal into fighting for the Crown.[23]

After considering the intelligence and recommendations from Allen, Arnold, and Hay, Congress reversed itself and, on June 27, directed Major General Schuyler to possess St. Johns and Montreal if he found it practical and not disagreeable to the Canadians.[24] In a letter to George Washington the next day, Hancock cited the new intelligence from the Albany Committee of Correspondence as the reason for Congress's dramatic change in military strategy. Hancock indicated that the orders were delivered directly to Schuyler and not through Washington as delay "might prove Detrimental to the Service."[25] A day after the Canadian invasion was authorized, Congress received a "number of letters and speeches from the Chiefs of the Stockbridge Indians." Writing to George Washington, delegate Richard Henry Lee indicated that Congress learned that "the Six Nations and the Canadian Indians are firmly disposed to observe a strict neutrality." So, if there was no imminent threat of a general Native American uprising against the Rebels, why did Congress authorize the discretionary Canadian invasion?

As opposed to concern over the Indians supporting the British, there is another explanation for Congress's apparent flip-flop. Upon learning of Fort Ticonderoga's capture, Congress recognized its lack of authority over the extra-legal Green Mountain Boys and the Massachusetts and

22. While this report is "hear say," Udney Hay ably served the Continental Army for the war's duration. Walter H. Crockett, "Soldiers of the Revolution Buried in Vermont, and Anecdotes and Incidents Relating to Some of Them," *Proceedings of the Vermont Historical Society* 1901–2 (1903): 102–6.
23. Dirck Swart, "Letter from the Albany Committee of Correspondence to the Continental Congress, June 21, 175," in *Minutes of the Albany Committee of Correspondence 1775-1778,* ed. James Sullivan, vol. I (Albany, NY: New York State Division of Archives and History, 1923), 93.
24. Continental Congress, "Tuesday, June 27, 1775" (Philadelphia, PA, June 27, 1775), https://memory.loc.gov/cgi-bin/query/r?ammem/hlaw:@field(DOCID+@lit(jc00246)).
25. "Letter from John Hancock to George Washington, June 28, 1775" (Philadelphia, PA, June 28, 1775), https://memory.loc.gov/cgi-bin/query/r?ammem/hlaw:@field(DOCID+@lit(dg001498)).

Connecticut militias' unapproved actions in the Champlain Valley (from a Congressional point of view). Congress likely issued its June 1 Canadian invasion prohibition to buttress its authority by banning further unsanctioned actions and not as a definitive statement on military and political strategy. In this manner, Congress established its prerogative to order or not order an invasion, a classic tactic used to assert a nascent political body's authority. Other evidence includes Congress sending the invasion prohibition directly to the "commander of the Forces at Ticonderoga."[26]

Further, Congressional delegate John Adams did not believe the June 1 prohibition against offensive actions in Canada was a settled issue. He averred on June 7, "It seems to be the general conclusion that it is best to go if we can be assured that the Canadians will be pleased with it and join."[27] However, a "go or no go" invasion decision was impossible on June 1. Beforehand, the Continental Army would have to be created, with the selection of a commander-in-chief, senior generals, and articles of war drafted. It would take Congress most of the month to accomplish these critical requirements before it could return to the Canadian invasion decision.

After instituting the requisite military organization and leadership, Congress plowed ahead based on an incoherent understanding of the situation compounded by delegating political control to military leaders. It is hard to understand why Congress would believe French Canadians (other than a few residents on the border with Vermont) would join the rebellion after their northern neighbors consistently rebuffed overtures to send delegates to the First or Second Continental Congress. Further, congressional members received promising intelligence solely from a few English-speaking merchants who sought to wrest business and political control from the vast French-Canadian majority. Congress expended little effort to inquire about the receptivity of the French speakers, including key community leaders in Quebec. Additionally, the invasion decision did not consider essential military campaign requirements such as funding, supplies, and a replacement Canadian government.[28] Even overcoming these obstacles, little thought went into holding Quebec City and the St. Lawrence Valley, given its openness to seaborne counterattack.

26. Thomson, "Resolve," June 1, 1775.
27. Adams to Warren, June 7, 1775," https://founders.archives.gov/documents/Adams/06-03-02-0012.
28. For a deeper perspective on Congress's failings, see Anderson, *The Battle for the Fourteenth Colony*, 345–53.

Further, Congress ceded civilian control by providing discretion to military leaders as to when and if they invaded Canada. As a result, Ethan Allen and Benedict Arnold could continue to agitate for an invasion subject only to General Schuyler's command. All three leaders had vested commercial interests in Canada.

It is understandable why the Continental Congress "looked North" at the rebellion's outset. Over the prior eighty-seven years, Native Americans, European empires, and North American colonists violently and continually contested the area between New England and Canada in five significant wars: King William's War (1688-1697), Queen Anne's War (1702-1713), King George's War (1744-1748), Father Le Loutre's War (1749-1755), and French and Indian War (1754-1763). In an early account of the Revolution, Mercy Otis Warren noted the strong Rebel interest in controlling Canada to secure the colonies' valuable Western frontiers. "This was important business, as whoever possesses Canada will in a great measure command the numerous tribes beyond the lakes."[29] While a northern conquest might have seemed natural to existing imperial powers, it is remarkable that an embryonic union of thirteen colonies espousing freedom from metropole control would choose to embark on its expansionist conquest hastily. While costly, the abortive Canadian invasion served a proper purpose. The Continental Congress never again delegated consequential political decisions to the military and retained civilian control over crucial military strategic choices, such as the controversial decision to defend New York City in 1776.

29. Mercy Otis Warren, *History of the Rise, Progress and Termination of the American Revolution, Interpreted with Biographical, Political and Moral Observations* (Boston: E. Larkin, 1805), 1:141.

The Story of Isaac Bissell–and the Legend of Israel Bissell

J. L. BELL

In April 1775, Isaac Bissell was a crucial link between the Patriots of Massachusetts and the government of neighboring Connecticut. His actions contributed to alerting many communities along the Atlantic coast about the outbreak of war in Lexington. Nevertheless, through a chain of circumstances, Isaac Bissell's name has been overwritten in history books.[1]

This story starts in February 1775, when two gentlemen from Connecticut visited the Massachusetts Provincial Congress, then meeting in Cambridge. The Bay Colony's rebel legislature had

1. This article draws from fine previous studies of how Joseph Palmer's April 19 message moved down the Atlantic seaboard in 1775, including John J. Scheide, "The Lexington Alarm," *Proceedings of the American Antiquarian Society*, 50 (1940), 49–79; Elizabeth Merritt, "The Lexington Alarm, April 19, 1775: Messages Sent to the Southwaid [sic] After the Battle," *Maryland Historical Magazine*, 41 (1946), 89–114; and Robert L. Berthelson, "An Alarm from Lexington," Connecticut Society of the Sons of the American Revolution, www.sarconnecticut.org/an-alarm-from-lexington/, and Massachusetts Society of the Sons of the American Revolution, massar.org/alarm-from-lexington/. Those articles did not have the benefit of Lion G. Miles's work highlighting documents about Isaac Bissell in the Massachusetts State Archives. See Miles, "The True Story of Bissell's Ride in 1775," July 21, 2004, at www.iberkshires.com/story/15001/The-true-story-of-Bissell-s-Ride-in-1775.html; and Miles, "Letter: Superhuman ride of Bissell is fake news," *Berkshire Eagle*, April 20, 2018, at www.berkshireeagle.com/archives/letter-superhuman-ride-of-bissell-is-fake-news/article_9d213ac1-c15d-5bc9-924a-cdea38674c26.html. Miles's influence can be seen in David Robinson, "The Shot Eventually Heard 'Round the World," *Colonial Williamsburg Journal*, vol. 28, no. 3 (summer 2006), 60–5, but that author was still reluctant to move away from the then-standard credit to Israel Bissell. As of this writing, Wikipedia includes entries for both Isaac Bissell and Israel Bissell, the latter supposedly taking over in Worcester from a man with a nearly identical name. This article presents a more plausible scenario.

convened on and off since the preceding October, defying Parliament's Massachusetts Government Act and preparing for war against the royal governor if necessary. That congress wanted allies, so its leaders were pleased to hear from William Williams and Nathaniel Wales, Jr.

Williams was the speaker of the Connecticut assembly, a militia colonel, and a son-in-law of his colony's elected governor, Jonathan Trumbull. Wales was a representative from the town of Windham. Both men lived in eastern Connecticut, closer to Cambridge than many of their colleagues. Back in May 1773, the Connecticut legislature had named Williams and Wales to its "standing Committee of Correspondence and Enquiry" with a mandate to "maintain a correspondence and communication with our sister Colonies" and "obtain all such intelligence" about the political conflict with the Crown.[2]

The official record of the Connecticut assembly says nothing about that body sending Williams and Wales to speak to the Massachusetts Provincial Congress in early 1775. The colonial legislature might have preferred a low profile for this potentially treasonous outreach. Arguably the two men were already empowered to consult with colleagues in Massachusetts because of their seats on the standing committee of correspondence.

Williams and Wales's visit shows up only in Massachusetts records. On February 15, the provincial congress named committees to converse with the two men—one to greet them, then a second to sit down with them in Ebenezer Stedman's tavern for a serious conversation. The official description of those discussions was spare and bland, but their importance was clear. Both committees included such high-ranking leaders as Samuel Adams, John Hancock, and Thomas Cushing (usually speaker of the Massachusetts house); members of the busy committee of safety and supplies; and top militia officers. Furthermore, though the congress was preparing to adjourn, it ordered that no members head home "until the conference with the committee from Connecticut is over."[3]

The day after the discussion at Stedman's, the Massachusetts congress named a committee of nine leading members (their mandate defined by yet another committee) "to correspond with the House of

2. Connecticut committee of correspondence: *The Public Records of the Colony of Connecticut*, Charles H. Hoadley, transcriber (Hartford: Case, Lockwood & Brainard, 1887), 14:156. Williams is well documented as a signer of the Declaration of Independence.
3. Massachusetts committees: William Lincoln, editor, *Journals of Each Provincial Congress of Massachusetts in 1774 and 1775* (Boston: Dutton & Wentworth, 1838), 105.

Assembly of Connecticut; and, if necessary, with the other neighboring colonies." That resolution made clear the mood of the assembly:

> While the iron hand of power is stretched out against these American colonies, and the abettors of tyranny and oppression are practising every art to sow the seeds of jealousy and discord among the several parts of this country, it is incumbent on us to take every step in our power to counteract them in their wicked designs; and . . . we are convinced, that the union now established throughout the several colonies can never be maintained without frequent communication of sentiments between them.[4]

In addition, as the Massachusetts congress prepared to recess, it authorized this committee to maintain ties with neighboring colonies during adjournments. Among the nine men given that authority was Joseph Palmer (1716–1788), a militia colonel from Braintree and member of the committee of safety and supplies. Williams and Wales went home to report to their colleagues.

On April 8, the Massachusetts Provincial Congress moved closer to war. The body voted "to make preparations for their security and defence by raising and establishing an Army." It decided to appoint "delegates . . . to repair to Connecticut, to Rhode Island and New Hampshire." Those delegates were to ask the neighboring colonies about "furnishing their respective quotas for general defence," or a combined army.[5]

The Massachusetts congress then chose members as its delegates. The contingent for Connecticut consisted of militia colonel Jedediah Foster of Brookfield and John Bliss of Wilbraham, soon joined by Timothy Danielson of Brimfield.[6] All three men came from towns in central Massachusetts close to the Connecticut border, making a journey to Hartford less onerous. Danielson, furthermore, had spent years in the neighboring colony as a Yale College student.[7] Foster later reported that Danielson "Immediately proceeded from Concord to Governour Trumbul with the papers as Directed by the Congress." However, "from the then Appearance of affairs," the Connecticut governor "did not think proper to Call the Assembly" to authorize

4. "to correspond": Lincoln, *Journals of Each Provincial Congress*, 106.
5. "to make preparations": Lincoln, *Journals of Each Provincial Congress*, 135.
6. Foster, Bliss, and Danielson: Lincoln, *Journals of Each Provincial Congress*, 136–7.
7. Danielson at Yale: Franklin Bowditch Dexter, *Biographical Sketches of the Graduates of Yale College* (New York: Henry Holt, 1896), 2:410–1.

raising troops.[8] Trumbull had already convened one special legislative session in early March and publicly proclaimed there was no need for another, so he would need a strong reason to reverse himself.[9]

On April 15, the Massachusetts congress adjourned, planning to gather again on May 10 in Concord. Already the conflict with the Crown was heating up. The previous day, HMS *Nautilus* arrived in Boston, bringing instructions from the London government for the royal governor, Gen. Thomas Gage. Britain's secretary of state for the colonies, Lord Dartmouth, had advised that it was time for Gage to "arrest the principal actors and abettors in the Provincial Congress." Patriot leaders were leaving Boston, apparently having received warnings of the imperial government's policy from a previous ship.[10]

On April 19, Joseph Palmer was staying with his son's in-laws in Watertown, about nine miles outside of Boston. As a member of the committee of safety, he knew there was an arms cache in Concord. Early that morning, Palmer started to receive reports that a British army column was moving west through Cambridge. Then came news from Lexington, further out. Palmer dashed off this message at "abt 8 o'clock":

> To all whom it may concern, be it known, that the Regular Troops have this morning kill'd six men near Lexington Meeting House; this news is brot: to Watertown by Mr. Sanger, who told me that he saw the men lie dead.
> J. Palmer
> of the Congress Com:tee[11]

8. "Immediately proceeded": Jedediah Foster to President of the Massachusetts Provincial Congress, April 23, 1775, Massachusetts Archives Collection, 193:57 (microfilm 7703487, images 272–3), Massachusetts State Archives. This letter is transcribed in Peter Force, compiler, *American Archives*, series 4 (Washington, D.C.: Clarke & Force, 1839), 2:378. Force modernized spelling and punctuation, and he read Danielson's name as "Davidson."
9. Trumbull and the legislature: The Connecticut assembly met in New Haven on March 2–10, focusing on militia organization, with a plan to reconvene on April 13; *Public Records of the Colony of Connecticut*, 14:388, 409. On April 4, Trumbull proclaimed there was no need for a second session that spring; *Norwich Packet*, April 6, 1775.
10. Leaving Boston: James Warren to Mercy Warren, April 6–7, 1775, in *Warren-Adams Letters* [*Massachusetts Historical Society Collections*, vol. 72] (Boston: Massachusetts Historical Society, 1917), 1:45.
11. "To all whom": Document sold by Heritage Auctions on June 8, 2017, historical.ha.com/itm/miscellaneous/joseph-palmer-historic-autograph-note-signed-jpalmer-19-april-1775-/a/997039-1064.s. There were several men named Sanger in Watertown at this time, including David Sanger, on the town's October 1774 committee to equip two cannon, and Samuel Sanger, first sergeant of the militia company, so it is not possible to identify Palmer's informant.

Two hours later, Palmer wrote out a more detailed dispatch to go to Hartford. He handed it to Isaac Bissell, a twenty-six-year-old blacksmith from Suffield, a town on Connecticut's northern border. It is unclear whether the Massachusetts Patriots had already hired Bissell as a dispatch rider or he happened to be in Watertown that day. Either way, Palmer made Bissell a courier to "Col. Foster of Brookfield, one of the Delegates" from Massachusetts to Connecticut. But the committee man did not seek to keep that letter confidential. Instead, Palmer addressed all supporters, and he probably encouraged Bissell to spread the news everywhere he went.

Palmer's letter said:

> Watertown / Wednesday Morning 10 Clock
>
> To all the Friends of american liberty be it known that this morning before break of Day a Brigade consisting of about 1000 or 1200 men Landed at Phips' Farm in Cambridge and marched to Lexington where they found a Company of our Colony Militia in arms; upon whom they Fired without any Provocation & killed six & wounded four Others[.] by an express this moment from Boston we find another Brigade are now on their March from Boston supposed to be about 1000[.] The Bearer Mr. Isaac Bissell [is] charged to alarm the country quite to Connecticutt and all Persons are Desired to furnish him with such Horses as they may be needed
>
> I have spoke with severall Persons who have seen the Dead & wounded[.] Pray Lett the Delegates from this Colony to Connecticutt see this
>
> they know
>
> J. Palmer
>
> one of the Com. of Safety
>
> Colo. Foster is one of the Delegates[12]

Palmer's primary goal was to help Foster and the other Massachusetts delegates to Connecticut convince that colony's government to raise troops. As a secondary purpose, he also wanted to rouse "all the Friends of American liberty" who might see this message along the way. But Palmer faced a challenge in raising that alarm. Back in September 1774, dire rumors of a British military attack in Boston

12. Alarm letter: Palmer's original letter does not appear to have survived. This transcription is based on "A true Coppy" filed in the United States Revolution Collection 1754–1928, Box 1, folder 22, American Antiquarian Society, Worcester. Other transcriptions say that Palmer wrote "near" ten o'clock, a detail this document's transcriber probably skipped. Thanks to Joel Bohy for sharing an image of this page.

had spread through rural Massachusetts and Connecticut, prompting thousands of militiamen to mobilize—only to learn that there had been no attack, no deaths, not even any injuries. Earlier that spring, contingents of British soldiers had marched out of Boston several times with no consequences. How could Palmer convince people that this time the redcoats really had killed people? When Palmer wrote, "Lett the Delegates from this Colony to Connecticutt see this / They know" me, he was trying to establish his credibility.

Isaac Bissell rode west with Palmer's letter, his route taking him safely south of the Concord road. In early afternoon he reached Worcester, another center of political resistance where the Massachusetts Provincial Congress was storing weapons. Local organizers probably gave him a fresh horse and a meal. During that stop, Worcester's new town clerk, Nathan Baldwin, quickly copied the letter Bissell was carrying.[13] To avoid unnecessary delay, Baldwin probably did not take extra time to check if he had exactly matched the original letter's spelling, capitalization, punctuation, and other small details; eighteenth century writers did not demand as much consistency in those matters as we do today. At the bottom Baldwin added a line authenticating his new page as reliable information, something like:

> A true copy taken from the original per order of the Committee of Correspondence for Worcester
> Attested Nathan Baldwin, Town Clerk
> Worcester April ye 19th 1775.[14]

The Worcester committee probably saved one copy of the dispatch for themselves, and they definitely sent a copy south with another rider.

Bissell continued west to Springfield, where another "true Coppy" of his message was made for that town's selectmen. On that copy the rider's name could be read as "Isaac Russell."[15] By April 20, Springfield

13. Baldwin elected clerk: *Early Records of the Town of Worcester: 1753–1783*, Franklin P. Rice, editor (Worcester, Mass.: Worcester Society of Antiquity, 1882), 254.

14. "A true copy": Language based on surviving copies derived from Baldwin's transcription with modern capitalization, punctuation, and abbreviation for clarity.

15. "Isaac Russell": This name appears in Alfred Minott Copeland, *Our County and Its People: A History of Hampden County, Massachusetts* (n.p.: Century Memorial Publishing Co., 1902) 1:75; and John Hoyt Lockwood, *Westfield and Its Historic Influences, 1669–1919* (Westfield, Mass.: n.p., 1922), 1:531. Copeland's second volume named Isaac Bissell correctly; 2:39–40. Henry A. Booth, "Springfield During the Revolution," *Papers and Proceedings of the Connecticut Valley Historical Society*, 2 (1904), 291, also read that name as "Isaac Bissell"—but guessed that the letter was signed "Z. Palmer." As this article shows, transcribing a handwritten document precisely can be a challenge, even in the best of conditions.

militiamen were marching east to Boston, eventually to serve in a regiment under congress delegate Timothy Danielson.

Isaac Bissell fulfilled his assignment to ride to Connecticut on the morning of Thursday, April 20. Early that day, Massachusetts delegates Jedediah Foster and Timothy Danielson learned about the outbreak of war and began telling politicians in Hartford. In Wethersfield, a few miles to the south, Silas Deane started a journal:

> Memo. / Thursday 20th April 1775 Mr. Isaac Sheldon of Hartford came over from Hartford half past Ten in ye. Morning with a Letter from J. Palmer informing that the Regular Troops fired, early the Morning before on a Number of people at Lexington and killed Six of them, that they then Continued their March for Concord, and that they had intelligence of another large Body of them on their march toward Concord on another Road—

Palmer's worry that people might doubt him turned out to be well founded. Deane went on: "The News was discredited, from the suddeness of its arrival, & other Causes." The very fact that Bissell had brought this letter so quickly, far ahead of any confirmation—its "suddeness"—ended up working against it. Deane went up to Hartford and met with other politicians, but they "Conferrd on the Intellgence Wh. was discredited."[16] The only action those men took was to send another express rider south to Middletown with the possible news.

In contrast, Massachusetts delegates Foster and Danielson had no doubts. They knew Palmer and trusted his report. Early on April 20 those two men "set out for Lebanon," home town of Gov. Jonathan Trumbull. They ran into the governor and other Connecticut politicians in the town of Norwich. He had already "Received the Tragical Narrative from Colo. Palmer," he told them, and now "Chearfuly Consented to Call the assembly of the Colony" the next week to raise an army.[17]

The next day, Williams, Wales, and the governor's son Joseph Trumbull wrote to John Hancock as president of the Massachusetts Provincial Congress:

16. Silas Deane journal: Christopher Collier, editor, "Inside the American Revolution: A Silas Deane Diary Fragment April 20–October 25, 1775," *Connecticut Historical Society Bulletin*, 29 (July 1964), 86–7. Berthelson, "An Alarm from Lexington," reports that the William L. Clements Library in Ann Arbor, Michigan, holds a manuscript copy of Palmer's letter signed by Silas Deane; it renders the name of Palmer's messenger as "Mr. Isaac Bissell."

17. "set out for Lebanon": Foster to Massachusetts Provincial Congress, April 23, 1775, Massachusetts Archives Collection, 193:57.

> Writs are gone out to Call the Genll. Assembly to meet at Hartford next Wensday—Every preparation is making to Support your Province—We have many Reports of what is doing with you, the particulars, we cannot yet get with precision—the Ardour of Our People is such that they can't be kept back;—The Colonels are to forward part of the best men & most Ready, as fast as possible; the remainder to be ready at a Moments warning—these are the present movements with us.

In the same letter, those Connecticut men pleaded for more information: "our Accots. are so various We know not what to rely on," they said. Yet another son of the governor, David Trumbull, was sent to find Hancock and gather all the information he could. Reflecting the importance of information in this conflict, Williams, Wales, and Trumbull advised Hancock and his colleagues to distribute the "most Authentic Accots. of the late Transactions, to forestall, such exaggerated Accots. as may go from the Army & Navy."[18]

By the time the Connecticut assembly met in formal session the next week, some of the colony's militia regiments were already helping to besiege Boston or on their way. Among those men was Isaac Bissell, a private in Capt. Elihu Kent's company from Suffield. At the start of 1776, Bissell signed up as a sergeant in Capt. John Harmon's company, Col. Erastus Wolcott's regiment. Bissell served through March 1776 and the British evacuation of Boston.[19]

On July 7, 1775, the Massachusetts Provincial Congress's committee of safety "Passed upon Mr. Isaac Bissel, a post rider's account, amounting, as by copy on file, for two pounds one shilling; and a certificate was given him for the committee on accounts."[20] Bissell took this paper to the man he understood was the congress's treasurer, who answered that "he Could not alow it unless atested by the Provenchal Congress."[21] On July 10, the full provincial congress assigned three men to "consider the account of Mr. Isaac Bissell."[22] But that committee

18. "Writs are gone out": Connecticut Committee of Correspondence (Williams, Wales, Trumbull) to President of the Massachusetts Provincial Congress (Hancock), April 21, 1775, Massachusetts Archives Collection, 193:52–4 (microfilm 7703487, images 264-6), Massachusetts State Archives.

19. Isaac Bissell's military service: *The Record of Connecticut Men in the Military and Naval Service During the War of the Revolution, 1775–1783*, Henry P. Johnston, editor (Hartford: Adjutant-General of Connecticut, 1889), 23, 385, 552.

20. Committee of safety action: Lincoln, *Journals of Each Provincial Congress*, 590.

21. "he Could not alow": Isaac Bissell to Joseph Palmer, March 20, 1776, Massachusetts Archives Collections, 303:162-1. Thanks to Joel Bohy for sharing images of these documents.

22. Provincial congress action: Lincoln, *Journals of Each Provincial Congress*, 484.

never finished the task before the congress dissolved in favor of a newly elected Massachusetts General Court, the official legislature. When Bissell asked about his money, congress members told him "they Could not doe any more bisness and it must be Put of till the assembly Sat and they took my order and Put it into the files."

Eight months later, the British military had pulled out of Boston, and Bissell's bill was still unpaid. In March 20, 1776, the rider wrote to his original contact, Joseph Palmer, now a member of the legislature's upper house: "Sir you may Remember when Lexinton Fite was you gave me an Express to Cary to hartford in Connecticut which I did." He recounted his attempts to get paid the previous July and concluded: "now Sir I Cant Neither get my order nor the money for I Cant Lite on any Body that Noes any thing abought it . . . and I think I Earn my money."[23] Within two days, Palmer passed on Bissell's request to the lower house.[24] On April 4, the Massachusetts House took up Palmer's petition on behalf of Bissell, assigning it to a one-man committee. Four days later, that became a three-man committee. On April 23, 1776, slightly over a year after Isaac Bissell completed his ride to Hartford, the Massachusetts General Court finally voted to pay him the £2.1s. he had asked for.[25]

Isaac Bissell married Amelia Leavitt, niece of his first company captain, on July 4, 1776. They had thirteen children between 1777 and 1801.[26] In July 1779, the British army attacked New Haven, and Bissell marched again as part of a militia alarm. At times of peace, he operated a blacksmith shop in Suffield, though that apparently did not always support the family well. In October 1778 he advertised "SIXTEEN HUNDRED weight of BOHEA TEA" for sale, "as I am in necessity for a sum of money in a short time." In March 1781 Bissell offered to sell

23. Bissell's petition: Bissell to Palmer, March 20, 1776, Massachusetts Archives Collections, 303:162-1.

24. Palmer's petition: Joseph Palmer to Massachusetts General Court, March 22, 1776, Massachusetts Archives Collections, 303:162-2.

25. Massachusetts General Court action: *Journals of the House of Representatives of Massachusetts* (Boston: Massachusetts Historical Society, 1982), vol. 51, part 1 (1775), 78, 96, 165. *The Acts and Resolves, Public and Private, of the Province of Massachusetts Bay* (Boston: Wright & Potter, 1918), 19:342. The payment went through John Bliss of Wilbraham, one of Massachusetts's three delegates to Connecticut back in April 1775, presumably because he lived near Bissell's home in Suffield.

26. Isaac Bissell's family: Benjamin W. Dwight, *The History of the Descendants of John Dwight, of Dedham, Mass.* (New York: John F. Trow & Son, 1874), 1:412–3. For Leavitt's connection to Capt. Elihu Kent, see Nathaniel Goodwin, *Genealogical Notes: or, Contributions to the Family History of Some of the First Families of Connecticut and Massachusetts* (Hartford: F. A. Brown, 1856), 147.

his twelve-acre farm north of town "For Hard, Continental, or State's Money," and he finally made that sale in 1788.[27] For a time, the Bissells moved to Hanover, New Hampshire, where Amelia died, but Isaac came back to Suffield. He died in 1822 and was buried in the town cemetery.

America does not remember Isaac Bissell's service as a courier. Instead, there have been articles, artwork, poems, and even a picture book celebrating *Israel* Bissell for carrying Joseph Palmer's message.[28] Indeed, many authors have credited "Israel Bissell" with riding all the way to New York, or to Philadelphia, or beyond.

As described above, in Worcester the town clerk, Nathan Baldwin, made a copy of Palmer's letter on the afternoon of April 19 and sent it south. As Isaac Bissell continued riding west, a second, unknown rider carried Baldwin's copy down to Brooklyn, Connecticut, arriving by eleven o'clock in the morning on Thursday, April 20. Daniel Tyler, Jr., then made another "true Copy" before he and his father-in-law, militia colonel Israel Putnam, set out toward Boston. By four o'clock that afternoon, that text had reached the town of Norwich.[29] That was the message that alerted Governor Trumbull and convinced him to summon the Connecticut legislature.[30] Ironically, Tyler's copy of Baldwin's copy of Palmer's letter turned out to be more galvanizing than the original sent to Hartford. Trumbull's response showed the value of spreading multiple copies of the dispatch.

That transcription which reached Norwich contained some errors—understandable given how two people had hastily copied a document in unfamiliar handwriting. The Tyler text named the first rider as "Israel Bissell" and rendered the Worcester clerk as "Nathan Balding."[31]

27. Isaac Bissell's sales: *Connecticut Courant*, October 27, 1778. *Connecticut Courant*, April 10, 1781. *Celebration of the Two Hundred and Fiftieth Anniversary of the Settlement of Suffield, Connecticut* (Suffield, CT: 1921), 172.

28. Artistic celebrations of Israel Bissell: Alice Schick and Marjorie N. Allen, *The Remarkable Ride of Israel Bissell as Related by Molly the Crow: Being the True Account of an Extraordinary Post Rider who Persevered*, illustrated by Joel Schick (Philadelphia: Lippincott, 1976). Poems included Gerard Chapman, "Israel Bissell's Ride" and Clay Perry, "I. Bissell's Ride," both published in the *Berkshire Eagle* newspaper in the 1950s. George Avison painted a mural of Israel Bissell at Roger Ludlow High School in Fairfield, Connecticut, in 1937. More recently, D. W. Roth painted an image for the Union Oyster House in Boston. Neither of those pictures includes Bissell's name, though, so they could just as accurately depict Isaac Bissell.

29. Brooklyn and Norwich alerted: Scheide, "The Lexington Alarm," 64.

30. Trumbull alerted: I.W. Stuart, *Life of Jonathan Trumbull, Sen., Governor of Connecticut* (Boston: Crocker & Brewster, 1859), 173.

31. Norwich transcription: The Norwich copy received from Daniel Tyler, Jr., of Brooklyn is reproduced in Scheide, "The Lexington Alarm," opposite page 50.

Naturally, those errors persisted when people used that document to make further copies. Tyler's rendering was printed in that day's *Norwich Packet* newspaper, widening the reach of the message.[32] Two days later, the same printers used that text again, alongside two later accounts of the battle, in a handbill headlined "Interesting Intelligence."[33]

The transcribed message continued south. Norwich mill owner Christopher Leffingwell copied it, signed off that his copy was as accurate as he could make it, and sent it on to New London. Leffingwell's paper arrived in that port at seven in the evening on April 20, and a committee of four men sent another copy on along the coast. But the text of the warning now named the original rider as "Trail Bissell."[34] That message arrived in Lyme after midnight and by noon had gone through the towns of Saybrook, Killingsworth, East Guilford, Guilford, and Bradford on its way to New Haven.[35]

The April 24 *New-York Gazette* reported: "Yesterday Morning we had Reports in this City from Rhode-Island and New-London, That an Action had happened between the King's Troops and the Inhabitants of Boston." People did not believe that news, probably remembering the false alarm back in September 1774. Then in the early afternoon an express rider trotted in from Fairfield, Connecticut, with an attested copy of Palmer's message. A committee of five men in Fairfield had combined that original dispatch with an April 20 letter from Ebenezer Williams of Pomfret to Obadiah Johnson of Canterbury, passing on more detailed (though not necessarily more accurate) news of the previous day's fighting.[36]

When Hugh Gaine printed all that text in the *New-York Gazette* and as a handbill, he named the original rider as "Israel Bessel" and the

32. Norwich newspaper report: *Norwich Packet*, April 20, 1775.

33. Norwich broadside: "Interesting Intelligence. Norwich, April 22, 1775, 10 o'clock, P.M. . . . Printed by Robertsons and Trumbull." After helping to spread this alarm in 1775, the Robertson brothers became Loyalists, leaving Norwich for New York in 1776.

34. Norwich to New London: Scheide, "The Lexington Alarm," opposite page 56. In this document the name "Balding" had reverted to the more common and correct Baldwin.

35. Lyme to New Haven: Elias Boudinot, *Journal or Historical Recollections of American Events During the Revolutionary War* (Trenton, NJ: C. L. Traver, 1890), 1. Boudinot or this book's transcriber rendered Lyme as "Lynne" and Killingsworth as "Shillingsworth."

36. Williams to Johnson: "How the News of the Battle of Lexington Reached Philadelphia," *Pennsylvania Magazine of History and Biography*, 27 (1903), 259–60. This article reproduces in facsimile a four-page manuscript in the collection of the Historical Society of Pennsylvania. A photostat of this document is in the U.S. Revolutionary Collection, box 1, folder 22, American Antiquarian Society. Both Williams and Johnson had been chosen militia colonels and both would command Connecticut regiments during the war.

man who wrote the letter as "T. Palmer."[37] But even without exact transmission, the multiple signatures on the papers had the intended effect: they convinced New York Patriots that the news was authentic. In a 1940 article for the American Antiquarian Society, John H. Scheide described a copy of the New York handbill with a note on the back in the handwriting of Patriot organizer Alexander McDougall. He recorded that the news arrived in New York City at about two o'clock on Sunday, April 23, and by four o'clock the city's committee of correspondence decided to forward "the intelligence by Mr. Moorbach express to the Southard."[38]

Moorbach set off "express to New Brunswick [New Jersey] with directions to stop at Elizabethtown and acquaint the committee there." The New Brunswick committee in turn were "requested to forward this to Philadelphia."[39] In Elizabethtown, Elias Boudinot recorded the path of the message that reached him, from Worcester through Fairfield.[40] Overnight the news went through New Brunswick, Princeton, and Trenton, and in each town at least two committee members signed off on a copy for the next stop. At five o'clock in the afternoon on April 24, five and a half days after the fighting had started, a copy of Joseph Palmer's dispatch and Ebenezer Williams's letter reached Philadelphia, the largest city in North America. Thirty-eight different men had signed off on copies.[41]

Those documents (without all the signatures) were published in a special two-page supplement to the April 24 *Pennsylvania Packet*; it called the first rider "Trail Bissel." The next day, the same text ran in the *Pennsylvania Evening Post*, naming "Train Bissel." By this time, Jedediah Foster was "Col. Forster," and his home town of Brookfield was dropped. The *Packet*'s version was also translated into German and printed in the April 25 *Wochentliche Philadelphische Staatsbote* newspaper. William and Thomas Bradford issued their version of the dispatch naming "Israel Bissell" in the April 26 *Pennsylvania Journal*, with a handbill following.

From Philadelphia, messengers carried the report to New Castle, Dover, and New Christiana, Delaware, then Head of Elk, Maryland. At Baltimore, the news arrived in time for Mary Katharine Goddard

37. Hugh Gaine's report: *New-York Gazette*, April 24, 1775.
38. "intelligence by Mr. Moorbach": Scheide, "The Lexington Alarm," 66–7.
39. "requested to forward": *Pennsylvania Magazine of History and Biography*, 27:261.
40. Elias Boudinot recorded: Boudinot, *Journal or Historical Recollections of American Events*, 1.
41. Thirty-eight signatures: Berthelson, "An Alarm from Lexington." Merritt, "The Lexington Alarm, April 19, 1775," 97–100.

to print the Palmer and Williams letters in the April 26 *Maryland Journal* and as another handbill.[42] This text named the first rider "Tryal Russell," and the Worcester clerk "Nathan Balding," but it also restored the phrase "Col. Foster, of Brookfield." Evidently by this time multiple copies of the dispatch had made their way south through branching paths.

Patriots in Baltimore sped copies to their delegates at the Maryland Provincial Congress meeting in Annapolis because "they should have notice before they adjourn." Four militia officers added a promise of "our Immediate and chearful assistance in the Seizing of the Arms & Ammunition at Annapolis." They also apologized for at first sending the delegates a "Coppy" rather than "the original Intillegence," reflecting continued concern about making sure each message looked as authentic as possible. Of course, what those men called the "original Intillegence" was also a copy, simply an earlier one.[43]

In Williamsburg, Virginia, John Pinkney reprinted the Palmer and Williams letters from an April 24 Philadelphia newspaper in a supplement to his *Virginia Gazette* issued on the evening of Friday, April 28. The next day, Pinkney's rivals John Dixon and William Hunter announced in a supplement to their own *Virginia Gazette* that "This morning arrived an express from the Northward," sharing the report from Philadelphia. Both these newspapers called the rider "Trail Brissel." Another handbill followed.

Riders and newspapers continued to carry Palmer's message south. The alert reached Halifax, North Carolina, on May 8, and four days later the *North-Carolina Gazette* in New Bern reprinted the Philadelphia article. This time the first rider was "Trial Brisset." By then other reports of the battle in Massachusetts were coming by sea. The committee-man's early alert, now carried by a dozen or more men in turn, had become anticlimactic.[44]

Eventually the American newspaper reports were reprinted in London. John Almon's *Remembrancer*, a round-up of news for the year, included a version "From a New-York paper April 24" that named "Israel Bessell" and "T. Palmer."[45]

42. Maryland handbill: Scanned at www.loc.gov/resource/rbpe.02800600/.

43. Maryland Patriots: Merritt, "The Lexington Alarm, April 19, 1775," 100–1. This article shows more April 1775 accounts following the same path to Maryland, endorsed at each stop by different men in the same way as copies of Palmer's letter.

44. News streams reaching North Carolina: Scheide, "The Lexington Alarm," 70–4.

45. London reprint: *The Remembrancer, or Impartial Repository of Public Events* (London: John Almon, 1775), 1:39, reflecting the spellings in the *New-York Gazette*.

In 1861, Henry Wadsworth Longfellow, one of America's most popular writers, composed "Paul Revere's Ride." That poem made the Boston silversmith into a household name, and it provoked widespread interest in details of the Lexington Alarm. For the first time families began to publicly discuss ancestors who had sent the signals from "the Old North Church," as Longfellow called that building and it irrevocably became. Local historians sought to identify other riders carrying important Revolutionary news. Americans claimed that honor for their ancestors, not always credibly.

Given that interest, historians paid more attention to the copies of Joseph Palmer's April 19 letter in archives and newspapers. Most of those transcriptions had been made along the eastern seaboard, not from the original sent to Hartford but from the "true copy" that Nathan Baldwin wrote out in Worcester and from other "true copies" made from that one. As those documents moved through Connecticut, the name of the first rider had mutated to "Israel Bissell." Some of those versions were printed, producing more copies. As a result, many of the documents available to scholars carried that name. Even though the rider's name continued to evolve into new forms like "Tryal Russell" as the message moved south, historians latched onto "Israel Bissell" as the true name of the rider. The multiple documents showing how Isaac Bissell had billed the Massachusetts government for his ride to Hartford remained unpublished in a state archive until Lion G. Miles began quoting them in 2004.

Furthermore, that chain of documents with the same basic text produced the misconception that one man rode all the way to New York or Philadelphia, switching horses along the way. This legend was embellished with details like the claim that his first mount collapsed and died as he rode into Worcester. At the time authors made that assumption, Americans were traveling long distances by railroad and had largely lost touch with the realities of travel in 1775. People more familiar with sending messages by horse would have known that couriers worked in relays, stopping for meals and sleep as well as fresh mounts. Spreading the alert from Watertown to Philadelphia in five days and seven hours took the work of many riders, and almost all of them were anonymous. The one exception was the New York reference to "Mr. Moorbach," but that name was not published until 1940. In the early 1900s, all the credit went to "Israel Bissell."

Researchers then found a man actually named Israel Bissell—a farmer from East Windsor, Connecticut, born in 1752.[46] He and his

46. Israel Bissell: Edward Church Smith and Philip Mack Smith, "Descendants of Israel Bissell," *The American Genealogist*, 27 (1951), 236–8.

brother Justus joined Captain Wolcott's Connecticut company in July 1776 and served for a month.[47] Later this Bissell family moved to a part of Middlefield, Massachusetts, that would become Hinsdale. Israel bought farmland, married Lucy Hancock in 1784, raised sheep, and fathered six children. He died in 1823 at age seventy-one, and was buried in Hinsdale under a stone that said nothing about Revolutionary War service.[48]

In the twentieth century, the ride of "Israel Bissell" was lauded in art, poetry, and song as a forgotten feat equal to or greater than Paul Revere's ride. In 1967 the local Daughters of the American Revolution added a bronze plaque to the grave of that Hinsdale farmer. It reads, "In Memory of Israel Bissell post rider from Watertown to Philadelphia alerting towns of British attack at Lexington April 19, 1775."[49] But all that celebration was just the result of a spelling error back on the frantic afternoon when the Revolutionary War began.

47. Israel Bissell's military service: *Record of Connecticut Men*, 618. The commander of this company is listed as Captain Wolcott with no given name; he may have been Erastus Wolcott, Jr., son of the colonel whom Isaac Bissell had served under earlier in the year. Smith and Smith posit that the man listed on this roll might have been Israel Bissell's namesake father because a family tradition said that man contracted dysentery during military service and died; "Descendants of Israel Bissell," 234–7. Smith and Smith also refer to a receipt for five shillings in exchange for ten half-days of work before June 1775 from a Captain Stoughton as evidence of earlier military service by the younger Israel Bissell, but soldiers did not work half-days.

48. Israel Bissell's family: *Vital Records of Middlefield, Massachusetts, to the Year 1850* (Boston: New England Historic Genealogical Society, 1907), 66, 11; *Vital Records of Hinsdale, Massachusetts, to the Year 1850* (Boston: New England Historic Genealogical Society, 1902), 74. Smith and Smith, "Descendants of Israel Bissell," 237–8.

49. Israel Bissell grave: Visible at www.findagrave.com/memorial/28200928/israel-bissell.

Two Soldiers, a Cask of Wine, and Thou(sand Lashes)

DON N. HAGIST

When Bryan McSweeny stepped ashore on Staten Island in August 1776, it must have looked like a paradise. He had spent the previous three years in Jamaica, in a tropical climate that was often fatal to Europeans; now, he saw a verdant landscape and felt temperatures similar to his native town of Macroom in County Cork, Ireland. But unlike peaceful Jamaica, which had avoided the violence of the recent Carib War, Staten Island was the staging point for a new British military offensive in the rebellious American colonies.*

McSweeny was a private soldier in the 50th Regiment of Foot. He had volunteered for the army in 1768—during peacetime and for most of the American Revolution the British Army was an all-volunteer force—and now had eight years of soldiering under his belt including his three years in Jamaica. The regiment was ordered from that island to join the massive military buildup on Staten Island. But the disease-prone Caribbean climate had taken its toll on soldiers' health, leaving the 50th under strength. There were other regiments on Staten Island that had been in North America for several years and also needed more men. Rather than add a newly-arrived regiment that was not fit for service into the order of battle, the army's commander, Gen. William Howe, directed that the regiment be drafted.

*All of the material for this article is in the British National Archives, Kew, Richmond, Surrey, United Kingdom. James Gardner's career is documented on the 22nd Regiment's muster rolls, WO 12/3872. Bryan McSweeny's career is there, as well as on the rolls of the 50th, 54th and 20th Regiments, and his discharge, WO 121/12/371. The proceedings of their court martial are in WO 71/83 p. 41—48. Details about British army enlistment, drafting, and pensions can be found in Don N. Hagist, *Noble Volunteers: The British Soldiers Who Fought the American Revolution* (Yardley, PA: Wesholme, 2020).

Drafting, during this era, meant transferring soldiers from one regiment to another. This was a routine practice for the British army, a way to ensure that regiments on foreign service were brought up to strength with a portion of experienced soldiers instead of entirely with new recruits. In this case, the fit private soldiers of the 50th Regiment were drafted into other regiments on Staten Island; the rest would return to England, where the unfit men would be discharged while the officers, non-commissioned officers, drummers and fifers would begin an intensive recruiting campaign to rebuild the corps.

Bryan McSweeny and thirteen of his comrades joined the 22nd Regiment of Foot, which had been in America since arriving in Boston at the end of June 1775. Being drafted meant remaining overseas, but it also meant receiving a new enlistment bounty, equivalent to about two months' pay. Each soldier owned his uniform, and would not receive a new one until the regiment received an annual clothing shipment late in the year; for this reason, McSweeny continued to wear the unform of his previous regiment, a red coat with black lapels, cuffs and collar instead of the red with buff worn by the 22nd.

Within days of joining his new regiment, McSweeny was at war. The 22nd Regiment was part of the force that crossed from Staten Island to Long Island on August 22, then undertook a long nighttime march that outflanked rebel forces on August 27 in the Battle of Long Island; the regiment suffered only two casualties in this, one of the war's biggest battles. The regiment landed on Manhattan Island at Kips Bay in mid-September, and was part of the garrison of the city of New York while the main army commenced operations farther north on Manhattan and then in Westchester County.

Serving in the same company of the 22nd Regiment as McSweeny was James Gardner, a native of England or Scotland who had enlisted in March 1775 as the regiment was preparing to leave Ireland for America. On September 30, the two men were part of a detachment assigned to guard stores of provisions in the city starting at 8 o'clock in the morning. This was a twenty-four-hour duty assignment, with two or three hours at a time spent standing sentry and the rest in a guard room, available to turn out in case of an alarm.

No alarm came that night for the provision guard, but there was trouble elsewhere in the city. A British army officer was awakened in the middle of the night by a disturbance outside the house where he lodged. He went to the window and saw a crowd around the cellar door below, which dispersed when he opened the window. But about an hour later, he heard noises coming from the basement. This was only days after insurgents had started fires that destroyed a third of the city, so the officer was especially concerned about more saboteurs.

He roused the homeowner, who roused his servant, and the three of them went to investigate. They found the outside cellar door had been forced open, and perceived sounds from within. The officer found a nearby sentry and had him stand guard at the cellar door, then the officer, the homeowner and the servant went inside. With a candle they went from room to room in the darkened basement, finding no one, until they noticed an inner door broken open. They peered through the doorway to a room where casks of wine were stored.

In the room were two men. "One of them was sitting with a bottle with the neck broke, between his legs; and there were a great many broken bottles laying about, and a strong smell of wine," according to the officer. The homeowner recalled that "one of them hid away behind a Cask of bottled wine, and the other leaning over it, and the Cellar floor very wet, and many empty bottles broke and laying about," and one of them "had a bottle in his hand or between his legs; they were both very drunk, and one was vomiting." The three residents hauled the two intruders out of the basement—literally, as one of them needed to be dragged across the wine-wetted floor—took a bayonet from one of them (the other was unarmed), and proceed towards the main guard, the army post where disorderly people were put into custody.

One of the prisoners, the one who was standing when discovered, identified himself as James Gardner, on duty with the provision guard. He "walked very peaceably to the Guard and said that he was much ashamed of himself," saying that the other prisoner "had brought him into the Scrape." He then addressed the other prisoner directly, saying "he had told him what would happen." When the group arrived at the main guard between two and three in the morning, the residents turned their prisoners and the bayonet over to the captain of the guard, and said they'd return in the morning "to give a Crime." Gardner's comrade was too drunk to be responsive, so the sergeant of the guard "in order to rouse him gave him some slaps on the face, with his hand."

The homeowner arrived at the main guard at eight in the morning to lodge his complaint, only to find "to his great surprise" that both prisoners had been released. Remembering that Gardner was assigned to the provision guard, he went there and asked to see the men of the guard. Among them was Bryan McSweeny, who the corporal of the guard roused from sleep. He was immediately recognized, not only because he wore the uniform of the 50th Regiment, but also because his trousers were still wet with wine and he had marks on his face where the sergeant of the main guard had slapped him. He nonetheless had little recollection of the night's events.

Gardner was not in the guard room. He had been posted sentry. The corporal of the guard took the homeowner to him, who recognized him, and Gardner acknowledged that he had been brought to the main guard just hours before.

Bryan McSweeny and James Gardner were tried by a general court martial on October 3 and 4, 1776, charged with "having broke into the house of Mr. Loring in the Town of New York." In a common practice, they were tried together. The officer, the homeowner, the servant, the captain of the main guard and the corporal of the provision guard all testified for the prosecution. Their stories were all aligned, leaving little doubt that the soldiers were guilty of something; the only evidence in their favor was that "a side of mutton, a Turkey and a loaf of bread" as well as some bottles of wine were missing from the cellar, suggesting that others had also been marauding during the night.

Both prisoners denied having been the cellar. "Gardiner said that there being no room in the guard room to lay down, he went to walk the Street," according to the trial record, "and Swyney said that his trowzers was wetted by a Canteen of Water that he had Spilt." The thirteen officers who constituted the court were not impressed, found the two guilty, and sentenced them each "to receive one thousand lashes each on their bare backs with a Cat of nine tails," a typical punishment for this sort of crime.

No information has been found to indicate whether these sentences were carried out in full or in part. Harsh though the sentence sounds, it was common for part or all of the lashes to be remitted or pardoned. Surgeons (military doctors) attended corporal punishments to make sure prisoners were not in danger of death. It was, after all, corporal, not capital, punishment.

Both men continued their careers in the 22nd Regiment, which garrisoned Rhode Island from December 1776 through October 1779. James Gardner was not there the entire time; he died on October 24, 1777, of unknown causes.

Bryan McSweeny had a much longer career. When the war ended and the 22nd Regiment was reduced in size and ordered back to England, he was one of sixty-six men discharged in New York in September 1783. And he was one of forty-four who, rather than starting a new life as a civilian in the United States, immediately enlisted in another British regiment bound for Nova Scotia. Clearly he found the army an acceptable career in spite of his "scrape" and conviction seven years earlier. When the 54th Regiment left Nova Scotia in 1787, he was discharged once again, and once again re-enlisted, this time in the 20th Regiment of Foot—gaining his fourth enlistment bounty. He was discharged for the last time in October 1791, and crossed the Atlantic to go before the army's pension examination board at Chelsea Hospital. Now forty-one years old, having spent twenty-three years as a soldier, he was awarded a pension, well-deserved after a long career in spite of his run-in with military discipline.

The Terribile Ordeal of Capt. Bezaleel Beebe's Company

TIM ABBOTT

Sergeant Solomon Goodwin of Colonel Philip Burr Bradley's Regiment of Connecticut Levies kept an orderly book for Capt. Bezaleel Beebe's Company. On November 16, 1776, he added a poignant, personal note: "This Day was the Day that our friends & fellow Soldiers was either killd or taken who were on York Island. This fatal day was a most dismal day to us. In it fell the Flower & Glory of our Regiment, the chief and the best officers and Soldiers that their was in our Regiment."[1] Nearly half of Beebe's company had been present at Fort Washington on Manhattan Island when it was attacked and captured by a large British and Hessian force. Sergeant Goodwin watched helplessly from across the river at Fort Lee, noting, "I came from there on the 14th so I escaped with just the skin of my teeth, &c."

Col. Philip Burr Bradley commanded one of eight regiments of Connecticut State Levies called into service in May 1776 to strengthen the defenses of New York. Capt. Bezaleel Beebe of Litchfield, Connecticut commanded one of Bradley's companies raised primarily in Litchfield and Torrington. Captain Beebe was a veteran of the French and Indian War and served previously during the Revolution in the Northern Army as 1st lieutenant in Col. David Wooster's 1st Connecticut Regiment and in early 1776 as a militia captain with a company of three-month's men.[2] That year one of Beebe's soldiers, Robert Little of Litchfield, recalled marching to Norwalk and then taking a sloop to

1. Orderly Book, 1776 Jul 19–Nov 17, 1780, Litchfield Historical Society (LHS), *Beebe Family Papers*, Box 1, Series 2, Folder 2.6.
2. 1st Lieutenant's Commission, Litchfield Historical Society (LHS), *Beebe Family Papers*, Box 1, Series 2, Folder 2.2.; Alain Campbell White, ed., *The History of the Town of Litchfield 1720 -1920* (Litchfield, CT: Enquirer Print, 1920), 74.

New York, and being there in the city when independence was declared.[3] Bradley's Regiment soon crossed over to New Jersey and by the second week of August were part of the force protecting the West side of the Hudson River in Bergen County. During September and October they were in the vicinity of Burdett's Ferry and Fort Constitution, soon to be renamed Fort Lee.[4]

After the Battle of White Plains, Fort Washington at the northern tip of Manhattan became isolated from the rest of Gen. George Washington's army. Perched high above the river on Harlem Heights, the position was a strong one but not impregnable. Although three British warships had been able to pass upriver despite taking fire from the fortifications on either side of the Hudson, Gen. Nathaniel Greene believed Fort Washington was still of strategic importance, writing to General Washington on November 9: "I cannot conceive the Garrison to be in any great danger the men can be brought off at any time—but the stores may not be so easily removed—Yet I think they can be got off in spight of them if matters grow desperate."[5] His confidence was tragically misplaced, but it was shared by other general officers and so the fort was reinforced instead of evacuated.[6]

Colonel Bradley's regiment sent large detachments from Fort Lee drawn from each of its eight companies to support the garrison of Fort Washington. Sergeant Goodwin filed a weekly return for Beebe's Company on November 15, the day before the battle, listing two officers, four sergeants, two drummers and fifty rank and file present and fit for duty out of a total of seventy-six officers and men of all ranks on the company rolls. Two days later he mustered only three sergeants, one drummer and eight rank and file fit and present and a total of forty-one men remaining in the company. Goodwin added a new column under the heading "Alterations since Last Return" listing thirty-five or thirty-six "Killd & Taken Officers Privates."[7] As the senior noncommissioned officer present he now found himself in charge of what remained of Beebe's company. Bradley's regiment overall lost twelve

3. James Little Pension (W.8256), National Archives and Records Administration (NARA), (RG93) M804, Revolutionary War Pensions.

4. Bradley's Regiment, NARA, (RG93) M246, Revolutionary War Rolls, Folder 195, Roll 27.

5. Nathaniel Greene to George Washington, November 9, 1776, *Founders Online*, National Archives, https://founders.archives.gov/documents/Washington/03-07-02-0085.

6. Derrick E. Lapp, "The Fall of Fort Washington: The Bunker Hill Effect"?, *Journal of the American Revolution*, July 7, 2020, https://allthingsliberty.com/2020/07/the-fall-of-fort-washington-the-bunker-hill-effect/.

7. Orderly Book, 1776 Jul 19–Nov 17, 1780.

officers and two hundred and fifty-eight enlisted men, and by the end of the month could muster only two staff officers, seven company officers, and one hundred enlisted effectives.[8]

The attack and capture of Fort Washington on November 16, 1776 resulted in the loss of nearly 3,000 defenders, including fifty-nine killed and ninety-six wounded.[9] Three men from Beebe's company—Cpl. Samuel Cole and Pvts. Joseph Spencer and John Whiting—were missing after the battle and presumed killed.[10] Pvt. John Weed was also thought to have been killed, but he must not have been present with the garrison because he subsequently marched through New Jersey with the remnant of the company and filed a successful pension application on his service that made no mention of being in the battle.[11]

Captain Beebe and thirty-three enlisted men from his company became prisoners of war. Pvt. James Little was one of them, having been wounded in the right side while fighting on the lower lines before retreating into the fort.[12] The prisoners from Fort Washington were first kept in an open field, then marched to Harlem Village and crowded into buildings where they spent the remainder of the night and several more days shivering under guard. Another member of Beebe's company—Pvt. Oliver Woodruff of Litchfield—remembered that they were held "without anything to eat or drink even the skin of a Potato except the pith of an old cabbage stump which he found in the garden."[13]

A few days later the prisoners began an arduous march down to captivity in New York. Private Little provided a lengthy, chilling narrative of their suffering as part of his pension application. "[B]eing formed into platoons," he wrote, they "were marched through the British and Hessian Army and were Insulted, kicked, beat with the butt of their Guns, some were knocked down and robd of our Hats and Blankets which was afterwards severely felt as most of us had only summer clothing."[14] The men staggered from exhaustion but were not permitted to halt or given food or drink and "forced by our extreme thirst," said Private Little "to sip from our hands the muddy water in the Road." Upon reaching the city, the captives became objects of great interest to its Loyalist inhabitants:

8. Bradley's Regiment, NARA.
9. Lapp, "The Fall of Fort Washington."
10. White, *The History of the Town of Litchfield*, 77.
11. John Weed Pension (S.23999), NARA.
12. James Little Pension (W.8256), NARA.
13. Oliver Woodruff Pension (S.14885), NARA.
14. James Little Pension (W.8256), NARA.

> The Ladies and Gentlemen from the City came to see the Yankey Prisoners, when Sergt [John] Cotton Mather asked a Lady who appeared to be much affected at our situation, if she Could not give him something to Eat She went and soon returnd with and gave him a small Loaf of Bread after thanking the generous Woman he turned and said Comrades you shall share with me and twenty-four of us shared in the Loaf.[15]

"We were separated for Quarters," remembered Private Little, with the prisoners from Beebe's company distributed among several places of confinement. Little was sent to a church that had been converted to a prison:

> five of my Company with a great Number of others were put in the North Chapel . . . We drew three days Allowance my share which was of Bran Bread was about a double handfull mouldy and full of Worms with two ounces of Pork . . . I ate the whole and then went three days more without food so that in eight days I had one meal.[16]

The other five men with him were Zebulon Bissell, Aaron Stoddard, John Parmelee, Joel Taylor and Phineas Goodwin. None of the five made it home to Litchfield.[17]

Private Woodruff "with eight hundred and fifteen others was imprisoned in New Bridewell then unfinished with loose floors and no windows—first food after captivity [the previous Saturday] was on Thursday morning."[18] Private Woodruff remained in the Bridewell jail until sometime in January, 1777 "without fire suffering more than has ever been written or told." Pvt. Remembrance Loomis was the only other man there from Beebe's company.

There were by now over five thousand American soldiers held captive in New York, including those taken during the Battle of Long Island and the chaotic retreat of General Washington's army from the city in mid-September. Not only the Provost and Bridewell jails but also city Hall, two sugar warehouses, churches and the troop transports *Whitby* and *Grosvenor* now served as prisons. Even had they been inclined to provide adequate food, clothing and shelter to so many men who had been taken in arms while in open rebellion, the enormity of the logistical challenge far exceeded the capacity of the occupying

15. James Little Pension (W.8256), NARA.
16. James Little Pension (W.8256), NARA.
17. White, *The History of the Town of Litchfield*, 76, 77.
18. Oliver Woodruff Pension (S.14885).

British authorities. Instead, a fatal mix of neglect, incompetence and abuse led to the deaths of hundreds during that winter.[19]

Captain Bebee was able to move about within the confines of the city while on parole. He spent the next few months diligently trying to determine what had become of the men from his company. His record—"An Account of the Prisoners Names and Places of Confinement"—is a grim litany of death with few survivors.[20] Twenty-eight of his men died in prison or of diseases contracted there, including from an epidemic of smallpox. Pvt. Isaac Grant of Judea in Litchfield, a prisoner from Capt. Benjamin Mills' company of Bradley's regiment, remarked that after first being held in a church and then being transferred to the prison hulk *Grosvenor*, he "had the smallpox in the natural way."[21] Connecticut still prosecuted people for getting inoculated without state sanction, and it is doubtful that anyone in Bradley's regiment had been exposed to smallpox before now.

Most of the prisoners from Beebe's company were confined in one of the notorious Sugar Houses: massive six-story stone buildings. Pvt. Enos Austin died there of smallpox on December 4 and there were many more deaths to follow.[22] Private Little alleged that several of the healthiest prisoners held with him in the New Chapel were forcibly impressed into British service. Later in December he and many of the sickest men were moved into the prison ship *Grosvenor* where nearly all of them suffered from smallpox. Among those who died on the *Grosvenor* were Cpl. David Hall and Pvts. Gershom Gibbs, Isaac Gibbs, Alexander McNeil, Timothy Stanley, Samuel Vaill and Solomon Parmelee; of the latter, Captain Beebe wrote that he "went on board the ship, and I fear he is drowned as I cannot find him."[23]

By this time, both Pvts. Oliver Woodruff and Isaac Grant were also on the *Grosvenor*. Woodruff misremembered the name of the prison ship as the *Glasgow*, a different vessel that was later used for a cartel,[24] but he was very clear that the hulk "moved from New York Harbor in Hell Gate where she cast anchor where she lay for 10 or 12 days during which time 28 of the Prisoners died from disease occasioned by hard treatment and hunger."[25] Private Little described the ship as "a two

19. Edwin G. Burrows, *Forgotten Patriots: The Untold Story of American Prisoners During the Revolutionary War* (New York: basic Books, 2008), 45-52.
20. White, *The History of the Town of Litchfield*, 76, 77.
21. Isaac Grant Pension (R.4195), NARA.
22. White, *The History of the Town of Litchfield*, 76,77.
23. Ibid., 77.
24. Burrows, *Forgotten Patriots*, 63.
25. Oliver Woodruff Pension (S.14885), NARA.

decker and so crowded that there was not room for us to lie down."[26] The *Grosvenor* was not a hospital ship but a place to quarantine sickened and contagious men. Those from Beebe's company and their fellows on board struggled to survive on "about three pints of Burgoo or Water Gruel without Salt in a Bowl for six men in the morning and at night about a handful of Kennel Biscuit . . . but when the Small Pox began to rage our case seemed deplorable, Indeed death and distress was on every side."[27]

James Little recounted bitterly how the bodies of the dead "were hoisted on deck a Cannonball fastened to them and then thrown overboard with a shout of there goes Another Damd Yanke Rebel."[28] Although the men were given the option of going ashore to bury their dead, he could recall only one instance when this was done, with disastrous consequences. Solomon Gibbs of Beebe's company died on the ship on December 29, 1776. His teenaged son Isaac convinced one of their fellow townsmen from Litchfield, Alexander McNeil, to help him bury his father. "[T]o go abroad from the Confined air in the hold of the Vessel provd almost Instant Death," Little observed grimly. His messmates Gibbs and McNeil "got so chilled & frozen that they died soon after their return . . . My last messmate young Gibbs before he died [on Jan 15, 1777] was frozen from his feet to his hips."[29]

Little and Woodruff endured unimaginable horrors while on the *Grosvenor*, their "situation hopeless and pitiless faint and feeble confined in the putrefied stagnated air of the hold of the Vessel & covered with Vermin."[30] Finally, after about six weeks, those who had smallpox were visited by a doctor and according to Little about forty were removed to a house on shore where nearly all of them were dead within a fortnight. His fellow townsmen Isaac Grant from Bradley's Regiment and Elihu Grant, who had been detached from the 19th Continental Regiment to serve in Knowlton's Rangers, survived in the house with him.[31] Isaac Grant described how after most of his companions died, he was visited by Levi Allen, the Loyalist brother of Ethan Allen, who interceded "with the Commissary of the Prisoners and got him out of the hospital and he was billeted out in the city and clothed by him."[32] Little also recalled that Allen, formerly a resident of Salisbury, Con-

26. James Little Pension (W.8256), NARA.
27. Ibid.
28. Ibid.
29. Ibid.
30. Ibid.
31. Elihu Grant Pension (R.4194), NARA.
32. Isaac Grant Pension (R.4195); James Little Pension (W.8256), NARA.

necticut, brought them clothing. At this time Oliver Woodruff remained on board the *Grosvenor* and Sergeant Mather somehow was still alive in the Sugarhouse. There were not many more of them left.

On February 20, 1777, a cartel ship deposited about two hundred sick and starving men at Milford Neck on Long Island Sound, and around the same time at Rye, New York "the Commanding Officer gave a receipt for nineteen almost dead men."[33] Among these paroled survivors were eleven from Beebe's company who were left to shift for themselves and make their way home as best they could. Many died on the road, among whom were Barnius Beach, Zebulon Bissell who got as far as Woodbury, Elisha Brownson, Remembrance Loomis, Timothy Marsh and Oliver Marshall. Thomas Mason died shortly after he arrived home in Litchfield.[34]

A few survived. James Little, who started walking at Rye, was so weakened that he stopped in Danbury and was taken in by a friend until his father arrived from Litchfield to care for him. Oliver Woodruff and Noah Beach made it back to Litchfield. Both Elihu and Isaac Grant also arrived home at Judea together, and by some miracle Sergeant Mather survived the Sugarhouse and made his way back to Sharon, Connecticut. Daniel Benedict also made it back to Litchfield County, but that was all. Oliver Woodruff was correct, however, when he recounted in his pension that "out of the thirty three of Captain Beebe's company that were made prisoner, only two beside himself ever arrived at home" in Litchfield.[35] Including the three men lost at Fort Washington, the detachment from Beebe's company suffered an 86 percent death rate. If the same held true for their fellows from the other seven companies of Bradley's Regiment who were at Fort Washington, there may have been as few as thirty-six enlisted men who survived their ordeal and quite possibly even fewer. Capt. Noble Benedict reportedly lost all but two of twenty-eight enlisted men who served with him at Fort Washington.[36]

Remarkably, Isaac Grant, James Little and Oliver Woodruff recovered their health and soon returned to service. Little remained in the militia and responded to the Danbury Alarm in April 1777. Grant joined his old commander Colonel Bradley in the new 5th Connecticut

33. Oliver Woodruff Pension (S.14885), NARA.

34. White, *The History of the Town of Litchfield*, 77.

35. Oliver Woodruff Pension (S.14885), NARA.

36. Royal R. Hinman, *A Historical Collection From Offical Records, Files, &c., of the Part Sustained by Connecticut During the War of the Revolution* (Hartford, CT: E. Gleason, 1842), 137. Hinman claims Benedict had fifty men in his detachment, but a subsequent return records twenty-eight enlisted men taken with Benedict on November 16, 1776. Bradley's Regiment, NARA, (RG93).

Regiment of the Continental Line. Woodruff shipped on a privateer out of New London in 1778 during which "nothing occurred of importance" and returned to port after a cruise of thirty days. Sgt. Solomon Goodwin dusted off his old orderly book in 1780 and accepted a warrant as sergeant major under Bezaleel Beebe, now colonel of a regiment of state troops guarding Horse Neck on Long Island Sound.[37]

Late in life while living in Vermont, James Little tried to qualify for a pension and was frustrated by a bureaucracy that failed to credit him for sufficient time in service. His application was "rejected by the Secretary for the war department on account of my enlistment being only for eight months," he declared,

> Notwithstanding I was taken prisoner and kept over the time that is considered sufficient to come within the Law to be entitled to a Pension. I would take the liberty to forward my declaration that the whole subject may be before you and in addition to what is there stated may I be permitted to mention some of the cruel treatment I underwent while a Prisoner.[38]

Both Little's and Woodruff's harrowing records of neglect and inhumanity while in prison are a poignant reminder that thousands of revolutionary captives died in New York from what one historian calls "a lethal convergence . . . of obstinacy, condescension, corruption, mendacity, and indifference."[39] There are many contemporary accounts like these, too many to ignore.

The impact of all those losses on their home communities defies the imagination. Both John Parmelee and his uncle Solomon were gone, as was Gershom Gibbs who entered the fort a few days before the battle as a substitute for one son and then died in captivity along with another. The father of Pvt. Noah Barnum, one of the men in Captain Benedict's company of Bradley's Levies, learned that his son died of hunger in prison after having attempted to eat a piece of brick. Wild with grief and anger, he reportedly went out the following day and shot and wounded a Loyalist neighbor who was working on his own land.[40] This war, like all wars, was filled with trauma and marked by inhumanity as well as courage.

37. James Little Pension (W.8256); Isaac Grant Pension (R.4195); Oliver Woodruff Pension (S.14885); Solomon Goodwin Pension (W.24,283), NARA (RG93) M804, *Revolutionary War Pensions*; Orderly Book, 1776 Jul 19–Nov 17, 1780, Litchfield Historical Society (LHS), *Beebe Family Papers*, Box 1, Series 2, Folder 2.6.

38. James Little Pension (W.8256) NARA.

39. Burrows, *Forgotten Patriots*, xi.

40. Hinman, *A Historical Collection*, 137.

Bacheller vs. Wilkinson: The Quest to Understand Benedict Arnold at Saratoga

COLIN J. WOOD

The common viewpoint on Benedict Arnold's role in the Battle of Bemis Heights on October 7, 1777 is based almost exclusively on the early nineteenth century testimony of James Wilkinson. That view holds that Arnold, after clashing with Gates over matters involving the Battle of Freeman's Farm on September 19, was without a command on October 7, but nonetheless boldly rode onto the battlefield and rallied flagging troops, ensuring victory at a key moment. But is Wilkinson a reliable source? He was, after all, a man steeped in controversy; Theodore Roosevelt said of him, "In all our history, there has been no more despicable character."[1] In 1787, Wilkinson worked as a double agent for the Spanish while being a senior officer in the American Army. Though his ultimate goal of delivering the states of Kentucky and Tennessee to the Spanish Crown failed, Wilkinson evaded capture and died in ignominy. He was relieved of duty and court-martialed during the War of 1812 and wrote a memoir in an attempt to clear his name.[2]

Wilkinson was present at Saratoga and witnessed the events of October 7. The account from his memoir in 1816 states that Arnold was not given command that day. He called Arnold a traitor he "would not offer injustice for," and called his own account a "statement of facts"

1. Robert Brammer, "General James Wilkinson, the Spanish Spy Who was a Senior Officer in the U.S. Army During Four Presidential Administrations," *Library of Congress Blogs*, April 12, 2020, https://blogs.loc.gov/law/2020/04/general-james-wilkinson-the-spanish-spy-who-commanded-the-u-s-army-during-four-presidential-administrations/.

2. Adam Henry and Earl Harbert, *History of the United States of America During the Administrations of James Madison* (New York, NY: Random House, 1986), 923.

against misinformation spread at the war's end.[3] Wilkinson gave Arnold the benefit of the doubt, asserting that it is "natural" for someone of Arnold's status to "feel irritated by the humiliating situation in which he found himself."[4] He continued by claiming Arnold was drunk and rode around the camp in a frenzied state.[5] As he put it, Arnold acted rashly and belligerently and even wounded an officer in his tirade.[6] During the engagement on Bemis Heights, Arnold was reckless and darted across the battlefield from left to right, riding through enemy fire.[7] Wilkinson finished his account with this final anecdote: "It is certain that he neither rendered service nor deserved credit on that day, and the wound he received alone saved him from being overwhelmed by the torrent of General Gate's good fortune and popularity."[8]

Most, if not all, historians ascribe some substance to Wilkinson's memoir. Though there are occasions where the comments of drunkenness and being underserved of credit are scrutinized if not rejected, the prevailing opinion is that Arnold was not given command on that day and decided to join the battle of his own volition.[9] This idea remained for nearly two hundred years of historiography until differing evidence emerged in 2016.

In August of that year, a letter was sold on the e-commerce website eBay; the seller and buyer of this letter are unknown, but historian Eric Schnitzer obtained a copy of it. He proceeded to authenticate and transcribe the letter and present it at Saratoga National Historical Park. The letter was dated October 9, 1777, and was a communication between New Hampshire Lt. Nathaniel Bacheller and his wife, Suzanne. His letter's contents provide a perspective contrary to that of Wilkinsons.

3. James Wilkinson, *Memoirs of My Own Times* (Printed by Abraham Small, 1816), 272. Something to note regarding this text is that it was written with the perspective of Arnold as a "traitor" which does not contextualize his character during this period of the war.
4. Ibid., 273.
5. Ibid.
6. Ibid.
7. Ibid.
8. Ibid.
9. Any scholarship before 2016 would have an account similar to Wilkinson's memoir. Amongst them is James Kirby Martin, *Benedict Arnold: An American Warrior Reconsidered* (New York, NY: NYU Press, 1997); Theodore Corbett, *No Turning Point: The Saratoga Campaign In Perspective* (Norman, OK: University of Oklahoma Press, 2012); Barry K. Wilson, *Benedict Arnold: A Traitor In Our Midst* (Montreal, QE: McGill-Queen's University Press, 2001); and after 2016, John F. Luzader, *Saratoga: A Military History of the Decisive Campaign of the American Revolution* (New York, NY: Savas Beatie, 2018).

Bacheller's regiment, led by Brig. Gen. Enoch Poor, was instructed to join Arnold's brigade at 2 in the afternoon on October 7. At that moment, the British engaged Patriot riflemen, and Arnold went out to view the conflict. General Gates arrived and called a dispatch rider to retrieve Arnold because he ordered the assault and feared Arnold would accidentally fire upon Col. Andrew Scammell's 3rd New Hampshire Regiment.[10] Arnold returned and told Gates the enemy's position. He implored Gates to reinstate his command, asserting, "It is late in the day, but let me have men, and we will have some fun with them before sunset."[11] Gates agreed, and the assault on Balcarres's Redoubt commenced.[12] This letter indicates that Arnold was given command on October 7, quite in contrast to Wilkinson's account of events.

There are other sources that help corroborate Bacheller's letter, and which in some ways accord with Wilkinson. In 1951, Charles W. Snell arranged an order of battle for the American forces at Bemis Heights. Snell found that Col. Daniel Morgan "had received special orders to act only upon orders received directly from Gates' headquarters." Later, Morgan left Gates' command and was under Arnold, causing subsequent strife between the two.[13] He asserted that Oliver Wolcott's brigade also joined Arnold.[14] Historian Samuel Woodruff continues this by claiming that Arnold and Morgan consulted each other before the battle.[15] This is consistent with Bacheller's letter stating that Poor's regiment was also under Arnold's command.

Returning to Wilkinson's account, his assertion that Arnold was drunk and acting belligerently is inconsistent with Snell's conclusions. Wilkinson described Arnold as grasping for power and riding through enemy fire in an attempt to rally "his" men. This is plausible if we accept that Arnold was beloved by the soldiery; Col. Henry Livingston once said Arnold was the "life and soul of the troops."[16] Perhaps, seeing Arnold's impassioned tirade, soldiers followed him out of sheer impulse.

10. Nathaniel Bacheller to Suzanne Bacheller, October 9, 1777 (transcript), Saratoga National Historic Park, Stillwater, NY.
11. Ibid.
12. Ibid.
13. Charles Snell, "A Report on the Organization and Numbers of Gates' Army, September 19, October 7, and October 17, 1777, Including an Appendix with Regimental Data and Notes," February 1, 1951, https://npshistory.com/publications/sara/gates-army.pdf.
14. Ibid.
15. Samuel Woodruff, *An Original, Compiled and Corrected Account of Burgoyne's Campaign* (Albany, NY: Munsell, 1844), 256.
16. Quoted in Stephen Brumwell, *Turncoat: Benedict Arnold and the Crisis of American Liberty* (New Haven: Yale University Press, 2018), 107.

But it was Gates who gave Arnold credit after the British surrender at Saratoga.[17] Moreover, his actions were praised by leaders such as Scammell and Poor.[18] This differs significantly from Wilkinson's sentiments, who believed that Arnold did not deserve credit. This inconsistency brings doubt as to whether or not Wilkinson was telling the truth. Bacheller's letter proves to be more consistent with other sources.

How does this change our understanding Arnold and the Battle of Bemis Heights? Firstly, it vindicates Arnold's actions as coordinated and not recklessly impulsive; secondly, it paints him as a collected, obedient, and professional commander instead of a sulking, drunken fool. Thirdly, this pivotal moment in Arnold's career, where he led the assault factored in turning the tide of the war, can now be viewed with a more professional perspective.[19]

As for Wilkinson, his testimony appears to be a ghastly falsehood. Wilkinson, a traitor in his own right, wrote his memoirs hoping to vindicate himself, but the truth of his treachery still became exposed. He wrote his description of Arnold at Saratoga to purposely defame him. Perhaps Wilkinson threw Arnold under the bus as a confession for his own treason.

ACKNOWLEDGEMENTS

I extend my fullest gratitude to Eric Schnitzer of the Saratoga National Historical Park for transcribing and giving me access to Bacheller's letter. I also want to thank Dr. Christopher Smith from Liberty University's Department of History for his assistance.

17. Ibid., 109.
18. Corbett, *No Turning Point*, 220.
19. For revised historiography with Bacheller's account see Brumwell, *Turncoat*. Kevin John Weddle, *The Compleat Victory: Saratoga and the American Revolution* (New York: Oxford University Press, 2021).

Henry Clinton's Plan to End the War

GENE PROCKNOW

The General Sir Henry Clinton papers at the William C. Clements Library in Ann Arbor, Michigan, contain a curious document, "A proposal to Subdue the Rebellion and a Sketch of the Necessary Rout for that purpose." The British military plan envisioned a summer campaign attacking north from New York City to capture the Hudson River and Connecticut River valleys with a force of sixteen thousand soldiers, supported by naval ships and landing craft.[1] Clinton's principal biographer, William Willcox, does not reference the campaign plan in his authoritative monograph.[2] While historians have thoroughly analyzed Gen. John Burgoyne's 1777 attempt to capture the Lake Champlain and Hudson River Valleys from Quebec, no historian has interpreted Clinton's previously overlooked plan.[3] The plan's obscure nature and London's strategic shift to counter the French entry into the war have left it unaddressed, to the detriment of better understanding Clinton's generalship.

At the time of the British planning, Clinton served as second in command to Gen. William Howe. Placing Clinton in charge in New York City, Howe led a tactically successful campaign to capture the Rebel capital city of Philadelphia but failed in the strategically important objective of thoroughly defeating Washington's army. Clinton's principal orders were to defend New York City. However, when the

1. Henry Clinton, "A Proposal to Subdue the Rebellion and a Sketch of the Necessary Rout for That Purpose" (August 1777), Henry Clinton Papers Volume 29, Folio 13, William C. Clements Library.
2. William B. Willcox, *Portrait of a General: Sir Henry Clinton in the War of Independence* (New York: Alfred A. Knopf, 1964).
3. The most recent account of General Burgoyne's 1777 invasion is Kevin John Weddle, *The Compleat Victory: The Battle of Saratoga and the American Revolution* (New York, NY: Oxford University Press, 2021). Another excellent account is Dean R. Snow, *1777: Tipping Point at Saratoga* (New York, NY: Oxford University Press, 2016).

New York commander learned of Burgoyne's distress in the Saratoga region, he led an attacking force up the Hudson River to relieve pressure on Burgoyne and potentially link up with his army at Albany.

Initially, Clinton's expedition experienced success. He executed a victorious multi-prong attack on Fort Clinton and Fort Montgomery, astride the Popolopen Creek, a few miles south of West Point. His daring, circuitous march to the relatively undefended rear of these forts led to their capture.[4] However, as his command traveled further up the Hudson River, Patriot forces strengthened, and progress slowed. Howe, never keen on supporting Burgoyne's efforts, ordered Clinton to detach several thousand troops and send them to reinforce the British Philadelphia garrison. As a result, Clinton recalled the attacking regiments to New York City, and his Hudson Valley expedition ended.[5] However, the general's initial success demonstrated that British forces could sever New England from the other colonies with the proper number of troops and experienced leadership. This experience led General Clinton to believe that the Hudson Corridor was the key to winning the war, and either he or a subordinate officer developed a detailed campaign plan to accomplish this objective.[6]

The unsigned and undated twelve-hundred-word plan commences with a two-pronged attack, one up the Connecticut River and the other up the Hudson River. The document calls for an army of ten thousand troops to strike the Connecticut River Valley from Long Island Sound. The objective of this attack was to capture Hartford, Connecticut. The plan is peculiarly silent on the rationale for capturing Harford or any other purposes for this substantial force. However, the planners believed that the region between the Connecticut and Hudson Rivers contained many residents who would side with the King if British troops secured the area.

The campaign's second prong was to proceed up the Hudson River and recapture Fort Clinton and Fort Montgomery. Next, the British would execute a multi-directional attack to surround and invest the West Point fortress. Leaving a reserve force at Fort Clinton, the remainder of the troops would march to the hills west of West Point to cut off a Rebel retreat. Another group would land on the river's east

4. For the most detailed account of the Fort Montgomery and Fort Clinton battles, see William H. Carr and Richard J. Koke, "Twin Forts of the Popolopen - Forts Clinton and Montgomery, New York, 1775-1777," *Bear Mountain Trailside Museums* 1, republished October 2006 (July 1937).

5. Henry Clinton, *The American Rebellion Sir Henry Clinton's Narrative of His Campaigns, 1775-1782 with an Appendix of Original Documents*, ed. William D Wilcox (New Haven: Yale University Press, 1954), 81.

6. Clinton, *The American Rebellion*, 81.

side to capture Fort Constitution, located on an island in the Hudson River opposite West Point. A third force would pass West Point's guns at night to land north of the fort. With all avenues of escape cut off, the British Army would open batteries opposite West Point and bomb the Rebel fortress into submission.

After West Point's capture, the British would leave four hundred men at Fort Clinton (renamed Fort Vaughan) and an unspecified force opposite West Point to inhibit its reconstitution. Two-thirds of the British army would then march ten miles on the west side of the river to the Rebel post on Butter Hill near New Windsor. The remaining one-third would pass Butter Hill at night on flat boats under the cover of galleys. The amphibious force would land at Martler's Creek and capture Rebel forces encamped on Butter Hill in concert with the landward force.

Next, the army would march eight or ten miles into the countryside to collect cattle and destroy the "disaffected's" property. The British author believed this incursion would engender Loyalists to flock to the Royal standard. He would leave eight hundred soldiers to support the gathering of Loyalists. The main army would continue up the river, stopping at Fish Kills to destroy Rebel stores and barracks. The campaign planner envisioned another march into the country to collect supplies, destroy Rebel property, and gather additional Loyalist recruits. The British officer ordered the destruction of all boats to prevent the Rebels from crossing the Hudson.

The British author planned a landward approach to Poughkeepsie by employing a tactic similar to that he used at the Lower Hudson forts. After capturing the town, the British would leave three hundred soldiers and as many Loyalists as needed to establish fortifications. Next, the attacking force would cross the river at Kats Kills and march to Lunenburg. After capturing this town, the water route to Albany would be open, completing the territorial gains envisioned in the campaign plans.

Turning next to defending the newly captured river corridor, the British planner envisioned emboldened Loyalists joining the Royal Army and securing the river as a communications and supply corridor. Couriers would travel the countryside with messages for the Loyalists to assemble at fixed river landings on appointed muster days. The British believed that at least four thousand Americans would enlist under the King's banner. The author calculated that the British would need only two thousand muskets to properly arm the recruits, as many would bring their muskets. Army officers would administer oaths of allegiance to pacify the countryside and require two hostages in every district to ensure compliance with their pledges.

Further, all Hudson Valley residents must surrender arms and ammunition and join a Loyalist militia unit. The conscripted soldiers would serve under officers of their choosing to augment Royal forces until the end of the campaign, at most the first of December. In conjunction with the British Navy, the British author planned to station sixty to one-hundred-ton ships in intervals of fifteen to twenty miles between New York City and Albany. The ships would carry supplies and prevent the Rebels from crossing the river, cutting New England off from the rest of the colonies. After achieving the strategic objective of dividing New England from the rest of the rebelling colonies, the war-ending plan abruptly ends.

The two-and-a-quarter-page campaign proposal and accompanying illustrative map are unsigned and undated and not in Clinton's handwriting but scribed by a British secretary. Despite missing an attribution, the plan to control the Hudson River Valley is consistent with Clinton's views on winning the war and experiences in the Hudson Highlands. Clinton opined later in life that he "flattered myself with hopes that I had opened the important door of the Hudson ... and prevented the rebels from ever shutting it again . . . it would have probably finished the war."[7] Additionally, the uninscribed plan contains strategies and tactics used by General Clinton during his Fall 1777 Hudson Valley campaign, including waterborne attacks on both sides of the river, attacking rebel forts from the more vulnerable landsides, and using watercraft to more speedily transport troops than the rebels who trod poorly maintained roads through rugged territories.

While the unattributed plan exhibits Clinton's thinking, other British leaders proposed schemes to capture the Hudson and Connecticut River corridors. Patriot turned Loyalist William Smith wrote a confidential note to Frederick Howard, 5th Earl of Carlisle, who served as a Peace Commissioner, advocating a movement into the region between the Connecticut and Hudson Rivers to rally the purported large number of loyalists in the area.[8] The New York Royal Governor and Major General William Tryon proposed a similar, though more audacious, fast attack plan up the Hudson Valley to capture Albany and enlist the purported many loyalists in the region. While aiming at similar objectives, the Smith and Tryon plans differed in the number of troops, campaign tactics, and methods to punish Rebels. Additionally, Clinton categorically rejected Tryon's plan as too risky:

7. Ibid.

8. William Smith, *Historical Memoirs of William Smith, 1778-1783*, ed. William H. W. Sabine (New York: New York Times & Arno Press, 1971), 43–44.

> He apprehended Mr. Tryon's Designs were to burn the Villages. He said the proper Mode for conducting the War was to seize the Highland Forts, and make a Lodgment there of 6000 Men, to put 8000 more on the coast of Connecticut, and act by Detachments from New York and Rhode Island in a variety of Occasional Descents favoring the main Bodies.[9]

Therefore, Clinton or a member of his staff is the most likely author of the Clements Library document ("Clinton Plan") and not Governor Tryon or Jurist William Smith. Furthermore, Clinton thought enough of the plan to retain a copy among his papers.[10]

Similarly, one can infer that Clinton drafted the plan, or ordered it drafted, after October 1777, as the Clinton Plan refers to Fort Vaughan, which he renamed from Fort Clinton after its capture on October 6, 1777. The document provides another hint as to its preparation time by specifying the initiation of the Hudson and Connecticut Valley campaigns before May. After achieving success in the fall of 1777, the British could have developed the attack plan before the 1778 summer campaign season. However, it is less likely that the British created the plan in 1778 – that year, Clinton focused on a compelling defense of the vital New York City while the bulk of Howe's command garrisoned Philadelphia. In late 1777, the British commander worried more about protecting New York City and its critical harbor. Clinton assessed in his memoirs that his forces were "too low to admit of more than the strictest defensive (6142 rank and file fit for duty)."[11]

On March 8, 1778, Lord George Germain appointed Clinton as successor commander-in-chief to Howe. Accompanying his orders, Germain assumed responsibility for deploying British North American forces to reflect France's entry into the war. The American Secretary ordered Clinton to abandon Philadelphia, freeing up troops for the West Indies, St. Augustine, Pensacola garrisons, and offensive operations in the Southern Colonies. Germain issued discretionary orders for Clinton to raid the New England coast to destroy privateers and cut off supplies for Washington's army.[12]

9. Henry Clinton quoted in Smith, *Historical Memoirs*, 41.
10. Clinton retained numerous documents to counter second-guessing by superiors and politicians. After the war, he employed many of the saved papers to justify his actions and avoid criticism.
11. Clinton, *The American Rebellion*, 84.
12. Lord George Germain to Henry Clinton, March 8, 1778, in K. G. Davies, ed., *Documents of the American Revolution, 1770–1783: Colonial Office Series* (Shannon: Irish University Press, 1972), 15:57.

Despite his superior's focus elsewhere, Clinton continued to see offensive opportunities in the Hudson Valley before the 1779 summer campaign season. The British general asserted,

> And, when the attention of the enemy should by these operations be turned to the southward, it was planned that the armament should suddenly return and join in a move I proposed up the North River against the rebel forts that covered King's Ferry. And, should the English and West Indies reinforcements join me at that critical moment (as was promised and fully depended on), it was my intention to extend my views even to the attacking the works at West Point.[13]

While Clinton did not receive sufficient forces to conduct a full-scale attack up the Hudson Valley, he did attack as far north as Stony Point in an attempt to recapture a portion of Burgoyne's convention troops transiting the river on their way to prisoner-of-war camps in Virginia. This attempt failed due to arriving late at the crossing point. However, Clinton established a post at Stony Point, which Brig. Gen. Anthony Wayne famously seized on July 16, 1779. After this defeat, Clinton continued to look for ways, such as Maj. Gen. Benedict Arnold's treason to capture West Point. Eventually, Clinton gave up on a Hudson Valley operation due to the lack of forces and explicit orders to focus efforts on the southern theater.

While nothing came of Clinton's projected Hudson Valley campaign, the plan's existence demonstrated that Clinton sought promising, aggressive offensive opportunities. Due to more significant geopolitical issues, he did not possess sufficient latitude to resource and execute his plans. By the time of Clinton's appointment as commander in chief, war planning necessarily shifted to London due to the French entry into the war. Given the need to confront French forces globally, Lord Germain relegated Clinton to a tactical commander in the former thirteen colonies with fewer resources and vague and discretionary orders. Given that all strategic plans emanated from London, Clinton never sent any plan to Lord Germain, unlike William Howe, who bombarded his superiors with four military alternatives to end the war over five months.[14]

Although the "Clinton Plan" demonstrated considerable local knowledge and military insights, it was not sufficiently complete to execute successfully. The plan offered copious details on the Hudson

13. Clinton, *The American Rebellion*, 122.

14. For a discussion of General Howe's plans and interactions with Lord George Germain see John Fortescue, *The War of Independence: The British Army in North America, 1775–1783* (London: Greenhill Books, 2001, reprint of 1911 edition), 52–65.

River attack vector and none on the Connecticut River grouping, resulting in several unaddressed questions. Why deploy a more substantial force on the Connecticut River? What were the planner's objectives in this region? Additionally, the plan does not address contingencies such as a counter-attack from Washington's main army. Finally, General Wayne's daring nighttime attack and successful capture of the Stony Point fortress demonstrate that accomplishing "Clinton's Plan's" objectives might be easier than holding them.[15]

The Clinton Plan belies the commonly held view by contemporaries and some historians that Clinton was overly passive and unaggressive.[16] Its existence demonstrates that Clinton was a skillful strategist who developed a workable strategy to end the war, informed by his perceptive, unmatched on-the-ground experiences.[17] The "Clinton Plan" represented early thinking of what the British commander would have done if he possessed sufficient war planning latitude from London with adequate military resources. Finally, the plan's existence gives credibility to Washington's focus on controlling the Hudson Highlands and keeping its river crossing open to transit soldiers and supplies.

15. For a description of the Rebel attack on Stony Point, see Henry P. Johnston, *The Storming of Stony Point on the Hudson Midnight July 15, 1779* (New York: James T. White & Co., 1900).
16. For a summary of the views of fellow officers and colleagues on Henry Clinton, see Andrew Jackson O'Shaughnessy, *The Men Who Lost America: British Leadership, the American Revolution, and the Fate of the Empire* (New Haven: Yale University Press, 2013), 224–25. An eminent military historian assessed, "Caution was Clinton's watchword." John W. Shy, *A People Numerous and Armed: Reflections on the Military Struggle for American Independence* (Ann Arbor: University of Michigan Press, 1990), 206. Another historian opined, "He overestimated his difficulties and then did not really try to overcome them." Robert Middlekauff, *The Glorious Cause: The American Revolution, 1763-1789* (New York: Oxford University Press, 2005), 598. A British historian averred that Clinton possessed "strategic timidity," "played the game safely" and was "a very capable general in the field," but crippled by self-distrust." Piers Mackesy, *The War for America: 1775-1783* (Lincoln: University of Nebraska Press, 1992), 144, 515, 213.
17. Only George Washington served longer as a senior commander than Henry Clinton.

Cato: A Tragedy–The Enduring Theatrical Mystery at Valley Forge

SHAWN DAVID MCGHEE

The Valley Forge winter of 1777-78 is an integral part of America's national narrative.[1] For many citizens, the name "Valley Forge" relates both a physical and intellectual landscape, specific spatial geography in Pennsylvania and a certain emotional acreage representative of the enduring suffering many Americans embraced during the revolution. At the end of that challenging encampment, Gen. George Washington permitted a performance of English Whig Joseph Addison's *Cato: A Tragedy* (perhaps at Bake House) on Monday, May 4, 1778.[2] The Continental Congress had, however, prohibited theater-going (and other cultural rites) in 1774 in its effort to pressure Parliament into repealing the Coercive Acts and purify Americans of perceived moral corruption. Just why the commander in chief allowed this theatrical engagement to take place given the political circumstances remains a point of contention among scholars.

Washington saw the play many times over the course of his life and, in some respects, modeled his own private and public behavior after that Roman senator.[3] According to historian Gordon Wood, Addison's

1. This work is indebted to Director of Visitor and Community Engagement Adam Gresek of Valley Forge National Historical Park. He allowed the author a careful and informative investigation of the interior of Bake House, which is not open to the public. Throughout he remained generous with his time and patient with the author's methods, a bounty to this present work. Ranger Steven Walter also offered his time and knowledge regarding *Cato* at Valley Forge. This essay is better informed due to their consideration.
2. Mark Evans Bryan, "'Slideing into Monarchical Extravagance': Cato at Valley Forge and the Testimony of William Bradford Jr.," *William and Mary Quarterly* 67, no. 1 (2010): 123-144.
3. Peter Henriques, *Realistic Visionary: A Portrait of George Washington* (Charlottesville, VA: University of Virginia Press, 2006), 81-82; H. C. Montgomery, 'Washington the Stoic," *Classical Journal* 31, no. 6 (1936): 371-73

Cato impressed upon Washington "what it meant to be a stoical classical hero" committed entirely to the public weal.[4] Researcher Henry Wiencek claimed Valley Forge represented "the darkest moment of the Revolution" and, presumably to raise morale, Washington convened his officers to witness a performance of *Cato*.[5] Both Peter Henriques and Richard Norton Smith similarly claimed Washington staged the play to inspire a demoralized army at the nadir of the war.[6] Ron Chernow theorized the general approved the play to "buck up his weary men" and remind subordinates their sacrifice mimicked the glorious suffering of the ancient Romans.[7] Mark Evans Bryan recently argued that Continental officials held the play for "an exclusive entertainment" that offered a "display of Georgian gentility by young officers keen to garner the attention of Washington and the major generals."[8] Which is it? Did Washington authorize the play to remind soldiers that sacrificing for the public good was a timeless expression of republican virtue? To revivify an otherwise downtrodden officer corps? To create the proper social environment for rank-conscious climbers to compete for favor and position? Or is there something else at play here?

Most historians who contemplate this controversial performance analyze it from the vantagepoint of the Valley Forge winter encampment. This parochial perspective naturally lends itself to the "sacrifice and/or inspiration" school of thought: Washington quietly offered the production to ingrain in his men the necessity of self-denial and resurrect their desire to press on after surviving a difficult winter.[9] But even this narrow view is difficult to rationalize considering Addison's text. If the general hoped to "buck up his weary men" with a play, why *Cato*? After all, despite the unshakable virtue the tragic hero displays over the course of five acts, he fails to protect Rome from Julius Caesar's imperial ambitions. And when Cato learns of Caesar's arrival at Utica, the senator chooses suicide over surrender. Shortly before his corporeal body

4. Gordon S. Wood, "The Greatness of George Washington," in Gordon S. Wood, *Revolutionary Characters: What Made the Founders Different* (New York, NY: Penguin Books, 2006), 36.

5. Henry Wiencek, *An Imperfect God: George Washington, His Slaves, and the Creation of America* (New York, NY: Farrar, Straus and Giroux, 2003), 36.

6. Henriques, *Realistic Visionary*, 81; Richard Norton Smith, *Patriarch: George Washington and the New American Nation* (New York, NY: Houghton Mifflin Company, 1993), 269.

7. Ron Chernow, *Alexander Hamilton* (New York, NY: Penguin Books, 2004), 107.

8. Bryan, "'Slideing into Monarchical Extravagance,'"123-144.

9. Willard Stern Randall, *George Washington: A Life* (New York, NY: Henry Holt and Company, 1997), 43; Henriques, *Realistic Visionary*, 81; Smith, *Patriarch*, 269; Chernow, *Hamilton*, 107.

expires, he learns that Pompey's son has arrived from Spain to combat Caesar. Had Cato lived to lead the Romans, his son Portius laments, their combined forces may have rescued the republic from impending despotism.[10] On the surface at least, this plotline is not exactly inspiring. If viewers imagined Cato and Rome as stand-ins for Washington and the United States and likewise Caesar as George III (as contemporary Americans did), the play gloomily predicted a certain if virtuous American failure.[11]

But what of staging the play to allow junior officers to curry favor with their superiors and jockey for promotions? Bryan's argument is compelling, and it is likely that some men who attended and others who performed in *Cato* hoped to replicate their British counterparts' aristocratic environment. But Washington approving a performance of Addison's work presents a different problem. Why would an obedient and disciplined commander in chief, who sought to embody and model republican virtue, blatantly disregard the Continental Association's eighth provision which specifically prohibited theatrical performances? Moreover, why would the general support a form of entertainment that he, as a former delegate of the First Continental Congress, identified as detrimental to the American cause? To get to the root of this political problem, a broader historical context is necessary.

Prior to the publication of *Cato* in 1713, Joseph Addison penned numerous essays commenting on, among other topics, politeness and politics. Through these writings, he hoped to promote gentility and civic pride among British subjects, arming them with a moral compass and shared sense of identity. A "Human Soul without education," he remarked, is no different than a block of marble. Only a talented sculptor can transform lifeless stone into a work of art, and only scholastic training, following this logic, can prepare the mind to realize its vast potential. Education, Addison concluded, enabled men to "recover our souls out of Vice, Ignorance and Prejudice." Addison aimed to nurture refinement through his essays and "contribute something to the polishing of Mens Minds."[12] Addison's literary exercises continued a tradition of intellectual and cultural cultivation in fashion since at least the early sixteenth century, when Italian knight Baldassare Castiglione published *The Book of the Courtier*.[13]

10. Christine Dunn Henderson and Mark E. Yellin, eds., *Cato: A Tragedy and Selected Essays* (Indianapolis, IN: Liberty Fund, 2004).
11. Roger E. Stoddard, "Notes on American Play Publishing, 1765-1865," *Proceedings of the American Antiquarian Society* 81 (1971): 161-90.
12. Joseph Addison, *Spectator* 215 in Henderson and Yellin, *Cato*, 131-34.
13. Henderson and Yellin, "Introduction," in ibid., xv.

Through *Cato*, Addison likely hoped to continue this behavioral proselytization. He based his plot mainly on Plutarch's *Life of Cato the Younger* and Sallust's *The War with Catiline*.[14] Addison, throughout his composition, portrayed the title character as virtue embodied, a public figure dedicated solely to Rome who suppressed his private wants for the public good. Cato's unswaying commitment to the state, as depicted by Addison, earned that Roman admiration from the entire political spectrum of contemporary Britain despite his obvious association with a political faction. The historical Cato caucused with the *Optimates*, a loose fraternity of Romans that worked to uphold senatorial power against encroachments on its authority from dictatorial tyranny above and mobocracy below. Historians typically cast Caesar as a member of the *Populares*, reformers who advocated for a more equitable distribution of Rome's resources.[15] Addison, intimate with the destructive force political factions could potentially unleash upon communities (with both the English civil wars and the 1688 Glorious Revolution tattooed on the minds of most eighteenth-century subjects), warned readers of the perils of toxic partisanship. Parties, he explained, "spoil good Neighborhood, and make honest men hate one another." Faction creates "a dreadful Spirit of Division" that "rends a Government into two distinct People." It is, he continued, fatal to men's virtue and morality and destroys common sense. Finally, he warned "A furious party Spirit . . . exerts it self in Civil War and Blood-shed . . . and extinguishes all the Seeds of Good-nature, Compassion and Humanity."[16] Addison's play channels these sentiments, issuing a stern reminder of political extremism's bipartisan dangers. Once the play debuted in London in 1713, both Whigs and Tories claimed Cato as their own.[17] A liberal writer channeling a conservative figure united, however briefly, a fractured political community through theatrical patriotic valor and selflessness.

14. This can be gleaned from Addison's dialogue in *Spectator* 169, in ibid., 127-31.
15. There is fierce debate among classicists about the utility and viability of using *Optimates* and *Populares* to describe factions in the Roman Republic, a debate well beyond the scope of this essay. Since Cato clearly stood up for the prestige of the senate and the *Optimates* are associated with this political objective, for the sake of brevity I have included the term's usage. Likewise, the eighteenth-century audience familiar with Addison's *Cato* remained deeply unsettled by the creeping presence of faction. See Erich Gruen, *The Last Generation of the Roman Republic* (Oakland, CA: University of California Press, 1974); M.A. Robb, *Beyond Populares and Optimates: Political Language in the Late Republic* (Stuttgart: Franz Steiner Verlag, 2010); Richard E. Mitchell, *Patricians and Plebeians: The Origins of the Roman State* (Ithaca, NY: Cornell University Press, 1990).
16. *Spectator* 125, in Henderson and Yelling, *Cato*, 123-26.
17. Henderson and Yellin, "Introduction," in ibid., xiii-xiv.

The work enjoyed critical and financial success; enthusiasts staged it throughout much of western Europe while translated editions appeared in Italy, Holland and France (among other polities). It likewise caught the imagination of most subjects in British North America.[18] New York hosted the first known colonial performance of *Cato* in 1732. Traveling actors next offered two productions at Charlestown, South Carolina, in November 1735. The show made its way to Virginia the following year and, by 1750, companies had staged the work at Philadelphia and again in New York.[19] Between 1732 and 1774 professional American thespians had staged *Cato* at least twenty-eight times with only *Romeo and Juliet* (barely) surpassing this figure.[20]

After 1765, the play met the moment for colonists, offering the best popular expression for how ostensibly pure and virtuous Americans might respond to the policies of a politically unaccountable Parliament. As observed by historian Forrest McDonald, "That most of the founding generation read or saw it or both is unquestionable."[21] Washington freely borrowed lines from its pages throughout his life (most notably in his Farewell Address) while editor Isaiah Thomas's *Massachusetts Spy* included a verse in his gazette's masthead for a good portion of the 1770s. "Do Thou Great Liberty inspire our Souls—And make our Lives in Thy Possession happy," the heading thundered, "Or, our Deaths glorious in Thy just Defense."[22] Resistance theater of a different sort from December 16, 1773, however, brought the empire to its breaking point and, for American Whigs, promoted *Cato* from remarkable entertainment to requisite moral instruction.

The third and final imperial crisis resulted from perhaps a few dozen brazen American Whigs tossing 342 chests of the Royal East India

18. Christine Dunn Henderson and Mark E. Yellin, "'Those Stubborn Principles': From Stoicism to Sociability in Joseph Addison's *Cato*," *Review of Politics* 76, no. 2 (2014): 223-41; Randall Fuller, "Theaters of the American Revolution: The Valley Forge 'Cato' and the Meschianza in their Transcultural Contexts," *Early American Literature* 34, no. 2 (1999): 126-46; Hannah Filipowicz, "School for Patriots?: The Foundational Dramas of the American and Polish Revolutions Revisited," *Canadian Slavonic Papers* 52, no. 1/2 (2010): 19-45.

19. Katherine Harper, "Cato, Roman Stoicism, and the American Revolution," PhD diss. (University of Sydney, 2014), 71-72.

20. Bryan pointed this data out in "Slideing into Monarchical Extravagance," 123n2; see also Odai Johnson and William J. Burling, *The Colonial Stage, 1665-1774: A Documentary Calendar* (Cranbury, NJ: Fairleigh Dickinson University Press, 2001), 64-65.

21. Forrest McDonald, "Foreword," in Henderson and Yellin, *Cato,* viii.

22. Forrest McDonald, *Novus Ordo Seclorum: The Intellectual Origins of the Constitution* (Lawrence, KS: University of Kansas, 1985), 195-96; For the masthead, see, for example, *Massachusetts Spy*, September 29, 1774.

Company's tea into Boston Harbor.[23] Parliament responded by passing the Coercive Acts, punitive legislation designed specifically to demoralize Boston into submission. As a result, communities from New England to Georgia began calling for non-importation and non-consumption of British goods, some even going so far as to call for non-exportation of American resources.[24] And virtually all called for a "Grand Continental Congress" to direct a nationalized resistance movement and secure American liberty at all costs.[25] The First Continental Congress convened at Philadelphia on September 5, 1774 and closed its doors in late October.[26] Congress's actionable response to the Coercive Acts came in the form of the Articles of Association, itself something of a national code of conduct.[27] Over fourteen articles, the Continental Association: called for non-importation of slaves as well as British and Irish goods effective December 1, 1774; warned merchants, retailers and ship captains against price gauging and smuggling; declared those knowingly breaking the Association as individuals "inimical to the liberties of their country"; and advised colonists to limit slaughtering sheep to promote domestic textile production.[28] The eighth article holds the key to unlocking the *Cato* mystery. In that provision, Congress banned a range of popular pastimes such as horse racing, cockfighting, gambling, elaborate funeral processions and theatrical performances.[29] What lay behind Congress's condemnation of these social engagements reveals the nature of the moral crisis American Whigs felt threatened their political nation.

23. Benjamin Carp, *Defiance of the Patriots: The Boston Tea Party and the Making of America* (New Haven, CT: Yale University Press, 2011).
24. Shawn David McGhee, *No Longer Subjects of the British King: The Political Transformation of Royal Subjects to Republican Citizens, 1774-1776* (Yardley, PA: Westholme Publishing, 2024).
25. *Newport Mercury*, August 15, 1774; *New-Hampshire Gazette*, August 12, 1774; *Rivington's New York Gazetteer*, November 24, 1774; "Letter from a Private Individual to Peyton Randolph," October 20, 1774, in Peter Force, ed., *American Archives: Consisting of a Collection of Authentic Records, State Papers, Debates, And Letters And Other Notices of Publick Affairs, the Whole Forming a Documentary History of the Origins and Progress of the North American Colonies; of the Causes and Accomplishments of the American Revolution; and of the Constitution of Government for the United States, to the Final Ratification Thereof: Fourth Series*, 6 vols. (Washington, D.C., 1837-1853), 1:944.
26. Caroline Robbins, "Rights and Grievances at Carpenters' Hall, September 5-October 26, 1774," *Pennsylvania History: A Journal of Mid-Atlantic Studies* 43, no. 2 (1976): 100-18.
27. McGhee, *No Longer Subjects of the British King*.
28. Worthington C. Ford et al., eds., *Journals of the Continental Congress, 1774-1789*, 34 vols. (Washington, D.C., 1904-37), 1:78.
29. Ibid.

Many eighteenth-century theorists imagined polities as cycling through an organic lifespan: birth, maturity, decline and death.[30] In light of this, disinterested statesmen aimed to prevent the latter stages by remaining virulent and youthful through an enlightened allocation of a given political community's natural resources and labor pool.[31] For many American Whigs, Britain represented a modern Rome, a once-virtuous empire overrun with vice, effeminacy and self-interest rapidly devolving into a state of moral decline. Colonists hoped to avoid Britain's perceived plague of disposable wage earners, landless drifters, oppressive factory regime and debauched aristocracy.[32] And while British North America did not resemble England in terms of its commercial modernity, Whigs did sound the alarm over what many considered degenerate practices out of place in their American Sparta.[33] During the Coercive Acts Crisis, Congress sought to morally cleanse colonists by prohibiting cultural cancers many felt had infected an otherwise healthy body politic. The Continental Association's eighth article laid bare those ailments, aiming to "encourage frugality, economy, and industry" while promoting American agriculture, art and manufacturing. Congress further discouraged "every species of extravagance and dissipation" along with all "expensive diversions and entertainments."[34] These demands represent a fusion of classical virtue and Protestant morality and asked American Whigs to submit private desire to public demand and sacrifice luxuries some felt tainted republican simplicity.[35] For resistance actors familiar with Addison's *Cato*, that classical Roman effectively had lived by Congress's contemporary creed. Put another way, Congress asked colonists to commit to living like Cato.

30. "Gracchus," *Pennsylvania Packet*, October 17, 1774; see also See also Drew McCoy, *The Elusive Republic: Political Economy in Jeffersonian America* (New York, NY: W. W. Norton and Company, 1980).
31. "Lucius Publicola," *Pennsylvania Packet*, October 24, 1774; see also McCoy, *Elusive Republic*.
32. McCoy, *Elusive Republic*.
33. For some expressions that compared American purity with the classical world, see Samuel Adams to Thomas Young, October 17, 1774, in Harry Alonzo Cushing, ed., *The Writings of Samuel Adams*, 4 vols. (New York, NY: Knickerbocker Press, 1904-1907), 3:162-63; John Adams to Abigail Adams, September 20, 1774, Abigail Adams to John Adams, October 16, 1774, in L. H. Butterfield, et al., eds., *Adams Family Correspondence*, 13 vols. (Cambridge, MA: Harvard University Press, 1963-), 1:156-57; William Tudor to John Adams, September 26, 1774, in Robert J. Taylor, et al., eds., *The Papers of John Adams*, 18 vols. (Cambridge, MA: Harvard University Press, 1977-2016), 2:174-76.
34. Ford et al., eds., *Journals of the Continental Congress*, 1:76.
35. McGhee, *No Longer Subjects of the British King*.

Even before Congress issued the Continental Association, many colonists faulted theater-going for weakening civic virtue among Americans. The educated ought to model appropriate Christian behavior for the masses, one observer lectured in 1768, by avoiding profligate productions that contradicted biblical prudence.[36] Middling folk, some contended, should lead frugal and industrious lives out of, if nothing else, necessity; partaking in frivolous entertainments like plays only contributed to the misery of poorer families since attendees wasted resources they might otherwise have reserved for food and fuel. One critic advised upper-class women to avoid theater altogether for fear it would corrupt feminine virtue by exposing ostensibly pure ladies to profanity and vulgarity. Others warned that plays transformed men into women and all attendees into slaves, ultimately creating crowds of dependents incapable of defending the commonweal.[37] Another commentator blamed theater productions for "sinking the Athenians into effeminacy" and warned Americans of a similar fate.[38] This collection of attitudes made its way into Congress's eighth provision and most theater companies ended up shutting their doors or relocating outside the mainland colonies after 1774.[39] Despite the hostility Whigs expressed toward theater performances, however, American writers continued to dedicate their energy to writing plays for colonists to read during the crisis period. Appreciating the difference between public productions and private consumption is critical to fully grasping *Cato* at Valley Forge.

Going back to the classical world, playwrights often wrote morality and politics into their works, allowing productions to function as entertainment and vehicles of education (or indoctrination).[40] Historians David Shields and Fredrika Teute described eighteenth-century theater as "Britain's great school of manners and the engine of fashion."[41] This tradition continued during the crisis period as colonists picked up their quills to inculcate Americans into supporting the Whig cause with patriotic propaganda. Naturally public theatrical productions, fit with costumes, stages, intoxication and idleness, threatened the purity of the

36. *Boston News Letter*, October 30, 1760.

37. Ann Fairfax Withington, *Toward a More perfect Union: Virtue and the Formation of the American Republics* (New York, NY: Oxford University Press, 1991), 24-37.

38. "Philander," *New York Journal*, February 4, 1768.

39. Jason Shaffer, "'An Excellent Die': Death, Mourning, and Patriotism in the Propaganda Plays of the American Revolution," *Early American Literature* 41, no. 1 (2006): 1-27.

40. Peter Arnott, "Greek Drama as Education," *Educational Theater Journal* 22, vol. 1 (1970): 35-42.

41. David S. Shields and Fredrika J. Teute, "The Meschianza: Sum of All Fetes," *Journal of the Early Republic* 35, no. 2 (2015), 189.

republican ideal. Reading alone or in small groups in private spaces, however, allowed consumers to absorb the politeness and politics of a given work without the waste and extravagance associated with public performances.

During this period, Mercy Otis Warren wrote *The Adulateur*, *The Defeat* and *The Group*, each of which commented on or satirized revolutionary politics and war, casting favorable light on the American position. Hugh Henry Breckinridge crafted *The Battle of Bunkers Hill* and *The Death of General Montgomery*, the former lauding the righteousness of the American cause, the latter lambasting supposed British wickedness at Quebec.[42] And Philip Freneau, the "poet of the American Revolution," directed his verse to the imperial struggle, perhaps most famously in "The British Prison Ship."[43] This composition relates his first-hand experience of captivity's horrors. "Shut from the blessing of the evening air / Pensive we lay with mingled corpses there," he recounted, "Meagre and wan, and scorch'd with heat below / We loom'd like ghosts, ere death had made us so."[44] And while Americans likely read this literature with the intended pride or outrage writers' designed it to provoke, *Cato* still held an even deeper emotional connection with most colonists. For a people expected to sacrifice material and social convenience in an effort to save their suffering communities, nothing resonated more than the self-denial depicted in the pages of Addison's *Cato*.

On September 26, 1777, His Majesty's forces marched into Philadelphia, the rebel capital and meeting site of the Continental Congress, to settle in for the winter.[45] After considering several options, General Washington selected Valley Forge for his army's third winter encampment. Contrary to the mythology surrounding this pivotal decision, Valley Forge offered an excellent site for military quarters. The land's natural bounty supported thousands of farmers who produced dairy, flour and wheat for the wider Atlantic marketplace while forges, mills and furnaces diversified the local economy. The Schuylkill River served as both protective barrier and commercial highway while the landscape's elevation kept the Continental Army safe from potential

42. Shaffer, "'Excellent Die,'" 1-27.

43. For some literature on Philip Freneau, see Lewis Leary, *That Rascal Freneau: A Study in Literary Failure* (New Brunswick, NJ: Rutgers University Press, 1942); Jacob Axelrad, *Philip Freneau: Champion of Democracy* (Austin, TX: University of Texas Press, 1967).

44. Philip Morin Freneau, *The Poems of Philip Freneau. Written Chiefly During the Late War* (Philadelphia, PA: printed by Francis Bailey, 1786), 196.

45. Frederick Bernays Wiener, "The Military Occupation of Philadelphia in 1777-78," *Proceedings of the American Philosophical Society* 111, no. 5 (1967): 310-13.

surprise attacks. Finally, Valley Forge provided plenty of flat land, acreage utilized to construct an organized military community and train soldiers for the coming campaign.[46] Despite these available advantages, the army's condition initially remained dire.

Private Joseph Plumb Martin declared the army "in a truly forlorn condition" on its march to Valley Forge, made up of soldiers with "no clothing, no provisions and as disheartened as need be." Yet despite men remaining "weak, starved and naked," he explained, they "engaged in the defence of our injured country" determined to persevere.[47] Surgeon Albigence Waldo ruminated in his diary, "Why are we sent here to starve and Freeze—what sweet Felicities have I left at home; A charming wife—pretty Children—Good Beds—good food." He then described his current condition, "Here all Confusion—smoke and Cold—hunger and filthiness . . . There comes a bowl of beef soup—full of burnt leaves and dirt, sickish enough to make a Hector spue."[48] Washington assessed the situation in equally fatal terms that December. "What then is to become of the Army this Winter," he asked President Henry Laurens, as soldiers slept "under frost and snow without Cloathes or Blankets." The general harbored grave concerns over whether or not Continental forces would even remain intact during the encampment.[49] About eighteen miles east at Philadelphia, the material circumstances for the British Army were markedly different.

Surveying the comparative military camps that winter, Philadelphia loyalist James Allen ridiculed General Washington for being a "lame-spectator" to the ruthless success of British raiding parties. Allen estimated the Continental Army had dwindled to an embarrassing 5,000 men after calculating for desertions, disease and death. In contrast, he explained His Majesty's forces had spent the Philadelphia encampment enjoying "a very gay life the whole winter, [while hosting] many very

46. Wayne Bodle, *The Valley Forge Winter: Soldiers and Civilians in War* (University Park, PA: Pennsylvania State University Press, 2002); John Ferling, *Almost a Miracle: The American Victory in the War for Independence* (New York, NY: Oxford Press, 2007), 274-75; For the concept of the army as a military community, see Holly A. Mayer, *Belonging to the Army: Camp Followers and Community during the American Revolution* (Columbia, SC: University of South Carolina, 1996).

47. Joseph Plumb Martin, *Memoir of a Revolutionary Soldier: The Narrative of Joseph Plumb Martin* (Mineola, NY: Dover Publications, 2006), 58.

48. Albigence Waldo, "Valley Forge, 1777-78: Diary of Albigence Waldo, of the Connecticut Line," *Pennsylvania Magazine of History and Biography* 21, no. 3 (1897): 299-323.

49. George Washington to Henry Laurens, December 23, 1777, in Philander D. Chase, et al., eds., *Papers of George Washington: Revolutionary War Series*, 29 vols. (Charlottesville, VA: University Press of Virginia, 1985-), 12:683-87.

expensive entertainments."[50] The frequent festivities culminated that season with Gen. Sir William Howe's departing celebration following his resignation. Organized largely by Maj. John André, the eighteen-hour Meschianza unfolded on May 18, 1778, a fortnight after Continental officers staged *Cato*. This extravagant display of indulgence and opulence began in the afternoon with a flotilla of officers and gentry engaged in a *regatta* on the Delaware River as musicians performed spirited music on the river's banks. Later, a neo-feudal jousting tournament took place between British officers clad in medieval French garb and divided into two camps, the Knights of the Blended Rose and the Knights of the Burning Mountain. After this theatrical mock-combat, spectators proceeded to a feast, then a ball, before the penultimate offering: an elaborate show of fireworks. As perfectly described by historian John Ferling, the festivities ultimately concluded early the following morning with a round of speeches and toasts for every "conceivable object save one—a British victory."[51] Yet despite the carefree attitude on display, the British mood had turned considerably darker by the time officers staged the Meschianza. Attorney James Allen wrote, the "face of politics is much alter'd for the worse, a war with France being inevitable, as she has recognized the independence of America and entered into a commercial treaty with the united States."[52] Eighteen miles west at Valley Forge, the American mood had also changed by early spring.

Washington learned in late April that France had recognized American independence.[53] By May 3, President Laurens had officially informed Washington that treaties "between the Court of Versailles and the United States" had been read before Congress and would likely be ratified and published in the coming days.[54] On May 4, according to Lt. Col. William Bradford, Jr.:

> Cato was performed before a very numerous and splendid audience. His Excellency and Lady, Lord Sterling, the Countess and Lady Kitty, and Mrs. Green were part of the Assembly. The Scenery was in Taste—and the performance admirable.[55]

50. May 11, 1778, "Diary of James Allen, Esq., of Philadelphia, Counsellor at Law, 1770-1778," in *Pennsylvania Magazine of History and Biography* 9, no. 3 (1885): 435-36.
51. Ferling, *Almost a Miracle*, 295-96; for the best cultural analysis of the Meschianza, see Shields and Teute, "The Meschianza," 185-214.
52. May 11, 1778, "Diary of James Allen," 435.
53. William Heath to George Washington, April 21, 1778, James Bowdoin to Washington, April 23, 1778, in Chase, et al., *Papers of Washington: Revolutionary Series*, 14:580, 591-92.
54. Henry Laurens to Washington, May 3, 1778, in ibid, 15:21-22.
55. Paul Leicester Ford, *Washington and the Theater* (New York, NY: Dunlap Society, 1899), 26.

Scholar Mark Evans Bryan plausibly deduced this engagement took place inside Bake House. Bryan uncovered that weeks earlier, another officer had received a ticket for an entertainment but the "bakehouse" was too crowded to enter, lending strength to the position that future performances may have also occurred in that particular building.[56]

Just how exactly *Cato* unfolded is absolutely unknown. American legend holds that actors performed this tragedy outdoors before the entire army.[57] Indeed, as late as 1927, Valley Forge offered a similar amphitheater production before a large audience to (approximately) commemorate the 150th anniversary of that 1778 performance. Yet it almost certainly did not happen during the encampment *en plein air*. Bryan is again likely correct in concluding that organizers intended the Valley Forge performance exclusively for men of rank.[58] Historians have yet to uncover any contemporaneous evidence suggesting anyone other than officers enjoyed this spectacle. Even the intrepid and ubiquitous Joseph Plumb Martin made no mention of *Cato* in his memoir.[59] But if this performance catered to the officer corps, it is difficult to imagine leadership considering it a reproduction of British leisure and cosmopolitanism. After all, the deep communication networks imbedded in both Valley Forge and Philadelphia certainly informed Continental officers of the incomparable round of perpetual parties and festivities the British enjoyed at Philadelphia.

If the performance did take place inside Bake House and overcrowding sometimes rendered that space inhospitable, how exactly did the action unfold? Also, if Washington and other notable figures attended, this typically crowded space would likely have been even more congested than usual. These factors would have severely limited the building's available square footage for a practical theatrical production of *Cato*. But if Bake House's structural limitations are combined with Congress's cultural prohibitions, a credible scenario presents itself.

While some historians countenance an unlikely amphitheater performance and others a more plausible officer corps production, an equally convincing interpretation is that *Cato* at Valley Forge was not a theatrical display at all in the traditional sense. To avoid breaking the letter of the law as explicitly detailed in the Continental Association's eighth article while adhering to its spirit, Washington may very well

56. Bryan, "Slideing into Monarchical Extravagance," 127; see also Thomas Ewing, ed., *George Ewing: Gentleman Soldier at Valley Forge* (New York, NY: Thomas Ewing, 1928), 67.
57. Shaffer, "Excellent Die," 2-3; Fuller, "Theaters of the American Revolution," 128-30.
58. Bryan, "'Slideing into Monarchical Extravagance,'" 123.
59. Martin, *Memoir of a Revolutionary Soldier.*

have opted for a middle ground of sorts. Rather than elaborate costumes, rehearsals and props, scholars must at least entertain that what actually took place within the cramped walls of Bake House that spring evening was a table reading of Addison's work. After all, reading plays did not break the Association; in fact, Whigs considered reading a necessary and virtuous engagement during the crisis period.

The main hall at Bake House is approximately 17´ x 17´ (roughly 289 square feet) with a low ceiling. Given these constrained measurements, it is unlikely that a standing performance with a stage of any kind took place in this space. In short, the room that unequivocally remains from the original structure is a tight parlor that would struggle to seat fifty people comfortably, theatrical considerations aside.[60] Yet imagining several readers, maybe in improvised costumes, maybe not, seated by candlelight and reciting their parts in private quarters is less a stretch than a grand outdoor spectacle or even an indoor stage performance in such a small space. And any variety of large-scale performance would almost certainly have left behind more evidence. But holding an intimate reading shortly before revealing the Franco-American Alliance would have presented American officers with a more enviable politico-military position (through the play) than Addison left Cato's followers after the stoic senator's suicide. In this contemporary version, Cato (Washington) *lived* to join with Pompey's son (France) to *unite* against Caesar (George III). And throughout the recital, Addison's selfless lawmaker would have reminded the officer corps that they sacrificed in the name of their suffering country, just what Congress expected of Americans. In other words, a limited reading would not only have adhered to the self-denial mandated by the Continental Association; it would have amplified Congress's attempt at moral purification with an aural lesson in public sacrifice.

On Tuesday, May 5, the day after the *Cato* performance, Washington decreed "the Almighty ruler of the Universe" had intervened on behalf of the United States and recruited "a powerful Friend among the Princes of the Earth" to help Americans secure independence. After some military theatrics and thirteen cannon discharges, the army shouted "Long Live the King of France" before offering a final salute "To the American States."[61] The once-desperate Continental army

60. I am indebted to technician David Sutton for accompanying me and taking these measurements on August 1, 2023. His mechanical capabilities and structural knowhow better informed the author of the practical possibilities of Bake House's spatial order for this essay.
61. General Orders, May 5, 1778, in Chase, et al., *Papers of Washington: Revolutionary Series*, 15:38-41.

emerged that spring a more disciplined and organized institution.[62] Addison's *Cato* reminded the officer corps of their solemn responsibility to elevate the needs of the state above the wants of the self. General Washington probably expected the soldiery to absorb Cato's virtue from their superiors in what might be described as "trickle-down virtue." Valley Forge ultimately represented another in a series of profound crises that mimicked, however imperfectly, the darkest days of Rome. And American Whigs embraced a willingness to suffer as part of their proto-national ethos in a shared struggle to, in the eternal words of Addison's *Cato*, "Restore the commonwealth to liberty."[63]

62. Mark Edward Lender and Garry Wheeler Stone, *Fatal Sunday: George Washington, the Monmouth Campaign, and the Politics of Battle* (Norman, OK: University of Oklahoma Press, 2016).
63. For voluntary suffering as the sinews of American union and a primordial quality of a proto-national ethos, see McGhee, *No Longer Subjects of the British King*; for the closing quote, see Addison, *Cato*, in Henderson and Yellin, *Cato*, 36.

A Smart Engagement: Boat Fight at Stamford, June 24, 1778

SELDEN WEST

Very early on a hot summer's day in 1778, Moses Mather, Jr., son and namesake of the Patriot minister of Middlesex Parish (today's Darien), Connecticut, was seventeen years old and sitting in a whaleboat just offshore.[1]

Only two years before, whaleboats rarely had been seen in western Long Island Sound. But as enemies on both sides of the water realized how easily the craft could be converted from sailing to rowing and back again, or dismasted and stealthily carried up beaches to be hidden in the underbrush, by early 1778 their numbers had multiplied. In late March a New York newspaper reported uneasily, "We hear a number of rebel whale boats have been seen reconnoitering the north shore of Long Island."[2] By May Connecticut whaleboats had been plundering Long Island and capturing Loyalists and small British vessels for weeks.

On the morning of June 24 it was cloudy and airless by 5:00 AM, not a breeze stirring. There were five Connecticut whaleboats floating west of the Norwalk Islands, and it appears the men in them were bored.[3] Someone must have had a spyglass.

A becalmed sloop was spotted close to the Long Island shore beneath the cliffs of Lloyd's Neck, a peninsula halfway between Hunt-

1. Prisoner list: Muster-Table of His Majesty's Ship *Falcon*, June 25, 1778, Great Britain, The National Archives (TNA), ADM 36/B016, courtesy of Todd W. Braisted.
2. *New York Gazette and Weekly Mercury*, March 23, 1778.
3. Weather from logs of His Majesty's ships *Fowey*, ADM 51/375, *Falcon*, ADM 51/336, and *Raven*, ADM 51/771, and armed brigs *Diligent*, ADM 51/4163, and *Halifax*, ADM 52/1775, all TNA. Location of whaleboats: Thomas Painter, Connecticut, No. R6896, Collection M-804, Pension and Bounty Land Application Files, National Archives and Records Administration (hereafter Pension Files); number of whaleboats: ibid., and Thomas Painter, *Autobiography of Thomas Painter: Relating His Experiences During the War*

ington Bay and Oyster Bay. Loyalist refugees there supported their families by cutting firewood for the British military. The wood was loaded on small sloops and schooners that were escorted by armed vessels in groups to New York. Here was a solitary wood sloop, helpless.[4]

Thomas Painter, eighteen years old and in a whaleboat from New Haven, later recalled in a memoir written for his children, "In a short time someone proposed to go over and take that Sloop and tow her across the Sound. No sooner said, than it was agreed to by all hands."[5]

The decision was the height of daredevilry. Within a five-mile stretch the boys could also see riding at anchor three British sloops-of-war, the *Falcon*, *Raven*, and *Swan*, all of fourteen guns, and the brigs *Halifax* and *Diligent* of ten guns. Moreover, inside Huntington Bay lay the powerful twenty-four-gun frigate *Fowey*.[6] The raiders were gambling that they could dart in, seize the little sloop, and tow her away while the enemy ships lolled powerless without a breeze.

Unfortunately, sometime after 7 AM someone on the *Diligent* spied the five whaleboats approaching the wood sloop. Immediately her commander, Lt. Thomas Farnham, ordered two of the brig's 3-pounders fired to alert the rest of the British squadron. The *Raven* acknowledged the warning by firing two guns of her own.[7]

Lighthearted, the whaleboatmen decided they were still committed. "[W]e were quick at our oars, going for the Sloop," said Painter, "notwithstanding there were several Ships of War, lying in Oyster Bay, all in plain sight, and we in plain sight of them and they preparing and manning their boats to oppose us. But notwithstanding all this, Over we went—took the Sloop—and towed her with our boats, after having put about three men from each boat aboard the Sloop, to fight the boats which were coming up after us."[8]

They had hit a hornet's nest with a stick. Soon the enemy was swarming from all directions. Ships' boats, manned and armed, were launched from every British vessel in the area—the *Diligent, Halifax, Falcon, Swan, Raven,* and *Fowey*—quickly joined by Loyalist whale-

of the Revolution, privately printed, 1910; 20 (hereafter *Autobiography*). Painter's pension application and autobiography differ. *Fowey, Diligent,* and *Falcon* logs specify 5 whaleboats. In his autobiography Painter adds confusion by mentioning the schooner but according to period sources she wasn't involved until later.

4. It was identified as a wood sloop in *Raven* log, ADM 51/771, TNA.

5. Painter, *Autobiography*, ibid.

6. Ships listed in Records of the British New York Vice-Admiralty Court, Captured Ship: *Mehitable*, (Captured Ship: *Mehitable*) HCA 32/338/14/1, TNA.

7. *Diligent* log, ADM 51/4163, TNA, *Raven* log, ADM 51/771.

8. Painter, *Autobiography*, ibid.

boats from Oyster Bay. Painter recalled, "The boats coming up after us, were about 18 in number, and probably not less than 150 men."[9]

Painter and his captain, Elisha Elderkin, both experienced privateers, were two of the roughly ten men now on the captured wood sloop. "The Sloop having some Swivels on board, we made free use of them," Painter recalled.[10] The rest of the whaleboatmen bent to their oars, rowing with all their might. The ropes towing the sloop were taut.

Off Oyster Bay, the *Diligent* had made sail. With little wind, her progress was slow. Nevertheless she crept after them, her cannons firing twenty-one 3-pound shots at the fleeing whaleboats and their prize. The eighteen British boats were rowing furiously in chase. Meanwhile the raiders aboard the towed sloop blasted astern with their purloined swivel guns. Capt. John Stanhope of the *Raven* noted in his log the Americans' "very hot fire."[11]

The boats churned across the Sound. The *Diligent* was eventually left behind. Hours passed, men sweated in the muggy heat, and the overcast sky grew darker, as if a storm were approaching.[12] It seems the frantically rowing oarsmen on both sides were too focused to notice. It was the beginning of a solar eclipse.

At 9 AM British muskets began firing in earnest as the gap between hunters and quarry narrowed. Still, the five whaleboats towing the wood sloop were nearly across the Sound to safety at Stamford when they finally fell within range of the eighteen pursuing boats. There was an eruption of crossfire. "notwithstanding their superiority," Painter said, "we beat them off, on the first attack, and got the sloop almost over to the main."[13]

9. Ships allowed a prize share are listed in Captured Ship: *Mehitable*, ibid. Loyalist boats from Oyster Bay in *Diligent* log, ADM 51/4163, TNA; they are identified as from DeLancey's Brigade in *Royal Gazette* (New York), June 27, 1778. Boats coming up: *Autobiography*, ibid. Jackson in Daniel Jackson, Connecticut, No. S17512 (Pension Files), testified to eighteen boats.

10. Roughly ten: Painter (Pension Files). In his pension application, Painter stated "2 or 3;" in his autobiography, "about three." Yet there were only two from his boat and it is hard to believe each of five boats contributed three men to fight a few swivel guns, leaving all boats shorthanded.

11. Logs of *Diligent*, ADM 51/4163 and *Raven*, ADM 51/771, both TNA.

12. Grew darker: the moon's disk began crossing that of the sun at 8:48 AM. Eclipse predictions by Fred Espenak, EclipseWise.com, https://eclipsewise.com/solar/SEcirc/1701-1800/SE1778Jun24Tcirc.html#section3.

13. At 9 AM: Two log entries of *Diligent*, ADM 51/4163; Michael J. Crawford, ed., *Naval Documents of the American Revolution* (*NDAR*), Vol. 13 (Washington, DC: Naval History and Heritage Command, 2019), 193, transcribes this entry, "from 9 to 11 Continued fireing Musquestry"; it is "Continuel." *Diligent* was far out of range, as is later clear: "at Noon the

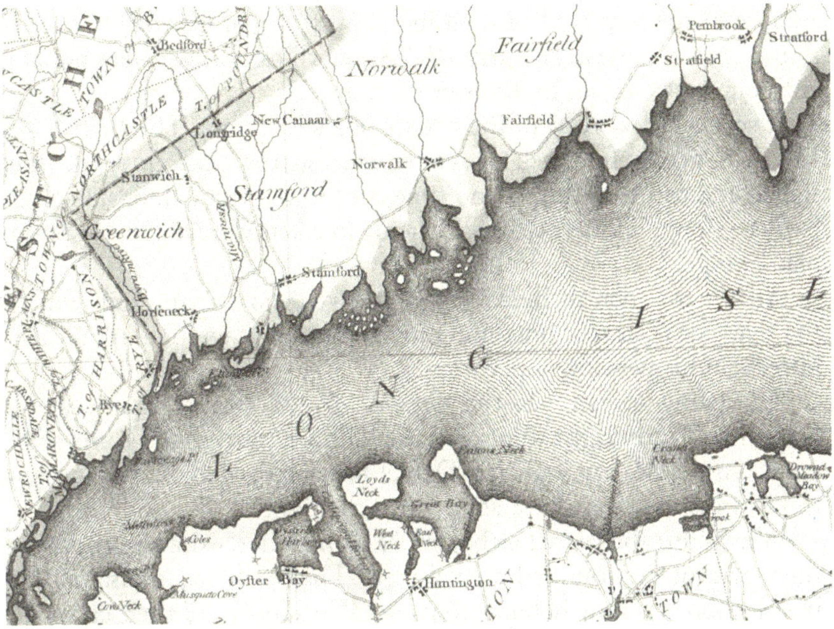

Detail from a 1776 map of Connecticut and Long Island. Stamford, Connecticut, is at lower left, west of Norwalk. (*Library of Congress*)

A visiting Rhode Island privateer sloop, the *General Arnold*, came out of Stamford harbor to their aid, accompanied by a privateer schooner, the *Mehitable,* under Capt. Daniel Jackson of Wilton Parish, Norwalk. Both were small coastal vessels, only twenty-five and ten tons burden respectively, and in the faint wind neither could move nimbly, but together they brought nine more swivel guns and two 2-pounders to the fight.[14]

At 10 AM for several minutes the dim light was swallowed in an eclipse of 93 percent totality. The boat fight raged on. Fifteen miles away in Fairfield, the Rev. Mr. Andrew Elliot and others were straining to see what was happening. He wrote to his father, "During the late

armed Boats & Prize Vessels Joind Us off Loyds Neck." Farnham was describing the musketry of the boats.

14. Came out: reconstructions, including eighty-six-year-old Jackson in Daniel Jackson (Pension Files), put them at Huntington, but period records are clear they were captured off Stamford. *Falcon* log, ADM 51/336, TNA, specifies both emerged from Stamford harbor at 10 AM. Guns: Captured Ship: *Mehitable,* ibid; Captured Ship: *General Arnold,* (Captured Ship: *General Arnold*), Records of the British New York Vice-Admiralty Court, HCA 32/338/14, TNA. Both had most recently been in Greenwich.

Eclipse of the Sun we heard an incessant firing of Cannon and small Arms . . . the sky was so dark—the Air so thick that we were not able with our best Glasses to discover the Cause."[15]

It seems at least one of the enemy boats was sunk. The British and Loyalists briefly fell back. However, even as the sky lightened, "they rallied and came up the second time, and rowed right alongside of the [stolen] sloop," Painter wrote.[16] Enemy muskets were blazing at point-blank range.

At this the men in the Connecticut whaleboats panicked. Four of the five "cut their tow lines and ran of[f] and left us," Painter recalled bitterly in his pension application.[17]

The panic spread. On the *General Arnold*, twenty-four-year-old Capt. Paul Cartwright went over the rail to escape, as did some of his crew. On the *Mehitable*, Capt. Daniel Jackson battled on, but it seems three of his men may have abandoned the fight.[18]

Why didn't the last whaleboat flee? Conscience, exhaustion, or were there grievously wounded men aboard? The result was the same. The wood sloop was now helpless to move. Without wind, their crews depleted, the privateer sloop and schooner weren't in much better shape. Soon they were surrounded, and the British boats "attacked with the greatest fury." Shortly after 11 AM, the wood sloop, the two privateers, and the whaleboat all surrendered.[19]

By early afternoon, the enemy had shepherded all prisoners and prizes back to Huntington Bay. The weary Americans were taken aboard the ship *Fowey*, where they were threatened with hanging at the yardarm. "Thus ended our Whale Boat Cruise," wrote Painter, "and

15. At 10 AM: Eclipse predictions by Fred Espenak, EclipseWise.com. "Late Eclipse": Andrew Eliot, Jr. to Andrew Eliot, Sr., June 26, 1778, in Bernadine Fawcett, *Missing Links to the Culper Spy Ring?* (Conshohocken, PA: Infinity Publishing, 2005), 203.
16. The moon's disk moved off that of the sun completely at 11:20 AM. Eclipse predictions by Fred Espenak, EclipseWise.com. Andrew Eliot mentioned "boats" sunk but as logs for *Diligent* and *Raven* clearly state five stole the sloop, four cut their tow lines, and one was captured, any boat sunk must have been the enemy's; Fawcett, *Missing Links*, 203. They rallied: Thomas Painter, *Autobiography*, ibid.
17. Ran off: Painter (Pension Files).
18. Capt. Paul Cartwright: in Captured Ship: *General Arnold*; the sloop's papers indicate a crew of twenty-five; there were only eight (seven men and a boy) when she was taken. In Captured Ship: *Mehitable*, Daniel Jackson testified that there had been thirteen hands, officers included, but this was changed to "ten" "when she was taken." How many had been aboard either when the action started is unknown, as is the number killed.
19. With greatest fury: Andrew Eliot in Fawcett, *Missing Links*, 203; 11 AM: log of *Diligent*, ADM 51/4163.

a more foolish and fool hardy transaction is not to be found upon record[.]"[20]

In fact, the escapade was so completely hare-brained that both sides tried to ascribe a logical motive. In New York, the *Royal Gazette* declared that the whaleboats were attempting an attack on the woodcutters at Lloyd's Neck when they were cut off by boats manned by a detachment from DeLancey's Brigade—which also had seized two armed rebel brigs covering the assault. The competing paper stated that in their effort to attack the woodcutters at Lloyd's Neck, the whaleboats had been convoyed by the *Wild Cat* galley and a tender recently captured from the *Raven* sloop-of-war. Meanwhile, in Connecticut, Andrew Eliot assumed the whaleboats had been returning from a trip plundering civilians on Long Island, referring in disgust to "their shameful Voyage."[21]

Just what had been the cost of this impulsive lark to steal a low-value wood sloop? The sleepy morning had exploded into a barrage of cannon fire and musketry, "a smart engagement of several hours." In his log, Capt. John Henry of the *Fowey* recorded that twenty-five Americans were captured and twenty-three killed. This tallies closely with Eliot's initial information that forty-four Americans were killed, wounded, or missing. A week after the fighting the *Connecticut Journal* reported, "We lost 24 Men, 5 or 6 of whom are supposed to be killed or wounded." It seems impossible to discover exactly how many American casualties there were. (On the British side, "we had not One man hurt," Captain Henry noted with satisfaction.) How many of the prisoners taken up onto the *Fowey* were wounded? Was Captain Henry given a miscount, or did two prisoners die of wounds overnight? What is clear is that the next morning, twenty-three American prisoners, guarded by seven marines, were transferred from the *Fowey* to the sloop-of-war *Falcon*.[22]

20. Threatened: Painter (Pension Files) and Painter, *Autobiography*, 21.
21. Attack on the woodcutters: *Royal Gazette*, June 27, 1778; competing paper: *New-York Gazette and Weekly Mercury*, June 29, 1778; shameful Voyage: Andrew Eliot in Fawcett, *Missing Links*, 203.
22. Smart engagement: *Connecticut Journal*, July 1, 1778, Capt. John Henry: *Fowey* log, ADM 51/375; This tallies: Andrew Eliot in Fawcett, *Missing Links*, 203; We lost: *Connecticut Journal*, July 1, 1778; not one man: *Fowey* log; twenty-three prisoners: Muster-Table of His Majesty's Ship *Falcon*, ADM 36/B016, TNA, courtesy of Todd W. Braisted; marines: *Falcon* log, ADM 51/336, TNA; *New York Gazette and Weekly Mercury*, June 29, 1778, said, "Thirty Men were made Prisoners, and two killed, without any Loss on our Side." Did these two die on the *Fowey*?

Most of this little band of prisoners did not know each other. Since Elderkin's New Haven whaleboat had been one of those to cut its towline and escape, neither he nor Thomas Painter recognized anyone in the group. It seems likely that Moses Mather of Darien had been among those in the staunch last whaleboat. There were Rhode Island men from the *General Arnold*, and Fairfield County men and Long Island refugees from the *Mehitable*. And sprinkled among them were three boys under the age of sixteen.[23]

All week the cloudy, breathless weather persisted, punctuated by heat lightning. The *Falcon* moved ponderously toward New York, its boats "towing and rowing the Ship up Sound" to Hart's Island, where the prisoners were put on a tender for the city.[24]

Five days after their capture, the group was delivered to the prison ship *Good Hope*, anchored in the mouth of the Hudson River off the western edge of Manhattan, not far from the Cortlandt Street ferry stairs. During their incarceration the prisoners would hear the ferry to New Jersey pass first on one side of the ship, and then the other.[25]

If any man put aboard a prison ship could be considered to have luck, they were lucky. The *Good Hope* was a new prison ship. Formerly a Danish merchantman, a cargo ship of 700 tons burden, the *Good Hope* had been captured by the British in the Chesapeake, brought to New York, condemned as a prize in a Court of Admiralty, and sold to a private owner. The rental agreement was less than two weeks old. She had not yet been hulked, and, more critically, when they arrived June 29, she was not yet crammed and festering with sick prisoners.[26]

23. Muster-Table of His Majesty's Ship *Falcon*, ADM 36/B016; Muster-Table of His Majesty's Ship *Ardent*, ADM 36/7824, TNA, courtesy of Todd W. Braisted. The twenty-three prisoners were listed on the *Falcon* and then again, some with descriptions, on the *Ardent*: Wm. Havens, Master; Wm. Johnson, Mate, John Dunwell, Lieut.; Palmer Cleveland, Boasn.; Jno. Finch, Sr. Mate; John Sweet, Seaman; Geo. Havens, Boy; Daniel Jackson; Jna. Seymour, Gunr.; Isaac Raymond, Clk., Saml. Conclin, Seaman, Moses Mathers; Thos. Provoce; Richd. Provoce, Seaman; Peter Stonard; Jno. Thatcher, Boy; James Sawyer, Captn.; Benjamin Stonard or Leonard, Seaman; Jno. King; Abm. Cooper, Boy; Thomas Painter, Elisha Elderkin, Master. Painter and Jackson were listed on *Falcon* but not on *Ardent*. Painter escaped; Jackson testified July 1 at New York's Vice-Admiralty Court. In his pension he said he was imprisoned on the *Prince of Wales* prison ship; perhaps he was returned there instead of the *Good Hope*.

24. *Falcon* log, ADM 51/336, TNA.

25. Painter, *Autobiography*, 21.

26. New: Painter, *Autobiography*, 21; Danish of 700 tons: British New York Vice-Admiralty Court, Captured Ship: *Good Hope*, HCA 32/344/2/1-25, TNA; sold: *Royal Gazette*, May 13, 1778; rental: Rif Winfield, *British Warships in the Age of Sail, 1714–1792* (Barnsley, UK: Seaforth Publishing, 2007), 353, courtesy of Three Decks, https://www.threedecks.org.

Nevertheless, thought Thomas Painter, she soon would be. "considering that I had not had the Small Pox, and that most likely it would soon be on board," he recalled, "and considering also that the Chance of our Exchange was Extremely bad, on account of our being Whale boat men (the worst kind of Privateers men), It therefore seemed to me, as if some way of Escape *must be contrived.*" The plucky eighteen-year-old had already urged the group to make a break for it. As the *Falcon's* tender was threading the narrows between Brooklyn and the city, the marine guards had lounged carelessly, and Painter was sure they could be overpowered. However, most of his fellow prisoners refused to try.[27] Perhaps the result of their last rash decision weighed heavily.

In his memoir and pension testimony Painter never mentioned casualties. But he definitely didn't aim to be one of them.

Soon the quick-witted young man had a plan that he shared with his captain, Elisha Elderkin. Each evening the prisoners were locked in the hold while the guard rested in their quarters between decks and two sentinels patrolled above. After sunset prisoners were allowed in pairs up through a narrow grated hatchway onto the deck for air. Painter had a junk bottle (a quart-sized bottle of thick dark glass). Perhaps if they both saved their small daily ration of rum they could collect enough to make the sentinels too drunk to notice them slip into the Hudson. They could swim to the jolly boat tied to the *Good Hope's* buoy, and once the tide carried them silently away from the anchored ships, they could row to safety. Elderkin immediately agreed.[28]

It took two or three weeks of scrimping to fill the quart bottle and to wait impatiently for a moonless night. At last the moment arrived. Everything proceeded according to plan. As the level of rum in the bottle diminished, the two sentinels became more and more "good Natured" and "happy," until they were paying no attention to duty—or to the grate securing the hatchway. More prisoners streamed up from below. Heels began thudding on the deck as desperate men scrambled up on the gunwales of the ship to jump into the Hudson or to climb

Winfield records the first rental agreement, June 16 to August 15, 1778. Not yet hulked: a year later, her sails and rigging, masts, spars, and yard were advertised for sale by Thomas Ludlow, Jr. *New-York Gazette and Weekly Mercury*, August 8, 1779. On April 24, 1780, Vice-Adm. Arbuthnot recommended discharging the *Good Hope*, ADM/106/1255/92, but on March 5, 1780, her prisoners, wrote Naval Commissary General David Sproat, "wilfully, maliciously and wickedly burnt the best prison ship in the world." *New-York Gazette and Weekly Mercury*, February 12, 1781.

27. Painter, *Autobiography*, 22.

28. Ibid., 23.

down the anchor cable. Painter became separated from Elderkin in the noisy confusion, but he, too, leapt from the cable into the water. He estimated that seven men were swimming for their lives in the darkness when the guards burst on deck and sounded the alarm.[29]

Fleeing prisoners were seized on the gunwales and while clinging to the anchor cable. The nearby ships helped scoop swimmers from the dark water. In the end, only Painter made his escape.[30] All the rest were quickly back aboard the *Good Hope*—where they sweltered.

The heat on a prison ship in a humid New York summer was torture. Robert Sheffield of Stonington had spent six days on one in early June. "The steam of the hold was enough to scald the skin and take away the breath, the stench enough to poison the air all around." That spring four prison ships at New York were jammed with skeletal men and disease was rampant. "The heat was so intense that (the hot sun shining all day on deck)," he reported, the prisoners were "all naked," many delirious, "all panting for breath." When Rear Adm. James Gambier arrived to take command at the end of May, men aboard the *Judith* prison ship sent him a petition on June 12 enumerating their distresses in horrific detail. The admiral promptly responded that he had "ordered a large commodious ship to be got ready immediately for the reception of the masters, mates, and gentlemen passengers—and another ship will be got ready in a few days, to thin the numbers on board of each prison ship, and to separate the well men from the sick." Three days later the rental papers were signed for the *Good Hope*.[31]

But if those in the hold of the *Good Hope* had (at least for a time) thinner numbers and (for a time) less exposure to disease, little could be done about the heat. It had been near 100° F at the end of June. After a July fortnight on the ship, Painter had been almost naked and

29. Account from Painter (Pension Files) and Painter, *Autobiography*, 23. In his pension application, he indicated a wider plot: "I however soon had Serious thoughts of making my Escape with a number of Others which I affected within two or three Weeks by means of a bottle of Rum . . . I cannot recollect the names of any who made this attempt Except Capt. Elderkin my boat Commander."

30. Painter, *Autobiography*, 24. Elderkin swam to shore in New York, stayed hidden four days, but was captured and returned to the *Good Hope*.

31. Robert Sheffield, a Long Island refugee in Connecticut, was captured in the spring of 1778 and put on a prison ship. He made his escape, arriving on June 19 back in Stonington, where he reported to Thomas Shaw: *NDAR*, Vol. 13, 192. Shaw wrote from Sheffield's facts the florid account that was printed in *Connecticut Gazette*, July 10, 1778; also, *NDAR*, Vol. 13, 333. Similar facts were submitted by prisoners on the *Judith* to Rear Adm. Gambier; Gambier replied the next day, June 13: *New Jersey Gazette*, August 8, 1778. The *Good Hope* was hired June 16: Winfield, *British Warships in the Age of Sail, 1714–1792*, 353.

it's likely the rest of his companions were also. In August a thermometer read in the nineties in the open air.[32] Conditions below decks would have been brutal.

Once again the prisoners captured at Stamford had something approaching luck. They had endured approximately five suffocating weeks on the *Good Hope* when details of a long-discussed cartel were finally hammered out. In early August the New York papers published a notice: "[A] general Exchange of *American* Marine Prisoners is now agreed on . . . 200 are already sent to Elizabeth-Town [New Jersey] . . . all those remaining, as well on Parole as in the Prison Ships, will be sent there by Thursday next the 13th Instant."[33]

In fact, the prison ships could not empty quite that quickly. According to a New London report of September 25, "All the American prisoners are nearly sent out of New-York, but there are 615 French prisoners still there." Records show that most of the twenty-two remaining Stamford captives were discharged from the *Good Hope* to various cartel vessels during the last week of August. Capt. James Sawyer and the boy Abraham Cooper had to wait until September 20. Capt. Daniel Jackson was released in October. The health of any of them was not recorded, nor how or when any reached their homes. But all survived imprisonment.[34]

Among those whose later careers can be traced, Daniel Jackson, gunner Jonathan Seymour, and seaman Richard Provost of the *Mehitable* would serve together again the following year under Capt. David Hawley on the Connecticut armed sloop *Guilford*. Thomas Provost joined the artillery at Stamford. Elisha Elderkin of New Haven returned to the boat service, taking prizes on the Sound with his armed whaleboat *True Blue*. The ever-resourceful Thomas Painter served at sea and on land. In July 1779, less than a year after the discharge from the *Good Hope*, a party of Loyalists crossed the Sound in a whaleboat and broke into the Darien home of the Patriot minister Moses Mather, Sr., described in a royalist paper as "a mischievous Puritan Priest . . . [who] from his Pulpit bitterly inveighed against his sovereign," carrying him off to New York along with four of his sons. This time luck was not

32. Near 100° F temperatures at the battle of Monmouth, June 28, 1778; 92° on August 5, 1778 in Franklin Bowditch Dexter, ed., *The Literary Diary of Ezra Stiles*, Vol. 2 (New York: Charles Scribner's Sons, 1901), 292.

33. *New-York Gazette and Weekly Mercury*, August 10, 1778.

34. New London report: *Maryland Journal*, October 13, 1778; dates of release: Muster-Table of His Majesty's Ship *Ardent*, ADM 36/ 7824, TNA, courtesy of Todd W. Braisted. In October: Daniel Jackson (Pension Files).

with Moses Mather, Jr. Eight weeks later he died of disease in one of the city prisons at age eighteen.[35]

Although previously whaleboats had made the occasional appearance, the spring of 1778 had marked the true beginning of Long Island Sound's whaleboat war. That summer the number of boats on both sides skyrocketed. By August, George Washington put Lt. Caleb Brewster in command of a Continental whaleboat for intelligence work, just as in New York William Tryon commissioned Connecticut refugees to spy in whaleboats for Britain. By 1781 both the Patriot coast of Connecticut and the Loyalist northern shore of Long Island would be described as "infested" with whaleboats.[36] They were in constant use for privateering, raiding, plundering, kidnapping, and smuggling. For five years men would fight ferociously and often die in whaleboat battles on the Sound.

The madcap, reckless snatching of a wood sloop and the ensuing "smart engagement" at Stamford were merely notes in the prelude.

35. Serve together: *Rolls and Lists of Connecticut Men in the Revolution: 1775-1783* (Hartford: Connecticut Historical Society, 1901), 243; Thomas Provost, Connecticut, No. S17028 (Pension Files); Elisha Elderkin, Connecticut, No. W17758 (Pension Files), Thomas Painter (Pension Files), Mischievous Puritan: *Royal Gazette*, July 31, 1779. The gravestone of Moses, Jr. says he was nineteen but he died two months before that birthday. https://www.findagrave.com/memorial/18137372/moses-mather.

36. Infested: in Connecticut, Benjamin Tallmadge to Robert Howe, September 6, 1779, Litchfield (Connecticut) Historical Society, Tallmadge Collection, Series 1: Correspondence, Folder 8, Item 1; In NY: Royal Gazette (New York), September 9, 1782.

Major Peter Charles L'Efant: Artist and Engineer of the Revolution

DOUGLAS R. DORNEY, JR.

Major Peter L'Enfant is most well-known for his 1791 "wholly new" plan for the Federal City that would become Washington, DC. Fewer are aware of his previous experience during the Revolutionary War where he served as an aide-de-camp, engineer, and sometimes as an artist and light infantry officer. This military service, coupled with his fine arts education and post-war career as an architect were the near-perfect prerequisites for his most famous role as the author of the most important civic design project in American history.

Pierre Charles L'Enfant was born in Paris on August 2, 1754, and descended from a long line of artists. His father, also named Pierre, was a "Painter in Ordinary" to King Louis XV.[1] Before his son's birth, he was appointed an academician to the *Academie Royale de Peinture et de Sculpture.*[2] By 1771, the younger Pierre was at the academy receiving a fine arts education which also included the study of architecture, landscape architecture, science, and mathematics.[3] In contrast to many French officers who would serve in America as engineers or in the artillery service, there is no record that L'Enfant ever received any pre-war education or training as a soldier or engineer.

L'Enfant's *entrée* into the American war was a social connection with the playwright (and covert agent) Pierre-Augustin Caron de Beaumarchais. By mid-June 1776, Beaumarchais had received funding for the *Roderigue Hortalez & Cie*, a front organization whose sole purpose was

1. H. Paul Caemmerer, *The Life of Pierre Charles L'Enfant* (New York: DaCapo, 1970), 1-3.
2. Ibid, 5.
3. Kenneth R. Bowling, *Peter Charles L'Enfant: Vision, Honor, and Male Friendship in the Early American Republic* (Washington, DC: Printed for The Friends of the George Washington University Libraries, 2002), 4.

secretly procuring and delivering French and Spanish arms and war materiel to American rebels.[4] In August of that year, L'Enfant's name was on a list of several dozen men to serve in America with the promise of commission in the Continental Army.[5] In December 1776, he was on board the *Amphitrite,* the first Beaumarchais ship to sail for America.[6] Before departure, he was commissioned a brevet lieutenant in the French colonial troops, ostensibly to provide him a degree of protection from imprisonment should he be captured at sea.[7] On the ship, L'Enfant was under the temporary command of artillery expert Gen. Phillipe Charles Tronson du Coudray. It was likely at the latter's insistence that the *Amphitrite* returned to port after a few weeks due to a lack of provisions.[8] L'Enfant was in Nantes in February 1777, where Beaumarchais was worried about the young officer, ordering an assistant to provide him with funds for his sustenance.[9] The *Amphitrite* soon departed without L'Enfant, arriving in Portsmouth, New Hampshire in April, 1777.

By March 1777, Beaumarchais reported he had ten total vessels at sea.[10] L'Enfant's path and course to America is not clear, but he almost certainly departed on one of the remaining ships and was in Charlestown, South Carolina, with six other French officers in August 1777.[11] He could have possibly arrived there as early as May on a direct route, however, most of the Beaumarchais ships sailed for Santo Domingo or Martinique where they offloaded men and material and either returned to France or sailed to America.[12] L'Enfant's voyage roughly parallels Lafayette's journey to America, except that the latter man's ship appears to have departed later and arrived earlier in South Carolina. Lafayette's purchased vessel, *La Victoire,* sailed in March from

4. Brian N. Morton & Donald C. Spinelli, *Beaumarchais and the American Revolution* (Lanham, MD: Lexington, 2003), 47.
5. Caemmerer, *Life of Pierre Charles L'Enfant,* 25.
6. Tom Shachtman, *How the French Saved America: Soldiers, Sailors, Diplomats, Louis XVI, and the Success of a Revolution* (New York: St. Martin's, 2017), 55-56.
7. Caemmerer, *Life of Pierre Charles L'Enfant,* 9.
8. Silas Deane to Beaumarchais, "American Commissioners in France to the Committee of Secret Correspondence," *Naval Documents of the American Revolution,* William Bell Clark et al. ed. (Washington, DC: Government Printing Office, 1962 -), 8:531-533; 512.
9. Caemmerer, *Life of Pierre Charles L'Enfant,* 39-40.
10. *Naval Documents,* 8:650.
11. John Dorsius to Congress, August 19, 1777, Charles Town, SC, Papers of the Continental Congress, M247, Roll 94, Volume 7, Item 78, Page 113; Robert Howe to Congress, August 15, 1777, Charles Town, SC, PCC, M247, Roll 178, Item 160, Page 368.
12. *Naval Documents,* 8:956-7., 9:451; Elizabeth S. Kite, "Lafayette and His Companions on the "Victoire"," *Records of the American Catholic Historical Society of Philadelphia* Vol. 45 No. 1 (March 1934), 5.

Spain (bypassing the Caribbean) directly to South Carolina and arrived on June 13. Lafayette was already in Philadelphia (by late July 1777) by the time L'Enfant was first mentioned in Charlestown.

L'Enfant and the six other officers had arrived in York, Pennsylvania, by October 2. A few days later, they were being paid to "tender their services to the United States."[13] Preceding L'Enfant's arrival in Pennsylvania was Gen. Coudray, who wrote of L'Enfant as a "creature of B__ [Beaumarchais]" but also had "some talent for drawing figures . . . but nothing of use for an engineer."[14] Coudray drowned crossing the Schuylkill River in mid-September 1777.

Throughout the previous year Gen. George Washington, among others, noted the surfeit of French officers in America and the numerous difficulties in finding suitable positions for them. The predominant causes were their lack of knowledge of the English language, few open officer assignments, the unlikelihood of them raising American troops, their requests for high military ranks, and in some cases, the misrepresentation of their abilities and experience. By November 1777, Congress had granted funds to return forty of these men to Paris.[15] L'Enfant and most of his French companions who traveled from Charlestown with him were on the list.

By early 1778, L'Enfant was in Boston, seemingly awaiting passage back to France. Fatefully, he encountered the recently arrived Friedrich Wilhelm von Steuben who prevailed upon him to forgo his departure. Steuben soon requested a brevet commission of captain from Congress for L'Enfant to serve directly under him as his aide.[16] L'Enfant is not listed among Steuben's companions to Valley Forge, Pennsylvania, but is mentioned in Gen. Washington's general orders of May 5, 1778. "Captain Lanfant" was one of several officers directing the "Grand Parade" of troops and the *feu de joie* to celebrate the newly formed French alliance.[17] Soon after, Lafayette requested Washington sit for a portrait by L'Enfant. The work, drawn from life at Valley Forge, was held privately for a time, but its current whereabouts are unknown.[18]

13. Jerome Le Brun Bellocour to Congress, October 2, 1777, York Town, PA, PCC, M247, Roll 91, II, 275; Journals of the Continental Congress, October 4, 1777, 9:765.
14. Caemmerer, *Life of Pierre Charles L'Enfant,* 41.
15. Journals of the Continental Congress, November 7, 1777, 9:877.
16. Baron von Steuben to Henry Laurens, May 21, 1778, Valley Forge, PA, Henry Laurens Papers, South Caroliniana Library, University of South Carolina, Accessions 13612.
17. General Washington's General Orders, May 5, 1778, https://founders.archives.gov/documents/Washington/03-15-02-0039.
18. Scott W. Berg, *Grand Avenues: The Story of Pierre Charles L'Enfant, The Visionary Who Designed Washington, D.C.* (New York: Random House, 2000), 55.

Captain L'Enfant was likely at the Battle of Monmouth with General Steuben on Bald Hill reconnoitering the British retreat on the morning of June 28, 1778. Lt. Col. John Laurens noted that he, Steuben, and his "aides" were nearly captured by General Cornwallis's dragoons early in the engagement.[19] Another account notes only Steuben, Laurens, aide Benjamin Walker, and a "small dragoon escort" were present and pursued by Lt. Col. John Graves Simcoe and the Queen's (American) Rangers.[20] Steuben's other aide and secretary, Peter Stephen Du Ponceau, noted very little in his autobiography about the day, only that he was with the army during the battle.[21] While L'Enfant was not conspicuous in accounts of the battle, it would have been his first exposure to combat on a large scale. The experience, minimal as it was, may have influenced his decision in the coming months to relocate to the southern theater of the war.

In September 1778, an event came to light that could have proved disastrous to L'Enfant's future in the army. The previous November, while he was awaiting return to France, he reportedly wrote a letter to a French acquaintance critical of Congress and disparaging American officers and soldiers. This letter was captured and published in the New York newspaper *Royal Gazette* in June 1778. L'Enfant was quoted as writing that Congress "refused complying with any of their promises" and was guilty of a "breach of justice and good faith." In regard to his brothers-in-arms, they were "cowards of the first order … scared of the least noise, and ever ready for flight." In a subsequent letter to George Washington, L'Enfant attributed the account to a British attempt at disinformation, writing, "they have most villainously abused the liberty of the translator and have altered the words and phrases of my letter." L'Enfant closed by noting that his service and conduct in the previous year should stand to disprove the newspaper's claims and offered to write a disavowal letter to the *Gazette*.[22] Beyond this letter to Washington, there is no further word on the matter, including the rebuttal letter.

19. John Laurens, "*The Army correspondence of Colonel John Laurens in the years 1777-8*," William G. Simms ed. (New York, n.p., 1867), 202.

20. Mark E. Lender & Garry W. Stone, *Fatal Sunday: George Washington, the Monmouth Campaign, and the Politics of Battle* (Norman, OK: University of Oklahoma, 2017), 241.

21. James L. Whitehead, "Notes and Documents: The Autobiography of Peter Stephen Du Ponceau," *The Pennsylvania Magazine of History and Biography*, Vol. 63, No. 2 (April 1939), 212.

22. Pierre-Charles L'Enfant to George Washington, September 4, 1778, https://founders.archives.gov/documents/Washington/03-16-02-0550.

In the fall and winter of 1778-9, General Steuben with a select team of one American and three French officers settled in Philadelphia to write a manual of arms for the Continental Army. This volume, colloquially known as the "Blue Book," was formally entitled *Regulations for the Order and Discipline of the Troops of the United States.* L'Enfant's role in the volume, as the only man with artistic training, was to draft the eight "plates" or illustrations detailing camp and troop formations. The "Blue Book" was completed by April 1779 with General Washington's and Congressional approval. Congress awarded L'Enfant $500 for his efforts and officially promoted him to captain of engineers retrograded back to February 1778.[23] During this period, he began to sometimes use the anglicized first name of Peter in his correspondence. He was not, however, consistent in this usage as he most often initialized his name as P.C. L'Enfant.

Almost immediately after completion of the "Blue Book," L'Enfant "took leave" of Steuben to find distinction in what he termed the new "seat of war."[24] After a twenty-nine-day journey, L'Enfant arrived outside Charlestown, South Carolina in mid-May 1779. His first letter to Steuben implies he entered the city without opposition during the brief siege by British troops commanded by Gen. Augustine Prevost. Prominent in this letter is the description of the recently arrived Gen. Casimir Pulaski's first action in the theater, losing seventy-five men and four officers.[25] The account is consistent with the action known as the Old Race Track skirmish.[26] It was to be the first of many military defeats L'Enfant would experience in the coming year while with the American army

In Charlestown, L'Enfant joined his friend Lt. Col. John Laurens who also recently arrived but had already been wounded in battle at Coosawhatchie on May 3, 1779.[27] Before Laurens left Philadelphia, he had received approval from Congress to raise a regiment of enslaved

23. George Washington Papers, Series 4, General Correspondence: Continental Congress, April 3, 1779, Resolution Appointing of Pierre Charles L'Enfant to Corps of Engineers, Varick Transcripts, 1775-1785, Library of Congress.

24. L'Enfant to Washington, February 18, 1782," https://founders.archives.gov/documents/Washington/99-01-02-07839.

25. Edith von Zemensky & Robert J. Schulman (eds.), L'Enfant to Steuben, May 24, 1779, The Papers of General Friedrich Wilhelm von Steuben, 1777-1794, (Library of Virginia, microfilm), Roll I, 383-392.

26. David K. Wilson, *The Southern Strategy: Britain's Conquest of South Carolina and Georgia, 1775–1780* (Columbia, South Carolina: University of South Carolina Press, 2005), 108.

27. Gregory D. Massey, *John Laurens and the American Revolution* (Columbia, SC: University of South Carolina Press, 2000), 134.

soldiers in South Carolina.[28] L'Enfant was promised a light infantry command and promotion to major under Laurens.[29] When the South Carolina General Assembly overwhelmingly rejected the proposal, L'Enfant resumed his duties in the engineering corps.[30] Interestingly, he claimed that one reason Laurens' proposal was rejected was that the enslaved men were needed for a labor corps to construct the town's defenses. He sarcastically wrote to Steuben that no labor could be done without the enslaved men, including the felling of a single tree.[31]

There are many indications that L'Enfant was deeply unhappy with the state of affairs in the South. In letters to Steuben, he mused that if he did "a foolish thing in America it was to come to this province."[32] He described the difficulty traversing the many creeks and rivers, the eroded spirit of the local population, the vastly inflated currency, the lack of initiative of American officers, and uncoordinated military operations.[33] As one example, he described a June 17, 1779 engagement (possibly referring to the battle at Stono Ferry), where Gen. Benjamin Lincoln did not wait for Gen. William Moultrie to attack a British position.

L'Enfant's first direct combat experience came on October 8, 1779, the day before the failed French-American main assault on British-occupied Savannah, Georgia. According to the prevailing sources, L'Enfant was seriously wounded while leading five men to set fire to the abatis in front of the town's fortifications.[34] One account notes the men succeeded in setting fire to the abatis but the wood, being recently cut, was too moist to remain alight.[35] In the ditch before the entrenchments, he either suffered burns or, more likely, was wounded by musket fire in one or both legs. One observer reported him dead, judging by the severity of the wound. In contrast to other battles he described, L'Enfant was proud of the bravery exhibited on the occasion. In 1782, he recalled to General Washington that "it is without partiality, I say that never were greater proofs of true valor exhibited than at the assault at Savan-

28. Ibid, 131-132.
29. Berg, *Grand Avenues*, 58.
30. L'Enfant to Washington, February 18, 1782," https://founders.archives.gov/documents/Washington/99-01-02-07839.
31. L'Enfant to Steuben, Steuben Papers, August 8, 1779, Roll II, 4-6.
32. Berg, *Grand Avenues,* 58
33. L'Enfant to Steuben, May-December 1779, Steuben Papers, Roll I: 383-392, 438-441; II:4-6, 148-154.
34. Wilson, *The Southern Strategy*, 157.
35. Charles C. Jones, Jr. (ed.), *The Siege of Savannah, 1779 as Described by Two Contemporaneous Journals of French Officers* (Albany, NY: Joel Mussel, 1874), 27.

nah. Never was there a more favorable moment for the troops of this Continent."[36]

By December 1779, L'Enfant had largely healed from his wounds but remarked on the "impotency" of his leg. Given that and the state of finances, he requested funds so he could be removed from Charlestown.[37] L'Enfant was still there when 150 British ships arrived off the South Carolina-Georgia coast in mid-February 1780.[38] He recalled posting himself "wherever he could render the best service."[39] This certainly entailed assisting in the ongoing fortification efforts but it also briefly involved a skirmish north of the town. Mounted on horseback, he noted joining Lieutenant Colonel Laurens on March 30, attacking the vanguard of a column of German jaegers and British light infantry three miles north of the town.[40] It was very likely his last direct involvement in combat during the war.

During the night of April 25, Gen. Louis Duportail, L'Enfant's commanding officer and commandant of the corps of engineers, arrived in the town by traveling through the woods in the dead of night, bypassing British patrols.[41] Duportail immediately assessed that the defenses would not withstand a prolonged assault. In contrast to the siege of the previous year, the British now had sufficient troops in addition to heavy artillery. With the British army and navy virtually encircling the town, he unsuccessfully recommended the evacuation of the garrison.

After the surrender of Charlestown on May 12, L'Enfant received a partial parole and was confined to Christ Church Parish, north of Charlestown. He simply described the experience as "my hard captivity."[42] The circumstances of his confinement may not have been too different from General Duportail, who was held fifteen miles from Charlestown and despaired over the oppressive heat, sandy soil, insuf-

36. L'Enfant to Washington, February 18, 1782," https://founders.archives.gov/documents/Washington/99-01-02-07839.
37. L'Enfant to Benjamin Lincoln, December 4, 1779, Boston Public Library, https://archive.org/details/lettertogeneralb00lenf/mode/2up.
38. Carl Borick, *A Gallant Defense: The Siege of Charleston, 1780* (Charleston, SC: University of South Carolina, 2012), 31
39. L'Enfant to Washington, February 18, 1782," https://founders.archives.gov/documents/Washington/99-01-02-07839.
40. Borick, *A Gallant Defense*, 105.
41. Elizabeth S. Kite, *Brigadier-General Louis Lebègue Duportail, Commandant of Engineers in the Continental army, 1777-1783* (Baltimore, MD: Johns Hopkins University, 1933), 172
42. Berg, *Grand Avenues*, 764.

ficient diet, and being covered with insect bites.[43] By November 1780, Duportail, General Lincoln, Lieutenant Colonel Laurens, and several other higher-ranking officers were exchanged. Duportail's only regret in leaving the theater was that his fellow French engineers were staying behind (Colonels Cambray, Laumoy, and Captain L'Enfant).[44] L'Enfant did not leave the vicinity of Charlestown until his general parole in July 1781 which restricted him to a distance of twelve miles from any military garrison.[45] As he was not yet fully exchanged, he did not join Duportail in engineering of the siegeworks at Yorktown in October 1781.[46] It was not until January 1782 that L'Enfant was finally exchanged for Lt. de Heyden of the Anspach Yagers.[47]

The year after the surrender of Yorktown proved to be an exceptionally creative period for L'Enfant. By April 12, 1782, he was noted as "on furlough" from the corps of engineers at West Point.[48] The reason for the release from duty was the announcement of the birth of the dauphin, heir of King Louis XVI. L'Enfant was directed to Philadelphia where he was granted the honor to design and erect a temporary pavilion for the French-American celebration. Held on July 15, 1782, the event was attended by Washington, Lafayette, Rochambeau, French Ambassador La Luzerne, leaders from Congress, and hundreds of others. L'Enfant's design for the pavilion received particular attention, being hailed for its classical elegance and grace.[49] This small project was a breakthrough for his later career. Immediately after the war, it led to numerous architectural and design commissions, culminating in the designs of Federal Hall in New York City and, most famously, the plan for the nation's capital.

Sometime during 1782, L'Enfant painted two sweeping panoramas of the fortifications of West Point on the Hudson River and General Washington's headquarters at Verplanck's Point. The latter watercolor painting details what is believed to be "the only known wartime depiction of Washington's tent by an eyewitness."[50] The seven-and-a-

43. Kite, *Duportail*, 177.

44. Ibid., 180.

45. James Dudley Morgan, Thomas Attwood Digges, William Dudley Digges, and Pierre Charles L'Enfant, *James Dudley Morgan collection of Digges-L'Enfant-Morgan papers*, Library of Congress, microfilm, Reel I, 23-24.

46. Kite, *Duportail*, 228.

47. *Digges-L'Enfant-Morgan Papers*, Reel I, 26.

48. Kite, *Duportail*, 228.

49. Berg, *Grand Avenues*, 63.

50. Jennifer Schuessler, "Washington's Tent: A Detective Story," *The New York Times*, November 15, 2017, https://www.nytimes.com/2017/11/15/arts/design/washingtons-tent-a-detective-story.html?_r=0.

Detail of General Washington's tent, panorama of Verplanck's Point by Pierre L'Enfant, watercolor, c. 1782. (*Museum of the American Revolution, Gift of the Landenberger Family Foundation*)

half-foot-long painting was recently purchased by the Museum of American Revolution in Philadelphia and is the feature of a current online exhibit.[51] Along with the elaborate pavilion design, the paintings are the first examples of L'Enfant's emerging "*en grand*" artistic vision which would come to be one of his defining characteristics.

Before the July *fête*, disconcerted by a younger officer's promotion to major, L'Enfant wrote to General Washington seeking a promotion.[52] By May 1783, a Congressional committee which included Alexander Hamilton finally promoted L'Enfant to brevet major.[53] Now a field officer, L'Enfant was almost immediately requested by Washington to design a badge to be issued to the founding members of the Society of the Cincinnati. Boldly disregarding Washington's desire for an oval design, L'Enfant proposed the bald eagle emblem which became the iconic hallmark of the society.[54] He also created designs for the society's medal and membership certificate.[55] L'Enfant sailed for

51. "Among His Troops, Washington's War Tent in a Newly Discovered Watercolor," Museum of the American Revolution, https://www.amrevmuseum.org/virtualexhibits/among-his-troops.
52. L'Enfant to Washington, February 18, 1782," https://founders.archives.gov/documents/Washington/99-01-02-07839.
53. Journals of the Continental Congress, May 2, 1783, 24:324.
54. Elizabeth Kite, *Duportail,* 252; George Washington Papers, Series 4, General Correspondence: L'Enfant to Washington, June 10, 1783, Varick Transcripts, 1775-1785, Library of Congress.
55. Berg, *Grand Avenues,* 65.

Paris in November 1783 to have the badges manufactured and to personally induct French officers into the society.[56] He returned from France in 1784 and became one of the very few French Continental officers to remain in America after the war.

It is hard to envision that Pierre—or Peter—L'Enfant would have been selected to formulate the plan for the nation's capital had he not been a Continental Army officer. While he certainly would have been qualified for the position without his military service, it was the connections with men like Washington and Hamilton that proved to be critical to his appointment. However, these military bonds were not infinite and immutable. L'Enfant's intransigence and "artistic temperament" during the latter part of 1791 proved to be too much for Washington and the District commissioners. L'Enfant's dismissal or resignation (accounts vary) from the post certainly negatively affected his career trajectory. While he was later offered some payment for his work, opportunities for significant design commissions, and even a teaching position at West Point, he was too proud to accept them. Beyond the problems of his occupation was his wounded sense of honor. Perhaps the greatest slight one might have bestowed on the artist and designer was not even being credited with the capital design on engravings of the published plan.

Major Peter L'Enfant died on June 15, 1825, in Prince George's County, Maryland. A modest obituary in the *National Intelligencer* did credit him as being the "author" of the plan of Washington DC.[57] He may have remained an obscure figure if not for the *City Beautiful movement* of the late nineteenth century. With the movement's heightening of the public's appreciation of civic architecture came the belated recognition and admiration of the brilliance of L'Enfant's plan. By 1908, the esteem for L'Enfant rose to such a degree that plans were made to reinter his remains within a new public memorial. He was the first foreign-born man to receive the honor of lying in state at the U.S. Capitol. Soon after, his remains were finally reinterred on a prominent hill in Arlington National Cemetery overlooking the city he designed. On the one-hundredth anniversary of his death, a second memorial marker was placed at his original gravesite in Maryland.

In the years after the war, L'Enfant was often described by those close to him as the "old major." Others less acquainted with him may have been under the impression his first name was "Major" and not

56. Ibid, 71.
57. Ibid, 292.

Peter, judging by the way some addressed him. Certainly contributing to this was L'Enfant's attire; being observed wearing a blue military coat on his many visits to government claim offices. All aspects of his life considered, it is clear that Peter L'Enfant's sense of honor and identity were very closely tied to his major's commission. This military identity extended further into the twentieth century where his two epitaphs prominently note his military rank of major. The readers of these inscriptions may go so far as to contemplate what alternative form and shape the nation's capital city might have taken had it not been for Maj. Peter Charles L'Enfant of the Continental Army.

The Moses Ogden Myth: Misremembering the Battle of Connecticut Farms

TIM ABBOTT

General histories of the Battle of Connecticut Farms, New Jersey that was fought on June 7, 1780 tend to miss their mark with the very first shots. The intrusion of local myth impacts our understanding of the sequence of battle and distorts some of its key elements. In the process, the battalion that suffered nearly half the Continental casualties that day –Spencer's Additional Regiment– barely rates a mention except in association with a fondly recalled legend that does not hold up to scholarly scrutiny.

Between eleven o'clock and midnight on June 6-7, 1780, Hessian Generalleutnant Wilhelm Reichsfreiherr von Innhausen und Knyphausen started moving the first of five divisions across the narrow saltwater channel between Staten Island and Elizabethtown Point. It was a massive expedition totaling nearly 6,900 British, German and Loyalist units from the New York garrison including Hessian and Ansbach *jägers*, companies of light infantry and grenadiers, musketeers, dragoons, artillery, pioneers and baggage.[1] The only forces available to oppose them were scattered elements of Gen. William Maxwell's Jersey Brigade and local militia. Of such odds are heroes made and legends born.

ENSIGN OGDEN'S MYTHICAL PIQUET

The British commander leading the first division of General Kyphausen's expedition was Brig. Gen. Thomas Stirling (1731-1808). He would soon be severely wounded at a crossroads in the dark, giving

1. Samuel Steele Smith, *Winter at Morristown 1779-1780; The Darkest Hour* (Monmouth Beach, NJ: Philip Freneau Press, 1979), 62-63.

rise to the story that a young officer serving in Spencer's Regiment named Ens. Moses Ogden led the piquet that fired that volley. This, in turn, has led historians to mistakenly conclude that Spencer's entire regiment was on the front lines at the outset of the battle. No less an authority than the National Archives Records Administration, in a "Founders Online" footnote to a May 28, 1780 letter from Gen. George Washington to General Maxwell, attests that Maxwell "ultimately placed two regiments at 'The West farms' and two regiments (Col. Oliver Spencer's and Col. Elias Dayton's) at Elizabeth."[2] The citation for this statement comes from Ward's *General William Maxwell and the New Jersey Continentals*, and Ward relies on Fleming's *The Forgotten Victory*.[3] Where modern histories of Knyphausen's raid are concerned, all roads lead to Fleming, and Fleming is sometimes unreliable.

Although regarded today as a prolific and quite competent historian, Thomas Fleming was better known in 1973 as an historical novelist when he wrote *The Forgotten Victory*, and his treatment of the Battles of Connecticut Farms and Springfield is novelistic both in tone and approach. It is an engaging read but rife with questionably-sourced anecdotes, and one of these concerning Ensign Ogden has profoundly influenced subsequent historiography of the battle, perpetuating what the evidence shows to be two significant errors: young Ogden's alleged connection with the wounding of Brigadier General Stirling, and the placement of Spencer's Additional Regiment prior to the battle. The latter of these mistakes has been aided and abetted in recent years by an overreliance on a near contemporaneous account by the ambitious Lieut. Col. William S. Smith of Spencer's Regiment, who elevated his personal role that day while obscuring those of his superiors, including Colonel Spencer.

As told by Fleming, Col. Elias Dayton of the 3rd New Jersey Regiment (who was certainly near Elizabethtown that night) placed nineteen-year-old Ensign Ogden, a scion of a prominent branch of the local Ogden family, at an advanced post with a dozen men. As the first division of the invading force advanced in the darkness up the old King's Road, it was fired on by Ensign Ogden's piquet, badly wounding

2. George Washington to William Maxwell, May 28 1780, https://founders.archives.gov/documents/Washington/03-26-02-0148.

3. Harry M. Ward, *General William Maxwell and the New Jersey Continentals* (Westport, CT: Greenwood Press: 1997), 150; Thomas Fleming, *The Forgotten Victory; The Battle for New Jersey—1780* (New York: Readers Digest Press, E. P. Dutton & Co., 1979), 95-96, 99, 155, 310. Fleming also cites *Revolutionary History of Elizabeth*, Elizabeth Public Library as a reference for Moses Ogden's role.

Brigadier General Stirling in the thigh. This first blow supposedly delayed the advance for several hours, buying time for the Continentals under Colonel Dayton and the rest of the Jersey Brigade under Brigadier General Maxwell to converge on a stronger defensive position a few miles beyond Elizabethtown at Connecticut Farms.[4]

Whoever fired those shots must have been a hero, and local boy Moses Ogden fits the bill. His sister Ann married Lieut. Col. Francis Barber of the 3rd New Jersey, a prominent staff officer. His first cousins were Col. Matthias Ogden of the 1st New Jersey and Capt. Aaron Ogden, also of the 1st New Jersey but serving at this time as Maxwell's Aide de Camp.[5] Ens. Moses Ogden was the junior officer in the colonel's company of Spencer's regiment. Tragically, as New Jersey militiaman Aaron Hatfield would later recall in his nineteenth century pension declaration, Moses Ogden did not survive the day and "was killed at the engagement at Connecticut Farms with a musket ball shot through his forehead."[6]

Here, then, was a hero and a martyr whose short life had purpose. Ensign Ogden was the only Continental officer to die during the battle, and his headstone in the 1st Presbyterian Churchyard in Elizabeth, New Jersey, adorned with crossed swords and angel's wings, bears the inscription:

> IN MEMORY OF
> Moses Ogden
> who was killed at
> Connecticut Farms
> June ye 7th, AD 1780
> In the 20th Year of his Age
> This lovely Youth
> Adorn'd with Truth
> A brave Commander shone
> His soul emerging from its Dust
> With his Progenitors we trust
> Shall shine in Realms unknown[7]

4. Fleming, *The Forgotten Victory*, 98.
5. William Ogden Wheeler, *The Ogden Family in America; Elizabethtown Branch* (Philadelphia: J.B. Lippincott Company, 1907).
6. Aaron Hatfield Pension declaration (S.23245), NARA M246 *US Revolutionary War Pensions.*
7. William Ogden Wheeler and Edmund D. Halsey, *Inscriptions on Tombstones and Monuments in the Burying Grounds of The First Presbyterian Church and St. Johns Church at Elizabeth, New Jersey, 1664–1892* (New Haven, CT: Tuttle, Morehouse & Taylor, 1892), 81.

The problem with this story is that despite diligent investigation, no contemporaneous reference to Moses Ogden's piquet has come to light. His cousin Aaron Ogden made no mention of it in a letter to his father Robert Ogden on June 15, 1780 nor in his posthumously published *Autobiography*.[8] Nor did his brother-in-law Lt. Col. Francis Barber say anything about it in his many surviving personal letters. Colonel Dayton's papers and surviving letters contain no such account either.[9] Nor did Brigadier General Maxwell say anything in his after action report to Gov. William Livingston.[10] Nor does it appear in the correspondence of Col. Israel Shreve of the 2nd New Jersey Regiment, including a highly important but overlooked letter to his wife "Polly" on June 12, 1780.[11] Nor did Lieutenant Colonel Smith of Spencer's regiment mention it in his lengthy November 10, 1780 account to General Washington of certain irregularities in command at the Battles of Connecticut Farms and Springfield.[12] Nor do any published newspaper accounts of the day. Maybe there was once such a letter or article, but if so, none has been discovered.

None of the nineteenth century histories that cover Brigadier General Stirling's wounding attributes it to Ens. Moses Ogden's sentries either. Neither Barber and Howe's anecdote-rich *Historical Collections of the State of New Jersey*, nor Lossing's *Pictorial Field-Book of the Revolution*, nor Hatfield's *History of Elizabeth* nor Irving's *Life of Washington* mention the Moses Ogden story.[13] Ricord's 1897 *History of Union*

8. Wheeler, *The Ogden Family*, 135; *Autobiography of Col. Aaron Ogden of Elizabethtown* (Patterson, NJ: The Press Printing and Publishing Co., 1893).

9. Elias Dayton (1737-1807), Revolutionary War Officer Papers, MG 94, New Jersey Historical Society, Newark, NJ.

10. William Maxwell to William Livingston, June 14, 1780; New York Public Library, William Livingston papers 1749-1782, Correspondence, vol. 2, item 171 (three pages, folio).

11. Israel Shreve to Polly [Mary] Shreve, June 12, 1780; Israel Shreve Letters, University Archives and Special Collections, Prescott Memorial Library, Louisiana Tech University, Box 1, Folder 007. See also William Y. Thompson, *Israel Shreve, Revolutionary War Officer* (Ruston, LA: McGinty Trust Fund Publications, 1979).

12. William S. Smith to Washington, November 10 1780, https://founders.archives.gov/documents/Washington/03-29-02-0114.

13. John W. Barber and Henry Howe, *Historical Collections of the State of New Jersey; Containing a General Collection of the Most Interesting Facts, Traditions, Biographical Sketches, Anecdotes, Etc. Relating to its History and Antiquities, With Geographical Descriptions of Every Township in the State*, (New York: S. Tuttle, 1846); Benson J. Lossing, *Pictorial Field-Book of the Revolution Vol. I* (New York, NY: Harper and Brothers, 1851); Edwin S. Hatfield, *History of Elizabeth* (New York, Carlton & Lanahan, 1868); Washington Irving, *Life of George Washington* (New York: G.P. Putnam and Company, 1855-1859).

County, New Jersey contains the earliest known reference to "an outpost of twelve men" but says nothing about the officer in command of it.[14] Elizabeth's "Minuteman Statue", erected in 1905 at the site of the crossroads where the first shots were fired, bears a plaque that gives equal time to the wounding of Brigadier General Stirling and the counterattack led by Brig. Gen. Edward Hand that reached that point the following day. It makes no mention of Ens. Moses Ogden.

Fleming did not conjure his story out of whole cloth. Rather, he seems to have relied on a file entitled "Revolutionary History of Elizabeth" at the Elizabeth Public Library, which plucked it from an equally murky account provided by James Madison Drake in his 1908 *Historical Sketches of the Revolutionary and Civil Wars.*[15] A newspaper publisher and Medal of Honor recipient, Drake states in the introduction to his book; "The sketches of the Revolutionary War are founded upon legends I fondly heard when a youth from revolutionary sires and their descendants, as well as official reports and statements appearing in the newspapers of the period."

Drake claims that Colonel Dayton placed the piquet, which indeed he could have done as the senior Continental commander on the front lines. He also claims that Moses Ogden commanded it:

> 'Fire!' rang out the clarion-like voice of Ensign Moses Ogden, an Elizabethtown boy of nineteen years, and the next instant, from the brazen muzzles of thirteen muskets poured forth a sheet of flame and death-dealing missiles into the serried ranks of the invading host, the proud and haughty general—Sterling—being unhorsed by a ghastly wound in his right thigh.[16]

There is a good deal more from Drake along these lines: stirring stuff, to be sure. In another part of his narrative he claims that it was Ensign Ogden's own shot that hit Brigadier General Stirling, never mind that he would not have been armed at this stage of the war with a firelock but rather a platoon officer's spontoon, if such were available, and a sword.[17] Fleming, by way of variation, has Ensign Ogden telling his men to aim—in the dark—for the mounted officer and then growling his command, but the writer clearly draws on material from Drake's

14. Frederick W. Ricord, *History of Union County, New Jersey* (Newark, NJ: East Jersey History Company, 1897).
15. J. Madison Drake, *Historical Sketches of the Revolutionary and Civil Wars* (New York: The Webster Press, 1908).
16. Ibid., 45.
17. Ibid., 62.

Historical Sketches and Drake provides no sources whatsoever for his account.[18]

Having placed Ensign Ogden with the piquet, Fleming goes further than Drake and concludes that because he was from Colonel Spencer's Regiment, Spencer's had to be the other battalion posted with Colonel Dayton's 3rd New Jersey near Elizabethtown. He places Colonel Spencer himself with Dayton on Jelf's Hill outside of town as they conferred with Capt. Aaron Ogden, but offers no documentation other than the alleged presence of Ensign Ogden of Spencer's Regiment with the piquet.[19]

A more likely interpretation, common practice at the time, is that an advanced piquet at this post was a detachment comprising men from more than one company, and in the case of larger detachments might have included men from more than one regiment. We know from the pension declaration of one of Spencer's men—Pvt. Henry Williams, who was wounded later that day—that on the night of the invasion he was with a piquet at Bound Brook in Camp Town, west of Newark.[20] Moses Ogden could have led such a detachment between Elizabethtown and DeHart's Point, but it does not follow that Spencer's Regiment was nearby.

Since no mention of Ensign Ogden's heroics has yet come to light prior to Drake in 1908, the identity of the other Continental regiment reported to be near Elizabethtown is not necessarily Spencer's. In fact, other participant accounts clearly show that the main part Spencer's regiment was not at Elizabethtown, but rather posted at West Farm (Camp Town) with General Maxwell.[21] These accounts have not been carefully considered before now, obscured by the repetition of the Moses Ogden legend by Fleming, and Ward, and the National Archives, and as recently as 2020 in Edward Lengel's *The Battles of Connecticut Farms and Springfield 1780*.[22]

18. Fleming, *The Forgotten Victory*, 96.
19. Ibid., 100.
20. Henry Williams Pension declaration (W.18353) NARA M246 *US Revolutionary War Pensions*.
21. Henry Williams (W.18353) NARA M246 *US Revolutionary War Pensions*; Henry Johnson to Mr. and Mrs. Lambert Johnson, June 13, 1780, Henry Johnson Letters, 1778-1780, Collection 429, Henry Johnson letters, 1778-1780, Library and Archives, Monmouth County Historical Association, Freehold, N.J.; Smith to Washington, November 10 1780; Israel Shreve to Polly [Mary] Shreve, June 12, 1780.
22. Edward Lengel, *The Battles of Connecticut Farms and Springfield 1780* (Yardley, PA: Westholme, 2020), 15, 24.

The death of the young Moses Ogden later that day is true enough and his loss must have been keenly felt for his family to have erected the sort of memorial stone that adorns his grave. However, as with the "shot heard round the world," there is no credible evidence for whomever may have fired the musket that wounded General Stirling, nor how many men fired, nor who may have been in command of them. Nineteenth and twentieth century estimates range from a single sniper to as many as sixty.

It now seems Drake, born in 1837 when the veterans of the Revolution were old men, repeated folklore that was carried forward by subsequent chroniclers as fact. One cannot prove a negative, but when there is no better positive evidence than Drake's, it casts the whole matter into real doubt. It is a good story, but it is not good history and there is no credible evidence for it. It should no longer be considered the preferred narrative.

A MISREMEMBERED AMERICAN DEPLOYMENT AND SEQUENCE OF BATTLE

Where were the various elements of the Jersey Brigade deployed at the outset of Knyphausen's raid and during the Battle of Connecticut Farms? There are other factors to consider aside from the Ensign Ogden legend, and these relate to who was in command of each of the regiments on that day (and their subsequent reputations). Based on contemporaneous sources, here is their disposition:

Col. Elias Dayton was at or near Elizabethtown, where he and the bulk of his regiment, the 3rd New Jersey, had been stationed for several weeks and from whence he had maintained an ongoing correspondence with Washington through the end of May.[23] Aside from piquet posts scattered between Newark and Rahway, the rest of the Jersey Brigade was based in the vicinity of West Farm, about six miles northwest of Elizabethtown. Brigadier General Maxwell provided details in a critical after action report to Governor Livingston.[24] Capt. Aaron Ogden also wrote an important letter to his father Robert Ogden, and covered this period in his *Autobiography*.[25]

We also have the letter written from Basking Ridge Hospital by wounded private Henry Johnson to his parents. Private Johnson was

23. Elias Dayton to Washington, May 15, 19, 28 and 30 1780 and Washington to Dayton, May 17, 20, 29 and 31, 1780, *The Papers of George Washington*, Revolutionary War Series, vol. 26, *13 May–4 July 1780*, ed. Benjamin L. Huggins and Adrina Garbooshian-Huggins (Charlottesville: University of Virginia Press, 2018), 261.

24. Maxwell to Livingston, June 14, 1780.

25. Aaron Ogden to Robert Ogden, June 15, 1780, in Wheeler, *The Ogden Family*, 134-135; *Autobiography of Col. Aaron Ogden*, 12-14.

in Major Burrowes' company in Spencer's regiment. Johnson states, "We lay at Newark Mountain / A Bout twelve oclock at Night we was Alarmed and Marched to the farms [Connecticut Farms] and about Sun Rise We Etacted them [with] the Jersey Berguade."[26]

Johnson's letter places at least some of Spencer's men "at Newark Mountain," which corresponds to Maxwell's headquarters at West Farm. Aaron Ogden's *Autobiography* states that he "rode as fast as his horse could carry him [from General Maxwell], to the other two regiments of the Brigade whom he found paraded on the hill near the rear of Elizabeth Town river, and there received information from General [then Colonel] Dayton."[27] What was the other regiment that Captain Ogden found when he arrived at Jelf's Hill and conferred with Colonel Dayton?

There are no known letters from either Col. Matthias Ogden of the 1st New Jersey or Col. Oliver Spencer from this period. It is certain that Colonel Ogden was sick in Chatham and not on the field in command of his regiment.[28] Spencer's Lieut. Col. William S. Smith wrote a lengthy, highly significant letter to George Washington several months later that places himself at the heart of the action and casts Colonel Shreve of the 2nd New Jersey in a very dubious light.[29] Lieutenant Colonel Smith was an ambitious intriguer—not a rare trait among the officers of the Jersey Brigade—and Colonel Shreve was, by all accounts, a decent man but a lackluster commander. William S. Smith's star was rising and Israel Shreve's would soon diminish. Both the Shreve and Smith letters need to be considered together in order to track the movements of the 2nd New Jersey as well as both Spencer's and the 1st New Jersey regiments.

Subsequent historians, mislead by Fleming, erroneously conclude that Spencer's Regiment was at Elizabethtown with Colonel Dayton and the 3rd New Jersey, making Colonel Shreve's 2nd Regiment one of two (and not three) with Maxwell at West Farm during the first phase of the Battle. Shreve's own letter to his wife dated June 12, 1780 shows he marched immediately from his camp to Elizabethtown, was there with Dayton on Jelf's Hill as General Knyphausen entered the Town, and remained involved in the delaying action leading up to the

26. Henry Johnson to Mr. and Mrs. Lambert Johnson, 13 June 1780.

27. *Autobiography of Col. Aaron Ogden*, 13.

28. Maxwell to Washington, May 28, 1780, says "Coll Ogden is sick at Chatham." See also Aaron Ogden to Robert Ogden, June 15, 1780: "Colo. Ogden has been ill, but is now fast recovering."

29. Smith to Washington, November 10 1780.

stand at Connecticut Farms. Despite its known existence and availability in print since 1979, this document has not been given the consideration it deserves in recent histories.[30]

Shreve wrote to his wife Mary Shreve, whom he called "Polly,"

> on tuesday night the 7th [actually the 6th] of June between 11 & 12 oClock the Enemy Landed at Elizabethtown point, Our Piquets fired upon them Which Alarmed Camp. Immediately a Light Horseman Arived from Colo. Dayton who Commanded that they were Landed in force, We Immediately Caled in all Guards about Camp, and Marched towards Elizabethtown and fell in about 2 miles above the town upon the Connecticut farm Road.[31]

It is unlikely the 2nd New Jersey could have managed to join Colonel Dayton at this time and performed the delaying action Shreve described if they had marched all way to the outskirts of Elizabethtown from West Farm. Either the camp of the 2nd New Jersey must have been somewhat closer to Elizabethtown or Colonel Shreve got them in motion in record time. In any event, his must have been the other regiment that Captain Ogden found when he met with Colonel Dayton near the river after riding to the sound of the guns. Lieutenant Colonel Smith's November 10, 1780 letter confirms it:

> On the 7th of June after the Enemy had disposed Colo. Dayton & my self of the pass at Connecticut farms and oblig'd us to retire in the vicinity of Springfield, I met General Maxwell a little in front of the town advancing with the brigade; I then rejoine my command which was with the brigade and consisted of the first and fourth [Spencer's] regiments.[32]

Lieutenant Colonel Smith placed himself at Connecticut Farms but no closer to Elizabethtown. Most of Spencer's regiment was with Maxwell at his West Farm headquarters, along with the 1st New Jersey. Some elements of each regiment did engage at Connecticut Farms, based on what Brigadier General Maxwell, Colonel Shreve and Captain Ogden wrote, but only Colonel Dayton's 3rd New Jersey and Colonel Shreve's 2nd New Jersey were closest to the enemy at Elizabethtown during the open phases of Knyphausen's Raid.

This is not how the story has been told before. Colonel Spencer's Regiment, and not Colonel Shreve, has been falsely positioned with

30. Thompson, *Israel Shreve*, 67-69.
31. Israel Shreve to Polly [Mary] Shreve June 12, 1780.
32. Smith to Washington, November 10 1780.

Colonel Dayton based on the Moses Ogden myth. Before there was even the modern history profession, more prominent names and episodes from that day captured local imaginations and informed subsequent chroniclers. Elias Dayton was from Elizabethtown and lauded as a local hero. Israel Shreve was a West Jersey Quaker and did not enjoy the same reputation. Spencer's Regiment, as was common for its entire term of service, was a cipher as an "Additional" Regiment, yet it took half the casualties suffered by the Continental forces on that day.

When Fleming wrote *The Forgotten Victory*, he did not have access to the trove of digital data available to researchers today and he did the best he could with what he had. One would have had to dig deep into General Washington's correspondence back then to unearth Lieutenant Colonel Smith's letter, and the extensive collections of Colonel Shreve's letters at Louisiana Tech and the University of Houston were not then widely known. His enthusiasm for a great, untold story sometimes led Fleming into the realm of local legend, and it makes his engaging history of the Battle of Connecticut Farms somewhat less than authoritative, even though until Lengel's 2020 treatment of the battle it remained the only book-length study.

Lengel introduces the Lieutenant Colonel Smith letter into historiography of the battle, although historian John Rees had published a transcription of it long before it became available through "Founders Online."[33] The Smith account can be a valuable source of information for scholars but it needs careful handling. His letter must be considered in light of Lieutenant Colonel Smith's broader purpose in writing it: namely, to show his fitness for continued command at the expense of others. Although it provides exceptional details of what took place, particularly during the later and most critical phase of the battle at the first bridge over the Rahway River before Springfield where the majority of the Jersey Brigade casualties were taken, in matters of his own actions William S. Smith has proven to be a less than reliable informant.

Lieutenant Colonel Smith's November 10, 1780 letter to General Washington omits any mention of the role played at Connecticut Farms by his own colonel when Smith described his "command," even though orderly book evidence places Colonel Spencer with the Jersey Brigade on June 3, 1780, just days before the battle.[34] Smith represented

33. John U. Rees, "Eyewitness to Battle: New Jersey Brigade at Connecticut Farms and Springfield, June 1780," *The Brigade Dispatch*, vol. XXIX, no. 4 (Winter 1999), 20-22.
34. Orderly Book of Colonel Oliver Spencer's (Continental) Regiment April 9 - June 6, 1780, New York Historical Society—Reel 11, No. 110.

Brigadier General Maxwell, who would be driven to resign in July 1780 by his senior officers, as having left control of the battlefield to Lieutenant Colonel Smith at a critical moment. Colonel Shreve was a soft target both for Lieutenant Colonel Smith and for fellow intriguer Col. Matthias Ogden, as by late 1780 either Ogden or Shreve would have to yield to the other in the new arrangement of the Jersey Line.

Clearly, Lieutenant Colonel Smith was looking to his own advantage, and like Brigadier General Maxwell and Captain Ogden he wrote to a powerful patron or with an eye toward posterity with his reputation in mind. Only Colonel Shreve shared his thoughts in private letters to his wife without that filter, and neither Fleming nor Lengel make use of his accounts. Surviving muster rolls and pension declarations speak for themselves, and they show that Spencer's Additional Regiment must have been heavily engaged on June 7, 1780.

Only now that we understand that the wounding of Brigadier General Stirling and the death of Ens. Moses Ogden have been conflated into one event, and recognize the problematic nature of the Lieutenant Colonel Smith narrative, do we know where to place Spencer's Regiment at Connecticut Farms. Its true part in that battle is worthy of remembrance, as is the death of Ensign Ogden, one of eighteen casualties suffered in the Regiment that day. As one of Spencer's veterans would attest late in life, the men of this understrength and largely forgotten Additional Regiment "lost all, except their Country, their swords, and their honour," helping achieve American liberty "in barter for our blood."[35]

35. John Bell Pension declaration (S.12189) NARA M246 *US Revolutionary War Pensions.*

Caleb Brewster's Spy Boat Boys

PHILIP D. WEAVER

In researching one of the many projects I have in train, I ran across the Federal Pension Application file of Caleb Brewster. With all the public interest of late in him, Abraham Woodhull, Robert Townsend, and the Culper Spy Ring, I decided to take a more detailed look.

Brewster was first commissioned as the lowest-rated infantry officer, an ensign, in the 4th New York Regiment on November 1, 1776. Three months later, on January 1, 1777, he advanced to the rank of 1st lieutenant in the 2nd Continental Artillery. He was promoted to captain-lieutenant on June 23, 1780, was wounded on Long Island Sound in December 1782, and officially ended his military career on June 16, 1783.[1] Brewster "was placed on the pension list of the United States by a special act of Congress on the 11th Augt 1790."[2]

Except for Brewster being an officer in the New York line, the information was really out of my wheelhouse, so I relayed it on to author and spycraft aficionado John Nagy, who I had recently met. I also told him

1. Entry for Caleb Brewster, Frances B. Heitman, *Historical Register of Officers of the Continental Army During the War of the Revolution, April, 1775, to December, 1783, Reprint of the New, Revised, and Enlarged Edition of 1914, With Addenda by Robert H. Kelby, 1932* (Baltimore MD: Genealogical Publishing Company, 1982), 119. A captain-lieutenant was essentially a lieutenant performing the duties of a captain. Elements of the 2nd Artillery were stationed all over the New York-Connecticut region since they were founded, so an unattached artillery officer would probably attract less attention than one from an infantry regiment stationed miles away. It is highly unlikely that, with all his "nocturnal activities," Brewster ever served with the artillery in the field.

2. Brewster to J.C. Calhoun, Secretary of War, March 24, 1820, S.28367, *Revolutionary War Pension and Bounty Land Warrant Application Files, 1800-1900*, Record Group 15, National Archives Building, Washington, DC (National Archives Microfilm Publication M804, Roll 0332) (*Pensions*).

of a reference in the file to one of Brewster's men, Joshua Davis. John was intrigued, but he sadly passed away shortly after our meeting.

To honor John and to satisfy my own curiosity, I dug into the subject. I learned that the whaleboat men who ferried Brewster back and forth across Long Island Sound and attacked British shipping were actually skilled current and former soldiers organized into rotating crews, with more men attached to those crews as marines.[3] These enlisted men, mostly natives of Long Island and Connecticut, were transferred from different regiments as they were the most qualified for this particular service.

Following are brief accounts of the men I have been able to identify. Most served in Brewster's boat, while others were in boats under Brewster's overall command. Nearly all of them had been severely wounded or were in "reduced circumstances" that forced them to apply for financial assistance from the federal government in the form of a pension. It is these applications that form the nucleolus of their brief stories.

THE SPY BOAT FIGHT

Before getting to the men, here is background information on the legendary December 7, 1782's "Spy Boat Fight." Perceived to be much larger than what it actually was, this horrific hand-to-hand fight affected the lives of many of the participants and is reflected in their stories below. Due to the wounds he himself received, Brewster lost command of both his boat and the "Spy Boat" fleet.

In early December 1782, Brewster heard that Capt. Joseph Hoyt was in the Sound with three boats. Leaving three of his boats on the south-side of the Long Island to cover any escape, he gave chase with three others, including his own. Brewster eventually caught up to Hoyt. A couple of weeks later, Brewster told the story of the subsequent action to Maj. Gen. Henry Knox in gory detail:

> We got close up with two of the Enemy, with two of my boats; (the other sailing [heavily];) they proved to be Capt. Hart & Lieut. Johnson; their other boat sailing faster or by being [far] ahead of them at the first of the Chase, escaped; being to windward, I bore down on the largest boat, and in passing Johnson received a full [fire] from him at the distance of about [eight Rods], which wounded me through the body, and one man in the Head, who is since dead, of the wound; I reserved my [fire] untill close alongside the boat. I designed the attack, (leaving

3. Marines are soldiers that serve on land and afloat. The marines who served on the "spy boats" were not part of the Continental Marines.

> Capt. Rider to contend with Johnson) with a view of having time only [its] charge again, and board him; but the briskness of the wind and the quick way of the boat prevented our loading before we Grappled. and having but three bayonets. we were obliged to make use of the butts of our Muskets, which decided the business in a short time; when we found but one man but what was either killed or wounded; five in boat were wounded (including the one who died a few days afterwards.) two of us with balls, the other with bayonets; the Enemy being much better fitted, had the advantage of us, Hart having three large wall pieces, and a compleat sett of Kings Muskets with long bayonets, I received Several blows from Hart with the Iron [Rammer] of a wall piece which fortunately did not prevent me doing my duty though it caused a pulsing of Blood; Johnson in the mean time surrendred to Capt. Rider without much resistance having had two killed by the [fire] of a Swivel Gun from Rider, Seven of the Enemy are buried two more lie at Norwalk badly wounded the rest am informd are prisoners at West point.[4]

Brewster recovered from his wounds enough to return to the "spy boats," but was ultimately unable to continue. He wrote to President George Washington of his condition in 1792:

> Early in the war, on the shore of Long Island from an exertion of bodily labor in carrying the boat I commanded into a place of safety & concealment, I received a dangerous & incurable rupture which has ever since been subject to the painful & inconvenient application of those modes of local support which are common in such cases—On the 7th of December 1782 while in the aforesaid service in a bloody engagement with two armed boats of the Enemy I received a wound by a ball thro. my breast—With this wound I languished & was confined two years & a half under distressing chirurgical operations & a most forlorn hope of cure. The nature of these wounds together with the impairing of my constitution by the long continuance of my confinement have rendered me incapable of any labour that requires a considerable exertion & have reduced me to the melancholy condition of an invalid for life.[5]

4. Brewster to Henry Knox, December 21, 1782, Gilder Lehrman Collection, GLC02437.01755. Transcript at https://www.gilderlehrman.org/collection/glc0243701755, accessed August 19, 2023. Some words in the transcript are in square-brackets. presumably to indicate they are the best guess of the transcriber. Captain Rider is likely Capt. Valentine Rider referenced by Elizabeth Lockwood later in this article.
5. Brewster to George Washington, March 15, 1792, *Founders Online,* National Archives, https://founders.archives.gov/documents/Washington/05-10-02-0062, Accessed August 19, 2023.

William Wheeler, a local teenager, recorded the happenings of the "Spy Boat Fight" in his journal:

> Captain Caleb Brewster . . . with 3 whale-boats about midway of the Sound against Fairfield, met 3 of the enemy's boats, when an engagement commenced. The boat that opposed Brewster had a small piece & was leeward; there was a fresh gale & Brewster reserving his fire till within 8 or 10 rods of Hoyt, poured in a broadside & then another & boarded; there was a large Irishman in the enemy's boat, who walked several times fore and aft, brandishing his broad sword till Hasselton, a mighty fellow from the State of Massachusetts, snatched it from him & cut his throat from ear to ear; he died immediately.
>
> Capt. Brewster being wounded was several times struck on the back with the steel rammer of a gun by Hoyt. On board of Hoyt's boat all but one were killed or wounded. In Brewster's boat 4 were wounded—one (Judson Sturges) mortally.
>
> Another of our boats had a swivel (gun) which killed 2 men at one shot in another of the enemy's boats & they immediately surrendered: the enemy's third boat escaped.[6]

THE "BOYS"

ABNER BECKWITH: An outlier from those below who remembered the size of the whaleboat crews being larger, Beckwith explains that he served under Capt. Oliver Cornstock from April–July 1782 and that

> There were seven men belonging to the boat. Captain Cornstock was regularly commissioned by [illeg.] Trumbull Governor of Connecticut. They were not employed the whole of the time in cruising the Sound but were held in constant readiness to go whenever they were ordered and whenever they returned to New London were required to make a regular report of their discoveries. The employment was peculiarly hazardous. Several of the men were wounded and Captain Cornstock very severely—He belonged with this boat more than three months—They captured a sloop during the time; and carried her to New London where she was condemned & sold.[7]

There could be several reasons why Beckwith remembered seven men on the crew. It may have simply been a smaller boat or that he did not count the marines, but what is clear is that serving on these boats was quite stressful and very dangerous.

6. William Wheeler, *The Journal of William Wheeler*, reprinted in Cornelia Penfield Lathrop, *Black Rock, Seaport of Old Fairfield, Connecticut, 1644-1870* (New Haven, CT: Tuttle, Morehouse & Taylor Co., 1930), 34-35.
7. Deposition of Abner Beckwith, August 9, 1832, *Pensions* (S.12158, Roll 197).

ROBERT BRUSH: A Long Island native who lived in Connecticut during the war, he later settled in Pine Plains, Dutchess County, New York. Initially a Connecticut soldier, Brush fought in the 1777 battle of Ridgefield and was near Gen. David Wooster when he fell. While he was living in Norwalk, Connecticut:

> he was in the habit of going with Lieutenant Caleb Brewster. . . to Long Island whenever Brewster called upon him—that he continued to go with him for the space of three or four years—that the number of these expeditions varied from one to three & four times a month—and in duration from two days to a week or more That the object of said Brewster was to get intelligence from the British and it was their usual custom to start in the night and land on the Island at some place where they would not be discovered and lay concealed whilst Brewster went to some agent as he supposed whom he had on the Island & after obtaining the information he returned & they then embarked us secretly as possible for the mainland . . . . one time they were obliged to concealed on the ground for two weeks—the consequence of a snow storm—at other times he has been [out] one night & back the next—at other times they lay on the Island two or three days or more according as the information was obtained by Brewster more or less expeditiously or the danger of detection by the British required.[8]

Brush mentioned other incidents that occurred while he was rowing for Brewster:

> at one time they had a skirmish with a boat crew of a Privateer on the Island after they had landed at another with a boats crew which they captured—At another time they were chased by a Privateer and escaped in consequence of being to the windward, the crew of their boat rowing further against the wind than the Privateer could beat—At another time they were chased by a Privateer when going into Stradford [Connecticut] harbor—the Privateer at that time being to the windward of them but they succeeded in getting over the bar before the Privateer could do them any damage although within reach of her guns—At another time he recollects that [they] were lying on the Island concealed a party of horse commanded by one Ismail Youngs a tory came in search of them and passed within fifty yards of their concealment but not discovering them.[9]

8. Deposition of Robert Brush, October 13, 1832, *Pensions* (S.23555, Roll 387).
9. Deposition of Robert Brush, November 9, 1835, ibid.

Brush then explained that:

> Their crew commonly consisted of ten or twelve—recollects but few of them who went with them—but he recollects that one James Phillips—one Kinner—Dickenson—Veal—Van Horne—Foy—Soper and one Captain Conklin [most] generally went with them.[10]

After the war, Brewster, like he did for so many of his men, reported that "Robert Brush was a good and brave soldier" and "frequently volunteered his services on different occasions under me during the war on difficult and dangerous services, whilst I was engaged in secret service in Long Island Sound by order of General Washington."[11]

JOSHUA DAVIS: In 1776, he first enlisted in Capt. Danial Griffing's company of the 2nd New York regiment before joining Capt. Samual Sackett's company of the new 4th New York regiment later that year. Davis explained that, after three years, he was merged into the 2nd New York regiment due to downsizing, and there he remained for the duration of the war. He was soon detached and "employed in what was called the whaleboat service," but was still on the Continental establishment.[12]

A review of the muster rolls of Capt. Samual Sackett's company confirms much of what Davis described. One roll, dated, January/February 1780 shows Davis, Cpl. David Dickerson, and Jonathan Kinner listed as being "on Command at Norwalk in the Whale Boats by order of his Excellency."[13]

Davis briefly described that at this point he was

> serving for a Special Service on board a certain whaleboat under Captain Caleb Brewster, who commanded a small fleet and had a commission to cruise Long Island Sound in the Continental Service & that I served on board said boat till the end of the war of the Revolution.[14]

Davis's widow, Abigail, reported in greater detail that

> her Husband had been taken from the Land Service into a Company under the command of Capt Caleb Brewster to go to & from Fairfield to Long Island for the purpose of watching and getting Information

10. Ibid.
11. Deposition of Caleb Brewster, January 15, 1827, *Pensions* (S.23555, Roll 387).
12. Deposition of Joshua Davis, June 14, 1820, *Pensions* (S.14049, Roll 1839).
13. A Muster Roll of Captain Saml Sackets [Company] in the 4th New York Regt in the Service of the United States, January & February 1780, Revolutionary War Rolls 1775-1783, National Archives Microfilm Publications, M246, War Department Collection of Revolutionary War Records, Records Group 93, Roll 71, Folder 67.
14. Deposition of Joshua Davis, July 28, 1832, *Pensions* (S.14049, Roll 1839).

> from the enemy which service was performed in a Whale Boat . . . as often as once a Week and continued in said Whaleboat service until the Peace. . . . She has heard her husband say was that he was selected to go in the whale boat with Captain Brewster because he was a Long Island man as also was Captain Brewster originally from Long Island and her husband being acquainted with the harbors there, caused him to be taken from the land service and put into this.[15]

James Penfield "lived with his father in said Fairfield during the Revolution at a Place called Penfield's tide Mills on Long Island Sound and said Brewster made it head quarters for his Boat at said Mills."[16] He further explained that

> Joshua Davis belonged to Capt. Caleb Brewster's whale boat the latter part of the war and was one of his Principle men and cruised from said Town of Fairfield to and from Long Island to watch the enemy and was called a Spy Boat.[17]

Despite taking part in serious actions, like the "Spyboat Fight," Davis seems to have come out of the war unscathed. He later did admit that all the physical abuse caught up to him in his later years. He stated "that in consequence of the severe service which I performed during the war I have a confirmed lameness in my left leg and am sometimes so lame in my back as to almost unable to rise from my chair."[18]

Benjamin Dickerson: Another of Brewster's own men to receive a bayonet wound in the "Spy Boat Fight," he was a former 4th New Yorker who was part of the "advanced guard" at the Battle of Monmouth Courthouse. Dickerson explained that he had "belonged to the Company commanded by Captain Samuel Sacket in the regiment commanded by Colonel Henry Livingston (that he was detached with others therefrom into the boat-service on Long Island Sound when wounded, under Captain Caleb Brewster)."[19]

Davis explained that "Dickerson, himself & three others were detached from the army by the commander in chief, served under the command of Caleb Brewster in the Boat Service." Over time, this service "had become more dangerous," but they still "served with said Brewster until on or about the 7th day of December 1782, when said Dickerson was severely wounded by a bayonet in his right breast."[20]

15. Deposition of Abigail Davis, October 1, 1836, *Pensions* (S.14049, Roll 1839).
16. Deposition of James Penfield, November 16, 1836 *Pensions* (S.14049, Roll 1839).
17. Ibid.
18. Deposition of Joshua Davis, June 14, 1820, *Pensions* (S.14049, Roll 1839).
19. Deposition of Benjamin Dickerson, October 6, 1827, *Pensions* (S.27691, Roll 0810).
20. Deposition of Joshua Davis, April 26, 1820, ibid.

Backing up Dickenson's memory, Brewster specifically named the five men reassigned from the Continental line when he explained that

> he was requested to take the command of a boat to be employed under the immediate command of Gen. Washington in cruising in Long Island Sound, between the shore of said Island & the Connecticut Shore, for the purpose of obtaining information. & consent to take the command of a boat, for the purpose aforesaid, on condition that he might choose his men, which condition was [illeg.] to, & the deponent send to Gen Washington the names of David Dickerson, corporal, Zachariah Newkirk, Jonathan Kinner, Benjamin Dickerson, Joshua Davis who then all belonged to the New York line on the continental establishment, & said men were immediately sent to the deponent by General Washington.[21]

Brewster then explained that in the "Spy Boat Fight," Dickerson was

> dangerously wounded in the breast by a bayonet, which entered the right breast & pointed out under the shoulder blade, in a battle which was fought between the boat under the deponent's command & a British Barge in Long Island Sound, in which battle 17 out of twenty five men engaged were either Killed or wounded, & said British Barge was captured; & that said Dickerson lingered for a long time in consequence of his wound, & did not in consequence of said wound again join the service, as the aforesaid battle, terminated the service of the deponent & his crew, in the boat aforesaid & he declares that said Dickerson was a brave & faithful soldier & on consequence of his would aforesaid was neither called upon nor able to perform further service.[22]

DAVID DICKERSON: As an early federal pension applicant and to meet the requirements of the law, he emphasized his term of service stating that he entered the army

> on or about the month of December in the year 1776 in New Haven in the State of Connecticut with the Company commanded by Captain Samuel Sacket of the 4th regiment of the New York line commanded by Colonel Henry B. Livingston but was afterwards or [illeg.] to the Second New York regiment. That he continued to serve in said corps or in the service of the United States until the 7th day of June in the year 1783 when he was discharged from service in Newburgh in the

21. Deposition of Caleb Brewster, April 25, 1821, ibid.
22. Ibid.

> State of New York—That he was in the Battles of Monmouth & the Taking of Burgoyne.[23]

Dickerson made no mention of his detached service in the whaleboats or his rank of corporal.

JONATHAN HAZLETON: Not all of the "Spy Boat" crews were from Connecticut or New York. Many had roots in other northeastern states. Hazleton was a native of New Hampshire, but after the war he lived in Rhode Island, Maine, and ultimately settled in Connecticut.[24]

Davis explained that Hazleton:

> had previously belonged to the Regiment under the command of Col. Seeley, in the New Hampshire line, on the continental establishment and do further testify that said Hazleton served under said Brewster in company with me for more than two years following the Spring of the year 1780 & was constantly employed in the Service of the United States & that he was ever considered a faithful soldier.[25]

Jonathan Kinner then confirmed that

> Hazelton served under said Brewster for the term of two years at least and I understood . . . that he had been detached from the continental army by order of Gen. Washington.[26]

Hazleton's transfer from the New Hampshire line to the whaleboats remains unclear. There are no known existing muster rolls from that line, but an account book that included members of Joseph Cilley's regiment does survive. It shows that he enlisted for three years in the second company on February 12, 1777 and was discharged on January 25, 1780.[27]

HEZEKIAH HYATT: A Norwalk, Connecticut resident for most of the war, he served in the local militia for various short-term duties and lo-

23. Deposition of David Dickerson, May 6, 1818, *Pensions* (S.44145, Roll 0810).
24. Deposition of Jonathan Hazleton, November 7, 1831, *Pensions* (W.23194, Roll 1239).
25. Deposition of Joshua Davis, August 7, 1818, ibid. Col. Seeley is probably Col. Joseph Cilley who commanded the 1st New Hampshire regiment from April 2, 1777 to January 1, 1781. Enry for the 1st New Hampshire Regiment of 1777, *Encyclopedia of Continental Army Units: Battalions, Regiments and Independent Corps*, Fred Anderson Berg (Harrisburg, PA: Stackpole Books, 1972), 79.
26. Deposition of Jonathan Kinner, August 7, 1818, ibid.
27. Entry for Jonathan Hazleton, US, New Hampshire, Revolutionary War Records, 1675-1835, Cilley and Reid Regiments (2nd capture), 1776-1779, Regiments, 109, https://fold3.com/image/713075618, accessed August 20, 2023.

cations. Hyatt mostly made gabions or guarded the coast on land or in local boats on the edge of the sound. During this time, he was frequently detached from his company and

> served under other Captains in the Boat Service. He served under Capt. John Rich, Daniel Jackson, Simeon Crossman, Ephraim Marion, Caleb Brewster, and Valentine Rider. Rich & Jackson belonged to Norwalk & the other Captains deponent thinks were from Long Island. These Boat Captains generally had about twelve men each under command & Rich & Jackson has special commission from Governor Trumbull to search the coast & guard the Sound.[28]

JONATHAN KINNER: Enlisted in Capt. Samuel Sackett's company of the 4th New York regiment in February 1777, he stayed until "the consolidation of the Regiments of the New York line." He earned "a badge of Merit for six years faithful service."[29]

Brewster explained that:

> Kinner who now resides in the Town of Weston, in the county aforesaid, was for several years under my command and that he was a brave and faithful soldier. . .& that he is now by reason of his reduced circumstances in life, in need of assistance from his Country for support.[30]

Kinner was a lifelong friend of Davis and explained that:

> I have been well acquainted with Joshua Davis . . . from his youth to the present time as we were brought up within a few rods of each other, that we enlisted in the service of the United States, in Feb. 1777, in the Company of Samuel Sackett, in the regiment of Col. Livingston, in the New York Line, & that said Davis served in said Regiment & with me under Capt. Caleb Brewster to the termination of the revolution.[31]

The muster rolls of Sackett's 4th New York company from August 1778 thru June 1780 indicate that many of these men including Davis, Benjamin Dickerson, Cpl. David Dickerson, Kinner, and a new name, Peter Denney, were "on Command at Norwalk in the Whale Boats by Order of his Excellency." That phraseology does vary from one roll to another. Some of them appear to have gone in and out of the boat service.

28. Deposition of Hezekiah Hyatt, February 19, 1836, *Pensions* (R.5461, Roll 1386).
29. Deposition of Jonathan Kinner, April 4, 1818, *Pensions* (S.37131, Roll 1493).
30. Deposition of Caleb Brewster, April 4, 1818, *ibid.*
31. Deposition of Jonathan Kinner for Joshua Davis, April 4, 1818, *Pensions* (W.17698, Roll 760).

JARED LOCKWOOD: His service in 1776 has not been documented, but for the next three years he was an orderly sergeant in Ebenezer Steven's company of the 2nd Continental Artillery. According to his widow, Elizabeth, "he fought in the Battles of Flatbush and Brooklyn, where the British Army advanced on New York in 1776. And at the Battle of White Plains in the same year. And that he fought at the Battle of Monmouth in June 1778."[32]

After his discharge, she and Lockwood were married, but

> subsequent to their Marriage, her said Husband was engaged almost without interruption till the close of the War and the Proclamation of Peace, in various services—in cruising in the government armed boats in Long Island Sound and the East River, reconnoitering within the enemies lines, and in communicating with our friends within the enemies posts. That during those services he was at different times engaged under the following officers of various periods, with Captain Caleb Brewster, Captain Valentine Rider, Captain Jabez Fitch, and Lieutenant Andrew Mead, Captain Ebenezer Jones, and Lieutenant Samuel Heacock or Kickock. That said services were attended with great hazzards and fatiques, Many engagements occurred, and many prizes were taken and prisoners made. That her Hus ban was principally under the command of Captains Fitch and Jones. But this Declarant is unable to say under what enrollment her Husband acted.[33]

Most widows of war veterans were not the best on details of their husbands' service. Her case is also light on specifics, but particularly good on names and places. She mentioned various captains, and suggested the overall size of the operation. She also noted that, in addition to the Long Island Sound, the "Spy Boats" also patrolled New York's East River.

JOSEPH LYON: Enlisting out of Danbury, Connecticut, he was in various short-term regiments for the bulk of the war. For most of his time, Lyon served as a teamster in and around the Hudson Highlands. During his last nine-month enlistment, he claimed to have served as one of the guards at the execution of Maj. John André at "Tappen Bay."

He further explained that he saw action both before and during the "Spy Boat Fight:"

32. Deposition of Elizabeth Lockwood, December 7, 1836, *Pensions* (W.16639, Roll 1577). Orderly sergeants handled the administrative duties for the company and its commander. They would later be called first sergeants, a rank that still exists today.
33. Ibid.

> That he afterwards enlisted in the month of April 1781 at Fairfield in the State of Connecticut for the term of one year in a company commanded by Capt. Caleb Brewster of the Spy Boats on Long Island Sound. That he served in this company until the expiration of this year when he again volunteered his services without leaving the said company and continued with it until sometime in June 1782 when he received a furlough to go to Danbury when he would afterwards receive further orders from his Captain but was finally discharged from the army in December 1782. That during this enlistment he was in various engagements with the enemy, was at the taking of Fort Slongo, he was wounded by a bayonet at the taking of Hoyt of the British Whale Boat, the scar of which he now retains in his arm through which he was pinned to the boat in which he was engaged.[34]

Emery D. Potter, who appears to have not served with him, added to Lyon's gruesome story when he related that Lyons

> was with Capt. Brewster of the "Spy Boat Service," on Long Island, when he was engaged in several sever fights, particularly at the taking of Fort Slongo: while in that action he was pinned to the boat which he had boarded, by the Bayonet of a British, the bayonet pierced his arm above the elbow, & while in that condition he discharged his musket with his other hand through the heart of his antagonist; I have often seen the sear on his arm.[35]

STURGES OGDEN: An active militiaman for most of the war, Ogden also served as part of the seacoast guard in Fairfield, Connecticut. In addition,

> he served in Embodied Corps maintained by public authority for the protection of the lives & property of the inhabitants against attacks of the British who were in posesion of Long Island, and that he always served as a private soldier on land & as an oarsman & marine in the boat under said Capt Brewster and that his services were constant and uninterrupted.[36]

34. Deposition of Joseph Lyon, October 16, 1832, *Pensions* (S.23306, Roll 1608). The Battle of Fort Slongo occurred on October 3, 1781. Benjamin Tallmadge, organizer of the Culper Spy Ring, was a commissioned officer in the 2nd Light Dragoons, and, after being ferried with his men to Long Island via whaleboats, commanded the attack on the fort. Sgt. Elijah Churchill, of the 2nd Light Dragoons, was awarded the Badge of Military Merit, the forerunner of the modern Purple Heart decoration, for his actions in this and other battles in the region.

35. Letter from Emery D. Potter supporting Joseph Lyon's pension claim, December 18, 1835, *Pensions* (S.23306, Roll 1608).

36. Deposition of Sturges Ogden, May 23, 1833, *Pensions* (S.14049, Roll 1839).

According to Davis, in the spring of 1781 Ogden specifically "entered as a volunteer on board of the same boat in which I was under the same officers & continued in service with me the deponent on board of said boat till late in the fall of the same year."[37] This should answer any questions of whether Ogden was a member of Brewster's crew, but because of his short tour, he would not have been aboard for the "Spy Boat Fight."

BENJAMIN STURGES: From "Fairfield town and County in the State of Connecticut," Sturges served as a marine on board one of Brewster's boats.[38] At some point during his service he received a bayonet wound, probably from grappling with the crew of an enemy boat on Long Island Sound. As result of this wound, he had "difficulty breathing, pain, and lameness of the side all which have arisen from the thrust of a bayonet through the body on the left side just above the hip" for the rest of his life.[39]

HEZEKIAH STURGES: As part of the Sea Coast Guard of Fairfield, Connecticut, he served several short tours of duty over a three-year period. "In Spring of the year 1781 he enlisted and served in a nine oared boat commanded by Abraham C. Woodhull" for about ten months in Brewster's fleet cruising on Long Island Sound. Sturges explains "that in all his Land Service he served as a private soldier and in the Sea Service as an Oarsman and Marine."[40]

Benjamin Sturges confirmed that Hezekiah Sturges: "volunteered & served with me the deponent the same year commencing when I did & continuing in service for the same term of time on board of a boat commanded as before stated."[41] This means that they likely both served on Woodhull's boat.

CONCLUSION

For decades the actions of Brewster's whaleboat fleet were far better known than the secret work of the Culper Spy Ring, which was intentionally kept out of the public domain. These days, things appear to have reversed so that the whale-boaters and marines who secretly rowed across Long Island Sound and jousted with enemy vessels have been

37. Joshua Davis Deposition, July 28, 1832, ibid.
38. Deposition of Benjamin Sturges, November 1, 1819, *Pensions* (W.25073, Roll 2319).
39. Physician's & Surgeon's Affidavit, January 17, 1826, ibid.
40. Deposition of Hezekiah Sturges, April 23, 1833, *Pensions* (S.14601, Roll 2319). This was not the same Abraham Woodhull who was a member of the Culper Spy Ring.
41. Deposition of Benjamin Sturges, July 27, 1832, *Pensions* (S.14601, Roll 2319).

all but forgotten, but spy activities have been highlighted in various media outlets.

These oarsmen and marines are but a small sampling of all those who served in the "Spy Boat Service." There are still many others that need to be identified and their stories examined. I hope I have sparked some interest among researchers to take up the challenge to find out more about these mariners who served so bravely and sacrificed so much.

Charles Turner: One Soldier, Three Armies

TODD W. BRAISTED

On the muster roll of a Continental Army regiment stationed at West Point in 1779, is a note that a soldier, Charles Turner, had deserted on June 5 of that year. In and of itself, it's a routine entry, a common occurrence with every army of the period. The war saw thousands of such desertions from both sides, men who took matters into their own hands to unilaterally, not to mention illegally, end their military obligations. Seeing so many deserters, one can lose sight that each one of these men had a personal story to tell, experiences often unique to themselves. So it was for Charles Turner, starting with the fact that his name was not quite Turner.

When the war started for Charles Turner, he was better known by his comrades as Carl Tournier (or Tornier), a private soldier in the Prince Ludwig Regiment of Brunswick Dragoons, one of the contingent of troops from the German principality of Brunswick hired by the British to supplement their forces attempting to subdue the rebellion in America. The Brunswick troops arrived in Canada in 1776 and formed a large part of Lt. Gen. John Burgoyne's invasion of northern New York the following year. Although a cavalry unit, the Prince Ludwig Regiment arrived without horses and fought as infantry during the campaign. Tournier, with many of his comrades, was captured at the Battle of Bennington on August 16, 1777. Marched as a prisoner to Massachusetts, he spent months as a captive, finally deciding to enlist with his captors in May 1778. Tournier became Turner to his new officers, serving in Capt. Elisha Brewer's company of light infantry in Col. Samuel Brewer's battalion.[1] With his battalion he was sent to the

1. Muster Roll of Capt. Elisha Brewer's Company, 9th Massachusetts Battalion, West Point,

Hudson Highlands, garrisoning the lynchpin of the Hudson River defenses at West Point. In early June 1779, Tournier was part of a scout sent out under a lieutenant from West Point, taking the opportunity to slip away and desert when within three miles of the British garrison of Stony Point, at which post he arrived the next day.

Upon arriving within the British lines, the former dragoon was debriefed for whatever intelligence he could provide concerning the enemy. Perhaps the most fascinating part of Tournier's interview concerned his time at West Point. Fifteen months after providing detailed intelligence on the state of the fortifications and garrison, his interviewer, John André, would be captured with similar information on his person, provided by Continental Maj. Gen. Benedict Arnold. André of course would be executed at Tappan, New York for possessing information he had probably already heard from any number of deserters from West Point. The information changed over time, but there was a steady stream of it to the British.[2] Tournier's information on West Point was recorded by his interviewer:

> He has been in Garrison at West Point since Novr. last and gives the following account of the works, &ca. there—That there are three Forts, call'd Fort Putnam, Fort Arnold & Fort Webb, of which Fort Putnam is the principal, and besides the Forts, they have three Redoubts & a Fleche along the River; that the 1st Redoubt has in it 3 Guns, (the natures of them he does not know) the 2d Redoubt 2 long 12 Prs., the 3d Redoubt, 2 – 9 Prs. and the Fleche 3 – 18 Pounders & 1 – 12 Pr. In Fort Putnam there are 7 Guns, (the heaviest an 18 Pr. and 1 Howitzer, but no Mortars; in Fort Webb, (which is a paultry work, there are 3 Guns, one of which is a 9 Pr. & the other two 6 prs. Fort Putnam has a Chevaux de Frize and a Stone Wall round it, with a parapet upon it of Fascines & Earth. Fort Arnold has a Ditch, but he cannot tell the number of Guns in it, as many small ones were lately mov'd into it, but there are between 50 & 60 cannon in all the Point. General Parsons commands at West Point & the Garrison of the different works consist of 7 Regts. belonging to Massachusetts Bay & 2 from North Carolina, besides the militia, who lay in the woods. Their light Infantry (to which Tornier himself belong'd) is commanded by Major Hull, a very good

Point, June 12, 1779. Revolutionary War Rolls, M-246, Reel 38, Folder 17, National Archives and Records Administration (NARA).

2. A British intelligence book shows no less than five deserters from West Point being interviewed in late July 1780 alone, including three who had previously been in the British Army. Clinton (Sir Henry). Information of Deserters and Others, Not Included in Private Intelligence, Emmett Collection, EM. C*, New York Public Library.

> Officer and consists of 7 Companies of 60 men each, which are as many almost as some whole Regts. are compos'd of. This Corps of Light Infantry have taken post on a hill about ½ mile from Fort Putnam, which it commands & are building a Block house there. Fort Putnam is about half a mile from Fort Arnold & about the same Distance from Fort Webb. Fort Putnam lays so high that the Shipping can't incommode it, nor can they fire on the Shipping except from one Gun[3]

Once with the British, it is unknown what immediately became of Tournier. He may have been placed with other escaped Germans until an opportunity presented itself to return him to the Brunswickers still serving in Canada. Such a provision had been made by the British as early as September 24, 1778 when George Albus, a former Hessian lieutenant, was ordered to "take Charge of Such Non Commissioned Officers of the Private Men of the Brunswick Troops as have been Exchanged or who have made their Escape from the Enemy."[4]

The number of men making it to New York, such as Tournier, was sufficient enough for the British to make temporary use of them. Accordingly, on April 11, 1779, the Brunswickers "are to be mounted for the Present & do duty as Hussars, under Capt. Diemar of the 60th Regt., till they can be restor'd to their proper Regiments."[5] Friedrich de Diemar was a Hanoverian officer who had served two years on Minorca before being commissioned an officer in the 3rd Battalion of the 60th Regiment of Foot. Armed with a letter of introduction from Lord George Germain, he sailed to New York in the late summer of 1778 to offer his services to Gen. Sir Henry Clinton, commander of the British army in America, who had served with his father in the Seven Years War.[6]

While some of these German prisoners had escaped from their places of confinement, others, like Tournier, had enlisted in the Continental Army prior to escaping to the British. One who did so a month after Tournier, Henry Siebert of the Hesse Hanau Regiment, had ac-

3. Intelligence report of Charles Tornier, June 9, 1779. Sir Henry Clinton Papers, Volume 60, item 25, University of Michigan, William L. Clements Library (CL).

4. General Orders, New York, September 24, 1778. British General Orderly Book, September 11 to October 24, 1778, Early American Orderly Book Collection, No. 69, Reel 6, New-York Historical Society (NYHS).

5. General Orders, New York, April 11, 1779. Orderly Book of the 1st Battalion of Guards, January 1 to December 28, 1779, Early American Orderly Book Collection, No. 77, Reel 6, NYHS.

6. George Germain to Henry Clinton, August 7, 1778. Headquarters Papers of the British Army in America, PRO 30/55/1296, Great Britain, The National Archives (TNA).

tually been commissioned a 1st lieutenant in Col. Charles Armand's independent partisan corps before deserting with fourteen others from Crompond in Westchester.[7]

Finding himself back in British hands, albeit in a completely different army than the one in Canada, Tournier was officially reunited with some fellow Brunswickers on September 21, 1779 when he entered as a cavalryman in the Corps of Black Hussars, as Diemar's troop would be known due to the color of their distinctive uniform jackets.[8]

The formation of the troop had not been universally popular with the senior officers of the Brunswick forces. General Clinton had initially planned on making up the difference of pay of the Brunswickers to make it consistent with the higher pay given to cavalry soldiers in the British service. The problem was, according to Brunswick Gen. Friedrich Riedesel, the senior officer in North America from that principality, the Duke of Brunswick regarded these men as deserters from their corps and had ceased paying them. Exerting his authority, he informed the British he would "order them to be Claim'd when ever an opportunity offers of Sending them to Canada," which the British had little choice but to agree with, regardless of how useful they were at New York and how less so they would be in Quebec.[9]

Sooner or later, Tournier expected to be back in Brunswick service. For the moment, however, he was a soldier in His Britannic Majesty's Provincial Forces. Provincials, as they were commonly known, referred to standing regiments raised in North America under the authority of the British commander-in-chief. These were overwhelmingly Loyalists, Americans who favored the British cause. Placing what was in effect a German cavalry unit on the Provincial Establishment was the only practical way to pay and uniform them, as only the king of Great Britain could authorize a new British regiment, nor could the British create a new corps belonging to the army of another country, or in this case countries. So Charles Tournier had the distinction of being a soldier of the Principality of Brunswick, serving in a Loyalist establish-

7. Intelligence report Henry Siebert, July 1779. Clinton Papers, 231:8, CL. Muster Roll of Capt. George Schaffner's Company, Armand's Corps, August 14, 1778. Revolutionary War Rolls, M-246, Reel 115, Folder 16, NARA.

8. "General Roll of Captain De Diemars Hussars taken from the Muster Rolls New York 20th May 1781." ARC.278, Mrs. Milan Hulbert collection of colonial British America and early United States of America papers, Corps of Hussars: General Roll, taken from the Muster Rolls, Box 2, Folder 8, Center for Brooklyn History (CBH). See also recruiting notice of the corps, dated Kingsbridge, August 12, 1779. Best.4h Nr.3106 S.118, Staatsanwaltschaft-Marburg.

9. James Robertson to Clinton, New York, December 22, 1779. Clinton Papers, 83:39, CL.

ment, commanded by a Hanoverian holding a commission in the British Regular Army, officially being placed in the new troop of hussars on September 21, 1779.

Cavalry had not been taken into account when the Treasury ordered clothing for the Provincial forces during the first few years of the war, leaving Alexander Innes, the Inspector General of Provincial Forces, no alternative but to purchase, at expensive local rates, all the necessary uniforms and equipage for the mounted troops. These expenses were born by Captain Diemar himself; "the Hussar Dress and Equipage being unknown," the articles were not to be found in the Provincial Stores, necessitating their purchase by the captain, which cost he was still seeking reimbursement for after the close of the war.[10]

Tournier's troop is one of the handful of units for which an inventory of items issued to each soldier survives today. As opposed to the light blue coat and heavy dress of a Brunswick cavalryman, the new hussar was issued with a coat and jacket, a waistcoat, two pair of Osnaburgh trousers, a hair ribbon, a pair of leather breeches, a "great hussar coat," a neck stock, a stock buckle, two blankets, two pair of shoes, two pair of spare shoe soles, two pair of stockings, a pair of winter gloves, two shirts, a canteen, a watering cap, a pair of leather gaiters and a pair of boots with spurs. What was notably missing from this list of things issued to Tournier, and many other of the hussars, were the tools to wage war.[11]

In the two years or so that the troop existed as an independent corps, a total of 180 men passed through its ranks, although the average strength of the troop was generally around sixty of all ranks. The items Tournier did not receive, according to the return cited above, seem to have been in short supply throughout the career of the corps. For these 180 members, there were issued just 96 horses, 68 muskets, 64 carbines, 46 pistols and 83 broad swords. Many, like Tournier, had none of these items, making them useless in combat. One explanation could be that since men left the corps through reassignment or other reasons, their equipment and horses were passed along to others during the course

10. Diemar to Lord Thomas Sidney, Glueckstadt, October 28, 1786. ARC.278, Mrs. Milan Hulbert collection of colonial British America and early United States of America papers, Corps of Hussars: Correspondence, etc. 1779-1791, Box 1, Folder 30, CBH.

11. "Account of the Corps of Hussars raised in North America under the Command of His Excellency General Sir Henry Clinton K.B. by Captain Frederick de Diemar, in the Year 1779, 1780 & 1781 and accounting for Clothing, Saddlery, Arms, Accoutrements and Necessaries issued to the Hussars on the Outposts of the Army and what has been received from the Inspector Generals Office of Provincials." ARC.278, Box 2, Folder 9, CBH.

of the troop's existence. The paltry number of pistols, however, strongly suggest the troop was never complete with them.

Despite the logistical difficulties, the troop was quite active in the New York City area, particularly in 1779 and 1780, attached to the cavalry of the Queen's Rangers, British Legion, and even an ad-hoc light corps commanded by the famous Capt. Patrick Ferguson. During Tournier's tenure with the troop, they were involved in at least four notable skirmishes and an abortive attempt to capture George Washington at Morristown, an expedition turned back by the severe ice and deep snow of the intense winter of 1779-1780.[12]

The most notable action of the troop took place on April 16, 1780, when they composed part of 120 cavalry, joined to 312 infantry, sent to attack the Continental Army outpost of 250 men at Hopperstown (modern Ho-Ho-Kus), Bergen County, New Jersey. With the cavalry in the vanguard, the horsemen overwhelmed a picket guard at New Bridge before quickly moving a further nine miles to surprise the garrison. The post was a rotating detachment of 250 men drawn from the regiments at Jockey Hollow. This April it was commanded by Maj. Thomas L. Byles of the 3rd Pennsylvania Regiment, who had just paraded some of his men when the first horsemen galloped into view. As reported by Capt. Jonathan Hallett of the 2nd New York Regiment,

> Their approach was so rapid after the[y] was discovered by the Guards that it was impossible to collect our force before they was up with the Quarters of the Troops, Altho we had been under Arms this morning as was Customary with us daily. Majr. Byles took Post in the House with a party of Men, [in which he] defended himself for some time.[13]

Cornet George Spencer of the Queen's Rangers Hussars conceded, "Never was a House better defended."[14] The attackers tried unsuccess-

12. "One hundred and Twenty Dragoons were to cross the North River from the City of New York to penetrate by a particular Route to the Neighbourhood of Morris Town and in their Retreat to fall back upon a Body of Infantry posted at Newark Mountain Meeting to receive them." The cavalry seems to have been drawn from all those at New York at the time, principally the Queen's Rangers and 17th Light Dragoons. The attempt, originally intended for February 7, 1780, was delayed by inclement weather for three days before being ineffectually launched. Journal of events in the New York District, January 1 — February 24, 1780, Clinton Papers, 83:2, CL.

13. Jonathan Hallett to George Washington, Paramus, April 16, 1780. George Washington Papers, General Correspondence, 1697-1799, MSS 44693, Series 4, Reel 65, Library of Congress.

14. Spencer account, c-April 1780. Simcoe Papers 1774-1824, CL.

fully to force the door, having a man wounded in the process. Finally the attackers set fire to the house, and the occupants thought best to give up. Major Byles "as he opened the door to surrender, was unfortunately shot by one of Captain Deimar's huzzars, and died three days after."[15] Organized resistance ended at that point, with the loss of at least ninety officers and men of the Continentals dead, wounded, prisoners and deserters, as well as six militia wounded on the march. Diemar's troop had two men wounded among the thirty-seven casualties suffered by the attackers.[16] Assuming Tournier was involved in the action, it was his last as a hussar, and probably of the war.

With the passing of the harsh winter of 1779-1780, normal shipping could resume, particularly the passage to Quebec. Reinforcements previously committed to Canada, in the form of the 44th Regiment of Foot and the Hessian Regiment of Lossberg, were now able to sail there and join the Northern Army. Seeing an opportunity of restoring his Brunswick regiments to some semblance of respectability in point of numbers, General Riedesel demanded the return of men from that principality then serving under Captain Diemar. With no apparent legal right to keep foreign troops from serving in their own regiments, on May 15, 1780 the British bid adieu to forty-two hussars, among whom was Charles Turner. Captain Deimar's troop was instantly gutted, being reduced to just thirty-seven officers and men.[17]

While the loss of the Brunswickers was severely felt, it did not mean the end of the troop. Enlistment records for sixty members exist, just over one-third of the enlisted men, for the period 1779-1781. Only eleven are clearly identified as being from Brunswick. The remaining forty-nine came from across Europe and America, including Sweden, Prussia, Hamburg, Wurttemberg, Hanover, Holland, Frankfurt, Hesse-Hanau, Anspach, Hesse-Cassel, Hungary, Osnabrück, Switzerland, France, Pennsylvania, Ireland and England.[18] To be sure, language issues could prove a problem. Four deserters in early 1781 claimed to leave the corps to join the Queen's Rangers as they "did not understand the language." Of the four, one was from Ireland, one from England

15. Report of Captain Alexander Wickham to Lt. Col. John Graves Simcoe. John Graves Simcoe, *A History of the Operations of a Partisan Corps called the Queen's Rangers commanded by Lieut. Col. J. G. Simcoe, during the War of the American Revolution* (New York: Bartlett & Welford, 1844), 139-142.

16. *The Royal Gazette* (New York,) April 19, 1780.

17. "State of the following Corps under the Command of His Excellency Lieut. General Knyphausen, New York 15th May 1780." Colonial Office, Class 5, Volume 1110, folio 128, TNA.

18. Corps of Hussars Enlistment Certifications, ARC.278, Box 1, Folder 29, CBH.

and one from Sweden.[19] New recruits brought the unit back up to its former strength in just a few months. The troop took part in the actions at Connecticut Farms and Springfield, New Jersey in June 1780, but nothing thereafter. In the spring of 1781, Captain Diemar was recalled to his actual corps, the 60th Regiment of Foot, leaving the troop under its present commander, Lt. George Albus, and New Jersey native Benjamin Thomson for the remainder of the war. Albus and the other sixty-three hussars were officially added as a fifth troop of cavalry to the Queen's Rangers on April 25, 1781.[20] The troop was eventually given to Capt. William Sutherland, a British regular officer, but he never actually joined the corps in person.[21] The hussars mostly remained at New York City for the rest of the war, not joining their regiment under Cornwallis, and thereby being spared capture at Yorktown.

Upon returning to Canada, Tournier, now listed as "Karl Tornier," found a reconstituted Brunswick Dragoon regiment of four complete troops doing garrison duty. He remained with them in Quebec until July 7, 1783, when he was discharged. In the course of his career in North America, it is doubtful this son of Germany could have possibly envisioned the trail across America he would follow, the people he would meet, or the events he would take part in. If by chance he did return to Brunswick, or if he remained in Canada, he would have stories to tell.[22]

19. The four were found guilty of desertion and sentenced to 1,000 lashes each. At least three were sent on board a Royal Navy warship later that year, possibly in lieu of corporal punishment. Court Martial Proceedings of Edward Handlin, Samuel Forrester, Richard Perry and Ouly Johnston [Ole Uhanssan], New York, 19 February 1781. War Office, Class 71, Volume 93, p. 210-211, TNA.

20. "Muster Roll of the Troop of Hussars attached to the Queens Rangers Jno. Graves Simcoe Esqr. Lieut. Col. Commandant From 25 April to 24 June 1781." RG 8, "C" Series, Volume 1864, page 41, Library and Archives Canada.

21. See William Sutherland to Clinton, October 20, 1784. Clinton Papers, 200:19, CL.

22. Rolls of the Prince Ludwig Regiment of Dragoons, January 1, 1783. War Office, Class 28, Volume 10, folios 236-240, TNA.

Top Twenty Wartime Quotations from the Letters of Lucy and Henry Knox

PHILLIP HAMILTON

Lucy and Henry Knox experienced the American Revolution at its very center. Growing up in Boston, the couple had fallen in love and married just prior to the outbreak of hostilities. Shortly after war broke out on April 19. 1775 at Lexington and Concord, they fled the city and Knox volunteered his services to the gathering Continental Army. He then began a remarkable military career. Indeed, during the conflict, he worked his way into George Washington's inner circle, gained command of the army's artillery branch, and ended the war as a major general and one of Washington's most trusted lieutenants.

Frequently separated by the struggle, Henry and Lucy wrote scores of letters to one another. As with most couples during this age, they wrote for many reasons: they wished, first and foremost, to express their love for one another and desire to be together; they also wrote about the war's events (both great and small) as well as debated the Revolution's impact upon their marriage. These twenty quotations from their wartime correspondence demonstrate the Knoxes' involvement in and influence upon these events. They also reveal the deeply personal struggles of a newly-married couple attempting to come to terms with a world in the midst of momentous changes.

1. Henry Knox to Lucy Flucker, 1773

> I have been upon the utmost rack of expectation for above two hours past, expecting some message from you. Is there any thing I can say or do that will affect it. If there is command it and [it] shall be done. . .
>
> To the Coffee house tomorrow evening? Do you ask me? Or is it only like the banter affixed at the head of your letter? N- N- N- No. . . Let

> me hear from or see you. I could write a volume to you, but I write so much in a hurry as your woman is waiting, that you could not read.

These are the first surviving words that Henry Knox wrote to his future wife, Lucy Flucker. In 1773, Knox was just twenty-three years old, but he already owned a thriving bookstore in central Boston. Lucy, then seventeen, belonged to a prominent Tory family. Her father, Thomas Flucker, was a wealthy land speculator as well as the royal colonial secretary of Massachusetts Bay. The young couple met inside Knox's bookshop, where they found themselves instantly attracted to one another. Clearly written during the early stages of their courtship, this letter points to Lucy playfully toying with her suitor's affections. A full-blown romance soon blossomed, which would eventually grow into an enduring attachment lasting until the end of their lives. The couple married in June 1774 despite opposition from her parents. Unfortunately, no letters written by Lucy survive from this period.

2. Henry Knox to Lucy Flucker Knox, July 6, 1775

> Yesterday, as I was going to Cambridge, I met the General, who beg'd me to return to Roxbury again which I did. When they had view'd the works they express'd the greatest pleasure & surprize at their situation and apparent utility to say nothing of the plan which did not escape their praise

Henry Knox here briefly described one of the most important encounters of his life: his chance meeting with Gen. George Washington just days after the latter's arrival outside Boston to take command of the Continental Army. Something of an autodidact, Knox had read numerous works about military history, siege fortifications, and artillery prior to the war. After volunteering his services to the colonial forces, the self-educated bookseller had been tasked to help with the construction of earthworks in Roxbury, just south of British-occupied Boston. Henry dated this letter at 6 AM, indicating that he could not wait to share the exciting news with his wife. Knox clearly made an impression upon the Virginia commander-in-chief; Washington asked him to come to headquarters at Cambridge just days later so that he could learn more about him.

3. Henry Knox to Lucy Flucker Knox, November 16, 1775

> I lodg'd at Barkers and arriv'd here Yesterday in the most violent N East Storm that I almost ever knew. Keep up your Spirits, my dear Girl, I shall be with you tomorrow night & don't be alarm'd when I tell you that the General has order'd me to go to the West Ward as far as Ticon-

> deroga, about a three Weeks Journey. Don't be afraid, there is no fighting in the Case. I am going upon buisness [*sic*] only

Knox had so impressed Washington (and many other officers in the army's camp) that by the middle of November 1775, the young bookseller had not only received a colonel's commission from the Continental Congress, but had also been named to command the Continental Army's artillery branch. As Henry explained in this hastily scrawled note, the general had just ordered him to travel to Fort Ticonderoga to retrieve nearly five dozen British cannon captured there the previous spring by patriot forces. This letter also reflects Knox's concern for his wife. Six months pregnant with their first child, she was anxious for her husband's safety. He, therefore, sought to reassure her that he would be safe throughout his upcoming mission.

4. Henry Knox to Lucy Flucker Knox, December 17, 1775

> My last Letter mention'd that I was just going of Lake George about 36 miles in length. We had a tedious time of it altho the passage was fine, in coming back it was exceedingly disagreable. But all danger and the principal difficulty is now passed &, by next Thursday, I hope we shall be able to set out from hence on our way home with our very valuable & precious Convoy. If we have the good fortune to have snow, I hope to have the pleasure to see my dearest in three weeks from this date . . . We shall cut no small figure in going thro' the county with our Cannon, Mortars &c drawn by eighty Yoke Oxen

This letter, penned in the midst of the Ticonderoga expedition, displays Henry Knox's near-unfailing good humor and optimism. He had just gotten fifty-nine cannon across Lake George. Although he found the passage exceedingly difficult and exhausting, he was now confidently prepared to set off for Albany before heading across the snow-covered Berkshire Mountains. During this journey, Knox would successfully lead more than a hundred teamsters and forty-two ponderous horse- and ox-drawn sleds. In his last line, he appears to grasp the magnitude and importance of his accomplishment.

5. Henry Knox to Lucy Flucker Knox, ca. March 5–17, 1776

> My only Love,
>
> I rec[eive]d your letter by my brother which gave me the most sensible pleasure. You tenderly ask what is become of me. "No evil has happen'd" but an excessive hurry of business has prevented my paying my Lucy that tribute of affection which is so justly her due . . . Certain it is they (the enemy) are packing up & going off bag & baggage. How

> far or where is yet uncertain. If to New York, my Dear Lucy must prepare to follow them as we are Citizens of the World, any place will be our home & equally cheap

Because he had successfully transported the nearly sixty heavy guns to the American encampment surrounding Boston, Knox gave Washington and the Continental Army the needed firepower to compel the British to withdraw from the city or else face destruction. Knox was undoubtedly excited about the British retreat, but he also correctly predicted that New York City would become the next great theater of war. He could not imagine, however, what lay in store for both him and his wife.

6. Lucy Flucker Knox to Henry Knox, April 29 or 30, 1776

> Is my Harry well. Is he happy. No, that cannot be when he reflects how wretched he has left me. I doubt not, but the plea of his little girl, as he used fondly to call me, must sometimes draw a thought from him tho surrounded with gaiety and scenes of high life. The remembrance of his tender infant must also greatly affect him when he considers it at so great a distance from its Father, its natural guardian, in a place exposed to an enraged enemy and almost defenceless

This is Lucy's first surviving letter to her husband. She reflected here on her loneliness without "my Harry" beside her, while imagining him enjoying a convivial lifestyle. She also indirectly prodded Knox into inviting her to New York City by invoking their newborn daughter. "Little Lucy," as her parents typically called her, had been born the previous February, and her mother understood how much Henry missed the child. This letter did the trick. A week after receiving it, Henry invited his wife and daughter to join him in the city.

7. Henry Knox to Lucy Flucker Knox, July 4, 1776

> My dearest Love,
>
> I regret & feel the keenest pain and anxiety on the account of the precipitation with which you and the Ladies were oblig'd to decamp. Your Harry scolding, the enemy approaching, all in Confusion. That was the moment I most dreaded of any thing, your being here and obliging me to feel the highest pangs. I most earnestly long to hear how you are and [that] you keep your spirits

On the morning of July 1, Henry and Lucy had just sat down to breakfast in their lodging on Broadway when they suddenly observed scores of British warships sailing up New York harbor and heading toward the southern tip of Manhattan. The previous week, this British fleet had been spotted off Long Island and was clearly heading toward the city. Thus, Henry had been urging his wife to leave. But the strong-willed Lucy had adamantly refused to go. Furious at both himself and her, he now shouted at his wife that she and their baby must depart immediately. Dissolving into tears, Lucy reluctantly obeyed. This was, in all likelihood, the first time Henry had ever raised his voice to his young spouse. This event also signaled the start of the New York-New Jersey campaign, which would last until the end of the year.

8. Lucy Flucker Knox to Henry Knox, July [8?], 1776

> My only friend,
> I will go to N[ew] Haven, indeed I will; but first must beg your patience to read this, which I think will shew that I am not deserving of the severe censure that I have received . . . You are pleased frequently in your letters to remind me of my incapacity of judging for myself. I now assure you that I have a deep sense of my own weakness and ignorance and a very high opinion of the abilities of him in whose eyes mine are so contemptable

This is Lucy's first letter to Henry after they had so bitterly separated the previous week. She was obviously still angry with her husband for the treatment she had received upon leaving him. New Haven was where Henry had ordered Lucy and little Lucy to go on July 1. Because the Connecticut township was eighty-five miles away from New York City, Knox thought his wife and child would be safe there. However, Lucy had only gone as far as Stamford, a mere forty miles from lower Manhattan and a place from which she could easily return to the army. This quotation most certainly reflects Lucy's combative spirit and her willingness to stand up to her husband when she felt she had been wronged.[1]

9. Lucy Flucker Knox to William Knox,[2] September 20, 1776

> Dear Billey,
> Before you receive this you will possibly learn that your Brother is a

1. On July 11, Knox replied that he was "grieved and distressed" upon the receipt of this letter, believing that his wife's troubles were self-inflicted. Fearing too that she was about to return to the army camp, he admonished her, "I ever wished my Lucy to soar above the Generality of her Sex many of whom to be sure are trifling insignificant animals, dreading what never will come to pass." The back-and-forth bickering by letter continued for another week until Lucy at last reached New Haven.

2. William Knox (1756-1795) was Henry's younger brother and a constant presence in the couple's life together. Prior to the war, he assisted Knox in his bookshop. At the start of the conflict, William accompanied Knox on the Fort Ticonderoga expedition. In the fall of 1776, William was then living in Boston overseeing the reconstruction of his brother's store.

> prisoner but dont be frightened, he is not . . . The [artillery] brigade of course would have been taken had not your brother, who stayed to see the last gun off, ordered them into the fort at Ballards hill, which stratagem had the desired effect, the enemy thought we had made a stand there and, crossing the fields, took another road into the city which our people took the advantage of and joined their main body unhurt . . . I am going to York or wherever the army are to see your brother, after which I believe I shall come to Boston upon a visit

This letter to Henry's younger brother, William, came days after the British captured New York City. Following a series of heavy blows by British forces, Washington's army was compelled to retreat northward out of lower Manhattan in order to escape destruction. Because her husband had stayed behind until the last minute to extract his guns, false rumors began to circulate that he had been captured. As Lucy described Henry successfully saving his brigade, her pride in his military prowess is unmistakable. Her resolve to visit Henry, in spite of the inherent dangers involved, further speaks to her deep love for him as well as her own grit and determination.

10. Henry Knox to Lucy Flucker Knox, December 28, 1776

> Our army was scattered along the river for nearly 25 miles. Our intelligence agreed that the force of the enemy in Trenton was from two to three Thousand with about six field Cannon and that they were pretty secure in their situation & that they were hessians, no[t] British troops. A hardy design was form'd of attacking the Town by storm. Accordingly, a part of the army consisting of about 2500 or three thousand pass'd the River on Christmass night with allmost infinite difficulty, with eighteen field pieces. Floating Ice in the River made the labour almost incredible, however perseverance accomplished what at first seem'd impossible. About two oClock the troops were all on the Jersey side. We then were about nine miles from the object, the night was cold & stormy. It hailed with great violence, the Troops march'd with the most profound silence and good order. They arrived by two routes on roads at the same time about half an hour after day light to within one mile of the Town. The storm continued with great violence, but was in our backs & consequently in the faces of our Enemy. About half a mile from the Town was an advanced Guard on each road, consisting of a Captain's Guard. These Guards we forc'd & enter'd the Town with them pell-mell, & here succeeded a scene of war of which I had often conceived but never saw before. The hurry, fright & confusion of the enemy was unlike that which shall be when the last Trump[pt] shall sound . . . The Hessians lost part of their Cannon in the Town. They

> did not relish the project of forcing, & were oblig'd to Surrender upon the spot with all their artillery, 6 brass pieces, army Colors &c &c. A Colo. Rawle[3] commanded who was wounded . . . The troops behav'd like men contending for every thing that was dear and valuable. It must give a sensible pleasure to every friend to the rights of America

This letter describes the stunning American victory at the battle of Trenton in which Knox played an important role. Indeed, Washington had ordered his artillery commander, who possessed a deep baritone voice, to direct the Continental Army's nighttime crossing of the Delaware River. Coming after a long series of defeats, Knox's joy is palpable in this passage. Writing just thirty-six hours afterwards, he demonstrated both delight and surprise at their triumph. The letter also reveals the pride he felt in the outstanding performance of the soldiers, especially of his artillerymen. Henry would learn less than a week later that he had been promoted by the Congress to brigadier general.

11. Lucy Flucker Knox to Hannah Flucker Urquhart,[4] ca. April 1777

> Oh, my sister, how horrid is this war, Brother against Brother and the parent against the child. Who were the first promoters of it, I know not, but god knows and I fear they will feel the weight of his vengeance. Tis pity the little time we have to spend in this world, we cannot enjoy ourselves and our friends, but must be devising means to destroy each other . . . In our juvenile days, my Hannah, we little thought this Barbaras [i.e., barbarous] art would so soon have reached America, but alas her fruitfull fields of war [have] been covered with the dead and dying of the heartfelt

During the first two years of the war, Lucy's Tory family members refused to have anything to do with her, an event that naturally proved exceedingly painful to the young woman. In the spring of 1777, Lucy had heard rumors that her eldest sister, Hannah, was then living alone in Halifax, Nova Scotia. Desperate to re-connect with anyone from her

3. Hessian Col. Johann Rall (ca. 1726-1776) commanded the brigade that Washington 's army surprised and defeated. He died from his wounds.

4. Hannah Flucker Urquhart (1751-1820) was Lucy Knox's oldest sister. She had gone to Halifax when the British Army evacuated Boston in the spring of 1776. Unhappily married to a British officer named James Urquhart, Hannah was likely separated from him by the spring of 1777. She eventually made her way to London, at which point she had an affair with another military officer named Stephen Kemp. The Urquharts were never reconciled and finally divorced in 1787. That same year, Hannah married Richard Horwood, a young surveyor and cartographer who was seven years her junior. Although the two sisters would correspond after the war, Hannah never made any reference to this letter.

family, she wrote to her sister in the hope that she would receive this message. In this passage, she reflected upon the universal horror and tragedy of war. This letter is all the more remarkable because at the time Lucy was just twenty years old. It is unknown if Hannah ever received this epistle.

12. Lucy Flucker Knox to Henry Knox, April 30 or May 1, 1777[5]

> I have just come from a scene my Harry which has roused my very soul, in gratitude to my bountiful benefactor. A man who was inoculated at or about the time I was lay in the last agonies, his pock proved the purple sort and he, poor soul, must die. His brother had just arrived from his wife, who was near laying in [i.e., giving birth] and very impatient for his return. And, as a proof of her affection, had sent him some good things such as he might venture to eat . . . He is just now dead. What a stroke will it be to that poor miserable woman. . . . How do I know to what the dear partner of my Soul is at this minute exposed. Indeed, my Harry, I am serious, I cannot live at this distance from you

Lucy wrote this letter to her husband several weeks after she and little Lucy had received smallpox inoculations. The procedure, which Lucy had long contemplated and feared, was going well for her (she developed only twenty pox marks on her face), but her daughter was then showing alarming signs of a more serious outbreak. Adding to her anxiety was the fact that a soldier, who had been staying in a room next to hers, had just died from his inoculation. This tragedy led Lucy to write this letter, illustrating the uncertainty of life in this day and age and the terrible pain caused by sudden and unexpected death. Lucy's sympathy for the young soldier's widow further points to the grim situation facing women without a spouse. Several days later, little Lucy did indeed develop a serious case of smallpox, but survived, much to the relief and joy of both parents.

13. Lucy Flucker Knox to Henry Knox, June 3, 1777

> My Harry writes to me as if I lived in a land of plenty. Six pounds of best green tea is what I have endeavored to the utmost of my power to procure. I wrote you last week that I expected some, but it belongs to Bill Turner[6] and he refuses paper money for it. However, you shall have a couple of pounds by the first opportunity tho it were my last gunie [i.e., guinea] that purchased it. The horses fetched but seventy five pounds owing to your not entrusting me with the sale of them. I wished

5. Lucy mistakenly dated this letter April 31, 1777.

6. Bill Turner was a grocer in Boston's Cornhill section.

> to have had them sold separate, but master Wm[7] was of a different opinion nor could he be persuaded. You had better make me your future agent. I'll assure you, I am quite a woman of business

Lucy remained in Boston throughout the Philadelphia campaign of 1777. In this passage, she demonstrated her efforts to support her husband in the field by obtaining needed supplies. In a previous letter that summer, she explained how she had just forwarded to him a wagon filled with Maderia wine, sugar, sweet meats, pepper, and coffee. She now described for him her growing struggles with inflation, something that would only grow worse in the months and years ahead. Yet she also revealed a growing self-confidence in her ability to handle their family's finances without her spouse nearby.

14. Lucy Flucker Knox to Henry Knox, August 23, 1777

> Oh, that you had less of the military man about you, you might then after the war have lived at ease all the days of your life. But now I don't know what you will do. Your being long acustomed to command will make you too haughty for mercantile matters, tho I hope you will not consider yourself as commander in chief of your own house. But be convinced . . . that there is such a thing as equal command

Lucy demonstrated in this passage both her teasing sense of humor as well as a growing assertiveness within her marriage. It also indirectly points to a long-held wish she had that Henry would leave the army in order to restart his mercantile career. This, she believed, would place their family in a more secure financial position.

15. Henry Knox to Lucy Flucker Knox, December 3, 1777

> does my Lucy really want a proof of my Affection, is there nothing in this world that will satisfy her but deserting the cause in which I am engag'd and render'd my self eternally infamous and all my connections by resigning at a time my Country may stand in need of my little assistance. God Forbid.
>
> I attribute her feelings by no means to such a cause. I believe she is chagrin'd and unhappy to have lost her Father, mother, sisters and brother in this contest, and her husband full knows she has made such capital sacrifices at too great a distance for [him] to support her under this consideration of such great afflictions. Believe me my only and dearest Love, (if your affection is not diminished—what a thought!), that my Life shall be spent to make you happy.[8]

7. William Knox.
8. The punctuation of this last sentence has been slightly modified for clarity.

As the grueling Philadelphia campaign drew to a close, Knox was exhausted and dispirited. A letter he had just received from Lucy only added to his woes; his wife had once more urged him to leave the army, claiming that, if he truly loved her, he would do so. Knox revealed here his utter commitment to the American cause by saying that he would never quit the flag. Yet he also attempted to comprehend the war from her perspective. Having been abandoned by her family, he realized not only how much she had lost in this contest, but he also understood that he was all she had left in the world.

16. Henry Knox to Lucy Flucker Knox, June 29, 1779

> I long to see you [and] to be assur'd from your own lips that you are getting better daily. I long to hear the little prattle of my lovely Lucy and to see the expressive countenance of Julia.[9] I pant after domestic happiness and most heartily wish the time arriv'd when we shall turn our swords into ploughs[hares] and pruning hooks

This letter, written shortly after the war had entered its fifth year, reflected Henry Knox's growing exhaustion with a conflict that appeared to have no end. By this point, the British and American forces had settled into a stand-off around New York City and the New York–New Jersey Highlands. Then on an operation along the Hudson River, north of the two main armies, Henry wrote this letter from New Windsor to inquire about his family's health. In this passage, he referred to the well-known biblical passage from Isaiah 2:4 which states, "They shall beat their swords into plowshares, and their spears into pruninghooks" (King James version). Tragically, the couple's three-month-old daughter, Julia, died on July 2, just three days after Knox penned this note.

17. Henry Knox to William Knox, September 4, 1781

> I wrote you my dear brother from Kings Ferry about a week past, & informed you some movements were about to take place but it was improper for me to specify what they were. One object is now developed and known to be Lord Cornwallis. Our measures are such that if the respective parts harmonize, we hope to do something handsome and we extend our views pretty far south.
>
> This manoeuvere, though much thought of by me, deranges my little family and creates a distress known only to domesticated minds. The General & Mrs. Washington prefers Mrs. Knox to take a trip to Vir-

9. Julia Knox, born on March 29, 1779, was the couple's second child.

ginia and she seems inclined to accept of the offer for several reasons. Our little daughter at any rate will be left in this Town at a eminent boarding school. Master Hal[10] will be the companion of his mama, who is six months in her fourth pregnancy

Knox wrote to his brother from Philadelphia to inform him about the upcoming campaign against a British army then in Virginia. Henry explained that the operation had deranged "my little family" due to recent news the couple had received about Lucy's father, Thomas Flucker: he was gravely ill and perhaps close to death in London. The information left Knox's wife distraught. Thus, he wanted to stay by her side, especially since she was in the middle of her fourth pregnancy in five years. So upset was Henry that he brought the situation to the commander-in-chief's attention, whereupon Washington graciously invited Lucy to stay at Mount Vernon during the campaign. This note clearly points to the intertwined nature of the public and private spheres of daily life throughout the Revolutionary War as well as illustrates the close bond between these two men.

18. Lucy Flucker Knox to Henry Knox, September 29, 1781

> I wrote you on monday by Mr. Custis[11] and informed you that Lucy [their daughter] was fixed with Mrs. Bredo[?] in philadelphia . . . I need not ask you to forward any letters which mention the dear little girl, with all possible dispatch to her anxious mother. Will the time never come when we shall have a house of our own and our Children about us. If not, life is not desirable.
>
> I mett a very kind reception from the good Lady of this place[12] but my circumstances lead me ardently to wish for a home, and I see but one possible way to obtain one. You know my meaning. I wish for nothing inconsistent with your happiness and future peace. But could you reconcile it to your feelings, I think it would make me happy

Lucy wrote this note to Henry as soon as she reached Mount Vernon. Like many of their letters later in the war, this one focused on matters of family and home. Although Martha Washington made Lucy feel welcome, as soon as she reached the beautiful mansion on the Potomac, she longed to have a grand home of her own. In the following decade, Henry would indeed make Lucy "happy" when he built her a

10. Henry Jackson Knox (1780-1832) was Lucy and Henry's third child.
11. John Parke Custis (1754-1781), son of Martha Washington, had just left Mount Vernon for Yorktown in order to serve as a civilian aide-de-camp to his stepfather during the siege. The young man sadly caught a camp fever and died in early November.
12. Martha Washington.

twenty-four-room mansion in coastal Maine called Montpelier. Unfortunately, the expense of constructing this enormous house was partially responsible for the Knoxes' later financial difficulties.

19. Henry Knox to Lucy Flucker Knox, October 19, 1781

> Camp before York 8 oClock A.M. 19th October
> I have detain'd William[13] untill this moment that I might be the first to communicate good news to the Charmer of my soul. A glorious moment for America! This day Lord Cornwallis & his Army marches out & piles their Arms in the face of our victorious Army . . . They will have the same honors as the Garrison of Charlestown, that is they will not be permitted to unfurl their Colours <u>or play Yankee doodle</u>.

Written at headquarters outside of Yorktown, Henry wanted his wife to hear directly from him the wonderful news that Gen. Charles Cornwallis's British army was to surrender that day to the Continental and French forces after a three-week siege. His heartfelt joy comes through in this short epistle, as does his pride in their "victorious Army" to which he and his comrades had sacrificed so much over the previous six years. The reference to the "Garrison of Charlestown" referred to an American army in 1780 that had been forced to lay down its arms without being accorded the honors of war. Furious at the disrespect shown to Patriot arms, Knox now relished the retribution the Americans were taking.

20. Henry Knox to Hannah Waldo Flucker,[14] November 24, 1783

> Harlem, 7 miles from New York, 24 Novr. 1783
> My dear Madam,
> The kindness of Mr. Watson presents an opportunity [in] which I cannot omit to inform you of the health of part of your family whose happiness I assure myself is still dear to you. My Lucy is at West point with her three sweet children in perfect health. They will be in New York as soon as the british forces evacuate it which is intended tomorrow. . .. We are extremely anxious to hear from you in answer to our several letters. I wrote in May last and Lucy has written twice since once in June & the other in July or August.
> I beg my sincere ardent affections may be presented to Mrs. Waldo, Mrs. Urquhart, Capt. Flucker and Lady. . .. I hope I shall in some future day have the pleasure of being acquainted with.

13. Henry Knox's civilian servant.
14. Lucy's mother.

I am my very dear Madam
Your truly affectionate Son
HKnox

Knox wrote this letter the night before British troops departed and the Continental Army marched in to reoccupy New York City. With the revolution now successfully concluded, Knox's epistle pointed to the couple's hope to reestablish the bonds of familial affection that had existed before the war. Although Secretary Flucker had died the previous March, Henry and Lucy were hopeful that this letter, combined with the restoration of peace, would bring about a family reunion. Although Hannah Flucker responded in a positive vein, it quickly became apparent that she and her other children were largely interested in the restoration of their property seized during the war. Thus, the Knoxes would never see any of their kinsmen again.

German Soldier, American Rebel: Christopher Ludwick's Pursuits of Happiness in Revolutionary Pennsylvania

SHAWN DAVID MCGHEE

Popular narratives of the American Revolution rank Christopher Ludwick, at best, among the extras in the imperial *dramatis personae*, a bit player who performed as honest gingerbread baker or amusingly spoke of himself in the third person.[1] Fortunately, his limited historiographical presence more seriously depicts him as superintendent of bakers for the Continental Army and develops his critical role feeding soldiers during the war or risking his life coercing Hessian soldiers to defect to the American side.[2] Yet historians have left unmined a vital element of his story that spells out the universality of the American struggle for liberty. Christopher Ludwick left the Old World to settle in Philadelphia and, during the imperial crisis, became a fierce supporter of the Whig position. The broad objectives that motivated Ludwick to commit his personal blood and treasure to American resistance and, ultimately revolution, lie less in his embrace of colonial identity and more

1. Many serious websites support this observation, yet they are harmless and still include Christopher Ludwick's general life trajectory and contributions to the American war effort. And many of the qualities and characteristics typically covered originated from the best source material, Benjamin Rush, *An Account of the Life and Character of Christopher Ludwick, Late Citizen of Philadelphia, and Baker-General of the Army of the United States During the Revolutionary War* (Philadelphia, PA: Garden and Thompson, 1831).
2. See for example, E. Wayne Carp, *To Starve the Army at Pleasure: Continental Army Administration and American Political Culture, 1775-1783* (Chapel Hill, NC: University of North Carolina Press, 1984); John Bakeless, *Turncoats, Traders and Heroes: Espionage in the American Revolution* (New York, NY: De Capo Press, 1959).

in his opposition to general oppression and hierarchical privilege. Ludwick remained grateful that Pennsylvania had welcomed him, foreigner though he was, and provided space where his personal industriousness and amicability made social mobility possible. In return, he dedicated his life to helping strangers realize their potential while jealously guarding against what he considered political despotism and economic predestination.

Shortly after Christopher Ludwick died in 1801, his friend, Philadelphia physician Benjamin Rush, wrote the baker's first biography. Rush opened his short treatise lamenting how history had once been limited to studying "men who occupied the first ranks of society." But now, and "Happily for the world," he continued, scholars had expanded their investigative scope to include "successful talents and virtue . . . [in] those classes of people who constitute the majority of mankind." Rush designed his biographical sketch partly to unveil the positive impact religious instruction had on moral character, a microstudy using Christopher Ludwick to tell a wider story. Rush also aimed to inform contemporary middling men that personal work ethic, frugality and honesty could result in private wealth, independence and happiness. Yet the physician had at least one other motive for writing his account. He hoped "to rescue from the rapid oblivion of the grave, the name of a venerable and excellent citizen."[3] Benjamin Rush's work remains the foundation to any modern exploration into Christopher Ludwick.

Heinrich and Catherine (*nee* Hiffle) Ludwick welcomed a son, Christopher, into their home on October 17, 1720, at Giessen in Hesse-Darmstadt.[4] Heinrich was a prosperous baker and Christopher likely began learning that trade when he became old enough to labor.[5] Sadly, Christopher's mother died when he was twelve, but his father still managed to send the boy to a free school when he turned fourteen.[6] This suggests Heinrich's business was profitable enough for the baker to lose much (perhaps even all) of his son's labor while possibly hiring a journeyman to replace him. At school, two overworked teachers presided over about 300 students to at least a modicum of success: Ludwick advanced his reading, writing and arithmetic under their tutelage. Histo-

3. Rush, *An Account*, 5-6, 26.

4. William Ward Condit, "Christopher Ludwick, Patriotic Gingerbread Baker," *Pennsylvania Magazine of History and Biography* 81, no. 4 (1957): 365-90.

5. Rush, *An Account*, 6; "Christopher Ludwig, Baker-General of the Army of the United States during the Revolutionary War," *Pennsylvania Magazine of History and Biography* 16, no. 2 (1892): 343-48.

6. Condit, "Christopher Ludwick," 366.

rian William Ward Condit suggested that Ludwick's chaotic scholastic experience likely contributed to his future support for educating poor children.[7] Scholars should equally consider that Ludwick recognized the value of his education and appreciated the effort put forth by his grossly outnumbered teachers; this might equally have been the impetus behind his later investment in educating the disadvantaged.

When Austria joined Russia in its contest against the Ottoman Empire in 1737, Ludwick joined the Austrian Army as a baker. The war proved disastrous for that Germanic state as the 1739 Peace of Belgrade bears out; Austria ceded Belgrade, Serbia, Wallachia and even parts of Bosnia to the Ottomans.[8] This demoralizing agreement prompted Austrian forces to withdraw from the Balkans during the harsh winter of 1739-1740, and Ludwick was among a contingent of soldiers forced to traverse some 350 miles to Vienna.[9] Of the one-hundred men who began this impelled march, only twenty-five lived to see their destination, a skeletal Ludwick among them.[10] According to Benjamin Rush, the men had to walk through "a dreary country, and in extremely cold weather."[11] Sick, starved and virtually stark naked, Ludwick happened upon some Catholic peasants who selflessly offered the foreigner resuscitative victuals and shelter. He never forgot this act of mercy; in fact, it transformed him.[12]

In 1740, Ludwick took on garrison duties in Vienna, where he witnessed the public execution of the Austrian Army's commissary general on charges of fraud and theft; this act of retribution haunted Ludwick for the remainder of his days, perhaps even solidifying honesty as one of his fundamental characteristics.[13] He next found himself stationed in Prague among a force about three thousand strong.[14] When the War of Austrian Succession broke out in 1740, France surrounded Prague and settled in for a ruthless seventeen-week siege. When Austrian forces finally surrendered, Ludwick became a prisoner of war. He quickly enlisted in the Prussian Army, however, and served faithfully until 1742. From a Baltic port sometime later that same year, Ludwick traveled west, washing ashore in London.[15]

7. Ibid.
8. Condit, "Christopher Ludwick," 366-67.
9. Ibid., 367.
10. Rush, *An Account,* 7.
11. Ibid., 27; Condit, "Christopher Ludwick," 367.
12. Rush, *An Account,* 7.
13. Ibid.; 7; Condit, "Christopher Ludwick," 367.
14. Condit, "Christopher Ludwick," 367.
15. Ibid.

Historian William Ward Condit contrasted the relative political freedom of metropolitan London "to the continental despotisms under which [Ludwick] had lived." The Hessian baker, Condit remarked, must certainly have noticed the general absence of the state in ordinary life as opposed to its oppressive ubiquity back home.[16] By early 1743, Ludwick had enlisted in the Royal Navy as a baker on the *Duke of Cumberland.* He served for nearly three years, traveling through China, India and the East Indies. In Canton (Guangzhou, China), Ludwick purchased a bowl with a silver rim and had his name engraved on it. This bowl became something his compatriots would later associate with the intrepid sailor.[17] He returned to his father's home in 1745 only to discover the old patriarch had passed away, leaving his estate to his son. With a respectable inheritance at his disposal, he next made a series of rare poor decisions; he returned to London and, according to Rush, spent several months "enjoying the pleasures of that great city."[18] Once again penniless, he joined the British merchant navy, serving from 1745 to 1753. During his tenure, he visited Ireland, Holland, the West Indies and even continental North America while gaining a command of the English language along the way. By 1753, he had landed in Philadelphia, lugging along sixty English-manufactured suits which he promptly sold at a three-hundred percent profit.[19] Recognizing a paucity of pastry shops and bakeries in that city, he returned to London, intent on studying the craft of baking. He planned to return and settle in German-heavy Pennsylvania as a master artisan.[20]

In 1755, Ludwick stepped back into Philadelphia with a baker's arsenal—from gingerbread molds to pans—all manufactured in England. These articles, as noted by William Condit, represented "basic equipment unobtainable in . . . Pennsylvania."[21] Not long after arriving, Christopher Ludwick married widow Catharine England. Specializing in confectionary and ornate gingerbread, the artisan opened a high-end bakery in Letitia Court and immediately set about building an

16. Ibid., 368.
17. Rush, *An Account*, 16.
18. Ibid., 8.
19. Condit, "Christopher Ludwick," 369.
20. Ibid.
21. Ibid., 365. Both Benjamin Rush and William Ward Condit (the latter probably following Rush's lead) record 1754 as the year Ludwick arrived and took up permanent residence in Philadelphia. Ludwick's memorial tablet at his grave, however, clearly states his arrival as 1755. I have followed the date on the grave marker, since Ludwick would have overseen the final words he had to offer to both the living and the unborn.

honest independence.[22] Financially secure by 1764, he helped found the German Society of Philadelphia, an organization dedicated to aiding impoverished Germans and educating their children.[23] Ludwick had moved from military man to roaming adventurer to skilled craftsman to community leader within a compressed period of time, a remarkable trajectory for anyone.

Christopher Ludwick's work ethic and conviviality, over time, brought him impressive wealth, as he acquired nine houses throughout Philadelphia, a farm in nearby Germantown, 123 ½ acres in Lancaster County and a small fortune in specie.[24] He came armed with his craft's most advanced technology and, for nearly twenty years, built a reputation as an industrious, amiable and community-friendly artisan. Ludwick had seen the world—as a student, as a soldier, as a sailor—and had absorbed both the horrors of war and pleasures of living. He settled half a world away from his birthplace, his health, wealth and happiness intact. Imperial politics, however, were on the verge of reshaping the anglosphere, as a profound constitutional crisis threatened to tear the British empire asunder.

When news of the Coercive Acts reached Philadelphia in May 1774, Ludwick found himself elected to that city's Committee of Correspondence, possibly because of his leadership in the German community and fluency in English. At one meeting, local leader Thomas Mifflin urged settlers to contribute to a fund for purchasing arms to defend the city. Ludwick volunteered, "Mr. President, I am but a poor gingerbread baker, but put my name down for two hundred pounds."[25] This act both endeared Ludwick to the broader political community and revealed his own sense of outrage at Parliament's perceived tyrannical measures. On June 18 Philadelphians once again held "a very large and respectable Meeting of the Freeholders and Freeman," chaired by Thomas Willing and John Dickinson. This gathering drafted local resistance resolutions condemning the Boston Port Act as "unconstitutional [and] oppressive" to Bostonians and "dangerous to the liberties of the British Colonies." The resolutions next declared "our brethren at Boston as suffering in the common cause of America" before calling for a continental congress to speak for British North America and reestablish "peace and harmony" between the colonies and the metropole. Those in attendance elected forty-four individuals to a committee to take up subscriptions for Boston. Among those burdened with this

22. Rush, *An Account*, 9.

24. Rush, *An Account*, 10; Condit, "Christopher Ludwick," 370.

25. Rush, *An Account*, 10-11.

solemn business were Dickinson, Charles Thomson, Thomas Mifflin, Robert Morris and Christopher Ludwick. These were men, according to the resolutions, of "approved integrity, abilities, and sincere affection for the interest of this immense Empire." They also noted that constituents looked to these individuals for guidance during this moment of great public unrest and calamity.[26]

When the First Continental Congress convened on September 5, 1774, it designed to restore liberty and moral purity to colonial America. In October, it issued the Articles of Association, a code of conduct that asked Whigs to commit to material and social sacrifice. More specifically, the Association asked Americans to refrain from purchasing British and Irish goods, warned merchants and vendors against price gouging and asked butchers to stop slaughtering sheep so as to bolster domestic textile production. Congress also asked Americans to abstain from alleged frivolous and corruptive practices such as horse racing, cockfighting, gambling, theatergoing and wastefully extravagant funereal practices. In order to enforce these resolutions, Congress directed each town and county to elect a Committee of Inspection and Observation, vigilance squads tasked with patrolling their respective zones of austerity. Congress empowered these committees to condemn all those unwilling to commit to self-denial as "enemies of American liberty" in local gazettes.[27] Philadelphians elected Christopher Ludwick to their committee on January 23, 1775.[28]

Philadelphians embraced the Articles of Association as a means to preserve "our Just Rights and Liberties." They equally sought to inspire frugality and industry among freeman so as to limit wasteful consumption and mitigate colonial America's industrial dependence on England. John Dickinson and Thomas Mifflin again served alongside Ludwick on this committee.[29] In March, Ludwick attended a meeting at Car-

26. Peter Force, ed., *American Archives: Consisting of a Collection of Authentic Records, State Papers, Debates, And Letters And Other Notices of Publick Affairs, the Whole Forming a Documentary History of the Origins and Progress of the North American Colonies; of the Causes and Accomplishments of the American Revolution; and of the Constitution of Government for the United States, to the Final Ratification Thereof: Fourth Series*, 6 vols. (Washington, DC, 1837-1853), 1:426-27.

27. For the text of the Articles of Association, see Worthington Chauncy Ford, et al., eds., *Journals of the Continental Congress*, 34 vols. (Washington, DC: Government Printing Office, 1904-37), 1:75-80; For a contemporary treatment, see Shawn David McGhee, *No Longer Subjects of the British King: The Political Transformation of Royal Subjects to Republican Citizens, 1774-1776* (Yardley, PA: Westholme, 2024).

28. "City and County of Philadelphia Resolutions, January 23, 1775," in Force, *American Archives*, 1:1169.

29. "Proceedings of the Convention for the Province of Pennsylvania, Held at Philadelphia, January 23, 1775," in ibid, 1:1169-71.

penters' Hall to discuss a plan to establish "an American Manufactory of Woollens, Linens, and Cottons." His fellow attendees elected him as one of the managers for this ambitious project.[30] For two years, this successful endeavor provided cloth for the Continental Army, production ceasing only when a British army occupied Philadelphia on September 17, 1777.[31]

On June 3, 1776, Congress resolved that "a flying camp be immediately established in the middle colonies," drawing 10,000 men collectively from Pennsylvania, Maryland and Delaware (the majority coming from the former).[32] Though Congress never realized this quota, Ludwick volunteered for one of these mobile outfits, refusing both pay and rations for his service. According to Benjamin Rush, the fifty-five-year-old Ludwick looked to inspire his fellow militiamen with a love of liberty, lecturing them on "the degrading nature of slavery" and recounting how his homeland suffered from "poverty and misery" caused by "the rapacious hands of arbitrary kings and princes." In one instance, Ludwick learned that some militiamen, deeply dissatisfied with their rations, planned on deserting. The artisan approached them and, dramatically falling to his knees, pleaded "Brother soldiers . . . When we hear the cry of fire in Philadelphia, we fly there with our buckets to keep it from our houses." He then likened invading British forces to a similar crisis, warning that all must pitch in or "the great fire of the British army" will consume American liberty and property.[33] Ludwick's plea did the trick and, according to Rush's account, the would-be deserters remained in service.[34] Incredibly, Ludwick not only dissuaded colonists from deserting American forces; he also engaged in psychological warfare to recruit Hessian auxiliaries to join them.

On August 9, 1776, Congress created a committee to encourage "Hessians and other foreigners, employed by the King of Great Britain," to quit the fight.[35] On August 18, Washington called Ludwick to his Manhattan headquarters to discuss the latter infiltrating a Hessian camp on Staten Island. Shortly afterward, Ludwick, presenting as an American deserter, made his way to enemy lines. As Joseph Reed explained to William Livingston, Christopher Ludwick "puts his Life

30. "Philadelphia, March 16, 1775," in ibid, 2:140.

31. Condit, "Christopher Ludwick," 373.

32. Ford, et al., *Journals Congress*, 4:412-13; See also Francis E. Devine, "The Pennsylvania Flying Camp, July-November 1776," *Pennsylvania History: A Journal of Mid-Atlantic Studies* 46, no. 1 (1979): 59-78.

33. Rush, *An Account*, 11-12.

34. Condit, "Christopher Ludwick," 374.

35. August 9, 1776, Ford, et al., *Journals of Congress*, 5:640.

in his Hand on this Occasion in order to serve the Interests of America" and any discovery of his mission "must prove fatal" to him.[36] The baker failed to convert any Hessians on this particular mission, Washington later lamented to President John Hancock; Ludwick had, however, risked capture and potential execution in support of the so-called glorious cause.[37] When confronted with Hessian prisoners, Ludwick hoped to charm them with the liberty and bounty of the land. "Let us," he exclaimed, "take them to Philadelphia, and there show them our fine German churches. Let them see how our tradesmen eat good beef [and] drink out of silver cups every day." He next recommended that Continental forces "send them back to their countrymen, and they will all soon run away . . . and be as good whigs as any of us."[38] Washington and Hancock agreed, the latter going so far as to recommend that Ludwick "negotiate an exchange of the Hessian prisoners at Elizabethtown."[39] Ludwick was, of course, living proof of a white equality of opportunity in colonial Pennsylvania.

On May 3, 1777, Congress appointed Ludwick "superintendent of bakers . . . in the grand army of the United States," granting him, through Washington's approbation, authority to hire journeymen bakers and regulate their pay. That body also expected Ludwick to alleviate waste and fraud and regularly report back to delegates.[40] In fact, Ludwick had already tried his hand at producing bread for militiamen in 1776. Jonathan Bayard Smith, an officer in a Philadelphia flying camp, divulged to Congressman John Adams that his men complained incessantly about the poor quality of bread until Ludwick provided his services. Bayard favorably described Ludwick as "disinterested, except for the public good" and disserted that if "he had any ambition I believe it is to be found, and known to be, in serving the public." He closed by claiming everyone in Philadelphia as well as his present military camp testified to Ludwick's abilities and virtue, adding "Indeed the alterations

36. Joseph Reed to William Livingston, August 19, 1776, in Carl Prince, eds et al., *The Papers of William Livingston*, 5 vols. (Trenton and New Brunswick, NJ: New Jersey Historical Commission and Rutgers University Press, 1979-1988), 1:119.

37. George Washington to John Hancock, August 29, 1776 in Philander P. Chase, et al., eds., *The Papers of George Washington: Revolutionary War Series*, 30 vols. (Charlottesville, VA: University of Virginia Press, 1985-2022), 6:74-75.

38. Rush, *An Account*, 12.

39. Washington to the Board of War, November 16, 1776; Hancock to Washington, November 16, 1776, in Chase, et al., *Papers of Washington: Revolutionary War Series*, 7:161-62, 169.

40. Ford, *Journals of Congress*, 7:323-24.

here in the article of bread is truly great."[41] John Hancock, already impressed with Ludwick's veracity, abilities and character, equally expressed to Washington in 1777 that he had "no Doubt [Ludwick] will do to the entire Satisfaction of the Troops, and in such a Manner as to save considerable Sums to the Public."[42] Ludwick's probity may have been at least partly inspired by his witnessing the public execution of the unscrupulous Austrian commissary general in 1740.

Washington began to coordinate troop movements around Ludwick's whereabouts to keep his army tethered to a reliable food source whenever possible, asking the baker in chief to disclose where "you have erected public ovens that I may know where to apply for Bread when wanted." The general also commanded Ludwick to transport bread by wagon, empowering him to press vehicles into service when necessary. In late 1777, Washington summoned Ludwick to Philadelphia, instructing the German to leave the Morristown encampment under the supervision of capable hands. The general recognized that bread, along with Ludwick's unique talents, had become "an indispensable necessity."[43] Ludwick, in turn, kept the commander in chief abreast of the condition, locations and productive capacity of his ovens. In one exchange, Ludwick explained to the general that no flour at any encampment should be wasted, but instead "sent to the nearest Magazine as it will . . . make good Bread."[44] At Valley Forge, Ludwick constructed and supervised multiple bake houses throughout the military community, and as noted by William Ward Condit, resorted to "his best powers of cajolery" to pressure neighboring German families into supplying flour for the Continental Army.[45] Benjamin Rush recounted how Ludwick frequently dined at General Washington's Valley Forge Headquarters, mainly discussing the mechanics and logistics of baking for so many for such a prolonged period. Ludwick also became known for his nearly ritualistic toast at dinners, "Health and long life to Christopher Ludwick and his wife," which he followed by drinking from his Chinese bowl.[46]

41. Jonathan Bayard Smith to John Adams, August 28, 1776, in Robert J. Taylor, et al., eds., *The Papers of John Adams*, 20 vols. (Cambridge, MA: Harvard University Press, 1977-2020), 4:500.

42. Hancock to Washington, May 3, 1777, in Chase, et al., *Papers of Washington: Revolutionary War Series*, 9:335-36.

43. Washington to Christopher Ludwick, September 5, 1777, in ibid., 11:153.

44. Ludwick to Washington, January, 1780, in ibid., 24:339-40.

45. Condit, "Christopher Ludwick," 381.

46. Rush, *An Account*, 16.

The war years ravaged Ludwick's health and wealth. In a failed resignation attempt in 1781, he noted to Congress how he had "served his country honestly" during the war, "had his property ruined by the enemy," spent his private fortune supporting independence and saved the public "great sums of money." He closed by revealing his sincere desire to retire in his sixty-first year "with the loss of his right eye and a ruined constitution."[47] Congress quietly ignored his plea and, instead, proclaimed Ludwick had acted "with great industry and integrity in the character of principal superintendent of bakers" and was "hereby continued in that employment." That body also compensated him one-thousand dollars "in new emissions" for past services. Ludwick, ever the good public servant, stayed at his post.[48] He was with Washington's army at Yorktown and, following that Franco-American victory, provided his talents once again. Washington approached the baker and requested he produce six thousand pounds of bread for the defeated British forces. "Let it be good, old gentleman," he expressed to Ludwick, "and let there be enough of it, if I should want myself."[49] Ludwick continued his duties after the crescendo of the war, mostly working out of West Point alongside skilled French bakers.[50]

Christopher Ludwick suffered staggering private loss supporting independence. He had sold many of his properties to feed the American army, British forces had pillaged others while others still had fallen into a state of disrepair in his absence. Ludwick committed to a Spartan lifestyle for some time after the war, partly to support some in his kin network, partly to rebuild his private fortune. He began selling off what remained of his properties and investing the proceeds into interest-bearing bonds, a decision that steadily began placing the old soldier back on secure financial terrain.[51] He also petitioned Congress for reimbursement based on his "Zeal for the Cause of America," and reminded that assembly how his "Skill and Knowledge in the Baking Business" and personal honesty had "saved vast Sums" of public money while injuring "his own private Property, as well as his Constitution."[52]

47. *The Papers of the Continental Congress*, as quoted in Condit, "Christopher Ludwick," 384.
48. Ford, et al, *Journals of Congress*, 19:159.
49. Rush, *An Account*, 15.
50. Condit, "Christopher Ludwick," 385.
51. Rush, *An Account*, 17-18.
52. Christopher Ludwick, as quoted in Condit, "Christopher Ludwick,"386.

And he came armed with more than just personal grievance for the evidentiary record.

Ludwick had reached out to some major figures who attested to his character as well as his contributions and sacrifices during the war. Arthur St. Clair, William Irvine and Anthony Wayne praised his services and recognized both his public support for the war and his private loss in its pursuit. Timothy Pickering argued Ludwick's "disinterested Zeal, his indefatigable industry in the duties of his department, his unsullied integrity, the essential Services he rendered to the Army, and the generous Sacrifices he has made in the Course of the late Revolution" entitled him to some form of relief. Thomas Mifflin described the baker as "one of our first and most determined Whigs," noting his "disinterested Services in the Army and the great Sacrifice" of property he made to support the American Revolution.[53] A calculating Ludwick also reached out to Washington.

Ludwick wrote to the retired commander in chief on March 29, 1785. He warmly addressed Washington as "Your Excellency" and reminded the general of their friendship during the war before revealing he had been reduced to asking Congress for compensation for loss of property and wealth suffered while serving the Continental Army. Ludwick entreated the general to provide a written statement attesting to the baker's disinterestedness, intrinsic value to the public and crippling private loss; Ludwick hoped Washington would not "refuse me this favor."[54] The Virginian did not disappoint. He composed the following lines praising Ludwick:

> I have known Mr Christr Ludwick from an early period of the War; and have every reason to believe, as well from observation as information, that he has been a true and faithful Friend, and Servant to the public. That he has detected and exposed many impositions which were attempted to be practiced by others in the department over which he presided. That he has been the cause of much saving in many respects. And that his deportment in public life has afforded unquestionable proofs of his integrity and worth.[55]

Congress approved the modest sum of $200 for Ludwick's dedication to American liberty.[56]

53. Ibid., 386-87.
54. Ludwick to Washington, March 29, 1785, in W.W. Abbot, ed., *The Papers of George Washington: Confederation Series,* 6 vols. (Charlottesville, VA: University Press of Virginia, 1992-1997), 2:471-72.
55. Rush, *An Account*, 18-19.
56. Condit, "Christopher Ludwick," 388.

Ludwick slowly rebuilt his tattered fortune over the next decade, remaining a community leader in Philadelphia and "the Governor of Letitia Court," as his neighbors affectionately addressed him.[57] Sadly, his wife Catharine died in 1796, Benjamin Rush describing her as the baker's "faithful companion" and supporter in all of his "patriotic schemes." Afterward, the aging veteran moved into the home of Frederick Fraley, a former apprentice of his. When yellow fever swept through Philadelphia in 1797, Ludwick and Fraley selflessly remained in that city and, according to Rush, "assist[ed] in making bread for distribution among the poor, in that period of awful distress."[58] This episode may reflect Ludwick repaying his earlier Vienna experience in 1740, this time acting as provider rather than recipient of mercy. Ludwick married Sophia Binder in 1798, Binder herself suggesting they wed so the extravert Ludwick would not spend his final days alone.[59] During one of those final days, a salesman asked Ludwick to purchase a biography of George Washington. The usually generous Ludwick replied, "No, I will not, I am travelling fast to meet him, I will then hear all about it from his own mouth." On Wednesday, June 17, 1801, Christopher Ludwick set off to meet Washington.[60] *The National Intelligencer and Washington Advertiser* simply announced, "Died . . . Christopher Ludwick, baker general in the revolutionary army."[61] The following month, Benjamin Rush began publishing portions of his short biography in the *New Hampshire Gazette*.[62] Sometime before Ludwick's death, however, the old baker had attended to his will and memorial tablet for his grave.

Ludwick revealed his character, philosophy and sapience in his will and gravestone. In the former, he left equal and substantial sums to the German Reformed Church, German Society, Lutheran Church and University of Pennsylvania to educate impoverished children. He bequeathed Pennsylvania Hospital £100 for poor patients and left another

57. Rush, *An Account*, 9.

58. Ibid., 19; Not unlike the discrepancy between Ludwick's year of arrival, there is a minor dispute over when his wife passed away. Rush recorded the year as 1795, Ludwick's grave tablet claims the year as 1796. For the same reasons I listed in n21, this work follows the tomb's memorial.

59. John F. Watson, *Annals of Philadelphia and Pennsylvania, in the olden Time, Being a Collection of memoirs, Anecdote, and incidents of the City and Its Inhabitants, and the Earliest Settlements of the Inland Part of Pennsylvania, from the Days of the Founders . . .*, 2 vols. (Philadelphia, PA: J.B. Lippincott and Company, 1870), 2:56.

60. Rush, *An Account*, 20.

61. *The National Intelligencer and Washington Advertiser* (Washington, DC), June 22, 1801.

62. *New Hampshire Gazette*, July 28, 1901.

£200 to purchase firewood for Philadelphia's destitute. Ludwick recognized the communal value of education and directed his executors to invest his more than £3,000 of specie into public or private interest-bearing securities or dependable rental properties. They were to next apply the annual interest, his will decreed, to defray the cost of educating the poor, "without any exception to country, extraction [ethnic origin] or religious principles of their friends or parents." If Philadelphia incorporated a public school, Ludwick asked that his estate be vested into it. If, within five years, no school materialized, he demanded his estate be divided among the German Lutheran, German Reformed, English Episcopal, First and Second Presbyterian, Roman Catholic and African churches of Philadelphia as well as the University of Pennsylvania, "exclusively [for] educating poor children."[63] The Catholic investment was directly related to the generosity some poor Catholics offered an emaciated Ludwick in Vienna some sixty years earlier.[64] The generosity toward children of African descent expresses a remarkable liberality on the German's part, another example of his crusade against all forms of oppression. In fact, The Christopher Ludwick Foundation still offers educational grants and support today. For more than two centuries (in one form or another), Ludwick's fortune has been fighting economic oppression.[65] His grave tablet, the final thoughts Ludwick offered both living and unborn, is worth reprinting *in toto.*

CHRISTOPHER LUDWICK
In Memory of
CHRISTOHPER LUDWICK
AND HIS WIFE,
CATHARINE,
She died at Germantown the 21st September, 1796,
Aged eighty years and five months ;
He died at Philadelphia the 17th June, 1801,
Aged eighty years and nine months.

—

He was born at Giessen in Hesse D'Armstadt in Germany,
And learndt the Bakers trade and business ;
In his early life he was a Soldier and a Sailor, and visited the
East and West Indies ;
In the year 1755, he came to and settled at Philadelphia,

63. Rush, *An Account,* 24-26.
64. Ibid., 26.
65. For more information on the Christopher Ludwick Foundation, see https://ludwick-foundation.org/.

And by his industry and his trade and business,
Acquired a handsome competency, part of which he devoted
To the service of his adopted country in the contest
For the INDEPENDENCE OF AMERICA ;
Was appointed Baker General to the Army,
And for his faithful services received a written testimony
From the Commander in Chief
GENERAL WASHINGTON.
On every occasion his zeal for the relief of the oppressed
Was manifest; and by his last will
He bequeathed the greater part of his estate for the
Education of the children of the poor of all denominations,
gratis.
He lived and died
Respected for his integrity and public spirit,
By all who knew him.
Reader, such was Ludwick.
Art thou poor, Venerate his character.
Art thou rich, Imitate his example.[66]

Christopher Ludwick's grave rests in Germantown, Pennsylvania, at Saint Michael's Lutheran Churchyard, among hundreds of ancient tombs. What stands out today is his stone's superior craftsmanship. Most of the other markers in the graveyard are either cracked, missing, have fallen over or are weather-worn and virtually devoid of the inscriptions they once bore. Ludwick's memorial tablet is, by contrast, intact, perfectly legible and unique; it is the only monument in the cemetery elevated and resting on four stone pillars. It is also the only marker to offer visitors a brief account of the unique odyssey and moral principles once attended to by the bones entombed in the ground below. And Ludwick made certain to carve in stone his support for the glorious cause and "zeal for the relief of the oppressed."

Benjamin Rush wrote *An Account of the Life and Character of Christopher Ludwick* shortly after that gentlemen's passing. He sent a copy to Abigail Adams and she responded to the physician in a warm but deeply pessimistic fashion. Adams claimed Rush's account would be "read with pleasure by all Lovers of Virtue honor and Patriotism," happily recognizing the biography as "a model for youth." Yet she warned that few characters with those qualities remained in the current envi-

66. Christopher Ludwick's grave memorial at Saint Michael's Lutheran Churchyard, 6671 Germantown Avenue, Germantown, Pennsylvania.

ronment of "prosperity Luxery and dissipation." Adams noticed an unsettling new approach to religion, morals and politics and worried the republic would only last "until heaven in wrath punishes us" for wasting the fruits of "this fair land."[67] She composed this response, no doubt, in the aftermath of her husband's electoral defeat to Thomas Jefferson during the bitter presidential election of 1800.[68]

The principles of the American Revolution, at least on the surface, announced a universally appealing message to the global community: Colonists refused to let a perceived reckless and unaccountable body of elites threaten life, liberty and property. At a moment when many western Europeans gloried in their enlightened place in the world and cast Russia and Asia as oppressors of mankind, by late 1774 many British North Americans suddenly began to feel as if the British system had become just as corrupt as the most despotic foreign court. Christopher Ludwick had left one of those foreign courts after fighting for the pride and pomp of princes. He found independence and purpose in Philadelphia and, with his hard-earned wealth, contributed to helping others in need break the socio-economic cycle of poverty leading to failure. He was an opponent of all forms of oppression, advocate of private pursuits of happiness and champion of the downtrodden. When Americans Whigs joined against king and Parliament during the Coercive Acts Crisis, Ludwick stood with the resistance. After all, he had poured his life into Philadelphia; that city repaid him with acceptance, opportunity and security. And when it became clear the empire's troubles could no longer be resolved with words, the fiery craftsman once again resorted to war. A German soldier transformed into an American rebel, supportive of the common cause and all it had afforded him and all he felt it had yet to offer future generations of citizens.

67. Abigail Adams to Benjamin Rush, September 21, 1801, in eds., Lyman H. Butterfield, et al., *The Adams Papers: Family Correspondence*, 15 vols. (Cambridge, MA: Harvard University Press, 1963-2021), 15:127-28.
68. See John Ferling, *Adams vs. Jefferson: The Tumultuous Election of 1800* (New York, NY: Oxford University Press, 2004).

Liberty and Property: Cash Africa's American Revolution

TIM ABBOTT

The 1774 colonial census for Litchfield, Connecticut lists 2,554 people living in this western New England town. Of these, just forty-five are people of color, including those of African origin described as "negroes" and indigenous Americans counted as "Indians." Among fifteen "negro" males, eight are under twenty years old and seven are above.[1] During the Revolutionary War, four African American men from Litchfield enlisted in the Continental Army, and one of them—Cash Africa—served during all eight years of the conflict.

The name "Cash" appears just twice among Connecticut's known African American soldiers of the Revolution.[2] Possibly it derives from "Quash," a traditional name of West African origin that denotes a male child born on a Sunday.[3] There were several people with the surname "Africa" living in Litchfield and surrounding communities in the 1770s, but given how few people of color were counted in Litchfield in the 1774 census, it is highly unlikely that more than one of them would be named Cash Africa. The records of his name from this time period al-

1. *Public Records of the Colony of Connecticut*, Volume 14, ed. Charles J. Hoadly (Hartford: Brown & Parsons, 1887), 490.
2. David O. White, *Connecticut's Black Soldiers 1775-1783* (Chester, CT: Pequot Press, 1973).
3. John C. Inscoe, "Carolina Slave Names: An Index to Acculturation," *The Journal of Southern History* vol. 49 no. 4 (November 1983), 527-554.
4. The Litchfield County Court Minorities Collection at the Connecticut State Archives (RG003_LLC_Minorities) is an artificial collection consisting of photocopies of cases involving African Americans and Native Americans from the *Files* and *Papers by Subject* series of Litchfield County Court records. All originals have been retired and second copies have been inserted in the places where the originals were once located. The case in question, Africa v. Marsh (September 7, 1777) is located in Box 1 Folder 9 of the collection (hereafter Africa v. Marsh).

most assuredly refer to the same individual, including a court case from 1777[4] that notably took place while Cash Africa was in the army, but at a time when he was recorded as "absent."[5]

Although his origins remain obscure, it is possible to reconstruct a remarkable chronology of Cash Africa's adult life and experiences between 1774 and 1796 using surviving muster rolls, court records, newspaper advertisements, diary entries, letters, marriage records and labor contracts. Although some of these documents express his thoughts and motivations indirectly, none are his own words, nor are written in his own hand.

"Liberty and Property" was the watchword of the era, even emblazoned across a huge scarlet flag atop a seventy-eight foot liberty pole in a nearby Litchfield County town.[6] The story of Cash Africa that emerges from the historic record is one where property is central: its pursuit, defense, and the right to profit from one's own labor. It is also as story of racial discrimination that is sometimes overcome but never vanquished.

Cash Africa enlisted for the first time in May 1775, and his last muster took place in May 1783. That eight-year span is itself remarkable. It was no small thing for a Black man from Connecticut to have remained a soldier from the outset of the war until its conclusion, especially in the beginning when both Gen. George Washington and Congress actively discouraged African Americans from joining the Continental Army. There is also strong evidence that Cash Africa was compelled to enlist not just once, but three times as an enslaved person, and as one who had been "wrongly" held in bondage.

Within weeks of the outbreak of hostilities, Maj. David Welsh of Litchfield raised a company for service in Col. David Wooster's 1st Connecticut Regiment. Cash Africa joined this company. Although the enlistment roll is missing, the commission date of its officers was May 1, 1775 and recruiting from Major Welsh's Company would have taken place during that Spring. Colonel Wooster's regiment was soon dispatched for service at Harlem, New York, before being assigned to the Northern Department at the end of September 1775. Pvt. Cash Africa's name appears on a subsequent return with a discharge date of

5. Muster Roll of Captn. Catlin's Compy., Col. P. Bradleys Regt. for July, Incl. (dated August 11, 1777) and Muster Roll of Captn. Catlin's Compy., Col. P. Bradleys Regt. for August 1777 Incl. (dated September 12, 1777), NARA M246. US Revolutionary War Muster Rolls 1775-1783, Fold3.com, US Revolutionary War, https://www.fold3.com/collection/us-revolutionary-war-us), (hereafter NARA M246 US Revolutionary War Muster Rolls 1775-1783).

6. *The Connecticut Courant and Hartford Weekly Intelligencer*, July 12, 1774.

November 23, 1775, making him one of the very last in his company to be released from service.[7] He was likely present during the siege and capture of St. John's and the taking of Montréal.

He was soon back with the Northern Army, though not in a Connecticut regiment. In late November, 1775, Capt. Eleazer Curtis of East Kent (now Warren) Connecticut returned from service in the North with a new commission from Maj. Gen. Philip Schuyler authorizing him to raise an independent company in his home state for Continental service.[8] In mid-February 1776, Captain Curtis's company was incorporated into Col. Goose van Schaick's unnumbered Continental Regiment, raised on New York's establishment for service in the Northern Department. A careful review of two surviving rosters and lists of men from Captain Curtis's company shows that fifteen of them were from Litchfield, including Cash Africa.[9] Four of Colonel Van Schaick's companies, including Captain Curtis's, were send into Canada to help bolster the American forces under Brig. Gen. John Sullivan but soon joined them in retreat.[10] They were later stationed at Fort George, and Cash Africa finished his service under Colonel Van Schaick at Saratoga on December 7, 1776.

Within a month he enlisted once again, this time as one of ninety-two men credited to Litchfield as its quota for Continental Service in the coming year.[11] Two companies of Col. Philip Burr Bradley's 5th Connecticut Regiment recruited heavily in Litchfield. Cash Africa joined Capt. Eli Catlin's Company on January 16, 1777, enlisting for

7. *Record of Connecticut Men in the Military and Naval Service during the War of the Revolution, 1775-1783*, ed. Henry P. Johnston (Hartford: under the authority of the Adjutant-General of Connecticut, 1889), 40.

8. Philip Schuyler to Captain Eleazer Curtis November 16, 1775, Ticonderoga, New York, Northern Illinois University Digital Library, Document ID S4-V3-P01-sp32-D0015, https://digital.lib.niu.edu/islandora/object/niu-amarch%3A103360.

9. A list of names who have not yet received a bounty for service in the Continental Army from Captain Moses Martin & Lieut. Ebenezer Hills. Dated Fort George, Sept. 9 & 11th, 1776. On the back, dated Saratoga, Nov. 21, 1776 is a receipt from Moses Martin, Capt. and Ebenezer Hills, Lieut., that they received a bounty of 31 pounds four shillings from Major Ebenezer Curtis. Included in the list of names is Cash Africa. See also NARA M 246, A Muster Roll of the Late Captn Eleazer Curtis's Now Captn Moses Martin's Company in Colo. Goose Van Schaick's Battalion of the Forces Rais'd in the State of New York & Now in the Service of the United States of America Dated in Barracks at Saratoga December 17th 1776, Litchfield Historical Society, Litchfield, Connecticut.

10. Philip J. Schuyler to George Washington, June 15, 1776, in *George Washington Papers*, Library of Congress, Manuscript Division, MSS 44693: Reel 036, series: Series 4, General Correspondence, 1697-1799.

11. *Lists and Returns of Connecticut Men in the Revolution 1775-1783*, Collections of the Connecticut Historical Society, Vol. XII (Hartford: published by the Society, 1909), 53.

the duration of the war.[12] The first return that survives from Captain Catlin's company was filed on August 11, 1777 and lists Cash Africa "on command." The next month's return (dated September 11, 1777) merely lists him as "absent." He was back with his company by October 25, which at this time was with General Washington's main army in Pennsylvania.

During the time that he was absent, it appears that Cash Africa was in Litchfield raising charges in court against an elderly widow named Deborah Marsh. The charge was criminal trespass against his person and falsely holding him in slavery since September 1774. It is not clear how Cash Africa came to be enslaved by the widow Marsh, but the period during which he claimed to have been held against his will includes his consecutive enlistments in the regiments of Colonel Wooster in 1775, Colonel Van Schaick in 1776 and Colonel Bradley in 1777. There were other slave soldiers in the Continental Army at this time, enrolled by their enslavers, and it appears that Cash Africa was among them.

The record of the case consists of a single page that describes how the widow Marsh was summoned to appear in court on the fourth Tuesday in September, 1777 to answer to Cash Africa's claim of unlawful enslavement:

> That the Def[endan]t at Litchfield aforesaid on the 15th Day of September 1774 did an Assault make upon the Pl[aintif]f and did then & there with force & Arms unlawfully seise upon the person of the Pl[aintif]f and with the same force imprison the Pl[aintif]f and hold him to hard labour from that time to this writ, all which doings of the Def[endan]t made against the law & to the Damage of the Pl[aintiff] the sum of one hundred pounds lawful money to recover which with just cause the Pl[aintif]f brings this writ hereof[13]

Deborah Marsh was the widow of Col. Ebenezer Marsh of Litchfield who died in 1773. Several members of the Marsh family were noted for their loyalism, including Deborah's son, Capt. Solomon Marsh, who refused to turn out with his company for the Danbury alarm in April, 1777 and would later be cashiered by the Connecticut General Assembly for "a general neglect of the duties of his office, arising from an unfriendliness to the grand American cause &c."[14] Perhaps

12. NARA M246, US Revolutionary War Muster Rolls 1775-1783. See also *Rolls and Lists of Connecticut Men*, 68.
13. Africa v. Marsh.
14. *Public Records of the State of Connecticut, with the Journal of the Council of Safety and an Appendix*, Vol. 1 (Hartford: Brown & Parsons, 1894), 484.

this fact influenced the court, or perhaps the case he made against the widow Marsh was just too compelling, but Cash Africa won his suit and was awarded both the financial compensation he sought and his freedom.

No longer a slave soldier but still committed to military service for the duration of the war, Cash Africa returned to the 5th Connecticut Regiment in Pennsylvania. He spent the winter at Valley Forge, where he was listed "sick in camp" on a return from February 21, 1778 and "on guard" as of April 2, 1778. He took part in the Monmouth campaign, but from August through early November 1778 he was on detached service in Waterbury, Connecticut. He overwintered at the encampment of the Connecticut Line at Reading, continuing his service as of February 1779 in the Colonel's Company of the 5th Connecticut. In February and March 1779 he was "on command" at Norwalk and spent much of the remainder of the year on detached duty.[15]

On November 26, 1779, Cash Africa received a five-day furlough. Having failed to return by January 1, 1780, he was listed as a deserter, but returned on April 1, 1780.[16] His unauthorized time away does not appear to have affected how he was treated after his return to duty. He was "sick, present" that August, received another furlough in September 1780 and ended the year on "extra service" with Colonel Bradley.

Under the reauthorization of the Continental Army in 1781, the 5th and 7th Connecticut Regiments were consolidated into a new 2nd Connecticut Regiment under Col. Heman Swift of Cornwall. Cash Africa was initially assigned to Capt. Thaddeus Weed's Company, but later that May he was chosen to join Capt. John St. John's Light Infantry company, then on command in Virginia with Maj. Gen. Marie-Joseph Paul Yves Roch Gilbert du Motier de La Fayette, Marquis de Lafayette.[17] By June 1, 1781 he reached his company, now under command of Capt. Elijah Chapman and serving in Lt. Col. Jean-Joseph Sourbader de Gimat's Battalion of Major General Lafayette's Light Division. These troops shadowed the British army in Virginia, and were present but not engaged at the Battle of Green Spring on July 6, 1781. At Yorktown, Cash Africa would have been in the thick of the fighting on October 14, 1781 when Lt. Col. Alexander Hamilton lead Lieutenant Colonel Gimat's men in the assault on Redoubt. No. 10.

15. NARA M246, US Revolutionary War Muster Rolls 1775-1783.

16. Ibid. See also *Lists and Returns*, 228.

17. NARA M246, US Revolutionary War Muster Rolls 1775-1783. See also *Record of Connecticut Men*, 352.

After returning north, Cash Africa remained in the Light Company of the 2nd Connecticut until June 13, 1782 when he transferred into Capt. Ephraim Chamberlain's Company, and subsequently continued in the same company under Capt. Samuel Comestock. Captain Comestock's Company had both White and Black soldiers, in contrast to Capt. David Humphries' segregated 2nd Company of the 4th Connecticut Regiment which had only Black soldiers serving under White officers.[18] Cash Africa was assigned to General McDougall's Guard at Newburgh during December 1782 and January, 1783. He mustered for the last time on May 26, 1783 in the Hudson Highlands and was discharged with the rest of the Connecticut Line shortly thereafter.[19]

Eight years of military service had taken Private Africa on campaigns ranging from Canada to Virginia. Now that the war had ended, he returned to Litchfield and tried to reestablish himself with paid employment. He placed an advertisement in the local paper on April 5, 1785 claiming to know all "all Kinds of Cookery, and House-Work" and seeking a position either waiting on "a single Gentleman" or with a family.[20] He later sold his warrant for bounty land on October 7, 1789 to fellow Litchfield townsman (and land speculator) Benjamin Tallmadge.[21] He also hired himself out to Tallmadge for a season of work in 1788 "in the services of forty shillings per month." Tallmadge agreed to provide boarding and lodging as well as wages but reserved the right to cancel the agreement if Africa failed to act "in a becoming manner."[22] There were several enslaved people working for Tallmadge at this time, including one under contract from another enslaver, but only Cash Africa was free to negotiate the terms of his own labor.

Before this, however, Cash Africa did something that was commonplace among white men in Connecticut but highly unusual for a man of color. He placed an advertisement in the local newspaper claiming that his wife, Margaret, had abandoned him.[23] In the prescribed language of this kind of notice, he announced that she had "eloped from my bed and board" and that he would not be responsible for any debts she might incur in his name. A woodcut depicting a woman wearing a bonnet and carrying a walking stick accompanies the advertisement. A

18. White, *Connecticut's Black Soldiers*, 32-34.
19. NARA M246, US Revolutionary War Muster Rolls 1775-1783.
20. *Litchfield Weekly Monitor*, Litchfield, Connecticut, April 12, 1785.
21. NARA US Revolutionary War Bounty Land Warrant Record Card No. 5375.
22. Agreement that Cash Africa will serve Benjamin Tallmadge, May 19, 1788, Tallmadge Collection, Litchfield Historical Society, Litchfield, Connecticut.
23. *Litchfield Weekly Monitor*, Litchfield, Connecticut, Monday, July 2, 1787.

typical illustration for notices of this sort, the figure represents a White woman. This brief announcement—effectively a divorce—is the only record of Margaret Africa's existence.

Cash Africa married a second time. Church records from Sharon, Connecticut show that on May 6, 1792, Anna Jackson married "Cash Africa, of Litchfield."[24] There was a new community along the Housatonic River in Sharon established by Black former soldiers and their families along what is now called Guinea Road, named for the part of West Africa from which some of them had come to North America. Several members of Cash Africa's old regiment were living there, but he and Anna did not join them. Perhaps there were few prospects for work, or not enough money left from the sale of his bounty warrant for Cash to purchase land. Rather than stay in Sharon, Cash and Anna Africa returned to Litchfield.

It must have been a precarious existence. We know that they had at least two children together, thanks to the prolific writings of Dr. Elihu Hubbard Smith of Litchfield, whose diaries and letters from late 1795 and early 1796 contain a number of references to Cash Africa and his family.[25] Doctor Smith was a brilliant young man, a graduate of Yale College and a member of the New York Abolition Society. He was also a paternalistic busybody, and his writings concerning Cash Africa reveal deeply prejudiced views of the character and capabilities of Black people.

By 1795, Cash Africa had left Anna and their children behind in Litchfield and sought work in New York. It is not clear where Anna Africa and her family were living in Litchfield at this time, but their circumstances became a matter of interest both to Doctor Smith and to Mrs. Susan Tracy, also of Litchfield, with whom he had a long correspondence. These White citizens of Litchfield decided that Cash Africa was not meeting his obligations as a husband and provider and decided to do something about it.

Doctor Smith wrote in his diary on November 16, 1795, "I am to speak with Mr. Sands, in New York, (The gentleman who hires Cash)—a negro man of this Place—on the subject of sending part of his pay to his wife—who is here, & in great distress."[26] He then went

24. Lawrence Van Alstyne, *Born, Married and Died in Sharon Connecticut; A Record of Births, marriages and Deaths in the Town of Sharon, Connecticut from 1721-1879* (Press of the Pawling Chronicle: 1897), 6, 73.

25. *The Diary of Elihu Hubbard Smith (1771-1798)*, ed. James E Cronin (Philadelphia: The American Philosophical Society, 1973).

26. Ibid., entry of November 15, 1795, 89.

to New York, and in a subsequent letter to Mrs. Tracy he described how he met Cash by chance in the street and confronted him about the plight of his family back in Litchfield:

> The fellow promises *well.* That, you know, he always does. I have, however, found out with whom he lives; and, if he does not fulfill his engagements, I shall apply to his master. He promised to bring me five or six dollars, before Thursday noon. If he should, I shall take the liberty to inclose them to you, & have no doubts of your applying them, to their best use. He has further engaged to do something more, for his family, at intervals, as he shall be able. I hope to effect something for the poor animals, but fear it must be, as it is now, uncertain.[27]

It is clear that Doctor Smith's support for the abolition of slavery in no way extended to racial equality, or even fellow feeling for Cash Africa and his family whom he describes as "poor animals." In a second letter to Mrs. Tracy, he provided an update that reveals as much about his own character as it does the situation of Cash Africa and his family:

> When I was at Phila. Mr. Tracy gave me a letter, for Cash, from his wife, which, in the hurry of his passage thro' New York, he forgot. This I delivered, yesterday, to Cash; & at the same time, informed him that, notwithstanding his promises, his wife had recd. nothing. He assures me, that, on the very day I last spake to him, on this matter, he purchased seven yards of baize, (I think it was,) which he put in the hands of a man, who was going to Litchfield, & who engaged to leave it, at Seymour's Shop in Litchfield. He says that what he sent was sufficient to furnish his Wife & children, with short-gowns, & the children with petticoats. Of this I am no judge. On my representing to him the insufficiency of so small a provision, & urging him to do something more for them, immediately, he has promised to bring me something for them, to-morrow—in time to send by the Post: money, or clothing. I fear that this will turn out to be one of his old tricks; & that he neither has sent, nor will send, any thing. It may be well to inquire, whether any thing has been recd. At Seymour's; &, if he does not furnish me with some aid for his family, I shall apply to his master.[28]

From this exchange it is clear that there were at least two female children living with Anna Africa and they must have been quite young. Doctor Smith did not believe that Cash had purchased baize cloth to clothe his family, and clearly considered him willfully deceptive on the

27. Ibid., Letter to Mrs. Tracy, December 15, 1795, 105.
28. Ibid., Letter to Mrs. Tracy (in continuation), January 20, 1796, 124.

matter. What Cash Africa thought of this white man's interference in his life and work can only be guessed, but it struck at his core identity as a free man, a husband and a provider. He was up against the pervasive, near universal trope of the unreliable and absent Black male, and a systemic racism that would always stand in his way.

Cash Africa yielded to Doctor Smith's pressure, whose diary records,

> This day I recd. of James R. Smith, the master of Cash Africa—five dollars—which sum is part of the wages of Cash—& is, by his consent, advanced to me, for his Wife—who lives in Litchfield. I gave a receit, to this effect, to Mr. Smith.[29]

On February 27, 1796, Doctor Smith concluded the transaction; "While at Litchfield I paid Cash Africa's Wife the money which I had procured, of his master, for her. She gave me her receit.[30]

This is the last reference to Cash Africa that has come to light, but there is one further clue that indicates he may have remained for a while longer in New York. Notices appeared in the *Litchfield Monitor* for several weeks in January, 1800 that there were unclaimed letters at the post office addressed to Anna Africa.[31] It is unknown whether Cash eventually sent for his family or abandoned them. Although he would have been eligible for a Continental soldier's pension under the Act of 1818, there is no record that he ever applied for one, and by this time he may no longer have been alive.

His wartime service did not impress the White citizens of Litchfield. He was not honored as a Patriot during his lifetime, and a land speculator became the primary beneficiary of his bounty land warrant. Like many others, he sought work in the city when the countryside did not afford him a livelihood.

In the end, Cash Africa emerges as a survivor, a man with the strength of will to sue a White woman for wrongfully enslaving him, and the fortitude to endure eight years as a soldier. For him, as for many of his White compatriots, the Revolution and the peace that followed were about "Liberty and Property." In the pursuit of both objects, he gained his freedom and a measure of autonomy, even disavowing the debts of his first wife, Margaret, who possessed fewer rights than he. His own pursuit of happiness remained "a dream deferred."[32]

29. Ibid., entry of February 17, 1796, 132.
30. Ibid., entry of February 27, 1796, 134.
31. *Litchfield Weekly Monitor*, Litchfield, Connecticut, January 8, 15 and 22, 1800.
32. Langston Hughes, "Harlem," *The Collected Works of Langston Hughes* (Columbia: University of Missouri Press, 2001).

Isaac Shelby, Patrick Ferguson, and Fire & Sword: The Power of a Good Story

WILLIAM CALDWELL

A good story spreads like glitter on a craft table: one spill and suddenly it's everywhere. Readers picking up almost any history book about the American Revolution in the southern colonies will learn about the 1780 Battle of Kings Mountain and the plot point of British Major Patrick Ferguson threatening the Patriots of the southern backcountry. Some examples include:

In 1881, Lyman Draper wrote in his *Kings Mountain & Its Heroes* that "if they did not desist from their opposition to the British arms, he [Ferguson] would march his army over the mountains, hang their leaders, and lay their country waste with fire and sword."[1]

In 1925, J.D. Bailey said in *Commanders at Kings Mountain,* "Ferguson, hearing the mutterings of the gathering storm, paroled Samuel Phillips, a relative of Colonel Shelby, with the following message: 'That if they did not desist from their opposition to British arms he would march his army over the mountains, hang their leaders, and lay their country to waste with fire and sword.'"[2]

In 1997, John Buchanan included in *The Road to Guilford Courthouse,* "Deadly in intent and import, the message had been given verbally to Phillips by Ferguson: 'If they did not desist from their opposition to the British arms, he would march over the mountains, hang their leaders, and lay their country waste with fire and sword.'"[3]

1. Lyman Draper, *Kings Mountain and Its Heroes* (Cincinnati: Peter G. Thompson, 1881), 169.
2. J.D. Bailey, *Commanders at Kings Mountain* (Gaffney, SC: E. H. DeCamp, 1925), 97.
3. John Buchanan, *The Road to Guilford Courthouse* (New York: John Wiley & Sons Publishing, 1997), 208.

In 2001, Walter Edgar described in *Partisans and Redcoats*, "Meanwhile, as Ferguson marched into the western frontier settlements he sent a personal message to Colonel Isaac Shelby. If the residents of the region 'did not desist from their opposition to British arms, he would march his army over the mountains, hang their leaders, and lay their country waste with fire and sword.'"[4]

In 2011, Randell Jones depicted the situation in *Before They Were Heroes at Kings Mountain*: "He imparted to Shelby the direct and succinct message from Ferguson: 'If they did not desist their opposition to the British arms, he would march his army over the mountains, hang their leaders, and lay their country waste with fire and sword.'"[5]

In 2013, Melissa Walker explained in *The Battles of Kings Mountain and Cowpens*, "Ferguson paroled a Patriot prisoner on September 10, 1780, and sent him to Patriot militia commander Isaac Shelby with a message: if the backcountry men 'did not desist their opposition to British arms,' said Ferguson, he would 'march over the mountains, hang their leaders and lay their country waste with fire and sword.'"[6]

It appears almost required that one cannot speak about Kings Mountain or Patrick Ferguson without including the threatening message. The summarized story follows that Ferguson, frustrated at the constant harassment by Patriot partisans in South Carolina and North Carolina in the late summer of 1780, issued a threat of destruction to anyone who continued to oppose him as he organized the Loyalist militia. Ferguson released a Patriot prisoner to convey a threat of hanging Patriot leaders, burning homes, and laying waste to their countryside with fire and sword if resistance continued. The messenger brought this warning directly to Patriot Col. Isaac Shelby deep in the Blue Ridge Mountains, who began organizing the Overmountain Men to confront Ferguson.

Such villainous language and line-in-the-sand ultimatums seem more fitting for a movie than the pages of a history book. This plot point negatively shapes the reader's perception of Patrick Ferguson for the rest of the story and inspires encouragement for the Patriots as they reply to the threat by crossing the Blue Ridge Mountains and succinctly end the saga of Kings Mountain with the justified killing of Ferguson. It is important to learn all that we can about Ferguson's message since

4. Walter Edgar, *Partisans and Redcoats: The Southern Conflict That Turned the Tide of the American Revolution* (New York: HarperCollins Publishing, 2001), 116.
5. Randell Jones, *Before They Were Heroes at Kings Mountain* (Winston-Salem: Daniel Boone Footsteps, 2013), 378.
6. Melissa Walker, *The Battles of Kings Mountain and Cowpens: The American Revolution in the Southern Backcountry* (New York: Rutledge Publishing, 2013), 75.

so much of the story is built upon this cornerstone. How do we know that Patrick Ferguson sent this threatening message? How would it change the story if Ferguson did not send the threat at all? Where is the evidence that has put "fire and sword" into our national mythology?

In 1823 a pamphlet was published by Issac Shelby.[7] By this time, Shelby had been twice the governor of Kentucky, a general of Kentucky militia in the War of 1812, and renowned leading figure of the American Revolution. Within the sixth paragraph of his pamphlet, Shelby explained the events that had befallen the Patriot cause in the southern campaign of the American Revolution in the autumn of 1780. Shelby described how British Major Patrick Ferguson proceeded with an army of Loyalist soldiers away from the main British army around Camden, South Carolina and marched northwestward into the Blue Ridge Mountains. Shelby explained:

> At that place he [Ferguson] paroled a prisoner, (one Samuel Philips a distant connection of mine) and instructed him to inform the officers on the Western waters, that if they did not desist from their opposition to the British arms, and take protection under his standard, he would march his army over the mountains, hang their leaders, and lay their country waste with fire and sword. Philips lived near my residence, and came directly to me with this intelligence.[8]

This was the first published description of the infamous threat that birthed a stirring and increasingly popularized vision of the historical events: destruction hanging over the heads of the Patriots of the Blue Ridge Mountains, and a challenge issued which these sturdy backcountry settlers would never shrink from.[9]

If a powerful message such as this threat was sent out to the backcountry leaders, why does it not appear in any contemporary stories of the campaign? One account appearing in the *Virginia Gazette* of November 18, 1780 noted that Ferguson had "advanced as high up as Gilbert Town, in Rutherford County, and threatened to cross the mountains to the western waters,"[10] claiming that Ferguson's advance

7. The pamphlet was intended to settle a controversy regarding the conduct of William Campbell in the Battle of Kings Mountain, and the lack of thanks and honors bestowed on other leaders such as Isaac Shelby and John Sevier.

8. Isaac Shelby, "Pamphlet," in Draper, *Kings Mountain and Its Heroes*, 522.

9. While notes exist from an interview with Shelby pre-dating this pamphlet by eight years, the notes were not published until twenty-five years after the 1823 pamphlet. The story depicted in these earlier notes bears no significant differences.

10. Draper, *Kings Mountain and Its Heroes*, 522.

was enough provocation to stir the backcountry Patriot leaders to action. This account, published just six weeks after the battle, described Ferguson's movements as threatening but included no message of destruction. Arthur Campbell, commanding officer (and cousin/brother-in-law) of another Kings Mountain leader, recalled his understanding that it was not a threat from Patrick Ferguson that spurred the Patriots to action, but the plight of the Patriot refugees fleeing Burke County, North Carolina: "They arrived in the settlement on Watauga River, without their families, to the number of about one hundred and fifty men. Their tale was a doleful one, and tended to excite the resentment of the western militia."[11] In examining over 300 additional statements by men who were on the 1780 campaign with Isaac Shelby, we found none that include any mention of a message or threat from Patrick Ferguson.

However, once a reader passes the 1823 publishing of Shelby's pamphlet, references to Ferguson's infamous message begin to appear. In September 1845, the *Southern Literary Messenger* of Richmond, Virginia shared an article about the Battle of Kings Mountain written by Joseph Graham. Graham had served as one of the North Carolina colonels during the Kings Mountain campaign but was called away in the last minutes before the battle commenced. Graham's retelling of the events says this about the threatening message:

> Although Col. Ferguson failed to overtake the detachment of mountain men alluded to, he took two of them prisoners, who had become separated from their comrades. In a day or two, he paroled them, and enjoined them to inform the officers on the western waters, that if they did not desist from their opposition to the British arms, and take protection, under his standard, that he would march his army over the mountains, hang their leaders, and lay the country waste with fire and sword.[12]

At last, Graham's article gives us another version of the story that includes the threat. But being published twenty-two years after Shelby's pamphlet and still being a word-for-word retelling of Shelby's story calls its validity into question. Most detectives would be suspicious if two witnesses, separated by hundreds of miles and twenty-two years, wrote two nearly identical statements. What scenario is most likely:

11. Arthur Campbell, "Kings Mountain – A Fragment," in Draper, *Kings Mountain and Its Heroes*, 522.
12. Joseph Graham, "Battle of King's Mountain," in *Draper, Kings Mountain and Its Heroes*, 546-551.

these men just happened to use the exact same forty-four words in the same order; or Graham was copying Shelby's account because it was a good story?

But wait; there's more. There is a source that directly contradicts Shelby's popular version of events. Within the collected and published papers of British General Charles Cornwallis is a letter written by Patrick Ferguson explaining his plan: parole prisoners, send out a message, and convince the Patriot holdouts to rejoin the Loyalist militia. Attached to the letter is a full copy of Ferguson's proclamation dated September 9, 1780.[13] Ferguson spent 850 words explaining how the people had been misled by the Continental Congress. He suggested

13. Enclosed with a letter from Patrick Ferguson to Lord Cornwallis, September 14, 1780: *DECLARATION* Tryon County, Gilbert Town
September 9th 1780
The experience that the deluded inhabitants of the revolted American provinces have had of the falsehoods by which the rebel leaders have artfully excited them, against their duty to God and the King and their best interests, to involve their country in blood and misery will, it is hoped, by degrees open their eyes that they may at last listen to the calm voice of reason and truth.

They have been told that Britain, the land of liberty and toleration and chief support of freedom and the Protestant religion throughout the world, was about to introduce popery and slavery among her American descendents at the very time the rebel Congress was privately forming a league with France and Spain which, had it succeeded to their wish, would have banished real liberty and true religion from the face of the earth.

They were told that the savages were to be solicited to murder and lay waste and that the British troops were to assist them in desolating the country. Now, the only Indians employ'd since the invasion of Carolina are those of Catawbaw by the rebels, and even the Cherokee nation that followed the British troops to Savannah River to revenge the burning of their towns were refused leave and sent back; and the King's troops have exerted themselves to restrain the resentment of the loyalists and prevent bad men on both sides from aggravating the horrors of way by rapine and outrage.

They were told the King meant to enslave them at a time when He with His Parliament had by publick Act of the Constitution renounced all right of taxing American for ever and voted a restoration of all their antient rights and libertys to those Americans who should submit; but the chief rebels have industriously conceal'd and suppress'd these advantagious offers, knowing that all reasonable and honest men would gladly receive them. They were told that all those in South Carolina who had taken protection were forced to inlist, then in fact no protected man was suffer'd, much less compell'd, to bear arms, even in the militia, until he had given proof of his sincerity.

They were told that the protected men were maltreated and plunder'd by order, when in fact the authority of the King's officers was diligently employ'd to restrain the loyalists from retaliating the injuries that their innocent familys had suffer'd during the rebel government; and althou it is impossible at once to prevent every person amongst a numerous body of men irritated by oppression from taking their revenge, yet the good behaviour of our militia at present in Tryon County shows that the King's officers have exerted themselves with success to prevent desolation.

that the only reason Patriot leaders still actively pursued the war was to personally gain by plundering. The final section of this proclamation (the "stick" to the previously explained "carrots") explained what would happen to those Patriots who continued to resist:

> As to those rebels who continue the waste of human blood in a war without a just object or even a reasonable pretext, whatever fate may befall them and their property, it shall be the endeavour of the King's officers to protect their wives and familys from injury or insult and to pursue with equal vengeance those of their own party or of the enemy who shall offer any outrage or insult to the female sex or act the part of house thieves.[14]

Additional evidence of Ferguson's intentions is in a second proclamation forwarded to General Cornwallis where Ferguson directed the Loyalists to protect property, families, and those Patriots who were peaceful:

In a word, the King by proclamation, and in consequence of a solemn Act of His Parliament, holds forth to every American who is disposed to return to his duty an offer of the same free and happy government he formerly enjoy'd, with an exemption from taxation and fardon for all offences; and His officers are strictly commanded to protect to the utmost of their power all men who submit and all women and children of every denomination. Of course no man can have an interest in continuing to his country the miserys of war (particularly after its fate is decided) except those few who have either engross'd all the power or who by their extreme injustice and cruelty to individuals are become detestable to the best men of all partys, or otherwise who, having got a habit of rapine and plunder, wish to continue to rob in the confusion of the times. Under the last description are the partys lately from Georgia, Nolachuki, and some scoundrels of both sides, all of whom it is the duty and interest of every man of honest feelings to suppress and crush.

Wherefore every man that is not conscious of crimes that render him unfit to live in a state of peace in civil society has only to repair to his home and declare his submission, after which his person, his property and just rights as a freeman will be protected to the utmost until the re-establishment of civil government shall for ever fix and secure his libertys. In the mean time, should the publick service render it necessary to use his cattle, forrage or grain, the same receipts that are in the like case given to the loyalists he will receive from the British commanding officer – not waste paper like the bills of the rebel Congress, but equal to cash, insuring him of full payment in a few weeks.

As to those rebels who continue the waste of human blood in a war without a just object or even a reasonable pretext, whatever fate may befall them and their property, it shall be the endeavour of the King's officers to protect their wives and familys from injury or insult and to pursue with equal vengeance those of their own party or of the enemy who shall offer any outrage or insult to the female sex or act the part of house thieves.

14. Patrick Ferguson, "Proclamation – September 9, 1780," in *The Cornwallis Papers: The Campaigns of 1780 and 1781 in the Southern Theater of the American Revolutionary War, Volume II, Chapter 23: Correspondence between Cornwallis and Ferguson etc.*, ed. Ian Saberton (East Sussex: The Naval & Military Press Ltd., 2010), 150-152.

> They [the Loyalists] are strictly enjoined to offer no injury to the persons or property of those men wo have been of the rebel side who remain at home and shew a disposition for peace and submission, but to afford every protection in their power to them and to women and children of every denomination ... those who by plunder and outrage disgrace the name of loyalists will be punished even to death as scoundrels who wish to continue to their country the miserys of war, to distress the women and children and other innocent people, to destroy all the property on both sides, and to retard the progress of His Majesty's arms.[15]

From Patrick Ferguson's own pen: no fire, no sword, no laying waste to the country, no hanging of leaders – but is this enough evidence to say that Patrick Ferguson did not issue a threat?

If every retelling of the Ferguson threat originates from Shelby's 1823 pamphlet, and if it is Ferguson's own copy of his proclamation that serves as the main challenge to the threat's existence, how can the scales be tipped in favor of one over the other? Due to the unusual nature of Ferguson's Loyalists serving in the backcountry, detached from the main British army, the communication between Ferguson and Cornwallis was detailed and frequent. These letters provide additional insight into Ferguson's strategies while in the western Carolinas and show evidence of attempting similar lenient tactics. In Ferguson's letter to Cornwallis on September 14, 1780 when he forwarded copies of the proclamations, he had just finished chasing and scattering the Patriot militia of Charles McDowell at the Battle of Cane Creek on the 12th. Ferguson explained that they captured seventeen prisoners there and described his next steps:

> They gave themselves out for 400 but I know their numbers to a certainty to have been 220, part of whom are skulking in scatter'd partys in the mountains and part at home preparing to avail themselves of the inclosed declaration, which I found necessary to circulate by means of the men of most character and moderation among the prisoners, whom I have sent to their homes upon promise of fidelity to His Majesty's Government. The people here have been kept in total ignorance, and the authority of your Lordship's proclamation would work surprizing effects.[16]

Ferguson's mention of using paroled prisoners to spread the proclamation confirms that this is the same message supposed to have been carried to Isaac Shelby by parolee Samuel Philips. This letter reveals

15. Ibid.
16. Ibid.

Ferguson's encouraging belief that some of the "scatter'd partys" were already preparing to follow his orders and give themselves up. We also learn that Ferguson hoped that bringing information to the people would have "surprizing effects," and that multiple paroled prisoners were chosen to serve as messengers due to their character and moderation, that is, their trustworthiness to deliver the message correctly. This sounds like someone whose plan is working, not an officer frustrated at being foiled.

Elsewhere in Ferguson's letters we see a similar pattern of trying to contact community leaders to discuss the reasons to end the rebellion. Ferguson was aware that opening communication with key leaders could sway the loyalty of entire regions. This is evidenced in Ferguson's letter of September 19, 1780, when he explained to Cornwallis:

> I have avail'd myself of Mr Cathey, who has submitted and has great influence with Macdougle's [McDowell's] party, to write a letter by him requiring that Macdowal will do justice to his adherents and their familys by letting them know the easy and advantagious terms upon which they may come in; and as he is said to be a man of humane and peaceable disposition and will have an opportunity of returning to his family and of putting an end to the ruinous war here, those who have submitted think that he with most of his followers will return. The rebel inhabitants here have been kept much in the dark. They are surprized at their treatment and declare that few, if any, would have gone off had we not been misrepresented.[17]

This insight into how Ferguson felt about the backcountry Patriot leaders and the positive responses he received paints a picture of someone who is attempting a velvet-glove approach to reconciliation and not the iron-fist of hangings and destruction. His proclamation dated September 9 that was copied and enclosed with his letter on September 14 was not a one-off attempt to deceive Patriots into laying down their arms, but was the shining example of his strategy to win the hearts and minds of the backcountry.

Reading the letters of Patrick Ferguson, his surviving proclamations, and considering the pattern of his other interactions with civilians across western South Carolina and North Carolina, it becomes fair to claim that Ferguson did not send a message to Isaac Shelby threatening him with "fire and sword." So why did Shelby claim that he did in his 1823 pamphlet? There are several potential answers:

17. Ibid., 153-155.

When Samuel Phillips was released by Ferguson under promise to deliver the proclamation, the message was either intentionally or accidentally exaggerated into the threat that Shelby remembered.

Shelby received Ferguson's proclamation as written, knew of Ferguson's success in recruiting thousands of Loyalist militia throughout the backcountry, and feared Ferguson would have similar success in Shelby's own North Carolina mountains. By altering the message himself and spreading fear and anger, Shelby galvanized his Patriot militia and prevented Ferguson from swaying his neighbors to Loyalism.

Ferguson lied in his letters to Cornwallis, and while claiming to spread peaceful words was really issuing threats of destruction.

Shelby sat down in 1823, forty-three years after the events, and decided his story needed a little razzle-dazzle to sell the heroic aspects of his accomplishments. The worse the villain, the greater the hero.

There is another possible explanation that doesn't turn these historical actors into fibbing glory-seekers. Perhaps when Shelby received Ferguson's proclamation, he simply did not believe it. While Ferguson was talking the good talk of peace and protection, other British officers were heavy-handedly crushing Patriot resistance in their areas of operation. To suppress Patriot leaders such as Elijah Clarke, Francis Marion, and Thomas Sumter, British and Loyalist officers like Banastre Tarleton, James Wemyss, and Thomas Brown often resorted to brutal tactics during their 1780 campaigns, tactics that could be described as "fire and sword." Perhaps when Ferguson's message reached Shelby in mid-September 1780, Shelby did not actually read or hear the words "fire and sword," but looked out across the other parts of the South and chose to believe the reality instead of the promises.

We will never know how the American Revolution would have changed if Isaac Shelby had believed Patrick Ferguson's peace offers. Shelby's decision to paint Ferguson as the author of these threats secured in American legend an image of Ferguson as a wicked British officer leading a vengeful Loyalist army to hang Patriot leaders and lay waste to their countryside with fire and sword, despite this story (more than likely) being false. Shelby's story shines a heroic light on the men who took up arms to challenge and defeat Ferguson, while depicting the men who followed Ferguson as villainous traitors complacent in his schemes to destroy the peaceful settlements of the Blue Ridge Mountains. This is the story that has been repeated for centuries despite its questionable validity; a story that is more folklore than truth. Despite continued efforts to prove or disprove this catalyst event of the Kings Mountain campaign, "fire & sword" will likely continue to reappear in our Revolution mythology, just like those few sparkles of craft glitter that remain no matter how many times you've vacuumed – but that's the power of a good story.

The Battle of Kings Mountain: New Insights from Forgotten Documents

JIM PIECUCH

On January 4, 1881, historian J. Watts de Peyster delivered an address to the New-York Historical Society in New York City. The lengthy oration dealt with the Battle of Kings Mountain, fought on October 7, 1780, in South Carolina, where the Revolutionaries achieved a decisive victory over a force composed of Loyalists. Although de Peyster raised several important questions about the battle, and his remarks were later published in pamphlet form, his work vanished into oblivion, perhaps due in part to the publication of Lyman C. Draper's exhaustive study, *Kings Mountain and Its Heroes*, later that same year. Yet some of the issues that concerned de Peyster merit further inquiry, including the numbers engaged on each side, casualties, and the curious inactivity of six hundred Loyalist militiamen who were nearby but did not come to the aid of their comrades.

De Peyster may not have been an impartial researcher. He was a nephew of Capt. Abraham de Peyster of the King's American Regiment, who was Maj. Patrick Ferguson's second-in-command at Kings Mountain and surrendered to the Revolutionaries there. Although Captain de Peyster died more than twenty years before J. Watts de Peyster's birth, the nephew very likely wanted to defend his late uncle's reputation as both a Loyalist and an officer, since he devoted a portion of his address to defending the Loyalists' military service during the Revolution.[1]

1. J. Watts de Peyster, "The Battle or Affair of King's Mountain, Saturday, 7th October, 1780," microfiche, David Center for the American Revolution, American Philosophical Society, Philadelphia, PA, 1, 2.

Noting that "the Americans have had pretty much the full say" in describing events at Kings Mountain, de Peyster sought to balance the narrative using "the accounts of three Provincial officers present, who survived the conflict." These were Captain de Peyster, Lt. Anthony Allaire of the Loyal American Regiment, and Capt. John Taylor of the 1st Battalion, New Jersey Volunteers.[2] The historian de Peyster declared that he intended "to correct the mistakes into which the public have been led by a document, purporting to be a report" of the battle, an undated copy of which de Peyster found in the Horatio Gates Papers, housed at the New-York Historical Society.[3]

The document, undated and composed several days after the battle by American colonels William Campbell, Isaac Shelby, and Benjamin Cleveland, had been forwarded to the Continental Congress by Gates and was published in several newspapers, on the order of Congress, as the official report of the battle. It provided information on the numbers engaged along with the casualties on both sides.[4] De Peyster challenged the accuracy of the account, declaring that "this document, in my judgment, was not digested by the practical men who made the history, but was prepared by one experienced in such matters," that is, propaganda, "and carries within itself conclusive evidence of this fact." He also quoted Shelby's later admission that the report was "nothing more than a brief and harried account in general terms of the expedition and the battle, drawn up to authenticate the intelligence of our victory and to give tone to public report." Thus, de Peyster concluded that the document was primarily designed to shape "public opinion, to make military capital, and to satisfy the cravings of the Carolinian Whigs, famished by a series of defeats."[5]

According to the allegedly "official" report, the Revolutionaries' strength reported by their officers was 900, and the American commanders claimed to have found "provision returns" in the Loyalists' camp that showed Ferguson had led 1,125 men. Of these, 19 of the provincial troops were reported killed, 35 wounded, and 68 captured; Loyalist militia casualties were given as 206 killed, 128 wounded, and 648 captured, a total of 1,104 (incorrectly stated as 1,105 in the document). American losses were reported as 28 killed and 62 wounded.[6]

2. Ibid., 4.

3. Ibid., 1.

4. The document, labeled "Official Report," is reproduced in Lyman C. Draper, *King's Mountain and Its Heroes: History of the Battle of Kings Mountain, October 7th, 1780, and the Events Which Led to It*, reprint edition (Bowie, MD: Heritage Books, 2002), 522-524.

5. De Peyster, "King's Mountain," 1-2.

6. "Official Report," in Draper, *King's Mountain*, 521-522.

These figures have been widely accepted for more than two centuries. Draper, who has been criticized as a "hero-worshiper" and "maker of heroes," and who did not conceal his affinity for the "Overmountain Men" who lived west of the Appalachian Mountains and formed a large portion of the American force at Kings Mountain, nevertheless made a serious attempt to assess the strengths and casualties of the combatants.[7] Draper noted that the Overmountain Men spent the night of October 5 "making a selection of the fittest men, horses, and equipments for a forced march," ultimately choosing about 700 while leaving some 690 "footmen and those having weak horses" to follow. Perhaps fifty of those on foot reached Kings Mountain in time to participate in the battle, Draper noted.[8] The next day, October 6, the Overmountain Men arrived at the Cowpens, where they were joined by four hundred North and South Carolinians under Brig. Gen. James Williams, bringing the total to eleven hundred, not counting the men on foot. From there, 910 men, again not including those lacking horses, were selected to continue pursuing Ferguson.[9]

As for the Loyalists, Draper asserted that "the exact strength of Ferguson's force cannot with certainty be determined." He mentioned the "official report" and its figure of 1,125, but noted, without giving a source, that there was "some reason to suppose that about two hundred Tories left camp that day, perhaps on a scout, but more likely on a foraging expedition." That led him to assert, later in the volume, that "the Loyalist force under Ferguson at King's Mountain was eight hundred." Several pages later, however, Draper contradicted himself. He provided more detail on the two hundred-man foraging party, commanded by Col. John (or possibly Patrick) Moore, then declared that their departure from camp "would have left about nine hundred altogether . . . to fight the battle," leading him conclude that "the numbers of the opposing forces were about equal." Draper dismissed claims by Loyalist participants that Ferguson's force had been outnumbered.[10]

Regarding American casualties, Draper repeated the figures of 28 killed and 62 wounded from the "official" report and remarked that these were "more reliable" than those stated by Isaac Shelby in a letter of October 12, 1780, in which Shelby mentioned 29 killed and 54 wounded and added that the numbers were more likely 35 killed and

7. William B. Hesseltine, "Lyman Draper and the South," *Journal of Southern History* 19 (1953):20.
8. Draper, *King's Mountain*, 221-222, 221n.
9. Ibid., 226-227.
10. Ibid., 237-238, 293, 297-299, 298n.

50 to 60 wounded. Examining losses by unit, Draper did not find any sign of inconsistent reporting when he noted that the small number of militia from Lincoln County, North Carolina, "suffered considerably" while the much larger force of South Carolinians lost only their commander, General Williams, and one other man, both killed. Draper did find it "remarkable" that Col. William Campbell's unit lost thirteen officers killed compared to only one enlisted man, but he claimed the disparity resulted from "how fearlessly the officers exposed themselves" during the battle. Draper attributed the Americans' low casualties to the Loyalists firing too high, thereby often failing to hit the attackers.[11]

The exact losses among Ferguson's troops "can only be approximately determined," Draper stated. Campbell reported that 19 provincials were killed, 35 wounded, and 68 captured, with 206 Loyalist militiamen killed, 128 wounded, and 648 captured, a total of 1,104 casualties (Draper arrived at a sum of 1,103). Shelby's October 12 letter gave a considerably lower figure of 1,016. Like de Peyster, Draper believed the discrepancy resulted from the American leaders' wish to present Loyalist losses as "sufficiently large to make a decided impression on the minds of all classes, encouraging the friends of freedom, and equally depressing their enemies." To support this assertion, Draper quoted Lt. Col. Henry Lee's statement that "exaggeration of successful operations was characteristic of the times."[12]

Later historians largely followed either Draper, the "official" report, or some combination of the two, thus minimizing the numbers and losses of the Revolutionaries while maximizing those of the Loyalists, as a look at some accounts of the battle demonstrates.

John S. Pancake, author of an influential 1985 academic history of the southern campaigns, gave figures of 910 Revolutionaries and over 1,000 Loyalists at Kings Mountain, with casualties of 28 killed and 62 wounded for the former and 157 killed and 163 wounded too badly to be moved for the latter. In a more recent academic work, Stanley D. M. Carpenter stated that 900 Revolutionaries and 1,000 Loyalists participated in the battle, writing that between 119 and 157 Loyalists were killed and 123 mortally wounded, while the Revolutionaries suffered "few casualties" because "the Loyalists consistently fired too high." J. David Dameron's volume, written for a popular audience, reports the Revolutionaries numbering 910 and the Loyalists between 1,075 and 1,125, with the Americans losing 29 killed, 4 mortally wounded, and

11. Ibid., 279, 302, 305.
12. Ibid., 297, 300-302.

58 wounded and the Loyalists 244 killed, not including Ferguson, and 143 wounded. Dameron noted that Ferguson's troops "did not have clear fields of fire." The "Kings Mountain" page on the American Battlefield Trust's website closely follows the "official" report, giving figures of 910 Americans who suffered 90 casualties and 1,125 Loyalists of whom 1,018 were killed, wounded, or captured.[13]

De Peyster challenged these statistics in his forgotten address. Basing his estimate on the statement in Allaire's letter of January 30, 1781, which was later published in James Rivington's New York newspaper, de Peyster insisted "that Ferguson went into action with about nine hundred men." This did not match the number Allaire recorded in his diary entry for October 7, 1780, where he wrote that "Maj. Ferguson had eight hundred men." Allaire added that there were 70 provincial troops present, though he did not indicate whether these should have been added to the 800. In his letter, however, Allaire stated that Ferguson commanded 800 militia at Kings Mountain along with 100 provincial troops.[14] Allaire was in an ideal position to know the strength of the Loyalist force, since he served as Ferguson's adjutant, making him "responsible for the paperwork of the unit." Loyalist Uzal Johnson of the New Jersey Volunteers, the provincials' surgeon and close friend of Allaire—the two often collaborated when writing in their diaries—partially corroborated Allaire's initial estimate when he gave a figure of seventy provincials at Kings Mountain in his entry for October 7. Although Johnson did not include a number for the militia, he wrote that "the Amn. Vols. charged them [the Revolutionaries] with success and drove them down the Hill, but were not able to pursue, our Number being so small" in relation to the attackers, but as with one of Allaire's accounts, it is not clear whether Johnson was referring to the entire Loyalist force as "so small" or only the provincials.[15] Since Allaire and Johnson were in general agreement that their force numbered about

13. John S. Pancake, *This Destructive War: The British Campaign in the Carolinas, 1780-1782* (Tuscaloosa: University of Alabama Press, 1985), 117, 118, 120; Stanley D. M. Carpenter, *Southern Gambit: Cornwallis and the British March to Yorktown* (Norman: University of Oklahoma Press, 2019), 125, 126, 127, 128; J. David Dameron, *King's Mountain: The Defeat of the Loyalists, October 7, 1780* (New York: Da Capo Press, 2003), 46, 49, 51, 76, 80; "Kings Mountain," American Battlefield Trust, https://www.battlefields.org/learn/revolutionary-war/battles/kings-mountain.

14. De Peyster, "King's Mountain," 5; Lt. Anthony Allaire to unnamed, January 30, 1781, in Draper, *King's Mountain*, 516-517; Anthony Allaire, Diary, October 7, 1780, in Draper, *King's Mountain*, 510.

15. Uzal Johnson, *Captured at Kings Mountain: The Journal of Uzal Johnson, a Loyalist Surgeon*, eds. Wade S. Kolb III and Robert M. Weir (Columbia: University of South Carolina Press, 2011), xiii-xvi, 31.

nine hundred, that both Draper and de Peyster independently arrived at the same conclusion, and given the admitted tendency of victors to exaggerate their success by inflating the strength of the enemy, as well as the intent of Campbell, Shelby, and Cleveland to use their report to boost the Revolutionaries' morale, it is safe to conclude that Ferguson commanded about nine hundred Loyalists at Kings Mountain.

After addressing the issue of Loyalist numbers, de Peyster turned his attention to those of the Americans, declaring that just as the size of Ferguson's force had been exaggerated, that of the Revolutionaries had "been underestimated." Dismissing the claims of Loyalist participants—Allaire claimed the attackers were 2,500 strong, and Taylor's assertion that Ferguson's force was outnumbered 4:1 would have translated to 3,600 Revolutionaries—de Peyster began his calculation of American strength with the accepted account that three thousand men from west of the Appalachians set out after Ferguson. Whereas Draper and most historians since stated that General Williams of South Carolina and Col. Frederick Hambright and Maj. William Chronicle of North Carolina joined the Overmountain Men before the force was winnowed to 910 men, de Peyster argued that these reinforcements joined only afterwards, and their numbers should be added to the 910. Williams's 400 South Carolinians and the 60 North Carolinians would bring American strength to 1,360. Because Shelby stated that "Colonel McDowell's command had been considerably augmented during the march," de Peyster concluded that this was in addition to the reinforcement from the Carolinas, so "these accessions must have swelled the number to fifteen hundred at least." In support of his assessment, de Peyster noted that in their postwar histories of the Revolution, Lt. Col. Henry Lee gave this figure, and Lt. Col. Edward Carrington placed the Revolutionaries' strength at about sixteen hundred.[16] However, Lee and Carrington only served in the South later in the war; neither was present at Kings Mountain, although they undoubtedly drew some of their information from participants.

There is substantial evidence to support de Peyster's belief that the American force was reduced to 910 before the Carolinians joined the Overmountain Men. The "official" report stated that after Williams with 400 men arrived at the Cowpens on October 6 and united with the Overmountain Men, the officers decided to pursue Ferguson with 900 of the "best horsemen." Many participants contradicted that assertion. A veteran of the battle, North Carolinian William Lenoir,

16. De Peyster, "King's Mountain," 4, 5.

stated that when the American commanders realized that they would not catch Ferguson by pursuing with infantry, "orders were given for as many as had, or could procure, horses, to go in advance," leaving those without horses to follow. Lenoir wrote that "about five or six hundred" mounted men set out at dawn on October 6, leaving fifteen hundred "footmen" to follow. During their march, the horsemen were joined by Williams, though according to Lenoir, Williams commanded only "a few South Carolina militia." Another Kings Mountain veteran, Benjamin Sharp, was with the Overmountain militia and recalled afterward that they were "all mounted" and numbered between 1,500 and 1,800. "After hard marching for some time, we found our progress much retarded by our footmen and weak horses," Sharp stated, and "it was then resolved to leave the footmen and weak horses . . . to follow as fast" as they could. Sometime after the reduced force of Overmountain Men reached the Cowpens, Williams arrived "with several hundred men." It is notable that Shelby, who signed the "official" report declaring that the Carolina reinforcements joined the Overmountain militia before the 910 men were selected to continue the pursuit, contradicted that statement in an 1823 pamphlet. In an account that closely matched Sharp's description of events, Shelby wrote that 910 Overmountain Men were selected on October 5, "started about light the next morning" to find Ferguson, and were later met at the Cowpens by Williams, "with about four hundred men." Joseph Graham, a North Carolina officer who was not present at the battle but knew many of the participants, later wrote that the Overmountain colonels on October 4 "resolved, that they would select all the men and horses fit for service, and immediately pursue Ferguson"; the following evening, they chose 910 men and set off for Cowpens, where they were joined by Williams with almost 400 men and Hambright and Chronicle with an additional 60. Loyalist Alexander Chesney, who fought at Kings Mountain, wrote that "we were attacked before any support arrived by 1500 picked men . . . all of whom were armed with Rifles."[17] Taken together, the accounts other than the "official" report indicate an American strength ranging from Lenoir's 900 to 1,000 (if Williams's 400 are added in place of the "few" militia Lenoir claimed Williams led), to 1,370 if the 460 Car-

17. "Official Report"; William Lenoir, "An Account of the Battle of King's Mountain," Benjamin Sharp, "Battle of King's Mountain," Isaac Shelby, "Battle of King's Mountain," Joseph Graham, "Battle of King's Mountain," all in Draper, *King's Mountain*, 522, 548, 552, 555, 565; Alexander Chesney, *The Journal of Alexander Chesney, A South Carolina Loyalist in the Revolution and After*, ed. E. Alfred Jones, *The Ohio State University Bulletin* 26 (1921):17.

olinians are added to the 910 Overmountain Men. Nevertheless, historians continue to accept the version of events in which the 910 Americans who fought at Kings Mountain were chosen after Williams and Hambright united with the Overmountain militia, rather than before the junction of the two forces.

Another approach to calculating American numbers, utilized by Lawrence E. Babits in his landmark study of the 1781 Battle of Cowpens, involves the use of federal pension applications. Babits noted the discrepancy between the Cowpens account of British commander Lt. Col. Banastre Tarleton, who claimed he was opposed by 2,000 Americans, and that of American commander Brig. Gen. Daniel Morgan, who reported his strength as just over 800. For more than two centuries, historians adhered to Morgan's figure while vilifying Tarleton for exaggerating his enemy's strength as a ploy to explain the British defeat. Babits identified about six hundred American veterans who, in applying for pensions decades after the battle, testified that they had fought at Cowpens. He observed that in cases where the size of a unit was known, "the pension application rate is less than one to three or four. That is, one pension application equaled at least three or four Cowpens soldiers—and this is a low figure." Babits concluded from this analysis that between 1,800 and 2,400 Americans actually fought at Cowpens. Tarleton had been telling the truth.[18]

The same method can be applied to estimate the number of Revolutionaries at Kings Mountain. In 1990, historian Bobby Gilmer Moss published *The Patriots at Kings Mountain*, in which he identified more than seven hundred men who had participated in the battle. An examination of his sources shows that nearly six hundred soldiers were identified from their federal pension applications. Subtracting applications filed by family members after a veteran's death, and those of men who were not actual participants (for example, Josiah Brandon fought under Ferguson and switched sides after the battle, while John Caruthers had been captured a few days earlier and escaped during the action) leaves a total of 439 men who, in filing for pension benefits, declared under oath that they had been present at the Battle of Kings Mountain. Nearly all were in combat; very few—one man sent to find horses, another who fell ill after reaching the field, a third assigned to guard baggage—did not fight.[19] Using the same methodology as Babits, the

18. Lawrence E. Babits, *A Devil of a Whipping: The Battle of Cowpens* (Chapel Hill: University of North Carolina Press, 1998), 150.
19. Bobby Gilmer Moss, *The Patriots at Kings Mountain* (Blacksburg, SC: Scotia-Hibernia Press, 1990).

pension applications of Kings Mountain veterans clearly indicate that at least 1,300 Americans and as many as 1,750 fought in the battle.

De Peyster did not challenge the American casualty figures, but given Babits's findings on Cowpens, the accepted numbers may not be accurate. While Morgan reported American losses at Cowpens as 12 killed and 60 wounded, Babits's examination of pension records revealed the names of 24 killed and 104 wounded. Babits remarked that it was "unlikely" that Morgan "had accurate counts of the militia."[20] Moss indicated in his compilation those soldiers who were killed or wounded, though he made no attempt to arrive at a total. Given the unreliability of figures for militia units, the loss of numerous officers, and the haste with which the Americans withdrew from Kings Mountain to avoid the possible arrival of a British relief force from Charlotte, North Carolina, only thirty-five miles from the battlefield, it is almost certain that no accurate accounting of casualties was undertaken. Loyalist doctor Uzal Johnson, who was forced to treat wounded Americans after the action, provided probably the best account. Johnson wrote in his diary that fifty of the provincial troops "got killed & wounded," and that 225 Loyalist militiamen were killed and 72 wounded. "How many of the Enemy got kill'd is uncertain, not far inferior to ours if we judge from the Number of their wounded which was equal to ours, I being employed to dress them . . . enabled me to get the Number," Johnson wrote.[21] The editors of Johnson's diary note that his "figures for British casualties are higher than some consensus estimates . . . but he may well have been in the best position to know," and that Johnson's calculation of American losses was "also higher than most conventional estimates, but official reports from both sides often omitted the militia."[22] If, as Johnson asserted, the number of wounded on both sides was equal, that would mean about 100 Americans were wounded, and while his estimate of American killed, about 250, is undoubtedly high, it would still be significantly larger than the thirty or so given in most accounts. The disparity, as noted earlier, is usually attributed to Ferguson's men firing too high, but the Loyalist militiamen were experienced backcountry hunters and many had served alongside the Revolutionaries in the 1776 campaign against the Cherokee, so there is little reason to believe that their marksmanship was not on a par with that of their opponents. Maj. Gen. Nathanael Greene, in assessing British strength in South Carolina in August 1781, commented that the British had nearly one thousand

20. Babits, *Devil of a Whipping*, 151, 152.

21. Johnson, *Captured at Kings Mountain*, 31.

22. Ibid., 110n.

Loyalist militia with them, and that "the militia Tories from their being such exceeding good marksmen, will not be the least useful" of the British force.[23] Draper agreed, writing that the Loyalists at Kings Mountain, like their opponents, "were expert riflemen."[24] If the Revolutionaries' casualties were lower than those of the Loyalists, the difference was probably less than most accounts state, and more likely the result of Chesney's observation that the slopes of Kings Mountain were "covered with wood which sheltered the Americans" rather than the Loyalists' poor marksmanship.[25]

Another point de Peyster raised and termed one of Ferguson's "grievous mistakes" was making "an eccentric retreat which is inexplicable," when the Loyalists could have marched directly to join Lord Cornwallis's army in Charlotte. De Peyster suspected that Ferguson "may have been led to this last and fatal course by assurances of support which were not fulfilled. It is well known that there were six hundred Tories in arms within a few miles of the scene of his disaster, whose assistance might have converted it into a victory." These Loyalists "did not put in their appearance," and de Peyster angrily added that "it is to be hoped that they suffered due punishment for their delinquency." He also suggested that if the Loyalists, who were camped "within a few hours' march to the west," had come to Ferguson's aid, they could have "stampeded their [Americans'] horses and fallen upon their rear, the result would have been . . . fatal." The Revolutionaries were so preoccupied with Ferguson's troops in their front that "one hundred to one a fire in the rear would have made them skedaddle," de Peyster declared.[26]

Draper, too, noted the presence of the Loyalist militia not far from Kings Mountain, and speculated on their failure to join the action. Draper remarked that in their pursuit of Ferguson, the Revolutionaries "passed where several large bodies of Tories were assembled; one, numbering six hundred, at Major Gibbs', about four miles to the right of the Cowpens, who were intending to join Ferguson the next day." Later, he wondered why many high-ranking Loyalist militia officers were not with Ferguson. "It is not a little singular, that so few of the prominent Loyalist leaders, of the Ninety Six district, were with Ferguson," he re-

23. Nathanael Greene to George Washington, August 6, 1781, in Dennis M. Conrad, ed., *The Papers of General Nathanael Greene*, Vol. 9 (Chapel Hill: University of North Carolina Press, 1997), 139-140.
24. Draper, *King's Mountain*, 294.
25. Chesney, "Journal," 17.
26. De Peyster, "King's Mountain," 5, 6.

marked, naming among others "Colonels Cunningham, Kirkland, and Clary" along with Gibbs, as notably absent. "Some were doubtless with the party whom the Whigs had passed at Major Gibbs' plantation," and others were elsewhere in the vicinity of the battlefield, "but they were not at King's Mountain, when sorely needed, with all the strength they could have brought to the indefatigable Ferguson," Draper remarked. While conceding that "the Loyalists evinced no little pluck and bravery at King's Mountain," he implied what he believed to be the reason for the nearby Loyalist militia's failure to join Ferguson, quoting Thomas Paine's *American Crisis* wherein Paine alleged that "every Tory is a coward, for a servile, slavish, self-interested fear is the foundation of Toryism; and a man under such influence, though he may be cruel, can never be brave."[27]

The reason for the Loyalist militia's not marching to Kings Mountain was not cowardice, as is clearly shown in letters that Ferguson wrote to militia major Zacharias Gibbes shortly before the battle. Gibbes, an ardent Loyalist, was certainly no coward. He had fought the Revolutionaries at Ninety Six in 1775, was captured after the Battle of Kettle Creek in 1779 and sentenced to death but was instead banished, and then took the field after the British captured Charlestown in May 1780.[28] Gibbes included Ferguson's letters in his postwar claim for compensation, and the documents appear to have thus far escaped the notice of historians. On October 5, Ferguson, who was at "Buffaloe Creek within 3 Miles of Cherokee ford," addressed a message to Gibbes "or any other Officers of his Regt." After describing his location, Ferguson instructed the Loyalist officers

> to send any reinforcements that are marching to join me to thicketty, where they will inform themselves of my Situation & join me. Lose no time. If I should move to any other Side of The Country, so as to make it unsafe for to come to Camp by Cherokee ford, I will give Notice. Please to inform the Comg officers of Companys of your Regts of this & also send a Copy to a Captn. of Plummers to be sent round to the officers of that Regt: In case of accident the officers need not publish this, or snares may be laid for them on the road. those who march should have two or three men always advanced & one or two push'd out on each flank. they should not keep the road if they Suspect an Enemy, always advance impudently, under Cover of the woods so as

27. Draper, *King's Mountain*, 222-223, 294.
28. Zacharias Gibbes, Loyalist Claim, 1783, Great Britain Audit Office (AO) Papers 12/46/145-146, microfilm, David Center for the American Revolution, American Philosophical Society.

> not to show their numbers, upon any Enemy in their way, & at night lodge themselves in a Log house & have their knives ready.

Beneath his signature, Ferguson added: "If your People have any inclination to settle their country speedily there never was Such an opportunity if they are not expeditio[us] it will be too late & your District will be over run."[29]

Later that day, Ferguson sent Gibbes a second message. The note stated: "Sir I am now on my march to [illegible word] near King's Mountain. I wish not to have any reinforcements from you immediately as they may be Destroyed on their way. take Care of yourself—for some Days—Sumpter & Clark have joined Macdowal."[30] This previously unreferenced correspondence clearly explains why Gibbes and the Loyalist militia did not march to Ferguson's assistance. After originally ordering the militia to join him, Ferguson reconsidered and, believing that the danger to the militia was too great, canceled his earlier instructions. Perhaps Ferguson recognized that he was in a difficult position and knew that if his force were to be overwhelmed, keeping the remaining Loyalist militia intact would be essential to maintaining British control in the South Carolina backcountry. On the other hand, Ferguson may have concluded that he did not need the militia's aid and chose not to have them undertake a risky march through a region swarming with Revolutionaries. Whether it was for these or other reasons, the Loyalist militia cannot be accused of cowardice or neglect of duty. They followed the orders of their superior. Had the officers chosen, on their own, to march to Kings Mountain, there is no guarantee they would have altered the battle's outcome, de Peyster's claims notwithstanding.

Although much of de Peyster's address dealt with issues of personal concern to him, particularly as they related to his ancestor, he called into question many generally accepted aspects of the Battle of Kings Mountain. Examining the issues he raised concerning the strength and casualties of the opposing forces reveals that the Loyalists were somewhat fewer in number than believed, while the Revolutionary force was far larger than usually stated. Also, American casualties were likely somewhat higher than the traditionally accepted figure. Finally, de Peyster's criticism of the Loyalist militia's failure to join Ferguson can be answered through other forgotten documents: Ferguson's two letters

29. Patrick Ferguson to Zacharias Gibbes, October 5, 1780, in Gibbes, Loyalist Claim, September 12, 1783, AO 13/119/155.
30. Ferguson to Gibbes, October 5, 1780 (second letter of this date), in Gibbes, Loyalist Claim, AO 13/19/155A.

enclosed in Gibbes' Loyalist claim. Taken together, the analysis of issues discussed in the neglected work of de Peyster and the information contained in Ferguson's overlooked correspondence provide important new insights into the campaign and battle of Kings Mountain.

The Battle at the Village: Alabama's Miniature Bunker Hill

ANTHONY RONEY II

Ten days before General Morgan's momentous victory at Cowpens, a battle, or rather to some, a skirmish took place beyond the peripherals of the Continental Army on the Eastern Seaboard. Though all but forgotten by a majority of history books and locals, this action was the bloodiest Revolutionary War battle fought in modern-day Alabama and was quite possibly the key fulcrum of a power struggle in the vast colony of West Florida.

Stretching from the Mississippi to the Apalachicola Rivers, West Florida had been a hotbed for conflict since Spain declared war on King George III in May 1779. Bernardo de Gálvez soon commenced successful sieges against the British forces at Baton Rouge in September 1779 and Mobile in March of the following year. Following the capitulation of Fort Charlotte at Mobile on March 14, 1780, Maj. Gen. John Campbell soon found his headquarters at the capitol city of Pensacola, just slightly over fifty miles away, to be within striking range of the Spanish. The disputed territory between these cities, modern-day Baldwin County, Alabama and Escambia County, Florida, would then become the primary battlefront of the Gulf Coast campaign for the next fifteen months.

For the most part, this area at the time was nothing short of an uninhabitable wilderness dangerous to any person that set foot on its land. Aside from the few communities and plantations that existed on Mobile Bay and its tributary rivers, there were almost no settlements in the region. While there existed a road between Pensacola and Mobile, it was one that was heavily mired with thickets, felled trees, washouts, and depending on the weather, sometimes impassible creek crossings.[1]

1. "Observaciones hechas en el reconocimiento de el Village al Río Perdidos emprendida

Along with these, wild predators were a constant source of danger.[2] Raids carried out by Native Americans and partisans were a prevalent threat to both Spanish and British outposts, and particularly to vulnerable civilians. These conditions would heavily weigh on the operations and combatants that played out within the area.

While the frontier straddled the Perdido River, the most important location within this territory was the self-referentially named The Village. The largest settlement on the Eastern shore of Mobile Bay at the time, The Village (also known as La Aldea or the Village of Mobile) commanded an imperative strategic position in West Florida as it was the primary waypoint for the Pensacola-Mobile Road to cross Mobile Bay. Surrounding the community on the bayfront was a string of large plantations owned by prominent English West Florida officials such as Attorney General Edmund Wegg and Lieutenant Governor Elias Durnford, the commander who surrendered Fort Charlotte. These plantations, along with smaller nearby French communities, were raided by Native Americans on numerous occasions for their cattle, horses, slaves, or other valuables during the area's tenure as the seat of war. As The Village was under threat of this constant raiding from Great Britain's native allies, Spanish military officials deemed it necessary to establish a fortified post protecting it.[3] With this position under guard, the Spanish could control a clear avenue to cross Mobile Bay, create a base for forward operating posts in the Perdido region, and protect valuable cattle and drinking water resources.[4] This was indeed necessary as the community was directly attacked at least four times while under Spanish control during the war.[5]

The most coordinated and vigorous of these attacks occurred in January 1781. As General Campbell sought a foothold to retake Mobile and its surrounding communities, he ordered a joint naval and ground offensive to take the post at The Village. While sources vary on the exact number of troops in the attacking force, it contained approximately 180 to 200 regulars and militia, and 300 to 500 Native Ameri-

en 22 de julio de 1780," Mobile, August 1, 1780, Cuba 2359, Archivo General de Indias, Seville, Spain (AGI); Philipp Waldeck, *The Diary of Philipp Waldeck*, trans. Bruce E. Burgoyne, University of West Florida, John C. Pace Library, Special Collections, M1983-09.

2. Waldeck, *The Diary of Philipp Waldeck.*

3. Bernardo de Gálvez to José de Ezpeleta y Galdeano (confidential), New Orleans, July 18, 1780, Cuba 1377, AGI.

4. Ezpeleta to Gálvez, New Orleans, July 18, 1780, Cuba 4A, AGI; John Campbell to George Germain, Pensacola, January 5, 1781, CO:5/597, The National Archives, Kew, UK (TNA).

5. Ezpeleta to Gálvez. Mobile, January 20, 1781, Cuba 2359, AGI.

cans (precisely counted at 420), totaling a force as high as 700.[6] Supporting this force were two brass 3-pounder field cannons.[7]

General Campbell sought to overwhelm his adversaries with superior numbers, but starkly underestimated the Spanish forces at the post to be around 100 troops, possibly due to outdated intelligence.[8] The 190-strong Spanish force defended the redoubt at the time of the attack.[9] The fortification was described as consisting of a series of entrenchments, wooden and earthen palisades, and a central stockade with an officers' quarters.[10] Much of the structures were apparently somewhat dilapidated.[11] It was quadrangular with moats on all sides except that which faced the bay. A "serpent's tongue" (a narrow, external fortification that jutted out) was also constructed. The fort was located nearby the ferry and anchorage area.[12] Within and surrounding the fortification were the encampments of troops and militia. At the time of the attack, it was supplemented with two 4-pounder cannons.[13]

While the two opposing forces fought for the Spanish and British Empires, they would both represent prime examples of the diverse groups that participated in the American Revolution. Needing every able-bodied man in the Louisiana colony, Governor Gálvez had recruited a large number of Black and mixed-race militia from New Orleans known as the New Orleans Colored Militia. By 1781, this detachment had become experienced veterans, many distinguished by the campaign for West Florida. The involved Spanish regulars hailed from multiple corners of its empire: the regiments of Principe, Spain, Navarre, and Havana.

The British forces consisted of a wider-ranging group of combatants within their ranks. Men from the 3rd Battalion of the 60th Regiment of Foot made up about forty personnel in the assaulting force. Coming in with approximately sixty experienced men was the 3rd Waldeck Reg-

6. Ezpeleta to Pedro Piernas, Mobile, January 15, 1781. LEG, 6912, 4, Archivo General de Simancas, Spain (SGU); Ezpeleta to Gálvez. Mobile, January 20, 1781; Alexander Cameron to Germain, Pensacola, February 10, 1781, CO:5/82, TNA; Campbell to Germain, Pensacola, January 5, 1781.

7. Campbell to Germain, Pensacola, January 5, 1781.

8. Ibid.

9. Ezpeleta to Gálvez, Mobile, January 20, 1781.

10. "La Mobila en su Hora Decisiva," *Jose de Ezpeleta, Gobernador de La Mobila: 1780-1781* (Seville: Publications de la Escuela de Estudios Hispano-Americanos de Sevilla, 1980), chapter IX.

11. Ezpeleta to Gálvez, Mobile, January 20, 1781.

12. Ezpeleta to Manuel Cabello, Mobile January 10, 28, February 2, 1781, Cuba 116, AGI.

13. Ezpeleta to Gálvez, Mobile, January 20, 1781.

iment, which consisted of German soldiers from the Principality of Waldeck.[14] This regiment had been contracted out by Prince Friedrich Karl August to the British Army since 1776. The Waldeckers had seen action throughout the New York and New Jersey campaign, including taking a part in the successful assault on Fort Washington. The unit was transferred in 1778 to Jamaica, then West Florida in anticipation of Spanish hostilities.[15]

Strengthening the regulars were Loyalist provincial militia regiments from Pennsylvania and Maryland. This united corps of about eighty troops was commanded by Capt. Philip Barton Key, a future U.S. Representative and federal judge, and the uncle of Francis Scott Key.[16] Lt. Joseph Pinhorn led a small contingent of ten to twenty West Florida Royal Foresters, a volunteer group of provincial mounted rangers.[17] Elements of this unit had participated in previous attacks on The Village.[18] It is possible that this detachment of rangers also had Black soldiers, as there were claims that enslaved men were armed and uniformed under their commanders.[19]

Many secondhand sources state that the British in West Florida allied only with the Creek and Choctaw nations. However, numerous intelligence reports across the region provided information of various warriors from different tribes that were cooperating with either (and both) the British or Spanish governments. Along with the Creek and Choctaw nations, the Chickasaws, Uchizes, Tallapoosas, Alabamu and more took part in the raiding of settlements between Pensacola and Mobile, according to these reports.[20] Even within these native nations, there were extensive factions and divisions that uniquely aligned with the great powers in North America. With that said, a great majority of natives that took part in the January 7 attack were from the Choctaw tribe.[21] More well-established alliances were based on previous political connections, personal ties, or trustworthy promises from either the

14. Declaración de desertores, Mobile, March 2, 1781, Cuba 3A, AGI.
15. Waldeck, *The Diary of Philipp Waldeck*.
16. Declaración de desertores, Mobile, March 2, 1781; "KEY, Philip Barton." Biographical Directory of the United States Congress, https://bioguide.congress.gov/search/bio/K000159.
17. Declaración de desertores, Mobile, March 2, 1781.
18. Cameron to Germain, Pensacola, October 31 and November 30, 1780, CO: 5/82.
19. Memorial of Adam Chrystie, March 4, 1784, Audit Office 13/99/116-117, Library and Archives Canada.
20. "El Problema Indio," in Francisco de Borja Medina Rojas, *Jose de Ezpeleta, Gobernador de La Mobila: 1780-1781* (Seville: Escuela de Estudios Hispano-Americanos, 1980).
21. Campbell to Germain, Pensacola, January 5, 1781.

British or Spanish officials in the region, though these usually favored the British who had a longer standing in the region.

Commanding the British party was Waldecker Col. Johann Ludwig Wilhelm von Hanxleden. Throughout the West Florida campaign, Colonel von Hanxleden had earned high esteem from both the British and Spanish armies. Valiant and effective, he was considered by the Spanish to be the best officer for the British on the Gulf Coast during the campaign. Prior to the battle, he had been given the command of the primary fortification in Pensacola, Fort George, as he had an exceptional logistical and engineering skillset.[22] He possessed further qualities that his superior, General Campbell, did not demonstrate, such as consistently seeking for the better care of his troops. In addition to his glaring complaints of the treatment of German prisoners in the West Indies, he provided for his troops as often as he could to make their lives easier in the camp.[23] As proper food was scarce in Pensacola, he personally saw to the troops being fed a freshly slaughtered ox on a weekly basis to improve their morale.[24]

Perhaps even more important was Colonel von Hanxleden's willingness to work with and learn from the native nations that cooperated with the British. General Campbell saw their allies as unreliable and opportunistic. This led to distrust between the British and the natives. Whereas General Campbell assumed an arrogance over the natives, Colonel von Hanxleden felt they were effective allies and would work and fraternize directly with chiefs and warriors to strengthen their alliance.[25]

Unlike this planned assault in January, the previous three attacks had largely consisted of British-allied natives directed by a small number of British or Loyalists. As these natives (in this case largely Choctaws) from the previous assault on The Village had been significantly defeated, they sought revenge against the Spanish for their losses.[26] General Campbell took advantage of the eagerness of his allies by ordering for a full assault on the fortification, but with rank-and-file troops as the anchor of the force. He, like his Choctaw allies, felt that the Spanish detachment at the settlement was smaller and weaker than it actually was, and was ripe for another attack. He ordered

22. Waldeck, *The Diary of Philipp Waldeck.*
23. Daniel Krebs, *A Generous and Merciful Enemy: Life for German Prisoners of War During the American Revolution* (University of Oklahoma Press, 2013).
24. Waldeck, *The Diary of Philipp Waldeck.*
25. Ibid.
26. Cameron to Germain, Pensacola, November 30, 1780.

Colonel von Hanxleden to use his discretion to either take The Village by a full-frontal storming assault or by surprise.[27] The British war party departed from friendly territory on the morning of January 3.[28] William McIntosh, father of White Stick Creek chief William McIntosh Jr., and Farquhar Bethune would serve as direct commanders and translators for the Choctaw combatants.[29]

Though General Campbell had faith in his ground forces, he wanted to insure his victory with a two-pronged attack. A small naval fleet sailed out of Pensacola on the afternoon of January 4.[30] The ships were ordered to make their way to the mouth of Mobile Bay, then sail north, off the shore of The Village, a distance of about thrity miles. Commanded by Capt. Robert Deans, the fleet consisted of his flagship, the sloop-of-war *Mentor* with twenty-four guns, and the smaller sloop *Hound*. Their orders were to provide support for Colonel von Hanxleden and his troops and defend against any possible Spanish reinforcements coming across the bay from Mobile.[31] The fleet would have to find a way to sail past the coastal redoubt the Spanish had constructed on Dauphin Island at the mouth of the bay.

Reaching the pass of Mobile Bay on January 5, Captain Deans determined that he would elude fire from the redoubt by raising captured Spanish colors, pretending to be incoming friendly ships.[32] The trickery worked to perfection as they not only navigated the pass without a shot being fired but also captured a boat with Lt. Martin Galvano, five soldiers, and seven sailors coming to meet the presumed Spanish fleet. Learning that only about fifteen soldiers were left at their posts, Captain Deans decided to send a landing party the next morning to take the island. Though they were met with musket fire upon landing on the beach, then quickly overwhelmed and dispersed the defending Spanish; the British captured at least three soldiers including the remaining commanding sergeant, and several small arms. The British also burned the barracks on the island and took numerous Spanish slaves and heads of cattle.[33] While the supporting fleet enjoyed success in their raiding on the island, that would be the full extent of their accomplishments. The shallow bar halfway up Mobile Bay made it im-

27. Campbell to Germain, Pensacola, January 5, 1781.

28. Campbell to Johann von Hanxleden, January 2, 1781, AGI Cuba, 1233.

29. Cameron to Germain, Pensacola, February 10, 1781.

30. Robert R. Rea and James A. Servies, *The Log of H.M.S. Mentor, 1780–1781: A New Account of the British Navy at Pensacola* (University Presses of Florida, 1982).

31. Campbell to Germain, Pensacola, January 5, 1781.

32. Campbell to Germain, Pensacola, January 11, 1781, PRO CO:5/597, TNA.

33. Ibid; Rea and Servies, *The Log of H.M.S. Mentor*.

passible for any ocean-going vessel to attempt to reach the northern end. On the day of the attack, the most the supporting fleet could do was observe the smoke rising from the battlefield miles away. Knowing they were utterly useless for the assault, Captain Deans set sail that afternoon in an attempt to intercept Spanish ships off the coast of Ship Island.[34]

Despite a torrential downpour that night, the British assault force was right on schedule, reaching the Spanish stronghold before the dawn of January 7 at approximately 6 a.m. Two hundred yards away from the fort, Colonel von Hanxleden decided that he would split his forces in three to surround and take the complex by surprise. He ordered the first prong of the native forces commanded by Bethune and McIntosh combined with the contingent of Royal Forresters to sneak their way around to the backside fort, lying low between the Spanish forces and the bay, waiting for a signal by drumbeat to attack. He then organized his remaining troops into a single column, with his Waldecker Regiment in the front, and the British regulars and provincial militia in the rear. Capitalizing on the scarce light and dense fog, they swiftly and quietly advanced up the path and into the Spanish lines.[35]

Seeing only vague, shadowy figures in the dark, Sublieutenant Manuel de Cordova presumed the them to be friendly militiamen returning to trenches and ordered his men to hold their fire, which would lead to his immediate killing. Without a shot being fired, the attackers passed undetected through the New Orleans Colored Militia manning the outer trenches and came upon the main entrenchments of the regular Spanish forces. Upon passing the outer trenches, Colonel von Hanxleden had the British and provincial troops to go left and flank around the Spanish earthworks in order to penetrate a weaker spot in the defenses. The colonel and his forces did not expect the palisade that had been built and halted in confusion for a moment to assess the situation. In this suspense, all hell broke loose in the twilight as the commander of the fort, Don Ramon de Castro, realized the attack and ordered his men to open fire in a full coordinated defense of musket fire.[36]

34. Ibid; Campbell to Germain, Pensacola, January 11, 1781.
35. Benjamin Baynton to Peter Baynton, Pensacola, February 2, 1781, Pennsylvania State Archives (PSA), MG019, Sequestered Baynton, Wharton and Morgan Papers, 1725-1827, Part III, Baynton Family Papers, 1770-1827, Correspondence of Benjamin Bayton, 1777-1785; Campbell to Germain, Pensacola, January 11, 1781; Cameron to Germain, Pensacola, February 10, 1781; Ezpeleta to Gálvez. Mobile, January 20, 1781.
36. Ezpeleta to Gálvez. Mobile, January 20, 1781.

At the head of the column, Colonel von Hanxleden and some of his most trusted adjutants fearlessly charged into the muddied main trench that surrounded the stockade, with screams from both forces of their respective "long live the king!" Here, the British suffered their greatest loss right at the start of the action. After aggressive hand-to-hand combat with knives, bayonets, and musket volleys, the entrusted Colonel von Hanxleden was instantly killed with a musket ball to the forehead at the foot of the stockade, along with his lieutenant and adjutant Johann Heinrich Stierlin.[37]

While the Waldeckers were stopped in their tracks with the death of their colonel and his second-in-command, the British and provincial troops under Captain Key enjoyed greater success. Following their flanking maneuver, they dramatically climbed up the sandy-soiled rampart with fury while facing continuous musket volleys and grapeshot. After close quarters fighting, they stormed the left portion of the defenses and took control of one of the Spanish 4-pounder cannons. This forced the Spanish to retreat and defend the plaza of the fort. These positions were held for the next fifteen minutes. According to Spanish sources, though, an attack was made from the backside of the fort where there was no moat.[38] During the course of the battle one of the magazines of the fort was set on fire and produced a large plume of smoke.[39]

Benjamin Baynton, a lieutenant for the Pennsylvania provincials, wrote to his brother about the intense action he experienced, which led to his being wounded both by a musket ball and bayonet. He provided one of the only legitimate firsthand accounts that was not given for government or military purposes. He emotionally wrote:

> Out of five gallant sturdy fellows I had before the action singled out to follow me at my Side, and in case of necessity, assist me in mounting the works, only two are left to tell the story; and one of them, a Serjeant, who earnestly requested to attend me, dangerously wounded in two places. They fell fighting by my side. I have to lament on this occasion, beside several brave officers, a most faithful & affectionate servant, into

37. Ezpeleta to Gálvez, Mobile, January 20, 1781; Ezpeleta to Navarro, January 22, 1781, AGI Cuba, 1233; Benjamin Baynton to Peter Baynton, Pensacola, February 2, 1781; Campbell to Germain, Pensacola, January 7 and 11, 1781, PRO CO:5/597; Peter Chester to John Dalling, Pensacola, January 10, 1781, PRO CO:137/80; Campbell to Dalling, Pensacola, January 9, 1781, PRO CO:137/80; Campbell to Henry Clinton, Pensacola, January 7 & February 15, 1781, PRO 30:55/89.
38. Ibid.
39. Carl Philipp Steuernagel, *Carl Philipp Steuernagel Diary, 1773-1783*, trans. Bruce E. Burgoyne, University of West Florida, John C. Pace Library, Special Collections, M1983-09; Rea and Servies, *The Log of H.M.S. Mentor.*

> whose arms I fell when I received my wound. I cannot help mentioning the poor fellow, because I feel myself hurt at never having it in my power as I could wish, to show him the sense I had of his services, and particularly the warm attachment he manifested in the most eminent danger, and within three foot of the muzzles of the enemy's muskets.[40]

At the same time, the New Orleans militiamen that had been cut off by the assaulting troops from the fortification commenced to charge to the wharf on the bay, breaking through the enemy troops. The objective was to retreat to a supply boat that had arrived the previous afternoon. This would prove to be a damaging mistake. During this maneuver, the Choctaws and Royal Foresters, still lying in wait in this area, preyed upon the militiamen with musket fire. Much to the dismay of the militiamen, the boat had been moved further into the bay so that there could be no attempt at such a retreat. The fearful troops were so desperate that a few even attempted to swim and wade their way to the boat. Unfortunately, the pursuing natives closed in on these men in the water and proceeded to scalp them.[41]

With no other options, the surviving militiamen then turned and charged back the way they came. Though they fought aggressively to reach the fort, which was still being struggled over, they suffered additional casualties from the natives seeking to kill and scalp them, and from crossfire from the friendly Spanish positions. In one case a militia officer, Simón Calfá, was even bayoneted to death by confused Spanish troops when charging back into the fort. This counterattack nonetheless proved effective and helped swing the momentum of the battle in favor of the Spanish. In fact, the militia would later be praised by commanders for their counterattack in the battle.[42]

With the Spanish regulars' and militia's counterattack, the top commanders now dead, and the Choctaws having never attacked the fort, acting commander Captain Key decided promptly to retreat back to Pensacola, the natives serving as the rear guard. The action lasted a total of about six hours, finally ending around noon as the retreating force burned bridges behind them on the main road.[43]

40. Benjamin Baynton to Peter Baynton, Pensacola, February 2, 1781.

41. Ezpeleta to Gálvez. Mobile, January 20, 1781; Ezpeleta to Navarro, January 22, 1781; Campbell to Germain, Pensacola, January 7 and 11, 1781; Chester to Dalling, Pensacola, January 10, 1781; Campbell to Dalling, Pensacola, January 9, 1781; Campbell to Clinton, Pensacola, January 7 and February 15, 1781.

42. Ezpeleta to Gálvez, Mobile, January 20, 1781; Ezpeleta to Navarro, January 20 and 22, 1781.

43. Campbell to Germain, Pensacola, January 7 and 11, 1781; Baynton to Baynton, Pensacola, February 2, 1781.

Lieutenant Baynton intentionally recounted the battle in intensive detail which he felt would be "unpardonable" if he left any omission. He clearly sought to highlight the honor and gallantry of his troops in battle which he felt would be otherwise tarnished by the newspapers. Though he felt there was potential condemnation to do so as an officer and a soldier, he conveyed to his brother the sheer devastation his force faced:

> The particulars of this action you will I suppose see in the publick papers; but, this I will venture to assert, no action since the rebellion, (for the numbers) was more severe while it lasted, or where more honor has been reflected on the astonishing intrepidity of the British Troops. They pushed on upwards of two hundred yards through an incessant fire of grape & musket shot, from at least twice their number, entrenched up to their teeth. One continual sheet of fire presented itself for ten minutes. You may judge of the gallantry of the Officers, when you read in the papers that out of ten, six were killed and wounded. *It was Bunkers hill in miniature.*[44]

Though both sides suffered heavy casualties, the British assault had been a decisive defeat. The Spanish had suffered fourteen killed (including two officers), twenty-three wounded, and seventeen prisoners (sixteen of these from the action on Dauphin Island).[45] The British were initially dealt eighteen dead (including three officers), with twenty-three wounded.[46] Three of these wounded were taken prisoner, with one dying and the other two later being handed over to the British for medical care.[47] According to other escaped prisoners, many of the British wounded from the battle did not survive the three days heavy rain during the retreat and the rough conditions in Pensacola.[48] Juan Gros, the sole Spanish prisoner during the land attack, came upon a dreadful fate. A free Black militiaman from around New Orleans, Gros was soon sold into slavery by the British to a powerful Native American chief. Governor Gálvez himself made it a point to regain his freedom by making it a contingency in the articles of surrender after the Siege

44. Baynton to Baynton, Pensacola, February 2, 1781.
45. Ezpeleta, "Relacion de los Muertos, Heridos, y Prisioneros en el ataque del Destacamento de la Aldea el dia 7 de Enero de 1781", Mobile, January 15, 1781, S.G.U., LEG, 6912, 4.
46. Campbell. "Return of the Killed and wounded at Village opposite Mobile, the 7th January 1781", Pensacola, January 11, 1781, PRO CO:5/597; Ezpeleta to Gálvez, Mobile, January 20, 1781; Ezpeleta to Piernas, Mobile, January 10, 1781, AGI Cuba, 2359.
47. Ezpeleta to Piernas, Mobile, January 10, 1781.
48. Ezpeleta to Diego Josef Navarro, Mobile, January 26, 1781, AGI Cuba, 1233.

of Pensacola.[49] However, Gros would be enslaved for another eight years until his strenuously negotiated manumission by Spanish authorities and comrades. He would return to the service of the militia when his freedom was regained.[50]

The British defeat at The Village was a greater loss than statistics would indicate. General Campbell was no longer able to effectively commence offensive operations from Pensacola for the rest of the war. This included, of course, any advances towards The Village or Mobile. The Spanish secured the vital ferry point and base of operations with their victory and were now able to prepare for a siege of General Campbell's headquarters in Pensacola. But the greatest British loss, not just of the battle, but quite possibly of the entire Gulf Coast campaign, was the death of Colonel von Hanxleden. Because of his high regard and gallantry, the Spanish buried him with military honors by firing a rocket over his grave.[51] Furthermore, according to historian Max von Eelking, he was buried under a large and magnificent tree and had a fence constructed around his burial mound.[52] Contemporary sources and modern scholars remain consistent that the primary factor leading to the British defeat was the premature death of the colonel. Not only did his death leave the forces without a commanding officer, but it also prevented the signal for the delayed attack of the 400 natives lying in wait.[53]

The loss of this capable officer was the writing on the wall for the British in Pensacola. It was also met with anger as it was reported that General Campbell wanted to immediately counterattack as an act of vengeance but was restrained by his officers.[54] Indeed, the loss of this effective commander, along with two other esteemed officers, likely ended any chance of the British maintaining a foothold in West Florida. With such a casualty rate of exceptionally experienced, effective officers, and the halting of offensive capabilities, the British in Pen-

49. Ezpeleta, "Relacion", January 15, 1781; Bernardo de Galvez, *Diario de las Operaciones de la Expedicion contra la Plaza de panzacola concluida por las armas de S.M. catolica, Baxo Las Ordenes del mariscal de campo D. bernardo de Galvez* (Havana, 1781); Kimberly S. Hanger, *Personas de Varias Clases y colores: Free people of color in Spanish New Orleans, 1769–1803*, PhD Diss, University of Florida, 1991.
50. Hanger, *Personas de Varias*, 1991.
51. Steuernagel, *Carl Philipp Steuernagel Diary, 1773–1783*.
52. Max von Eelking, *Die deutschen hulfstruppen im nordamerikanischen befreiungskriege 1776 bis 1783* (Hannover: Helwing, 1863).
53. Campbell to Germain, Pensacola, January 7 and 11, 1781; Cameron to Germain, Pensacola, February 10, 1781.
54. Ezpeleta to Navarro, Mobile, January 26, 1781.

sacola were left with no momentum, far less leadership capabilities, and broken morale when the Spanish besieged Pensacola that March. When Pensacola fell, Spain regained full control over Florida.

Ironically, Lieutenant Baynton's concerns over being publicly branded as a disappointment never materialized. Though there were numerous firsthand reports and descriptions of the battle, it, along with the settlement it was fought over, have largely been forgotten. Compared to battles in the region from other eras like the Civil War, The Battle at the Village does not have a real imprint in the public memory. This is despite it being the bloodiest Revolutionary War battle in Alabama history. Why did this small yet regionally vital battle subside in notoriety? The answer: the people.

From 1763 to 1813, control of the Mobile area changed hands from the French to the British to the Spanish and finally, to the American government. While some settler families from each colonial era remained permanently, many left the area for places retained by their respective national governments after each conquest. As they departed with their belongings and families, so too did they take their memories. In essence, the majority of the Mobile area population in 1781 was eventually displaced by an American-centered population by the mid-1800s. Consequently, the collective memory of the Battle at The Village was all but forgotten except for those who sought out the history, like local authors and historical societies.

Unfortunately, this collective memory loss is a microcosm of the long-storied and rich history of the Gulf Coast. Unlike the Eastern Seaboard which never saw a major colonial administrative-population displacement (aside from Native American) and acted as the foundation of the United States' growth, the Gulf Coast regularly saw population changes in its early history. Every time a population was displaced, their connections and local accomplishments would effectively be erased from that area. Though these histories played a vital role for how the United States formed and operates today, many Americans, both at the national and local levels, now see this as peripheral or irrelevant.

The lack of awareness has now produced a detrimental situation where historical preservation of the battle site is virtually impossible. According to archaeologists, the area where this once important battle took place has now been decimated by virtually unrestricted suburban developments.[55] Unless awareness and scholarship of the rich history

55. Daniel T. Elliott, et al, *Revolutionary War/War of 1812 Historic Preservation Study* Vol. 1 (Ellerslie, GA: Southern Research, Historic Preservation Consultants, Inc., 2002).

surrounding the battle increases, the physical state of the battlefield will deteriorate further, and archaeological work will be even more hindered. Better education both at the local and state levels on the battle would contribute to increased advocacy for the preservation of the site.

In many ways, we can look to Colonel von Hanxleden as a symbol of the current historical status of the battle and its preservation. At one time, the colonel had a well-respected reputation and an impressive record. Now he rests in obscurity, lost to time in disturbed soil so far away from his home. He, along with his and his adversaries' valor and struggles, now lie underneath a suburban neighborhood which was once marked by a large and dignified tree.

Ramsour's Mill, June 20, 1780: The Beginning of the End of Cornwallis' Loyalist Illusion

SCOTT SYFERT

Following the surrender of the major coastal capital of Charlestown, South Carolina (present-day Charleston) to the joint army-navy expeditionary force led by Maj. Gen. Sir Henry Clinton and Vice Admiral Mariot Arbuthnot in May 1780, British land forces began to fan out across the Carolina interior to reestablish Royal control. When Clinton returned to New York in early June, command in the south transferred to Lt. Gen, Charles, Earl Cornwallis.

As late May gave way to early summer, British strategy was, first, to mop up any remaining Continental or militia forces outside of Charlestown. Second, to establish contact with population centers thought to be especially sympathetic to the British. Although it was not clear where and to what extent such sympathy existed, areas around Orangeburg, South Carolina and Cross Creek (now Fayetteville, North Carolina) were thought to be broadly loyal. Third, to establish garrison posts commanded by regular British officers at key junctions to subdue and overawe the local population, especially in predominantly Whig areas. Cornwallis intended to use these garrisons as rallying points where Loyalist militias could be organized, armed and trained by British officers.

The British began to establish forward posts in an arc across South Carolina. To the west, near the Indian frontier, he sent forces to take the existing fort of Ninety Six. In the center, a depot was established at the town of Camden, which could be supplied from Charlestown. North of Camden, two camps were set up, one on a high prominence on the Catawba River called Rocky Mount, and, roughly fifteen miles away, another on the Camden Road near Hanging Rock Creek. Finally, to the west, the 71st Regiment of Foot, Fraser's Highlanders. were sent to the village of Cheraw. The posts were close enough to support one another if attacked, but advanced enough to give warning of any approach by an invading Continental army, which was surely to arrive sometime that summer.

As Cornwallis explained the strategy in a letter to the British Secretary of State for the American Department, he began by "fixing posts of troops from the Pedee to the Savannah Rivers, to awe the disaffected and encourage the loyal inhabitants." In addition, Cornwallis "took every measure in my power to raise some Provincial corps and to establish a militia" for the defense and for the internal government of South Carolina.[1]

The keystone of this strategy was the raising of a large Loyalist army among the citizens of South Carolina. Once this was done, this local force could maintain order in the Carolinas, freeing the British army to advance north into North Carolina and, ultimately, Virginia. This presupposed, of course, that such a body of motivated and reliable soldiers existed in the Carolinas, ready to be animated. Was this true?

No one knew for sure, but London decision makers had long harbored this belief (or illusion). In this they were constantly reinforced by many former Royal governors, such as North Carolina's Josiah Martin, who endlessly lobbied them that the bulk of the population was loyal, and only required a spark to light the counter-revolution. This was the "Loyalist Gamble," that is, a bet that if properly motivated and energized, and more importantly armed and trained by British regulars, a pro-British local militia could be activated in the South. Whether this strategy was grounded in reality or wishful thinking remained to be seen.

As Cornwallis consolidated established his bases across South Carolina in early June 1780, he sent emissaries to establish direct communication with "our friends in North Carolina." It was imperative that these Loyalist leaders not rise up prematurely, before they could be supported by the arrival of British regulars. This would not happen until late summer at the earliest. If they did, and were defeated early in the campaign, it might entirely deflate and derail the Loyalist project upon which British strategy for the Carolinas depended. For the moment, Cornwallis advised the Loyalist leaders to gather their crops, make preparations to rise when called upon, but otherwise take no action.

1. "Cornwallis to Germain," August 20, 1780, *The Cornwallis Papers*, ed. Ian Saberton (Uckfield, UK: Naval & Military Press Ltd., 2010), 2:7-8.

Keeping the Carolina Loyalists quiet, however, was not going to be easy. Since the departure of British Governors and the capture of power by the Whigs in the spring of 1775, they had been on the defensive. "Unwilling to forego their allegiance to the Crown, many were imprisoned, brought to the whipping post, banished, subjected to confiscation, and executed for treason," writes one British historian.[2] In the lawless environment that followed, Loyalist homes were burned by revolutionary irregulars, sometimes acting as armed gangs, who "unrestrained by concepts of civilized behavior took advantage of the disordered times and practiced all sorts of enormities ranging from plunder and destruction of property to severe chastisement, murder, and rape."[3] Now, the tide had turned. With the British ascendant in the summer of 1780, revenge was foremost on their minds.

In early June, two North Carolina Loyalist leaders, Lt. Col. John Moore and Maj. Nicholas Welch, both from the foothill area in Tryon County due west of Mecklenburg, arrived back home. Both had been serving with the British army that spring, and were acting under Cornwallis's authority. Returning to his family's farm in early summer dressed in a tattered British regimental uniform and bearing an officer's sword, Moore brought first-hand accounts of the fall of Charlestown. Welch, also finely dressed in a red Regimental uniform, began freely handing out guinea coins "to allure some, whilst he endeavored to intimidate others by an account of the success of the British army in all the operation of the South, and the total inability of the Whigs to make further opposition."[4]

They issued a summons to those loyal to the Crown to meet and discuss their strategy at a well known assembly place, near a mill on the west side of the Catawba river. Moore's family lived about six miles from the mill, owned by Jacob Ramsour (sometimes spelled Ramseur). Moore's message was that they were to bring in their harvest, gather weapons and ammunition, and make themselves ready to fight when the British army moved north into their area, possibly later that summer.

Over the first few weeks of June, more and more volunteers arrived at Ramsour's Mill. By mid-June, there were nearly 1,200 men, many of them boys or teenagers. Moore and Welch had not brought supplies and weapons with them, so each man was supposed to have armed

2. Ian Saberton, *The American Revolutionary War in the South* (Tolworth, UK: Grosvenor House Pub. Ltd., 2018), 153.

3. Ibid.

4. William A. Graham, *General Joseph Graham and His Papers* (Raleigh, NC: Edwards & Broughton, 1904), 215.

South Carolina during the American Revolution. The Catawba River is at top left, with Ramsour's shown above Kings Mountain and Charlotte to the east. Ninety Six is at center left, with Orangeburg to the southeast, and Charleston at lower right. This map contains many places of significance to the Revolution. (*Library of Congress*)

himself. As such, of the thousand plus men, probably a third of them had no weapons at all.

Meanwhile, Whig partisans in the area had heard of Moore and Welch's unwanted arrival and the mustering of Loyalists, and were determined to break it up. Around Charlotte, Brig. Gen. Griffith Rutherford had mustered several hundred local volunteers in late May, following Buford's defeat and Lord Rawdon's expedition into the Waxhaw area along the North/South Carolina border. Maj. William R. Davie, of renown in the Waxhaws, had also gathered sixty-five mounted dragoons and infantry not far from Ramsour's. Other local leaders from the area had similar bands, and each were eager to fight.

Rutherford resolved to attack Moore's Loyalists at the first opportunity, and to this end marched on June 18 from Charlotte Town to the Tuckasegee Ford on the Catawba River, just twelve miles away. Rutherford ordered Col. Francis Locke to gather forces to supplement him, and once combined, they would attack the Loyalist encampment. Other local leaders and their volunteer forces, led by Joseph McDowell, David Wilson and others, grew Locke's militia band to 400 men. On the evening of June 19, this large body of inexperienced, largely untrained civilians was camped at Mountain Creek, sixteen miles from Ramsour's. After a council of war, they agreed to attack the next morning. Meanwhile, Rutherford had sent a messenger instructing Locke to have his forces link up with him for a combined attack. Due to some mistake or miscommunication, Locke never got the message. While Rutherford waited for Locke to arrive, Locke, unaware that Rutherford was near, prepared to attack the Loyalists on his own at sunrise on June 20. His men broke camp the night before, rode through the night, and were only a mile from the Loyalist camp at day break.

The Loyalists were deployed on top of a ridgeline clear of underbrush with scattered large oaks, 300 yards east of Ramsour's Mill. The right of their camp lay on the downward slope near the Tuckaseegee Road, roughly six hundred yards from their encampment. From the crest of the hill, they had an excellent field of fire down the slope, with only a few trees interspersed. To their rear was a large pond on which Ramsour's mill stood. At the base of the hill was a small glen, fringed with bushes near the road. A fence ran from the glen to the right of their line. A low fog shrouded the road and the hill that morning.

Moore had placed a dozen picket guards on the approaching road, but otherwise had not organized a defensive perimeter. The companies of approaching Whig horsemen, therefore, arrived completely unexpectedly through the morning fog before the sentinels had any idea what was happening. Surprised but recognizing enemy cavalry, they fired at the dragoons, and fled up the hill towards their camp.

The cavalry charged them, firing on the awakening men in camp, who scrambled from their tents, searching for their weapons and clothes. At first Moore's men were in confusion, but they recovered from their initial panic and poured fire back at the Whig horsmen.

The Whig dragoons, although having the element of surprise, were still greatly outnumbered, and as Moore's men began firing in earnest, they retreated in disorder back down the hill. As they reached the base of the hill, Locke's infantrymen, who had not been able to keep up with the charge, were only then arriving, and the two forces met in some disorder. The dragoons rode through and past them to reassemble, while the infantry faced uphill to fire at the Loyalists, taking what cover they could find.

Seeing the Whig cavalry retreat, the Loyalists crept slowly down the hill and proceeded to fire upon the disorganized scrum at the base of the slope from behind trees, wagons and baggage. The Loyalists' musketry fire, remembered Davie, "was well directed," and "the action became general."[5] In turn, the Whigs formed a firing line facing the camp from the fence, on their left, across the base of the hill, to the right. It was a fight "without order or system," recalled Whig soldier Joseph Graham, with round after round of musket shots thundering on the hill side, mixing smoke and shouts with the humid mid-summer morning fog.[6]

Few of the officers or men on either side that morning had fired their weapon at another man before. Many were very young, just teenagers, and probably a third of them, at least on the Loyalist side, were unarmed. Neither side wore uniforms, and thus would have been nearly indistinguishable from one another (as a slight mark of differentiation, the Whigs wore a piece of white paper in the front of their hats—which made them excellent targets for the Loyalist marksmen—while the Loyalists wore green sprigs).

For half an hour, the two sides exchanged gunfire. The lines crept forwards or back, depending on who was receiving the worst of the fire. At one point, the Whigs were pushed back into the bushes near the glade, as the Tory "fire became so destructive." Then a group of Whigs led by Capt. Joseph Hardin moved forward on the Loyalist's left flank along the fence line, and began a "galling fire on the right flank of the Tories."[7] Another group extended the line on the Tory left, and now the Whig firing line, properly formed and extended, threatened to turn both their flanks. Fired on from three sides, the Loyalists were gradually pushed back towards the crest of the hill.

5. Blackwell Robinson (ed.), *The Revolutionary War Sketches of William R. Davie* (Raleigh, NC: NCDCR, 1976), 7.

6. Graham, *General Joseph Graham*, 220-221.

7. Ibid., 221.

Crowded in together on the exposed hilltop in close quarters, neighbors and fellow churchgoers fired at close range at one another or fought hand to hand, swinging musket butts as weapons. The melee was general. "The lines was crossed and neither side couldn't tell one another apart," stated one witness.[8] As Graham remembered, "In this battle, neighbors, near relations and personal friends fought against each other; and as the smoke would from time to time blow off, they could recognize each other."[9] In one episode, two old friends, a Whig named Billy and a Tory "Dutchman," argued while swinging their gun butts at one another.

> The Dutchman cried out, 'Oh, stop, stop! I is not going to stand still and be killed like a damned fool neder [*sic*—neither],' and raised the butt of his gun and made a blow at Billy's head, which he missed, and one of Billy's comrades, whose piece was loaded, clapped his muzzle under the Dutchman's arm and the poor fellow fell dead.[10]

The sun continued to rise over the scrum of men fighting hand to hand on the exposed hilltop. By now, the Loyalists were being fired upon on three sides, both their flanks having been turned. Capt. Nicholas Warlick of the Loyalists tried to rally his men on the hilltop; those without weapons were told to retreat down the other side of the hill, and take cover across the mill pond. Seeing these men pull back may have triggered a broader collapse of their lines, as men panicked and ran. One Whig recalled:

> The fightin' went on for near an hour with hundreds of dead on both sides. The Tories had the advantage as they was on the ridgeline and hid by bushes and such. As our infantry got close they began to fight hand to hand with the butts of their guns as they didn't have no bayonet on 'em.[11]

When Captain Warlick was shot dead by a sharpshooter, the game was over, and mass panic set in. Running men splashed across the fast running creek. Others tried to swim the mill pond and drowned. The Loyalists

> retreated down the ridge toward the mill, exposed to the fire of the centre and of Captain Harden's company behind the fences. The Whigs

8. Pension statement of Samuel Patton of Rowan County, NC, in William Thomas Sherman, *Calendar and Record of the Revolutionary War in the South: 1780-1781* (Seattle, WA: Gun Jones Publishing, 2011), 184-5.
9. Graham, *General Joseph Graham*, 225.
10. Ibid., 222.
11. Patton in Sherman, *Calendar*, 184-5.

> pursued until they got entire possession of the ridge, when they perceived to their astonishment that the Tories had collected in force on the other side of the creek, beyond the mill.[12]

It made no difference. The Whigs were now too tired and disorganized to mount a further attack against the confused mass of men across the creek. Locke himself could only muster less than a hundred of his original 400 men, and thus feared a counter-attack should the Loyalists regroup. He sent messengers to Rutherford to reinforce him. But the Loyalists were broken as well. Moore proposed a ceasefire to gather the wounded, but it was really just a ruse to delay a further attack on his unorganized and defeated men in the woods across the creek. While Locke considered a response, Moore instructed the remaining Loyalists to flee in any way they could. Rutherford was now en route to the battlefield, but by the time he arrived a few hours later, the Tories were gone. It was over.

At least seventy men lay dead scattered along the slope of the ridge. A great number of officers on either side were killed, including Warlick, as was his brother, Philip. The two of them lie there to this day, on the hill summit, beneath a stone and a British flag. As the men on each side had no uniforms, it was not known which were Tory or Whig, but the proportion of fatalities was probably equal. Many were buried in a common grave at the summit. About 100 men on both sides were wounded. Fifty Tories were taken prisoner, and all of their weapons, provisions and horses seized. The evening of the following day, relatives of the soldiers on either side searched the hillsides looking to retrieve the bodies of their slain kin.

In the days and hours after the battle, Davie's cavalry was sent in pursuit of the scattered and retreating Tories. Many Tory militia leaders surrendered in the following days and, as Davie put it, "that district of country lying between the [Catawba] river, the mountains and [South Carolina] was entirely cleared of the Enemy."[13]

The battle of Ramsour's Mill was a shambles for the Loyalist cause, and smashed the promise of British friends in North Carolina, even before it could get started. Writing to the Secretary of State at the end of August, after which he had more time to reflect on the debacle in Tryon County, Cornwallis decried the Loyalists "having assembled without concert, plan or proper leaders . . . [and thus] were surprised and totally routed by the Son of Genl. Rutherford. Many of them fled

12. Patrick O'Kelley, *Nothing But Blood and Slaughter* (Harnett, NC: Blue House Tavern Press, 2004), 186.
13. William R. Davie, in Sherman, *Calendar*, 184.

into this Province [South Carolina], where their reports tended much to terrify our friends and encourage our enemies."[14]

Although the overall casualties were relatively insignificant, the moral effect was devastating. Rawdon was told that "the loyalists were completely scattered . . . this advantage on the part of the rebels may shake the fidelity of our new-formed militia on the borders unless the troops are present to awe them to their duty."[15]

The loyalist leaders, particularly Moore, took the blame for acting against Cornwallis's express instructions. "The folly and imprudence of our friends is unpardonable," wrote Cornwallis, continuing,

> I desire you will inform Lt. Colonel Hamilton that I wish him to come to town immediately, and would have him acquaint his officers before he leaves the regiment that, if I hear of any more instances of irregularity about recruiting or disobedience of orders, that I will put the regiment into garrison on Sullivan's Island.[16]

Moore was threatened with court martial. British Lt. Col. George Turnbull, commanding Rocky Mount, agreed, blaming "that weak silly man Moore, who led a parcel of those poor innocent devils of North Carolina into a scrape."[17]

Ramsour's Mill also set in motion a series of chain reactions that would lead to an unravelling of British strategy in the Carolinas. First, the perception that restoration of British rule was inevitable, following the fall of Charlestown and the massacre of Buford's detachment in late May in the Waxhaws, was checked. Second, the horses, muskets and other supplies that had been gathered to launch the loyalist project in North Carolina were lost to the Whigs. And of course, the loss of manpower both in terms of killed and wounded, as well as those who would now sit the campaign out, was considerable. Consider if Patrick Ferguson had had an additional thousand or more men with him at the Battle of Kings Mountain, which would occur just three and a half months later. The nascent loyalist army could also have been useful in fighting William R. Davie and Thomas Sumter's militias in the Charlotte and Waxhaws area, with implications for the later battles of Hanging Rock and Rocky Mount. But all that was in the future.

More importantly, just a few months into the southern campaign, the fragility of Cornwallis's Loyalist gamble was exposed, although

14. Ibid.
15. Saberton, *Cornwallis Papers*, 1:182.
16. Ibid., 1:185.
17. Ibid., 1:363-4.

Cornwallis and the high command had not yet lost hope that it might still work. Still, it might be argued that through ill discipline, poor leadership and the fortunes of war, the project of creating a motivated and reliable Loyalist militia appeared to have fallen at the first hurdle. In retrospect, of course, the Loyalist gamble was, in truth, an illusion, one that would take a few more months to fully extinguish itself. As the British military historian John Fortescue put it in his *History of the British Army*: "Of all foundations on which to build the conduct of a campaign [the Loyalist gamble was] the loosest, the most treacherous, the fullest of peril and delusion; yet … there was none [that was] more in favour with British ministers, with the inevitable consequence of failure and disaster."[18] Although it would take until the end of the year for the Loyalist Illusion to become manifest to Cornwallis and others, its disintegration began on the slopes of a small hill in Tryon County.

18. J.W. Fortescue, *A History of the British Army* (Uckfield, UK: Naval & Military Press Ltd.), 3:168.

Love, American (Revolution) Style: The Romances of Otho Holland Williams

DERRICK E. LAPP

The senate chamber of the Maryland State House was more crowded than usual. It was Tuesday, December 23, 1783. Congress had recently relocated to Annapolis, and now George Washington was in town to fulfill a promise he made to that body in Philadelphia eight years earlier.

"I went with several others to see Gen. Washington resign his Commission," Annapolis socialite Mary Ridout later wrote her mother, "Both Houses of the Assembly were present as Spectators" and the gallery overlooking the chamber was "full of Ladies."[1] On the floor below, other prominent citizens and soldiers came to witness the event as well. Among the crowd was Otho Holland Williams, one of Maryland's three general officers in the Continental Army. Williams was part of the delegation that met Washington when the commander-in-chief stopped in Baltimore—where the thanks of the town's inhabitants were offered on the "happy conclusion of an unequal, precarious and bloody War."[2] He then accompanied Washington on the final leg of the journey to meet with Congress in Annapolis. In the painting *General George Washington Resigning His Commission* by John Trumbull commemorating the event, Williams is depicted fourth behind the

1. Maryland State Archives: Mrs. James N. Galloway and Mrs. Frederick G. Richards Collection, 1784, MSA SC 358-1-2. Letter, M[ary] Ridout to Mrs. [Anne Tasker] Ogle, January 16, 1784.
2. Otho Holland Williams to George Washington, December 18, 1783, Papers of Otho Holland Williams, Maryland Center for History and Culture. Photocopies of 3 reels obtained by the author. Unless otherwise noted, all correspondence to and from Williams cited hereafter is sourced from the Papers of Otho Holland Williams.

Commander-in-Chief, dressed in his uniform, a blue coat faced with red in the style of the Maryland Line. But as momentous as the proceedings were, there was much more on the mind of Otho Williams that day than the affairs of state—he was in Annapolis also to attend to affairs of the heart.

The object of this affair was a young woman named Sophia. The "fascinating Sophia" as Williams once referred to her. He was smitten in what appears to have been a whirlwind romance filled with secret meetings and "clandestine letters . . . etc." It consumed his every thought. To one of his comrades from the army, Otho had to apologize for not writing back sooner due to his being "involved in a little love affair which postpones everything else."[3] To another close friend, he was less cryptic: "It is true, I am engaged to Miss S."[4]

Williams had a problem, however. Sophia's parents did not approve. "The father is biased by the mother, who is obdurate" in her opposition to the match—a match Williams, himself, characterized as "notorious." In frustration, he complained, "Sophia is so closely confined, or watched when she's from home, that I cannot possibly speak to her."[5] It made for a challenging courtship. "Once only" over the course of several weeks was Williams able to "press her to his heart," and even after months passed, he had to admit to a friend that he could give "no positive assurance of what is to be the result of my fond attachment" to Sophia. All he could do was "stand prepared for the worst, hope for the best, and commit my self to fortune."[6]

Fortune sent help in the form of Otho's comrade from the 1780-81 campaigns in North and South Carolina, Henry Lee. "Light Horse Harry" encouraged his despondent friend. "If the lady is worthy, she is sincere. If she is sincere, then she will elope," he advised.[7] Lee did his best to play matchmaker. He met with the family "on the Hill," located just outside Annapolis, and vouched for Williams. Sophia's parents were unmoved. "Every character of distinction, all the former friends of [Sophia's father] and even his [Sophia's father] own mother" were interested in Otho and Sophia's "favor," Williams complained. But her mother and father remained "inexorable."[8]

3. Williams to William Pierce, May 8, 1783.
4. Williams to Phillip Thomas, May 8, 1783.
5. Ibid.
6. Ibid.; Williams to William Jackson, September 22, 1783.
7. Henry Lee to Williams, December 15, 1783.
8. Williams to Thaddeus Kosciusco, August 1, 1783. Otho Holland Williams papers, Middle Brook, NJ, Baltimore, and elsewhere, 1778-1790, https://cdm16923.contentdm.oclc.org/digital/collection/p16923coll3/id/1494/rec/3.

None of the letters extant within the Otho Williams Papers housed at the Maryland Center for History and Culture give Sophia's last name, so it is hard to determine her identity definitively, but there are a few hints that point to a family name. We know she lived in Annapolis. Henry Lee, as noted above, mentions meeting Sophia and her parents "on the Hill." Another friend would later reference "Strawberry Hill" regarding Sophia's residence. There was a home known as Strawberry Hill in Annapolis, located on what are now the grounds of the U.S. Naval Academy. This home belonged to Richard Sprigg, a member of a wealthy, influential family of Maryland, and he had a daughter named Sophia. She was born in 1766 and would have been seventeen or eighteen at the time. Otho Williams was thirty-four.[9]

A week before Washington was expected to arrive in Annapolis, Henry Lee sent a note to Williams. "Get down here," he urged. The only option was for the couple to elope, after which Washington could smooth things over with the family. The idea was to declare the betrothal at one of the many balls being held in Annapolis the week of Washington's resignation. It was Sophia's "own plan" according to Otho. She was "prepared to . . . throw herself Under my protection," he related to Nathanael Greene, "when I was to bear [her] off . . . from . . . a full assembly of the most fashionable people at the Court of the United States." It was romantic. It was daring. But then Sophia got cold feet.[10]

Before the ball even started, Sophia sent Otho a note. She called it off. What's more, Sophia proposed they return their previous letters and pledges, and that "the only thing in which [he could] oblige her is never to see or speak of her again." Dumbfounded, Williams replied with a "delicate but poignant censure of her perfidy." But he was devastated. To Greene he admitted, "nothing can compensate for the wretchedness to which I have been wantonly exposed. I have suffered the extremity of mental misery."[11] It was a blow to his heart. It was a blow to his ego as well. Otho had quite an ego. Years later, as president of the United States, and while assessing the characteristics of possible generals to command the army, George Washington noted that

9. Alexander Skinner to Williams, September 9, 1784; A Biographical Dictionary of the Maryland Legislature 1635-1789 by Edward C. Papenfuse, et. al. p594., A historical marker on the grounds of USNA, located on Phythian Road near the entrance to the USNA cemetery notes the location and evolution of Strawberry Hill.

10. Henry Lee to Williams, December 15, 1783. Williams to Nathanael Greene, January 14, 1784.

11. Williams to Greene, January 14, 1784.

Williams was "a sensible man, but not without vanity."[12] "Sensibility" (a concept we would now term as sensitivity) was easily offended in gentlemen of that age, and in addition to his own emotional pain, Otho worried about his particularly sensitive friend Thaddeus Kosciusko.[13] Of the aborted elopement he warned Nathaniel Greene that Kosciuszko "will be petrified at all this if he hears of it," although he admitted to not knowing the Polish officer's whereabouts. "He promised to be here a month ago," complained Otho. Ironically, Kosciuszko was with Greene at the time.[14]

So far, I've not found the "smoking gun"—that definitive explanation, as to why Sophia backed out of the plan. Given that her parents opposed a marriage to Williams, this factor may be what ultimately influenced her decision. We can only speculate about the reason for the Spriggs' opposition (assuming this was indeed Sophia's family). Williams was a Continental general and well regarded for his service, especially his participation in the action in the Carolinas. That regard translated into his securing one of the most lucrative positions in the Maryland government—collections officer for the port of Baltimore. "You are now rich!" Otho's friend and fellow Maryland officer Samuel Smith exclaimed when he learned of the appointment. According to Sam, Otho had just secured "the hansomest appointment in this State," one worth 1,000 guineas, "against numerous and respectable competion."[15] So, presumably, wealth and prestige ought not have been the factor for Richard Sprigg and his wife to resist Otho Williams. Perhaps it was age. As noted above, Williams was seventeen years older than Sophia. Her eventual husband, John Francis Mercer, was, by contrast, only seven years Sophia's senior. The Mercers were married in 1785. Sophia Sprigg Mercer died in 1812.

Otho had come close to marriage before. Early in the war he was taken with a "most amiable creature," Maria Ogden, whom he referred to in 1778 as his "Dear Girl." Unfortunately, there was, as Otho phrased it, the "parity of our fortunes" to consider.[16] Samuel Smith was more blunt about the situation: "Marriage would ruin you," he cautioned. As

12. "Memorandum on General Officers, 9 March 1792," https://founders.archives.gov/documents/Washington/05-10-02-0040.

13. Charles Royster, *A Revolutionary People at War: The Continental Army & American Character, 1775-1783* (Chapel Hill: University of North Carolina Press, 1979), 85-95. See especially p. 89 regarding "sensibility".

14. Williams to Greene, January 14, 1784.

15. Samuel Smith to Williams, January 9, 1783.

16. Williams to Smith, December 23, 1778.

rampant inflation devalued the paper currency the Continental Army received, Smith pointed out that an officer's pay would not even "furnish clothes for yourself," let alone a prospective wife, and, Sam reminded Otho, "the girl has no fortune."[17] Smith's advice was anchored in experience. He had his and his family's dwindling finances to manage in the face of his own pending nuptials. Despite Samuel Smith's brave defense of the Delaware River forts following the fall of Philadelphia to the British in 1777 (for which he was awarded a sword by Congress), money and marriage proved the deciding factors in his decision to leave the army. Otho Williams, however, chose another course. "Adieu Maria," he lamented, "I never felt the weighty curse of poverty so heavily as at this instant."[18] He remained in the army. It was a testament to Otho's dedication to the cause. He would fight for American independence, giving up on love in favor of continued hardship in the Continental Army. One has to wonder, however, would he have acted differently had Maria come from wealth. Would he have married had a hefty dowry been available?

In a letter to Smith, Williams noted that Maria went back to Long Island. This suggests he probably met her while on parole in the town of Flatbush, following his capture at the Battle of Fort Washington. Regardless, Maria's name does not appear again in Otho's papers. The names of other women, however, do figure in correspondence between Otho and his friends. They wrote about ladies quite a bit, in fact. They compared notes, pointing out young ladies of particular interest. Samuel Smith was a notorious gossip. "Miss De Visme is a sweet girl," he informed Williams, and "Mrs. Provost's good disposition and elegant manners make up for her want of beauty." Another of Otho's friends, William Heth, asked Otho, during the latter's time in Petersburg, Virginia, "did you happen to meet a most accomplished little Sirene, Miss Briggs of Wales?"[19] (Wales in this case meaning a plantation in Dinwiddie County just west of Petersburg, Virginia.) And Thaddeus Kosciuszko, Nathaniel Greene's chief engineer in the Southern Department, related to Otho his adventures with the ladies in South Carolina, drawing their portraits and being chased by them. Fashionable women of America's elite class were practically an obsession for the officers in Otho's circle (most probably this was the case for many an en-

17. Smith to Williams, November 29, 1778.
18. Williams to Smith, December 23, 1778.
19. For a possible portrait of "Miss Briggs" see https://colonialvirginiaportraits.org/portrait/dorothy-pleasants-briggs-nicholas-mrs-john-nicholas/.

listed man as well—we just don't have as extensive a written record as that available in Otho's papers).[20]

It's not a wonder that fascination with the opposite sex proved such a popular topic for Otho and his friends. The war presented the chance for a greater number of people to mingle from across the former colonies than ever before. And young men were eager to attract the attention (and the affection) of young women. After the failed engagement with Maria Ogden, Samuel Smith tried to entice Otho to visit Philadelphia (after the British evacuated the city in 1778) to experience the pleasures of metropolis for himself. "Officers are much Caress'd here," Smith encouraged Williams, adding, "Arnold likes the Tory ladies and so would you." It was an interesting observation given the fallout that would result from Benedict Arnold's attraction to one Tory lady in particular—Peggy Shippen. Who was marrying whom became just as much a topic for gossip as the single ladies. A fellow officer who entered matrimony was said to have "gone to the gown." And as much as the unions were discussed, so too were the near misses. "Major Jack Stewart was dam'd nigh it," Smith joked to Williams, "How he escap'd I know not . . . her wedding cloth[e]s are made but . . . poor Kitty Crane, you must hug your sheets."[21] As for Sam, he did marry. His bride was a good Whig, Miss Margaret Spear, daughter of a prominent Baltimore merchant. Smith resigned from the Continental Army and revived his father's mercantile business and faltering fortunes. Years later, during the War of 1812, Smith would again earn martial fame as defender of Baltimore when the British invaded in September 1814.

Otho Williams appeared to bounce back after both the aborted engagement with Maria and the failed elopement with Sophia. After Maria he resumed the carefree lifestyle of an unmarried man. "I have been a happy—very happy Batchelor," he once bragged to his friend William Jackson, "successful, and enjoyed much pleasure."[22] Two episodes in particular hint at just how happy and successful, and the nature of that pleasure. The first involved a case of mistaken identity that worked in Otho's favor. "I have been none the better for [im]personating you when the little Smiling woman came to look for you in my Tent,"

20. Private Daniel McCurtin, for example, noted "the unfair number of fine ladies" in New England in the journal he maintained in 1775-1776, in Thomas Balch, *Papers Relating Chiefly to the Maryland Line During the Revolution* (Philadelphia: T.K. and P.G. Collins, Printers, 1857), 11.
21. Smith to Williams, November 29, 1778.
22. Williams to Jackson, November 20, 1785.

Otho teased Brig. Gen. Daniel Morgan while they were on campaign in 1781. "But I should now be none the worse if I should not have taken a violent cold."[23] Morgan's biographer, Don Higginbotham, chose to interpret this letter by Williams as informing the Old Waggoner that the "little Smiling woman" was distressed at finding that Morgan had left for Virginia. Higginbotham surmised that Williams "had wished to be in Morgan's shoes,"[24] when clearly it appears that Otho did more than just wish! (How else could he have caught "a violent cold"?)

The second episode involved an even more risqué exchange, this time between Otho and Maj. Edward Carrington, in which Carrington wrote:

> I was somewhat alarmed when I saw in the Postscript of your letter, that you were in & out with the Widow—but when I read further & found that this circumstance happened 8 or 10 times a day, upon a few moments reflection in your time of life, my approbations ceased. Upon the hole I wish you much good luck there my friend, but remember that I am coming & will again be the Father of that Family.[25]

Not having the previous letter from Otho to Carrington, we don't know who "the Widow" was, but the inuendo (the words underlined for emphasis are Carrington's doing) hints at a sexual relationship. Was Otho Williams a ladies' man? He seems to have been popular with women. Nathanael Greene's wife Catherine, herself a reputed flirt, seemed to have believed Otho was coquettish. She once teased her "amiable friend" that his rheumatism was "brought upon you for the tyranny which you have" shown the women. It was a curse visited upon him "for being an old bachelor when so many fine Ladies are in want of good husbands."[26]

It took a bit longer for Otho Williams to recover after Sophia shocked him in 1783. "The Circe" he would call her in later years. In light of his public embarrassment, he was grateful for the discretion of others. Most people, he informed Greene, "except a few particular friends observe a delicate silence on the subject," and those friends were sympathetic.[27] His bachelor pal, William Jackson, consoled Otho:

23. Manuscripts and Archives Division, The New York Public Library. "Nov. 8. Williams, [Otho Holland]. Camp Hillsborough. To Brigadier General Morgan," New York Public Library Digital Collections, https://digitalcollections.nypl.org/items/02af0e90-55ac-0133-b144-00505686d14e.

24. Don Higginbotham, *Daniel Morgan: Revolutionary Rifleman* (Chapel Hill: University of North Carolina Press, 1961), 183.

25. Edward Carrington to Williams, November 17, 1781.

26. Greene to Williams, November 12, 1782.

"Happiness is not the lot of mortals," he mused, and then offered a bright observation—Williams probably had a "very fortunate escape from a connexion, which promised so little happiness."[28] Life was better off without Sophia. Otho agreed. He didn't need her or any woman for that matter. In a display of bravado, he claimed to not "think less favorably of the Sex, than I formerly did."[29]

But other friends urged Williams to get back in the game, so to speak. Don't "condemn the whole sex because one very fair has proved herself faithless," urged "Light Horse Harry" Lee.[30] Otho immersed himself in his duties as collections officer for the growing port of Baltimore. He also busied himself as secretary for Maryland's chapter of the Society of the Cincinnati, taking a lead role in procuring and distributing the diplomas given to each member nationwide. But little by little, Williams did reignite his social life. In March of 1784 he reported to a friend how he spent an "afternoon in a clamorous conversation in a congress of belles and beaux."[31] A month later he was dedicating more time to the belles. While riding in the countryside around Baltimore with John Eager Howard, he "joined a more agreeable—more beautiful and more delightful—party of ladies, with whom we drank tea." It was so enjoyable, he informed a friend, that he later had "a multitude of them in my little parlor" and made plans for more parties "every fortnight while I am in Town this Summer."[32] And when not in town, traveling throughout the nation, Williams made sure to take note of the local ladies. For instance, while in Philadelphia for a meeting of the Society of the Cincinnati, Williams gushed how the city was "full of fine women."[33]

"The past is a foreign country" L.P Hartley famously mused, "they do things differently there."[34] But while reading through the letters in Otho Holland Williams' collection, the arc of his romantic life feels remarkably modern. Finances disrupted his first attempt at marriage. His fiancée left him broken-hearted and embarrassed by calling off his second attempt. During the years in between, Williams lived the life of an unrepentant bachelor. He and his friends discussed women, com-

27. Williams to Greene, January 14, 1784.
28. Jackson to Williams, February 27, 1784.
29. Williams to Greene, January 14, 1784.
30. Henry Lee to Williams, March 12, 1784.
31. Williams to Philip Thomas, March 12, 1784.
32. Williams to Thomas, April 27, 1784.
33. Williams to Thomas, May 11, 1784.
34. David Lowenthal, *The Past is a Foreign Country* (Cambridge: Cambridge University Press, 1985), xvi.

pared notes, joked about who had "gone to the gown" and who narrowly escaped. Romantic encounters became the subject of bawdy banter not dissimilar to locker room talk in the present day. And female friends chastised and teased him, urging him to settle down. Far from the stiff, formal society most perhaps envision or presume characterized the Revolutionary-era generation, the letters of Williams and his correspondents reveal attitudes and interactions between the sexes that resonate today. We can relate to Williams and the tumult of his love life.

Otho Williams made one more attempt at finding a bride, and the third time proved the charm. His friend Williams Heth mused that it was likely that Williams' "late mortifying if not dear bought experience" with Sophia, "qualified him to choose well."[35] Apparently Otho did choose well this time. Her name was Mary Smith, daughter of William Smith, a wealthy merchant and future congressman from Baltimore, but everyone called her "Polly." Friends congratulated Williams. Mrs. Randolph said Miss Polly Smith of Baltimore was a "sweet pretty little girl."[36] More importantly, Polly's parents approved of the union. In fact, William Smith was quite proud of his son-in-law, and would name his farm located just outside of Baltimore "Eutaw" in honor of Otho's celebrated participation in the Battle of Eutaw Springs. The two men would maintain a close correspondence, especially while Smith served in the first U.S. Congress.

The wedding of Otho Williams and Mary "Polly" Smith was in October 1785. The weeks building up to the event saw an anxious and busy Williams. He was "horribly hurried," he complained to a friend, Phillip Thomas, as he managed the renovation of his Baltimore home, rushing to make it ready in time. The whole town was discussing the upcoming event, speculating as to the date, but Thomas was warned by Williams not to divulge it. After the wedding, congratulations poured in. William Heth, Nathanial Ramsay, William Jackson, all wrote to wish "much joy" to Otho on his "change in situation."[37] To his bachelor pal, Jackson, Otho responded with the suggestion that Jackson inquire to a mutual friend whether matrimony is better than bachelorhood. Answering his own question, Williams exclaimed that he was "Happy even to the extent of my hopes—for my Girl is all I thought her and all I wish her."[38]

35. William Heth to Williams, October 23, 1785.

36. Ibid.

37. Jackson to Williams, November 9, 1785; Nathaniel Ramsay to Williams, November 19, 1785; Heth to Williams, December 5, 1785.

38. Williams to Jackson, November 20, 1785.

The happiness appears to have been genuine and mutual. Polly referred to her husband as her "dear general" and informed him that he was the first "gentlemen she ever honored with a letter."[39] Williams wrote how he liked to take his wife on moonlight walks. After traveling, Otho related to a close friend, he would take Polly in his arms when she would meet him at the door. The couple had four children, with whom Williams would play soldier in the house on rainy days. But as long as it had taken Otho Williams to find love, his marital bliss proved to be short-lived. His health impaired from campaigns and captivity during the Revolutionary War, Otho died in June 1794, just shy of nine years after his wedding. Polly deeply mourned the loss of her "dear general." A family friend invited her and the children up to Frederick a few months after Otho's passing, but she declined. An outbreak of yellow fever in Baltimore had forced the Williamses to leave town for her father's farmhouse. Polly was exhausted, caring for both her father and the children. Tired and melancholy, she confessed to the friend that she "had done more than she thought she could do."[40] The bright and vivacious Polly was replaced with sadness. Many years later, a family member recalled how "after her widowhood all smiles forsook her face."[41] Mary "Polly" Smith Williams died in 1795, just a little more a year after her husband.

39. Mary "Polly" Smith Williams to Williams, January 1, 1786.
40. Mary "Polly" Smith Williams to Thomas October 12, 1794.
41. Mrs. Mary Smith Williams White, granddaughter of Otho Holland Williams, cited in *The Baltimore Sun*, April 2, 1905.

A Life in Fragments: Arthur Bowler in Slavery and Freedom

JANE LANCASTER

In January 1792 forty-three-year-old Arthur Bowler left Halifax, Nova Scotia on his second Transatlantic journey. Captured in Africa almost thirty years earlier, enslaved in Newport, Rhode Island for nearly twenty years, a free man for ten, he was returning to Africa.

He left fragmentary clues buried in archives on three continents which illuminate an "ordinary" person caught up in extraordinary circumstances. While he was not a major historical figure, leaving no personal papers or images, fighting in no wars, these clues allow insight into slavery in urban New England before and during the American Revolution. They also illustrate the dislocations and opportunities resulting from American independence, as well as the complex and intertwined worlds of abolition and empire.[1]

Bowler's experiences contribute to the growing scholarship on Loyalists, Black and White, and also complicate treatment of the "back to Africa" movement, often seen as a negative step for formerly enslaved people.[2]

1. For a use of small clues to build the story of a life see Tiya Miles, *All that She Carried: The journey of Ashley's sack, a Black family keepsake* (New York: Random House, 2021). And for a brilliant account of an obscure life, see Linda Colley, *The Ordeal of Elizabeth Marsh: A woman in world history* (New York: Pantheon, 2007).
2. Cassandra Pybus, *Epic Journeys of Freedom: Runaway slaves of the American Revolution and their global quest for liberty* (Boston: Beacon Press, 2006); Simon Schama, *Rough Crossings: Britain, the slaves and the American Revolution* (New York: Harper Collins, 2006); Maya Jasanoff, *Liberty's Exiles: American loyalists in the revolutionary world* (New York: Alfred A. Knopf, 2011). A vital source is Graham Russell Gao Hodges, *The Black Loyalist Directory: African Americans in exile after the American Revolution* (New York: Garland Library of the Humanities in Association with the New England Genealogical Society, 1996).

FIRST CLUE: CESAR LYNDON'S ACCOUNT AND MEMORANDUM BOOK 1765

Our first glimpse of Arthur is when his name appears in an account book. On July 8, 1765 Cesar Lyndon wrote: "To cash to Arter Bowler for ye ord^{r} [. . .] or 18/ & 2 Coppers 1—0—6."[3] Arthur was selling something to the enslaved and literate Cesar Lyndon in Newport, Rhode Island.

The enslaved Cesar Lyndon was secretary and amanuensis to Josias Lyndon (1704-1778) who as Clerk to the Rhode Island General Assembly was a colleague of Arthur's enslaver Metcalf Bowler (1720-87). Merchant, privateer owner, politician and superior court judge, Bowler was speaker of the General Assembly.

Cesar Lyndon ran a number of businesses, renting plots of land to fellow slaves, leasing out piglets to be raised for a share of the profits when they were slaughtered, trading with merchants in Surinam, and buying silk dresses for his wife and silver knee buckles for himself. He was very far along a continuum from servitude to freedom, and it is likely Arthur Bowler's degree of unfreedom in Newport was also mild compared with say, a field laborer in the South or even in nearby Narragansett, Rhode Island.[4]

What Cesar was purchasing from Arthur is a mystery, but nevertheless this fragment of evidence provides several clues. Specie was scarce in the colonies, and Rhode Islanders had to manage the exchange rates between different currencies. Arthur, who we discover from a later clue was born in Africa, cannot have been in Newport long. Most slave voyages were suspended during the Seven Years War (privateering was more profitable) but he was clearly well known to Cesar Lyndon. He had a new name, he could speak enough English to communicate, and he could understand variable currencies. He also had sufficient latitude from his enslaver to be doing some trading on the side.

SECOND CLUE: A LETTER, 1774

A letter dated "Portsmouth Jany 14th 1774" was addressed in a flowing script, "To Mr Willm Vernon, Merch^{t} in Newport p Arthur." Metcalf Bowler, the writer, had recently sold his large Newport house and moved to nearby Portsmouth. The purchaser was William Vernon (1719-1806), one of Newport's most prolific slave traders, with over forty such voyages. He was, however, slow to pay and Bowler needed

3. Cesar Lyndon, "Account and Memorandum Book," Rhode Island Historical Society, Providence, RI, MSS 9004, v.10, pp. 82-84.

4. Jared Ross Hardesty, *Unfreedom: Slavery and dependence in eighteenth century Boston* (New York: New York University Press, 2018), 54-55.

his money, so in January 1774 he sent his "Servant" Arthur with a letter, explaining that as he was going to Boston the next day, he could not wait on Vernon in person "but have sent my servant with this, requesting you would without fail, deliver him, the two hundred Dollars you promised to have in readiness for me . . . I have inclosed a receipt for that sum."[5] This suggests that Arthur was a well-trusted and well-known "servant."

THIRD CLUE: THE BOOK OF NEGROES, 1783

Nine years later Arthur Bowler, now with a wife and daughter, appears in the Book of Negroes, a British list kept in case Americans wanted to claim compensation for their human property.[6] The British freed many enslaved people as part of the war effort, and now the war was over, they were evacuating three thousand Blacks and 27,000 white Loyalists from New York City, Arthur, Phebe and Betsy Bowler among them.

Accordingly, on November 19, 1783 they lined up to board a British transport ship, the *Nisbet*. They were among the last Blacks to leave New York, their names appearing towards the end of the second volume of the ledger. They had already acquired certificates saying they were free to travel, stating that the bearer had His Excellency Sir Guy Carlton's permission "to go to Nova Scotia, or wherever else [he or she] may think proper."[7]

A clerk transcribed Bowler's name phonetically as "Boler" and his former owner as "Medcalfe Bowler" of Portsmouth, Rhode Island. Bowler said he was thirty-four years old, and he had left Rhode Island in 1781. (The other fifty or so Rhode Islanders listed in the Book of Negroes left in 1779 or earlier). There was a column for a brief description of the passenger: the clerk thought Arthur a "stout fellow" which in the eighteenth-century denoted sturdiness and strength, not obesity. This clerk's vocabulary was limited—almost all the men and women on the *Nisbet* were either ordinary or stout, though one or two were "very ordinary" and some of the children were "likely." Phebe Bowler,

5. Vernon Family Papers, Box 49A Folder 12, Bowler, Metcalf, Newport Historical Society. The house at 46 Clarke Street, Newport, now known as the Vernon House, is a national historic landmark; it was Rochambeau's headquarters during the French occupation, and George Washington dined there.

6. There are two original copies, with significant difference; the copy in the US National Archives contains 2,555 names, while the British copy contains 3,000, which includes the 407 who were still enslaved. See https://www.bac-lac.gc.ca/eng/discover/military-heritage/loyalists/book-of-negroes/Pages/introduction.aspx.

7. https://www.uelac.org/Loyalist-Trails/2018/Loyalist-Trails-2018.php?issue=201836.

thirty-five, was an "ordinary wench" while their daughter Betsy, twelve, was a "likely girl." The clerk recorded Phebe and Betsy as being "born free in Portsmouth, Rhode Island."

Most of the earlier Nova Scotian evacuees landed in Shelburne (then called Port Roseway), which was now overflowing, so the *Nisbet* was taking its more than one hundred and fifty Black passengers to Port Mattoon, some thirty miles to the north.

About a quarter of the adults on the *Nisbet* were listed as belonging to the Wagon Master General's (WMG's) department. They had been driving the carts hauling British equipment and materiel, an activity vital to the British military operations, but by mid-November the task was nearly done. The Bowlers, however, do not have the initials WMG after their names. The clerk was, perhaps, tired or careless after inserting nearly one hundred and forty names, or the Bowlers were doing something else: many free and self-liberated Blacks worked for the British as laborers, servants or teamsters, or for New Yorkers as carters or carpenters, actors or jockeys, while the women worked as laundresses and servants.[8]

The peace treaty signed in Paris contained clauses instructing the British to return enslaved people to their masters, but Sir Guy Carleton, the British commander-in-chief, felt that anyone who had responded to earlier promises of freedom or who had joined the British before the end of the war, was a free person. He told George Washington he could not honor anything in the treaty "inconsistent with prior Engagements binding the National Honor, which must be kept with all Colours" and to do otherwise would be a "dishonorable Violation of the public Faith."[9] Washington, whose enslaved stableman Harry Washington was among the newly freed and eventual evacuees, was not best pleased.

As soon as the list was complete, the *Nisbet* was ready to sail to Port Mattoon.[10]

FOURTH CLUE: THE BIRCHTOWN MUSTER OF FREE BLACKS 1784

The Port Mattoon settlement failed within months, and the Bowlers moved south to Birchtown, a (segregated) Black township near Shelburne. It celebrated Brig. Gen. Samuel Birch, a British officer in New York who had signed many Blacks' certificates of freedom. The enslaved

8. Edwin G. Burrows and Mike Wallace, *Gotham* (New York: Oxford University Press, 1999), chapter 15.
9. William Smith, *Historical Memoirs of William Smith, 1778-1783* (W.H. W. Sabine, ed. New York: New York Times and Arno Press, 1971), 574, quoted in Jasanoff, *Liberty's Exiles*, 89.
10. See Hodges, *The Black Loyalist Directory*.

Blacks and indentured servants stayed in Shelburne with their White Loyalist owners or employers. Birchtown was soon the largest community of free Blacks outside Africa, and almost 1,485 Black Loyalists were there by the time the Bowlers arrived in the early summer of 1784. A close-knit and almost self-sufficient community emerged based around two churches led by formerly enslaved men, the Baptists under David George and the Methodists under blind preacher Moses Wilkinson.[11]

A muster prepared in 1784 lists twenty-one companies in Birchtown, formed for convenience in the distribution of food.[12] Arthur, Phebe and Betsy belonged to carpenter Scott Murray's company, which comprised forty men, women and children. Eight of the men, including Bowler, described themselves as laborers, a catchall term for anyone without a specific avocation; the company also included two sawyers, a clothier and a cook. It is very unlikely Arthur Bowler had been a laborer when he lived in Newport and Portsmouth, but in the short term there was no call for whatever skills he possessed. As a refugee he was prepared to do anything to survive.[13]

The British originally intended to supply rations for a year but land distribution was slow; clearing old growth forest with only hand tools was even slower, and crops remained unplanted, so the government distributed food for two more years. Later rations were only supplied to those who worked for the community: Birchtown settlers had to perform six days' labor for the town. This enforced labor was, not surprisingly, a source of tension. Nor was the food particularly appetizing or equally distributed, and before long the Blacks only got meal and molasses to supplement what they could catch or grow.[14]

The free Blacks also faced racial prejudice and they were in a bad bargaining position. White unskilled laborers demanded, and usually received, between two shillings sixpence and four shillings a day, while skilled Black carpenters were willing to work for one shilling a day, and Black laborers earned a mere eight pence, only one third of the White laborers' wage. The availability and indeed desperation of the free Blacks tended to force wages down, and White working-class men, particularly the demobilized soldiers who were also waiting for their land, resented this. Under such conditions, tempers flared.[15]

11. Schama, *Rough Crossings*, 226, Walker, *Black Loyalists*, 43.

12. *Muster Book of Free Black Settlement of Birchtown," 1784, Library and Archives Canada, MG 9 B9-14, item 1292*, https://www.blackloyalist.info/event/display/8.

13. Birchtown Muster, https://www.blackloyalist.info/event/display/8.

14. Jasanoff, *Liberty's Exiles*, 357, 160; and Walker, *Black Loyalists*, 32, 40, 44-45.

15. Walker, *Black Loyalists*, 46-7, 62.

Tensions came to a head on July 26, 1784 when there was a "Great Riot" in Shelburne. According to Benjamin Marston, the chief surveyor, "the disbanded soldiers have risen against the Free negroes to drive [them] out of Town because they labour Cheapr [than] they (ye soldiers) will." The rioting continued the next day when, according to Marston, "The soldiers force the free negroes to quit the Town—pulled down about 20 of their houses.[16]

Baptist preacher David George, who was still living in Shelburne, became the focus of White male fury when he baptized (at her request) a White woman. A mob of more than forty former soldiers swinging chains and ships' hooks pulled down his house, and then threatened to burn down the Baptist meeting house, but George stood in his pulpit until the protesters began beating him with sticks and clubs and forced him out. He moved his church to Birchtown, where he hoped to be safe.[17] Where Arthur Bowler stood in this uprising is unknown, but as he was in Birchtown, not Shelburne, he may have avoided the violence.

FIFTH CLUE: LAND DISTRIBUTION PLAN, 1787

The British had offered land to all the Nova Scotian Loyalists, White and Black, but distribution was slow. In December 1787, four years after he left New York, Arthur Bowler finally got his land. His name appears, along with one hundred and eighty-two others, on a deed which grants him a share of 6,382 acres of Crown land. Most of the grantees received either twenty or forty acres, but Bowler, who was granted Lot 107, received an allocation of thirty-two acres, perhaps because it was awkwardly shaped at the southern end of the grant. As it turned out, he never saw his land as it was some fifteen miles from Birchtown through uncleared forest. Two hundred years later it is a golf course. [18]

SIXTH CLUE: LIST OF THOSE WISHING TO GO TO SIERRA LEONE, 1791

By the late 1780s British food handouts had ended, the settlers had endured some poor harvests and food was in very short supply. As Boston King wrote in his memoir,

> Many of the poor people were compelled to sell their best gowns for five pounds of flour, in order to support life. When they had parted

16. Wilson, *The Loyal Blacks*, 92.
17. Diary of Benjamin Marston, 26-27, 1784, https://blackloyalist.com/cdc/documents/diaries/marston_journal.htm.
18. Bowler's Land Allocation appears in the Nova Scotia Land Papers 1765-1800 RG-6052-6, Nova Scotia Archives Halifax, NS, https://novascotia.ca/archives/landpapers/archives.asp?ID=1080&Doc=document&Page=201108174.

> with all their clothes, even to their blankets, several of them fell down dead in the streets, thro' hunger. Some killed and ate their dogs and cats; and poverty and distress prevailed on every side; so that to my great grief I was obliged to leave Birchtown, because I could get no employment.[19]

Given the problems in Birchtown it is not surprising many villagers were prepared to listen when Lt. John Clarkson, on leave from the Royal Navy, arrived in October 1791 offering to take them to West Africa. Financed by the Sierra Leone Company, and partly inspired by the formerly enslaved Thomas Peters' visit to London, Clarkson offered to take anyone discontented with Canadian winters and slow land distribution to West Africa. The directors of the Sierra Leone Company were philanthropic evangelical Christians, idealistic eighteenth-century gentlemen. They were also investors and hard-headed merchants, all part of the emerging liberal political economy of the late eighteenth century. Accordingly, they favored trade as a way of "civilizing" and converting the Africans, as well as providing a good return to their shareholders. Eighteen hundred people invested in the Sierra Leone Company, which had working capital of £235,000. The investors included such luminaries as physician Erasmus Darwin, industrialist Sir Richard Arkwright, inventor of the water frame, and Josiah Wedgwood, of pottery fame.[20] While some of the shareholders were altruistic abolitionists, others owned large slave plantations in the West Indies and were looking for new sources of raw materials. All of them expected returns on their investments, which had cost £50 a share, an enormous sum of money, almost a year's wages for a skilled worker.[21]

Bowler was one of the last to sign up, and one hundred and forty-eight Birchtown heads of households had given their name and their details before he finally went to volunteer. There were only six more Birchtown families to go. He told Clarkson he was a farmer and had a wife and a daughter. He was not yet farming his land, however; he exaggerated slightly and said he had been allocated forty acres but admitted he had not yet seen it. And he did not seem to have the tools to farm it, listing only one axe, two hoes and a spade among the imple-

19. Autobiographical memoir of Boston King, a fugitive slave from South Carolina who became a teacher and minister in Sierra Leone, serialized in 1798 in *The Methodist Magazine*, https://blackloyalist.com/cdc/documents/diaries/king-memoirs.htm.
20. Suzanne Schwarz, "A Just and Honourable, Commerce: abolitionist experimentation in Sierra Leone in the late eighteenth and early nineteenth centuries," 6, https://eprints.worc.ac.uk/5308/1/Lecture%202013%20PressRevised%20%281%29.pdf.
21. The sum could buy four horses or ten cows in 1790; https://www.nationalarchives.gov.uk/currency-converter/#currency-result.

ments of his trade. He did have some other possessions, and told the authorities he would take two chests, two barrels, a bed and a musket on his journey back to Africa.[22]

He was one of fifty-two Birchtown men who said they were born in Africa, while eighty-eight said they were born in the southern colonies, and four born in the West Indies. He was the only one who had been enslaved in Rhode Island. The total number of people amounted to more than five hundred and fifty, rather more than a third of the inhabitants of Birchtown.

Elsewhere in Nova Scotia and New Brunswick many more people signed up, and to Clarkson's surprise almost twelve hundred people said they wished to leave: he had expected to take about five hundred. He hired extra ships and purchased more provisions, and after several delays, not least by obstructive Whites unwilling to see cheap labor leave, they set sail in January 1792. This was not a good time to be crossing the North Atlantic in small ships – the weather was not kind, and they endured a harrowing eight weeks at sea. When the surviving Nova Scotian passengers arrived in Freetown in March 1792, they found nothing ready for their arrival. The officers and men sent by the Sierra Leone Company had arrived some weeks earlier but rather than set to work, they had stayed quarreling on the (appropriately-named) ship *Harpy*.[23]

SEVENTH CLUE: THE LEOPARD, 1792

Bowler's first glimpse of Sierra Leone was of a low, cloud-topped mountain above a sea of green trees. Early Portuguese sailors thought it resembled a sleeping lion, hence the name, the mountain (Sierra) of the lion (Leon). Arthur was probably born elsewhere in Africa, although Bunce Island, some twenty miles upriver from Freetown, was a major British slave castle and had processed the shipment of thousands of captive Africans to the New World.

The local tribes, though not actively unfriendly, were wary, as this was the second attempt to settle former slaves in the area.

Arthur Bowler built a hut, where on March 21 he and his family got a terrible fright. John Clarkson noted the event in his journal, writing:

22. The list of Blacks in Birchtown who gave their names for Sierra Leone in November 1791 appears at https://www.blackloyalist.info/source-image-display/display/114.

23. See *Clarkson's Mission to America 1791–92*, edited with an introduction by Charles Bruce Ferguson (Halifax NS: Public Archives of Nova Scotia, 1971), 2:67, 92. A transcript of John Clark's journal is "Black Loyalists: Our History, Our People," Canada's Digital Collection http://blackloyalist.com/cdc/documents/diaries/mission.htm.

> Early this morning a Leopard came into the streets of the town; one of the colonists Arthur Bowler coming home from a neighbouring thicket, saw the Animal stop at his hut which he had left open and knowing his wife and daughter were asleep, he shouted so loud as to alarm his neighbour and frighten the beast which ran off into the woods. I am much afraid that some of the children will some time or other be carried off by these animals, if they are suffered to leave their huts either early in the morning or late in the evening.[24]

Bowler, like all the other settlers, had a long wait for the surveyor to mark out the farm lots, and the first forty lots (of five acres rather than the promised twenty) were only distributed in mid-November. He had his little hut and a small lot in the town, but he, like most of the settlers, relied for much of his food on supplies from the company store. He had to pay for it by two days' work a week, clearing brush and building roads, which limited the time available for his own cultivation.

The lack of land spurred the settlers to action. Some of the men fished the teeming rivers with home-made boats, others took their muskets into the forest and hunted antelope and wild boar, fresh meat that would make a welcome addition to the company stores. Some of the far-sighted settlers had brought seeds from Nova Scotia, and pumpkins, beans and cabbage soon sprang up, perhaps sage and thyme flourished, though most of the seeds brought by the company from England failed. The local tribe grew rice, cassava, millet and kola nut, unfamiliar foods that became part of the settlers' staple diet.

EIGHTH CLUE: SIERRA LEONE CENSUS, 1802

Arthur Bowler was fifty-three and still in Freetown in 1802 when the British conducted a census. His adult daughter and grandchildren lived with him. The rather judgmental census taker noted in the margin she had "1 Boy and 2 Girls by as many Fathers I suppose."[25]

There was no sign of Phebe and Arthur was now married to the widow of Richard Richards, a prominent Baptist, who was one of the five "free Ethiopians" from the Halifax area who petitioned John Clarkson for permission to nominate Baptist teachers and preachers from "amongst themselves."[26] This strongly suggests Arthur was a Baptist, for the religious communities were tightknit.

24. Lt. John Clarkson Diary (19 March 1792–4 August 1792), University of Illinois, Chicago. Special Collections, Sierra Leone Collection, Box 1, Folder 4. My thanks to Suzanne Schwarz, University of Worcester, for this and other Sierra Leone references. Clarkson, *Mission to America*, 2:9.
25. 1802 Freetown Sierra Leone Census, The National Archaives, WO 1/352.
26. See https://blackloyalist.com/cdc/documents/diaries/mission.htm.

The two major denominations in Sierra Leone had very different political agendas, and the Baptists were far more accommodating to the British authorities, far less likely to protest what they saw as injustice, than were the Methodists. Governor Zachary Macaulay called the latter "Malcontents." In one of their letters to Clarkson, back in England, they complained, "We wance did call it Freetown but since your Absence—we have Reason to call it Slavery."[27]

There were numerous teething problems in Sierra Leone in the decade since Bowler and the other Nova Scotians arrived, though by 1802 many of the sources of friction had ended. Zachary Macaulay, governor of Sierra Leone from 1794 through 1799, began training young Nova Scotians to take over jobs formerly held by Whites. Apothecaries, surgeons, master shipwrights, ships' captains joined the ranks of Black schoolteachers and preachers, creating a Black middle class invested in the success of the colony.[28] Black militia officers sometimes commanded White soldiers, and Black farmers cultivated new cash crops, notably coffee. It became clear, however, that small farms could not support a family and many Nova Scotians abandoned their yeoman-farmer stance and turned to trade. Those who had received land hired local Africans as laborers, or the Jamaican Maroons (who arrived in 1800) as sharecroppers; after the British abolished the slave trade in 1808, they used Africans "recaptured" from slave ships by the Royal Navy as apprentices or indentured workers.[29]

The Nova Scotians wanted the freedom and self-determination they had long lacked, and wished to be treated as English men and women, with equal rights and privileges, while the directors of the Sierra Leone Company wanted to run the new settlement from London and expected it would yield a financial return for its shareholders. The directors wanted the settlers to plant and harvest cotton, indigo, tobacco, rice and coffee (all of which grew wild) to generate exports to replace the slave trade as a source of income for local tribes and provide a living for the free Blacks growing them. The Company's desire to generate cash crops grown by free labor in Africa was, however, incompatible with the Nova Scotians' desire to provide for themselves and their families on their own farms. Most Nova Scotians had been enslaved in the American South and they had no desire to replace plantation labor in Virginia or South Carolina with plantation labor in Sierra Leone.

27. See Wilson, *The Loyal Blacks*, 321.
28. He was father of Thomas Babington Macaulay, the historian. See Catherine Hall, *Macaulay and Son: Architects of empire* (New Haven: Yale University Press, 2013.
29. See Walker, *The Black Loyalists*, 260-61.

Arthur Bowler, who had probably not been an agricultural laborer during the years he lived in Rhode Island, would have been even less inclined. Only the presence of the respected and conciliatory John Clarkson kept a lid on the simmering discontent for the first year of the settlement. He allowed Blacks to serve on juries with Whites, he allowed women to vote, he listened to their complaints about reserving waterfront property for public buildings. In the absence of roads, access to the water was imperative, and he negotiated a compromise about the size of lots. As one official wrote, without Clarkson "I should scarce think it safe to stay among them."

The climate was also a problem. Delays in leaving Nova Scotia meant they had arrived at the very end of the dry season, leaving little time to build suitable shelter. The rains began on April 2, 1792 and the hastily built huts proved inadequate.

Between downpours the humidity was debilitating; "nothing made of Steel can be preserved from Rust," Clarkson wrote, "Knives, Scissors, &c look like rusty iron, our watches are spoilt by rust or laid aside useless . . . everything of linen put by for a time must be frequently aired lest it should mould and rot." The supplies brought from England rotted in the heat and hunger became an ongoing problem.[30]

Many people fell ill, though the Whites suffered more than the Nova Scotians. More than half the settlers were sick with malaria and "scarce able to crawl about." Arthur survived: perhaps he had some immunity from his African childhood. Most of the Black settlers recovered, but almost half of the Whites, especially the poorer Whites and the soldiers, died.[31]

In early April 1792 food supplies were running short, and the settlers were put on half rations. Meanwhile the settlers' "murmurings and resentments" grew as the council member responsible for creating the garden lots was sometimes too drunk to do his job. Festering anger grew, and as one of the councilors noted, "with hunger comes mutiny."[32]

Thomas Peters, who had been sergeant in the Black Pioneers during the American Revolution, and whose visit to England in 1790-91 partly inspired the Loyalist migration to Sierra Leone, was particularly

30. Pybus, *Epic Journeys*, 153-54; Clarkson, *Mission to America* 2:72; Rachel B. Herrmann, "Rebellion or riot? Black Loyalist food laws in Sierra Leone," *Slavery & Abolition*, Vol. 37 no. 4 (2016), 680-703.

31. Walker, *Black Loyalists*, 158-159n6, quoting the Sierra Leone Company's *Directors' Report*, 1794, 45-47.

32. Mortality figures from Walker, *Black Loyalists*, 159n6, quoting Clarkson papers IV and Dr. Taylor's diary, April 11, 1792; Councilor James Watt to Clarkson, April 27, 1792, quoted in Walker, *The Black Loyalists*, 149.

unhappy. He had a profound effect, particularly on the Methodists, persuading them the officials of the Sierra Leone Company were failing them, just as British authorities had in Nova Scotia. Clarkson sympathized to some extent with the settlers' discontent, later acknowledging they had been "deceived and illtreated through life . . . and seeing no probability of getting their land, they began to think, they should be served the same way as in [Nova Scotia] which unsettled their minds and makes them suspect everything and everybody."[33]

On or about April 7, 1792, one hundred and thirty-two people, approximately one quarter of the adult Nova Scotians, signed a petition asking that Peters be their "Speaker-General," which some interpreted as the people wished to elect Peters as governor.

Clarkson was furious and called all the Nova Scotians to a meeting under a large tree—possibly the large cotton tree that stood in the middle of Freetown until it collapsed in a storm in 2023—and announced, "either one or other of us, would be hanged upon that Tree before the Palaver was settled." Those of the Nova Scotians who had not signed the petition were confused: they "appeared much agitated not knowing what was the matter." The Bowlers would have been listening as Clarkson warned that the "Demon of Discord" would bring them "misery and guilt" and, warming to his theme, would hinder the improvement of the Black population throughout the world. He told them the "great anxiety" of the Sierra Leone Company was "to make use of them as instruments to spread the Blessings of Christianity through the wretched Heathen Nations of this vast continent," and that their actions jeopardized this aim. Whether Bowler or most of the others thought of themselves as "instruments" in spreading Christianity is open to doubt: although their Christian faith was sincere, it is arguable they were equally interested in being treated as men and gaining a competence for themselves and their families.

The settlers tried to explain to Clarkson that they were misunderstood, that they had merely appointed Peters their spokesman, but they eventually agreed to obey the laws of the colony—including the authority of John Clarkson. The grumbling continued, however, as did the influence of Peters, and Clarkson noted in mid-May some of the settlers "imbibed strange notions from Thomas Peters as to their civil rights."[34]

33. Clarkson, *Mission to America*, June 15, 1792, quoted in Pybus, *Epic Journeys*, 153 and Jasanoff, *Liberty's Exiles*, 297.

34. Clarkson, *Mission to America* 2:80-87, quoted in Jasanoff, *Liberty's Exiles*, 298, and n66; see also Pybus, *Epic Journeys*, 152-53, Walker, *Black Loyalists*, 151, and *The Philanthropist* Vol. V (1815), 35.

Where Arthur Bowler stood in this challenge to Clarkson's authority is not known: the original petition does not survive so the names of the one hundred and thirty-two complainants are lost, but many of them would have been Peters' supporters from Annapolis and New Brunswick, or Methodist followers of Boston King and blind preacher Moses Wilkinson. The Baptists under David George's leadership were more moderate, more inclined to support Clarkson.

CONCLUSION

Arthur outlived his former enslaver who died in poverty in Providence, Rhode Island, but not in disgrace: Metcalf Bowler spied for the British before returning to the Patriot side, but his treachery was not discovered until the 1920s.[35] His gravestone in St. John's burying ground in Providence is ironic, saying it was:

> Sacred to the Memory of the Hon. Metcalf Bowler Esq., who resigned his soul to God on 19th September 1789 in the 63rd year of his age. Having been repeatedly elected to several of the most important offices in this State, shows the confidence of the Public in his ability and Patriotism, and is the best eulogium of his Character. He served as Judge of the Superior Court, was 19 years speaker of the lower House of Assembly and was a member of the 1st Congress in 1768 the duties of which station he discharged with Honor and Ability.

Arthur, whose journey took him from Africa and back, was a free man after twenty years of enslavement, eight difficult years in Nova Scotia and an early encounter with a leopard.

Historian Ellen Gibson Wilson concluded that there were always two Freetowns. The Sierra Leone Company's experiment failed and the country became a British colony, but she believed it was a triumph for the realization of the Nova Scotians' wishes and dreams. Although the new life was hard, it was, she said, "immensely more challenging, exciting, and influential" than the lives they left behind. Even Henry Thornton, the guiding light behind the Sierra Leone Company, suspected this, saying some "happy consequences" may have emerged and "tho' I have lost £2000 or £3000 . . . I am on the whole a gainer."[36]

Arthur was a gainer, too.

35. See Jane Clark, "Metcalf Bowler as a British Spy." *Rhode Island Historical Society Collections*, Vol. XXII, no 4 (October 1930).
36. Thornton quoted in Wilson, *Loyal Blacks*, 407.

The Physical Challenges of Major General Nathanael Greene

SALINA B. BAKER

The American Revolution provides heroes like almost no other event in American history. In a society where most of us live in comfort, with good medical care and remedies for what ails us, we recognize the sacrifices the people of the eighteenth century made for the cause of American liberty and, eventually, to build a new nation. In newspapers, public pamphlets and private letters, they proclaimed their passion for a movement rarely achieved in their time—the idea of a republic free from the bonds of monarchial rule and their mother country, Britain.

As self-educated Rhode Island Gen. Nathanael Greene wrote to his wife, Caty, in June 1775, "I am determined to defend my rights, and maintain my freedom, or sell my life in the attempt."[1] At some time in his life he developed a limp and asthma. At twenty-eight, he was afflicted with a smallpox scar on his right eyeball that was often infected, a result of his 1770 inoculation. Before the war, Greene wrote to his friend, Sammy Ward, Jr., that he "was raised a Quaker, and amongst the most superstitious sort."[2]

Despite the seeming austerity of his childhood, legend holds it that a teenage Nathanael and his older brother, Jacob, jumped from their bedroom window to attend neighborhood dances with the knowledge that their father would horsewhip them if they were caught. Was jumping from a window the cause of Nathanael's limp? Was it congenital? Or was it from working the trip hammer in the Greene family iron forge that he managed and operated in Coventry, Rhode Island? There

1. George Washington Greene, *The Life of Nathanael Greene, Major General in the Army of the Revolution Vol. 1* (New York: Hurd and Houghton. Cambridge: Riverside Press, 1890), 84.
2. Ibid., 59.

is no documented evidence of the cause of the limp. But one can imagine him working in the iron forge, the smoke exacerbating his asthma and irritating his right eye.

On August 17, 1772, the iron forge burned to the ground. Five days later, Nathanael wrote to his distant relative, William Greene, who lived in East Greenwich, Rhode Island, "News of our misfortune in the destruction of the forge doubtless will reach you before this . . . I have had a most severe turn of the phthisic or asthma; I have not slept six hours in four nights, being obliged to sit up the last two nights."[3]

The forge was rebuilt and operating by the following winter. But 1772 was a difficult year for the Greene brothers' other business ventures. Their ship, *Fortune,* was confiscated by Royal Navy officer William Dudingston for failure to pay taxes on the cargo, a violation of the recently reinforced Parliamentary Navigation Acts. Parliament levied taxes on the colonies in previous years including the despised Stamp Act and the Townshend Acts, which were resisted with violence, deliberate evasion of duties, and nonimportation agreements among merchants. All the Townshend Acts—except for the tax on tea—were repealed in April 1770. The tax on tea remained a flashpoint and a contributing factor to the Boston Tea Party of 1773, in which angry colonists destroyed an entire shipment of tea in Boston Harbor.

In response to the Boston Tea Party and other acts of tea destruction, Parliament passed the Coercive Acts. One of these acts, the Boston Port Act, was meant to punish Boston until the cost of the destroyed tea was paid. With Boston under duress and only a day's ride north, Nathanael Greene was among those who petitioned the Rhode Island General Assembly to form a militia company—the Kentish Guards—for East Greenwich, Warwick, and Coventry. The petition was granted in October 1774. Contrary to Quaker doctrines that did not condone armed conflict, Greene joined the militia as a private and clandestinely procured a musket from Boston. Then he applied for lieutenancy. He was mortified when he was denied because of his limp. He wrote to his friend and captain of the militia, James Varnum:

> I was informed the gentlemen of East Greenwich said that I was a blemish to the company. I confess it is the first stroke of mortification I ever felt from being considered, either in private or public life, a blemish to those with whom I associated . . . If I conceive right of the force of the objection of the gentlemen of the town, it was not as an officer

3. Greene, *The Life of Nathanael Greene*, 65.

> but as a soldier, for that my halting was a blemish to the rest. I confess it is my misfortune to limp a little.[4]

When the first shots of the American Revolutionary War were fired in Massachusetts on April 19, 1775, the Kentish Guards set out for Boston. When they passed through Providence, teenager John Howland, who would fight in the war, remarked:

> I viewed the company as they marched up the street and observed Nathanael Greene with his musket on his shoulder, in the ranks, as a private. I distinguished Mr. Greene whom I had frequently seen, by the motion of his shoulder in the march, as one of his legs was shorter than the other.[5]

The governor of Rhode Island recalled them. A few days later, the Rhode Island General Assembly voted to raise a brigade of fifteen hundred troops known as the Army of Observation to defend the colony. Greene worked diligently on defense committees. According to tradition, the appointment to lead the new army was offered to two others who both turned it down. It was then offered to Greene. He accepted and was commissioned a brigadier general on May 8, 1775. He immediately began to grapple with the problems of raising, equipping and drilling his brigade, valuable lessons that would serve him the rest of the war.

It was impossible for his appointment to abrogate his limp even if it soothed his sensitivity to criticism. He led his new army toward Boston and arrived in Cambridge on May 23. They joined provincial New Englanders who were holding the British army under siege in Boston. The Battle of Bunker Hill was fought on June 17, while Greene was on a recruiting trip to Rhode Island.

On July 2 Gen. George Washington, the new commander-in-chief of the recently formed Continental Army, arrived in Cambridge. Greene was appointed a brigadier general in the new army. No one knows exactly what Greene and Washington said to one another at their first meeting, but we do know that they developed a strong, trusting relationship. In January 1776, sixty tons of artillery from Fort Ticonderoga arrived at Boston for the Continental Army. An attack on Boston was planned. Greene was sick with jaundice, and he wrote to his brother Jacob on the February 8:

> I am as yellow as saffron, my appetite all gone and my flesh too. I am so weak that I can scarcely walk across the room . . . I am grievously

4. Ibid., 49-50.
5. Ibid., 78.

> mortified at my confinement, as this is a critical, and will be to an appearance an important period of the American War.[6]

The cannon were mounted on Dorchester Heights overlooking Boston on the night of March 4, 1776. Greene had recovered, and he prepared flat-bottomed bateaux in anticipation of a retaliatory amphibious British assault from Boston. But there was no battle; with cannon staring down at them, the British army evacuated the city.

The Continental Army moved to New York. Greene was given command of a string of five strategic forts on Brooklyn Heights on Long Island. When the British army arrived in New York Harbor in June 1776, Greene worried that his fortified works and often sick troops would be vulnerable to a British assault. In August, he was promoted to major general. Despite his best efforts to issue orders to keep camps clean and his concerns about the soldiers' nutrition, he himself fell ill. By August 16, with battle looming, Greene was in bed with a raging fever. He was taken to a "healthy air house" in Manhattan. He helplessly heard the thunder of the battle taking place on Long Island and the destruction of American troops.

On August 30, Greene wrote, "I have not the vanity to think the event would have been otherwise had I been there, yet I could have given the commanding general a good deal of necessary information."[7] Col. Henry Knox agreed in a letter to John Adams reporting on the battle of Long Island.

> We had one chance and only one for the defence of New York and that they completly put into our hands, and which some of our Ge[nerals?], most vilely miss'd improving. The ignorance of the Grounds and the not occupying the passes on that Island sufficiently has been the sole and only cause of our subsequent Retreats and — had General Greene been fit for duty I flatter myself matters would have worn a very different appearance at present.[8]

General Greene was well enough to participate in the Battle of Harlem Heights on September 16 and events of the battle for New York that culminated in the loss of Forts Washington and Lee under his command. The Continental Army retired to Morristown, New Jersey, after their triumphant attacks on Trenton and Princeton that began the year of 1777 with new hope that the Patriots had a chance to win

6. Greene, *The Life of Nathanael Greene*, 143.
7. Ibid., 204.
8. Henry Knox to John Adams, September 25, 1776," https://founders.archives.gov/documents/Adams/06-05-02-0021.

the war. In the summer of 1777, the bulk of the British army embarked on a mysterious sea journey that sent Washington and Congress into a frenzy. The British armada sailed up the Chesapeake Bay and disembarked at Head of Elk, Maryland. General Washington sent Greene to reconnoiter the countryside for a good defensive position from which they could challenge their opponent and move stores out of the enemy's reach.

The mission was exhausting, and the army's position at Wilmington, Delaware, was untenable. On September 10, the British army began moving. In response, Washington drew up his main body at Chadd's Ford, Pennsylvania. Greene wrote to his wife:

> I am exceedingly fatigued. I was on horseback for nearly thirty hours; and never closed my eyes for near forty. Last night I was in hopes of a good night's rest; but a dusty bed gave me asthma, and I had very little sleep the whole night; but little as it was; I feel finely refreshed this morning.[9]

We cannot know how many nights Greene lost sleep due to his struggles with asthma. Yet Greene—whose twenty-four-hundred-man Virginia division was held in reserve during the Battle of Brandywine on September 11—endured the smoke from thousands of firearms, artillery and the scene of panicked Americans running for their lives after the British turned Washington's right flank on Birmingham Hill. Greene's division rushed to the rescue and formed a line that surprised and stopped the British from doing more damage to the Continental Army. Two weeks later, the British took Philadelphia.

On March 2, 1778, under pressure from Washington and a committee from Congress, Greene reluctantly accepted the position of quartermaster general. Two months before on January 1, he wrote to Washington to inform him that the officers in camp at Valley Forge had grievances over lack of spirits and vegetables. At the end of the letter, he wrote, "I have got a very disagreeable pain in one of my Eyes, or else I should have waited upon your Excellency."[10] He did not indicate whether it was his right eye with the smallpox scar, but later in the war he repeated the complaint.

The British had occupied Newport, Rhode Island, since December 7, 1776. In the summer of 1778, Washington sent Gen. John Sullivan

9. Greene, *The Life of Nathanael Greene*, 438.

10. Nathanael Greene to George Washington, January 1, 1778, https://founders.archives.gov/documents/Washington/03-13-02-0086.

to attack them. Greene's family home at Potowomut lay across Narragansett Bay from Newport. He asked Washington for permission to join the Patriot forces at Tiverton. Washington denied his request, citing that he needed Greene to attend to his quartermaster duties for the main army in New York and the Newport expedition. By mid-summer, Washington relented and wrote to Congress that it was advisable to send General Greene.

It was to be a joint expedition with French Adm. Charles-Hector, Comte d'Estaing and his fleet with four thousand marines. Greene had written to Sullivan in July, "You are the first General that has ever had an opportunity of cooperating with the French forces belonging to the United States."[11] A storm and a battle with a British fleet left d'Estaing's ships damaged, and he decided to sail for Boston for repairs. The decision infuriated Sullivan. He had ten thousand men besieging Newport, and he needed sea fire power. He sent Greene and Gen. Gilbert du Motier, Marquis de Lafayette to d'Estaing's flagship to beg him to reconsider. Lafayette later recalled that, as the two men stepped into a waiting skiff, Greene remarked to Lafayette, "If we fail in our negotiation, we shall at least get a good dinner."[12]

Greene never did get that good dinner. He was too seasick. Yet he fought through his nausea and penned a letter of negotiation. Admiral d'Estaing sailed away anyway. On August 26, 1778, Greene wrote to his wife, "I'm not very well in health. I have been a little troubled by the asthma, but have got over it."[13] The Battle of Rhode Island occurred on August 29 as Sullivan's troops abandoned their siege; two days later, from "Camp Tivertown," Greene wrote to Washington to report on the battle and complained about his asthma:

> I would write your Excellency a more particular account of the battle & retreat, but I immagin General Sullivan & Col. Laurens has done it already; and I am myself very much unwell have had no sleep for three Night & Days; being severely afflicted with the Asthma.[14]

Despite his health problems, Greene did not shirk his duties as quartermaster general. It was an exhausting job made more exhausting by the Continental Congress's inability to provide money and support. Congress further exacerbated the issues when they questioned Greene

11. Greene, *The Life of Nathanael Greene*, 100.
12. Ibid., 117.
13. Ibid., 123.
14. Greene to Washington, August 28–31, 1778, https://founders.archives.gov/documents/Washington/03-16-02-0439.

about the large receipts he and his deputies were receiving from their agreed upon one percent commissions. On April 24, 1779, from Philadelphia, Greene wrote to Washington that, "The business of financeing is in a poor way. There is no plan formd or scheme digested for mending our Money."[15] Greene told Washington in the same letter:

> I have desird Congress to give me leave to resign as I apprehended a loss of Reputation if I continued in the business. They are not disposd to grant my request at all. But unless they change the system or publish their approbation upon the present, I shall not remain long in the business . . . Nothing shall induce me to continue in the business; even if the profits is made five times as large as they are . . . No body ever heard of a quarter Master in History as such or in relateing any brilliant Action.[16]

Congress did not grant Greene leave to resign. His patience came to an end when "The two principal characters on whom I depended for support, and whose appointment under the former arrangement . . . are now left out" and Congress introduced "a new systim in the middle of a Campaign" that he thought was "a bold and dangerous experiment."[17] He wrote a scathing resignation letter to Congress on July 26, 1780, in which he pointed out, "My rank is high in the line of the army; and the sacrifices I have made on this account—together with the fatigue and anxiety I have undergone, far overballance all the emoluments I have derived from the appointment."[18]

On August 15, from his headquarters in New Jersey, Washington demonstrated his support and unwavering belief in his discontented major general and replied to the letter Greene sent him on July 27, 1780, with his resignation letter enclosed. "You conducted the various & important duties of it with capacity & deligence—entirely to my satisfaction—and as far as I had an oppertunity of knowing—with the strictest integrity."[19]

Greene's abilities never wavered in Washington's eyes. By the summer of 1780, three of Washington's major generals who Congress had appointed to command in the South had failed. Robert Howe surren-

15. Greene to Washington, April 24, 1779, https://founders.archives.gov/documents/Washington/03-20-02-0171.
16. Ibid.
17. Greene to Washington, July 27, 1780, https://founders.archives.gov/documents/Washington/03-27-02-0267.
18. Ibid.
19. Washington to Greene, August 15, 1780, https://founders.archives.gov/documents/Washington/03-27-02-0490.

dered Savannah, Georgia; Benjamin Lincoln surrendered Charleston, South Carolina; and Horatio Gates lost an army at Camden, South Carolina. After Gates's loss on August 16, Congress left the choice of commander of the Southern Army to Washington. He chose Nathanael Greene. On October 16, Greene accepted the appointment Washington's offered him in a letter written two days before. He was ill and asked for time to put his "domestic concerns" in order.

> However, it will not be possible for me to leave this place for several days, if I put my baggage in the least order, or my business in a proper train for such a long journey. Nor is my health in a condition to set out immediately, having had a considerable fever upon me for several days.[20]

Washington denied Greene's request for time. On October 20, Greene set out with his second-in-command, Gen. Friedrich, Baron von Steuben. Greene took great care to learn all he could about his command and to outfit the army. When he arrived in Charlotte, North Carolina, on December 3, he was unprepared for what he found: "the Embarrassments far exceed my utmost Appre[he]nsion, nor can I find a Clue to guide me through the complicated Scenes of Difficulties."[21] His army was "naked and destitute." There was only a "shadow" of government. Human misery abounded, and the war between Whigs and Tories was "savage."

Within two months, he was contending with another eye infection. On March 5, 1781, he wrote to Col. Henry Lee, Jr.,

> I am the most unfortunate of all Men, while I am distressed for want of officers, I am rendered incapable of business my self, by a violent inflammation in my eyes. I have been bleeding and physicking for several days to correct it, and in part have succeeded; but the inflammation is still troublesome and my eyes weak and painful.[22]

On March 18, Greene wrote to Washington from his camp near Guilford Courthouse:

> The service here is extreme severe, tho the officers and soldiers bear it with a degree of patience, that does them the highest honor. I have never taken off my cloaths since I left the Pedee. I was taken with a

20. Jared Sparks, *Correspondence of the American Revolution Vol. III* (Boston: Little Brown and Company, 1853), 116-117.
21. Richard K. Showman, Dennis M. Conrad and Roger N. Parks, ed. *The Papers of Nathanael Greene: Vol. VII* (Chapel Hill and London: University of North Carolina Press, 1989), xi.
22. Ibid., 395.

> fainting last night, owing I imagine to excessive fatigues, and constant watching. I am better to day, but far from being well.[23]

Greene wrote to Pennsylvania politician Joseph Reed the same day and reiterated what he told Washington, admitting, "We have little to eat, less to drink, and lodge in the woods in the midst of smoke. Indeed, our fatigue is excessive. I was so much overcome night before last that I fainted."[24]

On April 16, 1783, at his headquarters in Charleston, South Carolina, Greene received notification that preliminary articles of peace had been signed between the United States and Great Britain. He issued final orders to his troops on June 21, and then left Charleston in a carriage bound for Philadelphia. On September 13, he recorded in his journal that they stopped at Mount Vernon and then set out for Alexandria. "That evening I was taken very ill with a fever, after my arrival, which lasted me, with very little remission and no intermission, eight days. The constancy of the fever and the excess of the pain reduced me very low."[25]

Greene went home to his wife and children living in a rented house in Newport, Rhode Island. He took home with him a crushing debt of over £30,000 sterling, a guarantee he had signed in 1782 with a Charleston speculator to clothe his army when Congress was not forthcoming with the money needed to provision his Southern troops.

In April 1784 Greene received several letters from Washington protesting the decision that only one of the three Rhode Island delegates should go to Philadelphia to the May meeting of the Society of the Cincinnati because there was an "uproar" that the society did not meet the principals of Republicanism. Greene wrote that he "had the Honor of being appointed President of the Cincinnati of Rhode Island," but begged off the trip to Philadelphia, including his predisposition toward seasickness among his reasons:

> My indisposition is such I fear it will not be in my power to comply with your wishes if there was no other obstacle. I have a constant pain in my breast and am now so weak as to be incapable of bearing the fatigues of a Journey. Besides which the Doctor thinks it would be dan-

23. Greene to Washington, October 25, 1781, https://founders.archives.gov/documents/Washington/99-01-02-07269.
24. William B. Reed, *Life and Correspondence of Joseph Reed* (Philadelphia: Lindsay and Blakiston, 1847), 349-350.
25. George Washington Greene, *The Life of Nathanael Greene, Major General in the Army of the Revolution Vol. III* (New York: Hurd and Houghton. Cambridge: Riverside Press, 1871), 508-509.

> gerous to go by water for fear I might burst a blood vessel as I am very subject to sea sickness and the Vessels of the stomach are exceedingly uncoated. And he thinks it equally dangerous to ride for fear of the same evil. My complaint arose from a strain I got in Providence last Winter in making a violent exertion to save my self from a fall.[26]

Later that year Greene went to Charleston to try to clear some of his debt. On August 29 he wrote to Washington again, explaining his difficulties and that "The clamour raised against the Cincinnati was far more extensive than I expected."[27]

> My ill health and the distressing situation of my private affairs for some time past has claimed too much of my Attention to afford me either time or inclination to attend to any thing else. At the time of the meeting of the Cincinnati in Philadelphia I had a dangerous and disagree[able] pain in my breast. It had hung about me then upwards of two months; but by the use of balsam of firr soon after I wrote you from Newport I got better of it.[28]

Greene petitioned Congress for indemnity in case of loss on August 22, 1785, just two months before he wrote his will and moved his family to Mulberry Grove on the Savannah River in Georgia. He died there on June 19, 1786, at age forty-three from sunstroke a week after walking a neighbor's rice fields without a hat. His wife Caty inherited his debt. She filed an indemnity claim with Congress in 1791 and won with the help of Alexander Hamilton, Anthony Wayne and others who had served with her husband during the war.

On October 1, 1786, from his home in Hartford, Connecticut, Greene's friend and business partner, Col. Jeremiah Wadsworth, wrote to Washington:

> I am persuaded he was just before his death, or rather before he fell sick—in better Spirits than he had ever been before, since his arriveing with his family in Georgia—as he had good prospects of geting clear of his troubles with the crediters of Banks & Co. and a Contract with the French Nation for Timber was so nearly compleated as to promise him sufficient funds for all his other purposes. Mr Miller a Young Gentleman who went with him to Georgia & lived on terms of intimacy & confidence with him assures me the General was in good Spirits and

26. Greene to Washington, April 22, 1784, https://founders.archives.gov/documents/Washington/04-01-02-0221.
27. Greene to Washington, August 29, 1784, https://founders.archives.gov/documents/Washington/04-02-02-0056.
28. Ibid.

> that he is persuaded he died of a fever in the Head which might have been removed if the Physicians had understood his disorder he had for some time before had an inflamation in one Eye—which was almost done away, when he was Sezed at table with a Violent pain in his Eye & Head which forced him to retire, a fever ensued the Symptoms increased and a few days put an end to his existance.[29]

For all of his physical, emotional and mental suffering, Nathanael Greene never wavered in his determination "to defend my rights, and maintain my freedom, or sell my life in the attempt." When giving up or crumbling under pressure may have been an easier route than forging ahead and forging a new nation, Greene did neither. Much gratitude is due the man they called "The Savior of the South," who drove a British army out of the Carolinas and into Virginia where it surrendered at Yorktown. We owe it to remember this hero.

29. Jeremiah Wadsworth to Washington, October 1, 1786, https://founders.archives.gov/documents/Washington/04-04-02-0255.

The Athletic John Adams

JACK CAMPBELL

It is not often that one comes across inspiration for research from a trading card. But sure enough, when this author came across a card produced by Topps featuring John Adams, he was inspired. The card, part of a set commemorating Presidential connections to the game of baseball, mentioned how Adams had mentioned playing a game of "bat and ball" as a child.[1] Now, it appears the card was partially incorrect. The letter stating this does exist but was written to Adams' dear friend Dr. Benjamin Rush, not to Dr. Benjamin West as the card states.[2] Nevertheless, the inquiry begins. What was John Adams' relationship to the game of baseball, or sports in general?

The earliest known reference to baseball in print occurred in 1744 in *A Pretty Little Pocket Book*, a children's book printed in England; it was reprinted in America for the first time in 1783.[3] For one, this confirms that baseball's origins are not wholly American. But it does show that it existed in some form during Adams' lifetime. Another reference comes in the diary of a Princeton student in 1786.[4] These games likely looked different from our modern version of baseball but were still its ancestors. They were likely derived from games such as rounders or

1. John Adams, Presidential Pastime. *Topps.*
2. John Adams to Benjamin Rush, January 4, 1813, *Founders Online*, National Archives, https://founders.archives.gov/documents/Adams/99-02-02-5924.
3. *A little pretty pocket-book: intended for the instruction and amusement of little Master Tommy, and pretty Miss Polly: with two letters from Jack the giant-killer, as also a ball and pincushion, the use of which will infallibly make Tommy a good boy, and Polly a good girl: to which is added, A little song-book, being a new attempt to teach children the use of the English alphabet, by way of diversion.* (Worcester, MA: printed by Isaiah Thomas, 1787), https://www.loc.gov/item/22005880/.
4. Diary of John Rhea Smith, Nassau Hall, College of New Jersey. Princeton, 1786. Manuscript Division, Library of Congress, https://www.loc.gov/exhibitions/baseball-americana/about-this-exhibition/origins-and-early-days/baseballs-roots/earliest-mention-of-baseball/.

stool-ball.[5] It is hard to say when and where the modern game of baseball was truly invented, as claims range from Ancient Egypt to Medieval Europe to Colonial America.[6] Either way, a young John Adams evidently played some version of the game, displaying his athleticism while doing so.

When one thinks of our most athletic presidents, John Adams probably does not often come to mind. Famously short and stout, Adams was also known as being studious and rather stern. But as a young man, he was quite the athlete by his own admission. In that same letter to Dr. Rush, he wrote of "making and sailing Boats . . . Swimming Skaiting, flying Kites and shooting in marbles, Ninepins, Bat and Ball, Footbal . . . Wrestling and sometimes Boxing," all as a young man playing truant from school.[7] It got to the point that he wrote of his father's concern for his passion for sports instead of his studies.[8] Even as a young adult in 1759, he wrote of fond memories of his young sporting days.[9] It was not until he got to college that he wrotes of giving up his sporting ways in favor of studying.[10]

Even as an older man, Adams loved to use sporting metaphors in his writings. A 1782 letter to Edmund Jenings states, "Let Us keep up this Ball and Set all the litterary Sportsmen in Europe to play with it" in reference to trying to get foreign leaders to acknowledge American independence.[11] An 1811 letter describes the young United States as "a foot-ball between contending nations."[12] So today when we refer to an idea as a "home run," we can think back to how even John Adams used sporting metaphors as turns of phrase.

Adams also liked to acknowledge sports a feature of celebrations. On July 3, 1776, the day after what he considered to be the United States' true Independence Day, and the day before what we now con-

5. Library of Congress, "Origins and Early Days of Baseball," *Baseball Americana*, https://www.loc.gov/exhibitions/baseball-americana/about-this-exhibition/origins-and-early-days/.
6. Ibid.
7. "[Parents and Boyhood – from the Autobiography of John Adams]," *Founders Online*, National Archives, https://founders.archives.gov/documents/Adams/01-03-02-0016-0002.
8. Ibid.
9. "[Spring 1759 – from the Autobiography of John Adams] ," *Founders Online*, National Archives, https://founders.archives.gov/documents/Adams/01-01-02-0004-0005-0001 .
10. "[Parents and Boyhood]."
11. Adams to Edmund Jenings, August 28, 1782, *Founders Online*, National Archives, https://founders.archives.gov/documents/Adams/06-13-02-0165.
12. Adams to *Boston Patriot*, June 27, 1811, *Founders Online*, National Archives, https://founders.archives.gov/documents/Adams/99-02-02-5651.

sider it to be, Adams wrote to his wife Abigail that American independence "ought to be solemnized with Pomp and Parade, with Shews, Games, Sports, Guns, Bells, Bonfires and Illuminations from one End of this Continent to the other from this Time forward forever more."[13] While in France, he wrote of Sundays, "There are more Games, Plays, and Sports of every Kind on this day, than on any other, in the Week."[14] Just as sports are considered leisurely activities today, so were they in the days of John Adams. He even wrote of watching his grandson, also named John, taking part in sports while his father John Quincy left the boy in his grandfather's care.[15]

Nobody will ever mistake John Adams for American sporting legends such as Michael Jordan, Michael Phelps, or Willie Mays. Nobody will mistake him for the avid fans of sports that can now be found in his native New England. But what we see here is a much more human John Adams. A more relatable one. He liked sports, just as many of us do. He enjoyed them as leisurely or celebratory activities and recalled eschewing his studies in favor of them. There is something there that so many can now relate to. While we might view Adams as the stern old man in paintings, there was also a vibrant and athletic personality that he so deftly recalled in his own words.

13. Adams to Abigail Adams, July 3, 1776, *Founders Online*, National Archives, https://founders.archives.gov/documents/Adams/04-02-02-0016.
14. Diary of John Adams, May 10, 1778, *Founders Online*, National Archives, https://founders.archives.gov/documents/Adams/01-02-02-0008-0004-0010.
15. Adams to John Quincy Adams, September 8, 1820, *Founders Online*, National Archives, https://founders.archives.gov/documents/Adams/99-03-02-3835.

A Second Fight for Freedom: The Enslaved of Dr. James Craik, Chief Physician

MICHAEL M. WOOD

As Founding Fathers of the United States met in Philadelphia to declare that "all men are created equal," Thomas Craik Jr. was born into a family of people enslaved by Dr. James Craik on his Maryland plantations.[1] This was not unusual at the time; many of the colonial landed gentry relied upon slave labor to work their tobacco plantations, including George Washington himself. What makes this story unique is a series of records which allow us to document much of the family who were enslaved by Dr. Craik.

SLAVERY IN MARYLAND

Slavery is a dark chapter in history; the retelling of an enslaved person's story can never capture the pain and suffering of a life in bondage.

As lucrative as the colonial tobacco crop might have been, growing it was extremely labor-intensive. Maryland Governor Charles Calvert wrote in 1729, "Tobacco, as our staple, is our all, and indeed leaves no room for anything else. It requires the attendance of all our hands, and exacts their utmost labour, the whole year round."[2] By the mid-eighteenth century, the plantation economy of Maryland relied almost exclusively upon slavery to supply the extensive numbers of field hands the crop required.

By 1755 enslaved Blacks accounted for 33 percent of Maryland's total population; the concentration was even higher in the tidewater

1. Inventory of the estate of John Winter, probated April 30, 1799, Charles County Inventories 1798-1802, June Term 1799, (Annapolis MD, Hall of Records), 140-141.
2. Benedict Calvert, *Calvert Papers, Number two* (Baltimore: Maryland Historical Society, 1894), 70.

region.[3] In some tidewater counties, as much as half the population originated in Africa; many of the enslaved in Maryland originated in the Windward and Gold Coasts of West Africa, from Sierra Leone to Nigeria. Throughout the south, regular sales offering "fine, healthy Negroes" from the windward coast, were common.

At the outbreak of the Revolution, the demographics of Maryland's enslaved population had changed significantly; some 90 percent of the colony's enslaved people were native-born Americans. Political changes soon followed; in 1774 Maryland lawmakers officially ended the colony's participation in the international slave trade. In Virginia, a 1778 law required those importing slaves from another state to give an oath confirming that the enslaved person was not imported from Africa and was not brought into Virginia for the purpose of being sold.[4] Another, passed in 1792, stipulated that "slaves brought into this commonwealth, and kept therein for one year, shall be free, excepting those who may be inclined to remove from any of the United States, and become citizens of this State, if within sixty days after such removal, he or she shall take the following oath before some justice of the peace of the commonwealth."[5] These laws, and their required oaths, would form the basis for several Freedom Suits brought by those who had been enslaved by Dr. Craik.

DR. JAMES CRAIK

The Craik family was of great prominence in the Chesapeake Bay region. Dr. James Craik of Charles County, Maryland, was one of George Washington's oldest and closest friends, and the personal physician who attended to Washington on his deathbed. In his last will, Washington called him "my compatriot in arms and old and intimate friend."[6]

James Craik was born about 1730 in the Parish of Kirkbean, near Dumfries, Scotland. The son of William Craik, a member of the British Parliament, James studied medicine at the University of Edinburgh. In

3. Maryland State Archives, "*A Guide to the History of Slavery in Maryland*", p.4, https://msa.maryland.gov/msa/intromsa/pdf/slavery_pamphlet.pdf.
4. Virginia General Assembly, *A Collection of All Such Acts of the General Assembly of Virginia of a Public and Permanent Nature, as are Now in Force* (Richmond: Samuel Pleasants, Jun., and Henry Pace, 1814), Act of the December 17, 1792, p. 262.
5. Matilda Derrick, Lucy Derrick, Louisa Derrick, & Matilda Derrick v. George Mason & Alexander Moore, Supreme Court of the United States, January Term 1827, summary at "*O Say Can You See*", William G. Thomas and the Center for Digital Research in the Humanities, https://earlywashingtondc.org/doc/oscys.report.0013.002.
6. George Washington's Last Will and Testament, July 9, 1799, https://www.mountvernon.org/education/primary-source-collections/primary-source-collections/article/george-washingtons-last-will-and-testament-july-9-1799/.

1750 he immigrated to the West Indies to serve as a British army surgeon. He soon resigned his post and moved to Norfolk, Virginia where he opened a medical practice. Craik later maintained a farm at Vaucluse, near Winchester, and practiced as a surgeon based at Fort Loudon.[7]

In March 1754 he accepted a commission to serve as a surgeon in Col. Joshua Fry's Virginia Provincial Regiment, alongside Lt. Col. George Washington, during the French and Indian War. Craik was with Washington at Fort Necessity in 1755 and with Braddock later that year.[8] Washington wrote of him in letter to Adam Stephen on November 18: "Doctr Craik is expected round to Alexandria in a Vessel with Medicines, and other Stores for the Regiment; so soon as he arrives I shall take care to dispatch him to you."[9] Craik's land holdings would grow significantly as a result of his service in the war.

On November 30, 1760 he married Mariamne Ewell, daughter of Charles Ewell and his wife Sarah Ball Conway, first cousin to George Washington. They wed at Belle Aire, in Prince William County. After the marriage, Craik moved across the Potomac to Port Tobacco, Maryland.[10] Together, the couple would have nine children.

THE CRAIK PLANTATION

Craik's property in Maryland included the contiguous plantations of Prospect Hill, May Day, and the 234 acre Moore's Ditch, which he purchased in 1763. Here he built his home, La Grange, around 1770.[11]

Craik was a major land holder. He is known to have held land in Hampshire County "on the North River" as early as 1771.[12] He held at least 7,000 acres in the Great Kanawha River tracts of Virginia, as did George Washington, in part granted to French and Indian War veterans.[13] He also owned land in Kentucky, and in Allegheny County, Maryland—which he noted were given to him "by that state for military services"—as well as homes and lots in both Washington and

7. James Craik, https://www.mountvernon.org/library/digitalhistory/digital-encyclopedia/article/james-craik/.

8. James Craik, https://twitter.com/FtNecessityNPS/status/1093255374201913344.

9. George Washington to Adam Stephen, November 18, 1755, https://founders.archives.gov/documents/Washington/02-02-02-0178.

10. Gay Moore, *Seaport in Virginia, George Washington's Alexandria* (Alexandria: Garrett and Massie, 1949), 184-194.

11. Willie Graham (principal investigator), Maryland Historical Trust, "The Architecture of Domestic Support Structures in Southern Maryland", St. Mary's College of Maryland, 2020, pp. 46-47, https://mht.maryland.gov/Documents/research/contexts/FRRMary40.pdf.

12. *Virginia Gazette* (Purdie and Dixon), October 17, 1771.

13. *Alexandria Daily Advertiser*, October 15, 1805.

Alexandria.[14] The Great Kanawha River lands included those granted in December 1772 when the Virginia Council ordered that surveys be "immediately patented in the name of Dr. James Craik"; two parcels of 4,232 and 1,374 acres, noting that he "will fall short 394 acres of the 6,000 he has a right to, and be entitled at the next distribution to that quantity of land."[15]

In recognition of his service in the Revolution, he would be eligible for 500 acres under the Acts of 1796 and 1799, and under the revised pension acts, his descendants were awarded 6,000 acres on March 12, 1832.[16]

The historical record shows that Dr. James Craik, as well as his sons Judge William Craik, James Craik Jr., Adam Craik and George Washington Craik, were all slaveholders. Although the exact number of enslaved persons working on the Craik plantations in Maryland is unknown, a 1782 tax assessment shows that Dr. Craik held twenty-two people in bondage.[17]

Although by 1798 the Craik estate had been sold to Francis Newman, and Dr. Craik was living in Virginia, it was in 1798 on the La Grange property that Josiah Henson was born, the enslaved man later depicted in Harriet Beecher Stowe's *Uncle Tom's Cabin.*

THE REVOLUTION AND THE RELATIONSHIP WITH WASHINGTON

After the French and Indian War, Craik and Washington remained in close contact. Washington wrote of him with great praise:

> The habits of intimacy and friendship, in which I have long-lived with Doctor Craik, and the opinion I have of his professional knowledge, would most certainly point him out as the man of my choice in all cases of sickness. I am convinced of his sincere attachment to me, and I should with cheerfulness trust my life in his hands.[18]

In the autumn of 1770, when Washington explored lands along the Ohio River, he set out from Mount Vernon on the 5th of October in company of Dr. James Craik.[19]

14. Fairfax County Courthouse, Fairfax County Virginia Will Book, James Crsaik, Vol K1, 1812-1816, pp. 180-183.
15. *Virginia Gazette* (Rind), January 14, 1773.
16. M. G. Brumbaugh, *Revolutionary War Records, Volume 1, Virginia* (Lancaster: Lancaster Press, 1936), 97.
17. Maryland State Papers, Scharf Collection Online, 1782 Tax Assessment, James Craik, MDSA s1005_107_15-0004.
18. Letter to James McHenry, 3 July 1789, in John C. Fitzpatrick, ed., *The writings of George Washington* (Washington: USGPO, 1939), 30:351.
19. John W. Wayland, "Washington West of the Blue Ridge," *The Virginia Magazine of History and Biography*, Vol. 48, No. 3 (July 1940), 193-201.

As early as 1774, Craik was active in the movement against British rule, and in 1777, at Washington's behest, he accepted a position in the Continental Army. In his letter to Craik of April 26. 1777, Washington offered him two positions:

> Dear Doctor,
>
> I am going to address you on a subject which may lay some claim to your attention, as I do to your candor in the determination of the proposition. In the Hospital department for the middle District (which District includes the States between the North or Hudson's River, and Patowmack) there are at present two places vacant, either of which I can obtain for you: The one is Senior Physician, and Surgeon of the Hospital, with the pay of four Dollars and six Rations—Day, and Forage for one Horse: The other is Assistant Director General, with the pay of three Dollars and six Rations—Day; and two Horses, and travelling expenses found, according to Doctor Shippen's (W.) Director General's account, who also adds that he thinks this latter the most honourable and desirable of the two.[20]

Craik accepted Washington's offer in May 1777, but as he was actively inoculating people against smallpox, he made it clear that he would not be able to report to camp immediately:

> At the Same time that I Solicite for this Appointment I must inform you that in case my immediat attendance at Camp is necessary, it will not be in my power to Comply with it as I have Some familys under Inoculation near Fredericksburgh whom I am not certain that I could leave under three or four Weeks from this time.[21]

Washington's reply, until recently unpublished, read "I have referred the request contained in your letter to the Director General who knows how far it is in his power consistently with the good of the service to prolong your absence."[22] Director General Dr. William Shippen Jr. did authorize Craik's commission and delayed arrival at Valley Forge, but asked in return that Craik "assist & direct Dr Tilton one of our senior Surgeons who writes me he has near 1100 Carolinians, officers

20. Washington to James Craik, April 26, 1777, https://founders.archives.gov/documents/Washington/03-09-02-025.

21. Craik to Washington, May 13, 1777, https://founders.archives.gov/documents/Washington/03-09-02-0404.

22. The Raab Collection, Ardmore, PA, letter in a private collection, "May 31st, 1777, "General George Washington Manages the First Major Inoculation Campaign in American History and the Continental Army Medical Department", https://www.raabcollection.com/presidential-autographs/washington-medical-als.

included, under inoculation at Dumfries, Alexandria & Georgetown."[23] Craik's work against smallpox was not without its dissenters, although he and Washington were of a like mind. While Craik was inoculating private citizens, Washington ordered that all soldiers that came through Philadelphia be inoculated.[24]

When Washington's leadership was questioned in the winter of 1777-1778, it was Craik who warned him of the "Conway Cabal," a group of men wishing to replace Washington with Horatio Gates. In January 1778, Craik wrote to his friend warning that

> you are not wanting in Secret enemies who would Rob you of the great and truely deserved esteem your Country has for you . . . If they are your Enemies every honest man must naturally conclude they are Enemies to the Country and the Glorious Cause in which we are engaged, and will no Doubt most Streneously exert every Nerve to dissapoint their Villainous intentions.[25]

In 1781 Craik was promoted to Chief Physician and Surgeon of the Army, a commission that he held until the end of the war. He was instrumental in setting up the hospitals that provided medical support to the French troops in Rhode Island during their stay in 1780 and 1781.

Although exaggerated, Craik's grandson James Craik D.D. (1806–1882), recalled that the doctor was with Washington in "every battle that he fought from Great Meadows to Yorktown."[26] Craik was certainly at Yorktown in October 1781, reporting to Washington on the casualties of the battle: "In the Hospitals at Williamsburg there are about four hundred sick and wounded, at Hanover Town about two hundred, and upwards of six hundred reported sick in the army—those in Hanover Town."[27]

23. William Shippen, Jr. to Washington, June 2, 1777," https://founders.archives.gov/documents/Washington/03-09-02-0593.

24. National Park Service, Smallpox, Inoculation, and the Revolutionary War, Boston National Historical Park, https://www.nps.gov/articles/000/smallpox-inoculation-revolutionary-war.htm. See also), Letter to James McHenry, July 3,1789, *The writings of George Washington*, 7:102-106.

25. Craik to Washington, January 6, 1778, https://founders.archives.gov/documents/Washington/03-13-02-0126.

26. "Boyhood Memories of Dr. James Craik, D.D., L.L.D. Rector of Christ Church, Louisville, Ky., 38 Years," *The Virginia Magazine of History and Biography*, Vol. 46, No. 2 (April 1938), 135-145.

27. Craik to Washington, October 23, 1781, https://founders.archives.gov/documents/Washington/99-01-02-07237.

After the war, at Washington's suggestion, Craik settled in Alexandria, Virginia, and became Washington's personal physician.[28] He was admitted as an original member of the Society of the Cincinnati of Maryland in November 1783.[29]

Craik was clearly a popular traveling partner. When in September 1784, George Washington again set out to visit his lands "west of the Apalacheon Mountains," he "set out myself in company with Docter James Craik."[30]

Craik continued to serve as Washington's personal physician during his lifetime. Letters between the men, as well as Craik's medical ledgers, indicate that he was a regular visitor at Mount Vernon. He was there as often as twice a week, providing services to Washington's household and his enslaved population, including inoculating them against smallpox.[31]

In the midst of the Quasi-War with France, a limited naval war against French privateers who were seizing U.S. shipping, in November 1798 Washington called the country's most senior officers together and tasked them with identifying senior officers who should be recommended to President Adams for commissioning.[32] On the recommendation of Washington, Dr. James Craik was selected as Physician-General of the Army.[33]

Craik was present at Washington's death bed on December 14, 1799. Washington told him, "Doctor, I die hard; but I am not afraid to

28. National Museum of the United States Army, *Biographies, James Craik*, https://www.thenmusa.org/biographies/james-craik/.
29. James Schmidt, *The Maryland Line and the Creation of the Society of the Cincinnati, Maryland State Archives*, 2019, https://msamaryland400.com/2019/10/25/the-maryland-line-and-the-creation-of-the-society-of-the-cincinnati/. See also: Journal and Correspondence of the Council of Maryland, 1781-1784, Maryland Archives Online, 48:483-484, https://msa.maryland.gov/megafile/msa/speccol/sc2900/sc2908/000001/000048/html/am48—483.html.
30. *George Washington Diaries*, 4:14, https://founders.archives.gov/documents/Washington/01-04-02-0001-0001.
31. James Craik, Invoice for services provided, November 14, 1791, Box: 24, Folder: 1791.11.14, RM-873; MS-5334, Mount Vernon Ladies' Association, Washington Library, https://archives.mountvernon.org/repositories/3/archival_objects/4946. See also Amy Speckart, "New Perspectives on Haberdeventure Plantation in Charles County, Maryland, 1770–1787." The Organization of American Historians and The National Park Service (February 2022), 41, https://www.nps.gov/thst/learn/historyculture/upload/508_THST-Final-508-3.pdf. See also J. M. Toner, "A Sketch of the Life of Dr. Gustavus Richard Brown," *Sons of the Revolution in State of Virginia Quarterly Magazine* 2, no. 1 (January 1923), 18-19.
32. Robert Gough, "Officering the American Army, 1798," *The William and Mary Quarterly* Vol. 43, No. 3 (July 1986), 460-471.
33. *Aurora General Advertiser*, Philadelphia, July 20, 1798.

go; I believed from my first attack that I should not survive it; my breath can not last long." Afterward, the other doctors were dismissed and only Craik remained in the room. Washington spoke, requesting to be "decently buried" and to "not let my body be put into the Vault in less than three days after I am dead."[34] Craik publicly recounted Washington's passing with the words,

> I, who was bred among scenes of human calamity—who had so often witnessed death in its direct and most awful forms, believed that its terrors were too familiar to my eye to shake my fortitude—but when I saw this great man die, it seemed as if the pillar of my country's happiness had fallen to the ground.[35]

The death of Washington while in Craik's care did not seem to impact his renown as a doctor. Many physicians in colonial North America were trained through apprenticeships, and every two years, in 1799, 1801 and 1803, Dr. Craik advertised for "A Young Man of Good Character" to apprentice with him in the "study of medicine."[36]

Craik's documented record of caring for the health and well-being of others would appear to stand in stark contrast to his position on human slavery; to his credit, he did actively care for the health of his enslaved population and made an effort to keep enslaved family groups together. Perhaps he, like his friend George Washington wrote in 1799, was "principled against this kind of traffic in the human species" and felt that "To hire them out, is almost as bad, because they could not be disposed of in families to any advantage, and to disperse families I have an aversion."[37]

POSTWAR SLAVERY

The "importation" of enslaved people from Maryland to Virginia was already subject to a duty of 20 percent, but the Act of 1785 further stipulated that enslaved persons "born in another state and brought into Virginia" after the date of the act would be freed after spending one year in the state. As such, clandestine importations were rampant.[38]

34. Mount Vernon Ladies' Association, Washington Library, Center for Digital History, Digital Encyclopedia, "Death of George Washington," https://www.mountvernon.org/library/digitalhistory/digital-encyclopedia/article/the-death-of-george-washington/.
35. *The Pennsylvania Gazette*, May 18, 1814.
36. *Alexandria Daily Advertiser*, June 24, 1803.
37. Robert Lewis to Washington, August 17, 1799, https://founders.archives.gov/documents/Washington/06-04-02-0211.
38. Donald M. Sweig, "The Importation of African Slaves to the Potomac River, 1732-1772," *The William and Mary Quarterly*, Vol. 42, No. 4 (October 1985), 518-519.

As they were considered taxable property, records of the names of those held in bondage on any given plantation can be inaccurate; even more difficult is establishing family groups and ancestry amongst enslaved peoples. Additionally, the practice of loaning or selling slaves between plantations complicates the historical record. Tracing the family history of persons enslaved in the eighteenth century is especially difficult, made more so by the general practice of using only given names to identify enslaved people.

The number of persons held in bondage by the Craik family increased in the years between 1782 and 1790. In the 1790 census, the Craik family reported holding twenty-four enslaved people in Maryland—in addition to those imported by Dr. Craik to Virginia—counting them among the larger slaveholders in the area.[39]

BOUGHT, SOLD, AND HUNTED

Slave labor was a valuable commodity in Maryland; thus aside from being considered part of an inheritance, these persons and their labor were rented, traded and sold as active commodities.

The average value of an adult male slave in the southern colonies in the early 1780s was $1,110. Because a runaway slave represented a loss of capital, slaveholders actively pursued runaways, both through local sheriffs and with vigilante justice. Those who ran away from the Craik estate included "Josh the property of Craik's estate well known in town as a fiddler and much marked with the small pox"; a five dollar reward was offered for delivering him to the town gaol.[40] In June 1798, James Craik placed an announcement in the local newspaper advising that two people had "Absconded" from his plantation, "a negro man named Joe, and a mulatto girl named Ann." He warned anyone "harboring or employing them," that he "shall in such case persecute the offender as the law directs."[41]

After his death, the estate of James Craik placed an advertisement offering "20 dollars reward" for the return of "a negro wench name Jenny . . . about 25 years old . . . runaway from the late residence of Dr. James Craik." For those wishing to pursue the bounty, her possible whereabouts were given: "it is believed that said wench is lurking in Charles County, most probably in the neighborhood of Port Tobacco, or Allen's Fresh, where she has relations."[42]

39. 1790 United States Federal Census, Maryland, Charles County, William Craik, p. 10. 1790 Virginia census records were lost.

40. *Hall's Wilmington Gazette*, August 24, 1797.

41. *The Columbian Mirror And Alexandria Gazette*, June 12, 1798.

42. *Alexandria Gazette, Commercial and Political*, February 9, 1815.

Despite his relocation to Virginia, James Craik initially retained his properties and slaves in Maryland; these were not transferred to his son William until 1796.[43] William Craik, who had been elected to Congress that year, sold all his Charles County lands and many of his slaves, the sales finalized by 1798.[44] William predeceased his father in 1807. At the settlement of William's estate, it was noted that "all my negroes not herein otherwise disposed of" shall be left to "my much beloved and respected father and mother for and during their natural lives," stipulating that after their deaths that four specific "negroes" and their "future increase" should go to his father and mother, then after their deaths to his nephew James Craik, "son of my brother George Washington Craik" (1774-1808). The four enslaved people named in this document were "Archibald and his wife Betsy and her future increase," "Rose and her future Increase" and "Lewis."[45]

The slaves of William Craik "otherwise disposed of" appear to have been transferred to John Winter Sr. (1712–1781, m. Elizabeth Bruce). Winter was a tobacco farmer who owned multiple plantations in Charles County; The Meadows, Meadows Marsh, The Old Gray Plantation, Orphin Loss, Grays Fancy, Westwood Manor, St. Thomas' Manor and Nanjemoy. When John Winter Sr. wrote his will in 1780, he named his "one Negroe man named Tom Craik, his wife Jude, her daughter Chloe, Victory, Beck, Hezekiah, Tom, Matilda, all children of Tom Craik & his wife Jude" to be left to his son John Winter, Jr., as well as a silver can, four silver spoons, and other "property."[46]

John Winter Jr. (1761–1799, m. Elizabeth Mason) died in 1799; the administrator Richard Mason presented an inventory of the "goods and chattels" belonging to the estate. Rather than simply listing the total number of enslaved people, as was commonplace, Winter provided the names and ages of the enslaved. These included:

> Thomas Craik Sen. aged 64, Adam aged 35, Gerard a carpenter aged 35, Thomas Craik Jr. aged 23, Samuel aged 12 [listed twice], Notly aged 12, Gerard aged 10, John aged 10, Thomas aged 7, Levy aged 3, and the women Mary aged 65, Chloe aged 36, Rebecca Sen. aged 30, Ann

43. Charles County Deed Books, Liber IB 2/47.
44. Webster et al., *In Search of Josiah Henson's Birthplace* (St. Mary's City MD: St. Mary's College of Maryland, 2017), 24.
45. Chancery Court Records, 1807 William Craik of Alexandria, (Richmond VA, Library of Virginia), Index No. 1827-023.
46. Will of John Winter, probated February 6, 1781, Register of Wills Charles County, AF 7.590, 590-593.

> aged 20, Juda Sen. aged 16, Rebecca Jr. "on the east shore" aged 14, and Juda Jr. aged 5.[47]

The "value" recorded for Thomas Craik Jr. was eighty-five pounds. The names of at least seven of the twenty-two slaves John Winter Jr. claimed in an earlier tax assessment, including Tom's wife Jude Craik and her children Victory, Beck and Hezekiah, do not appear on the 1799 list. As Jude does not appear in any later records, she might have died before 1799. Her daughters Beck and Victory do appear in later records, as does one slave named Hezekiah, of the right age to be Tom Craik's son. A Hezekiah, born about 1779, appears on the 1795 inventory of the estate of Thomas Winter of Charles County, the son of John Winter's first cousin.

The people enslaved by John Winter Jr., including the Craik family, would pass in large part to his son John Winter II, who died before 1801, the enslaved persons passing to his sister, Eliza Winter (b. abt. 1788), listed as "nearest of kin" in the inventory of his estate that was recorded on October 15, 1801. The document lists twenty-three enslaved people:

> Tom Crack Sen. aged 70 years, Adam aged 45 years, Tom Crack Jun. aged 30 years, Gerard carpenter aged 45 years, Sam aged 14 years, Notley aged 13 years, Gerard aged 11 years, John aged 9 years, Thomas aged 6 years, Levi aged 5 years, John aged 2 years, Hezekiah aged 1, and the women Chloe aged 40 years, Beck aged 30 years, Vick aged 36 years (author's note: poss. Tom's daughter, Victory), Anney aged 25 years, Jude Crack aged 21 years, Beck aged 15 years, Jude aged 7 years, Peggy aged 4 years, Priss aged 1 years, Jenny aged 20 years and Moll aged 60 years.[48]

As was the case in the inventory list taken in 1799, Jude Craik and her son Hezekiah were not recorded, perhaps sold to another plantation, deceased, or simply overlooked. Victory and Beck Craik—who were not included in the 1799 inventory—were recorded in 1801, clearly showing that these inventory lists were not always definitive. The ages of enslaved persons were often estimated, as can be seen by the variations between the two lists. Of importance, this inventory uses the spelling "Crack", which Tom Craik used in later years.

47. Inventory of the estate of John Winter, probated April 30, 1799, Charles County Inventories 1798-1802, June Term 1799, (Annapolis MD, Hall of Records), 140-141.
48. Inventory of the estate of John Winter, October 15, 1801, Charles County Maryland Inventory Accounts, June Term 1802, (Annapolis MD, Hall of Records), 491-492.

THE FREEDOM SUITS

At the close of the eighteenth century, several former slaves of Dr. James Craik sued for their freedom.

The Virginia slave importation laws required that anyone bringing an enslaved person into the state must "take an oath within 60 days after his removal" confirming that the person was not imported from Africa and was not brought into Virginia for the purpose of being sold. This law, and its legal interpretation by the courts, formed the basis for many slaves to sue their enslavers for their freedom.

Before his relocation to Virginia, Dr. James Craik held twenty-two slaves on a plantation of 495 acres.[49] Exactly when and how many were later brought with him to Virginia is unclear, as well as whether Craik took the correct oath required by the State of Virginia. Those who sued testified that Craik imported them into Virginia around the year 1792. It is these importations that would later cause Craik to be subpoenaed to appear in court.

Enslaved people were often backed by Quakers, or other opponents of slavery, when they sought freedom through the judicial process. Dr. Craik faced freedom lawsuits brought by Joseph Harris, Betsy Scarlett, Ann Williams, Mathilda Thompson and Ann Caruthers, but the outcome of these cases is unknown.[50]

In 1799, the enslaved Rose, noted in the estate settlement of William Craik, sued for her freedom. In the case of "Negro Rose, Harry, & Joe v. James Kennedy Jr.," Rose claimed that James Craik brought her into Virginia in 1792, and she claimed to be free because her owner had not taken the oath prescribed by the Act of Virginia of December 17, 1792.

The case took nearly three years, with James Craik summoned to testify twice, in July 1801 and in April 1802. The jury initially found for the plaintiff Rose, but on appeal the defendant (James Kennedy Jr.) produced a certificate by T. Hooe, a justice of the peace, of an "oath taken by the owner on the 28th of December, 1792." The jury then ruled for the defendant. Rose and her children remained enslaved.[51]

49. Amy Speckart, "New Perspectives on Haberdeventure Plantation in Charles County, Maryland, 1770–1787," *The Organization of American Historians and The National Park Service* (February 2022), 27, 125, www.nps.gov/thst/learn/historyculture/upload/508_THST-Final-508-3.pdf.

50. Gloria Whittico, "The Rule of Law and the Genesis of Freedom: A Survey of Selected Virginia County Court Freedom Suits (1723-1800)," *Alabama Civil Rights & Civil Liberties Law Review*, 9.2 (2018), 463.

51. N*egro Rose, Harry, & Joe v. James Kennedy Jr.*, United States. Circuit Court (District of

DEATH OF DR. JAMES CRAIK

Dr. James Craik and his wife, Mariamne Craik, died within months of each other, he in February 1814 and she in April 1815. The well publicized story of his attentiveness at Washington's death bed contrasts vividly with his own passing, which came quietly in Alexandria. Even his own obituary was but one line—the rest of the notice being about his attendance to Washington in 1799.[52] His resting place in the cemetery of the Old Presbyterian Meeting House remained unmarked until 1928, when descendants placed a slab in his honor.[53]

In his last will, dated June 5, 1813, Dr. Craik left "my said wife Mariamne her heirs and assigns forever the following slaves to wit Parker, Janney, Myrtilda and her children, Mary, Paris [possibly Tom Craik's daughter Priss], Lucy, William and Matilda, and all the future increase of the said Janney Myrtilda, Mary, Lucy and Matilda."[54]

Apparently Dr. Craik had remained active and in good health in his old age, continuing to practice medicine until just a few years before he died. He himself reflected on his later years, saying, "Age was as a lusty winter—frosty but kindly."[55]

His wife moved to Alexandria after her husband's passing, but followed him in death not long afterwards. Her will dated April 10, 1815 mentioned only "my woman, Myrtilla and her children," specifying that "if they are sold they must be sold for a term of years—they must not be sold for life out of the family."[56]

THE SUPREME COURT

In an 1805 case, Loudon v. Scott, the court ruled that a slave brought into Virginia in 1802, by a person removing from Maryland, and omitting to take the oath within sixty days after his removal, was entitled to freedom. This precedent case triggered others to sue, including "Myrtilda, Mary, Lucy and Matilda," who James Craik had left to his wife Mariamne in 1814 and she in turn left to her daughters.

Matilda filed a Petition for Freedom in 1822. She argued, as had Rose in 1799, that James Craik had violated the law of 1792 which

Columbia)—Alexandria (Washington, D.C.), summary at "*O Say Can You See*", https://earlywashingtondc.org/cases/oscys.caseid.0383.

52. *The Pennsylvania Gazette*, May 18, 1814.

53. *Richmond Times-Dispatch*, October 9, 1928.

54. Fairfax County Courthouse, Fairfax County Virginia Will Book, James Craik, Vol K1, 1812-1816, pp. 180-183.

55. *Alexandria Gazette Commercial and Political*, February 10, 1814.

56. Alexandria City Courthouse, Alexandria City Virginia Will Book, 1815-1821, Mariamne Craik, Vol 2, 1810-1831, p. 56.

forbade slaves to be brought to Virginia for the purpose of selling them. A separate case was filed for her minor son William, who was held in bondage by others.[57] Matilda claimed, "on the grounds of negress Matilda, their mother, having been removed in the year 1792 from Charles County in the state of Maryland to Fairfax County in the State of Virginia, by a certain Doctor Craik," that she and her children were free.[58]

She lost the case in October, but was immediately granted a new trial. On June 13, 1823, she won her freedom—but it would be short lived. The defendant appealed in August and the issue went to the Supreme Court of the United States, whose judgment in January 1827 reversed the lower court:

> One James Craik, through whom the plaintiffs in this court make title, some time in the year 1792, brought Matilda from the state of Maryland into Fairfax county, in Virginia, and there settled and resided until his death, in all about two and twenty years. During this time, the three children of Matilda were born, and the whole continued to be held by him in slavery, during his life, and at his death, were bequeathed to his wife, who bequeathed them to the wives of Moer and Mason. The whole time which elapsed from the bringing of Matilda into Virginia to the commencement of this suit, was thirty years.

Matilda and her children remained in bondage. There was, however, one exception.

TOM CRAIK'S MANUMISSION

By the time of the Missouri Compromise of 1820, Maryland's laws regarding slavery, as revised in 1796, remained in force, making it difficult for slaveholders to free their slaves. The rules for granting manumission required that the enslaved person be "of healthy constitution and sound in mind and body, capable by labor to procure them sufficient food and raiment with other requisite necessities of life." The law was additionally restrictive by allowing only enslaved people under the age of forty-five to be offered their freedom. Previously, persons up to the age of fifty could be manumitted.[59]

57. William Derrick v. David Read & Silas Read, summary at "*O Say Can You See*", https://earlywashingtondc.org/cases/oscys.caseid.0422.
58. Matilda Derrick, Lucy Derrick, Louisa Derrick, & Matilda Derrick v. George Mason & Alexander Moore, Supreme Court of the United States, January Term 1827, summary at "*O Say Can You See*", https://earlywashingtondc.org/doc/oscys.report.0013.002.
59. *Proceedings and Acts of the General Assembly*, 1796, Chapter LXVII, Volume 105, p. 255, Archives of Maryland Online, https://msa.maryland.gov/megafile/msa/speccol/sc2900/sc2908/000001/000105/html/am105—255.html.

Thomas Craik Jr. was forty-four years old in 1821, living in bondage under Elizabeth Winter in Alexandria. Whether motivated by his approaching age limit, influenced by the increasing abolitionist movement, or through a personal change of conscience, Eliza Winter gave Thomas Crack Jr. his freedom on October 25, 1821.[60]

> State of Maryland Charles County
>
> I hereby certify that Thomas Crack the bearer hereof a black man about forty four years of age five feet six inches high having a large black mole near the corner of his left eye, is a free person, and was liberated by a certain Eliza Winter of Charles County, by deed manumission bearing date on or about the twenty fifth date of October in the year of our Lord one thousand eight hundred and twenty one, and enroled among the record of Charles County Court, and I further certify that the said Thomas Crack was born and raised in Trinity Parish in the county and state aforesaid.
>
> In testimony whereof I have hereto subscribed my name and affixed the seal of Charles County Court this thirtieth day of October in the year of our Lord one thousand eight hundred and twenty one.
>
> John Barnes Clerk Charles County Court

In the census of 1830, Thomas Crack Jr. is recorded as a Free Colored Person, living alone in Allens Fresh, Charles County, Maryland. The hamlet of Allens Fresh borders directly on Trinity Parish, where Thomas was born. He had finally returned home, a free man.[61]

EPILOGUE

Members of the enslaved family of Tom Craik lived in bondage for a full century; with certainty from the birth of Tom Craik Sr.'s first son in about 1776 until the Virginia Constitutional Convention resolved to abolish slavery on March 10, 1864.

The existence of this rare sequence of documents allows the story of the enslaved Craik family to be partially reconstructed. These documents may be unique to this family, but the story they represent is exemplary of many others who lived in bondage during this period.

60. John Barnes (Clerk of the Charles County Court), Manumission papers of Thomas Crack, original document dated 1821, privately held, digital copy in the personal collection of Michael M. Wood.

61. Bureau of the Census, 1830 U.S. Federal Census, Allens Fresh, Charles, Maryland, Series M19, Roll 56, (Washington DC, NARA, 1830), 138.

Whether Thomas's father, Tom Craik Sr., lived long enough to see his son achieve freedom, no record exists. Elizabeth Winter is not recorded holding any persons in bondage after 1821. As for the rest of Tom's family, we can only speculate.

Don Diego de Gardoqui: Hero of the Revolution, Schemer Against the Republic

TYSON REEDER

When Don Diego Gardoqui stepped onto Philadelphia's docks in May 1785, he was a hero of the American Revolution. A merchant from Bilbao, Spain, Gardoqui, forty-nine, had early on in the war transformed his trade connections with Massachusetts into a pipeline for delivering the arms and supplies desperately needed by American troops. Following the war, Spanish King Carlos III named Gardoqui chargé d'affaires to the new nation. With diplomatic experience representing Spain to the Court of St. James, excellent English, and the esteem of US leaders, Gardoqui was the natural choice.

Learning that Congress had relocated to New York City, Gardoqui headed for the new capital with a mission to exploit weaknesses in the American union of states and advance his sovereign's interests. By the time Gardoqui departed New York City four years later, Americans no longer thought of him as a savior of the Revolution. Thanks to his scheming, he had become a scoundrel of the early republic.[1]

The 1783 Peace of Paris ended the war, but it left over one hundred thousand square miles in dispute between the United States, Spain, Georgia and Indigenous nations. Spain held New Orleans, which meant that it controlled the mouth of the Mississippi River. In 1784,

1. Alfonso Carlos Saiz Valdivielso, *Diego de Gardoqui: Esplendor y Penumbra* (Bilbao, Spain: Muelle de Uribitarte, 2014), 113–116, 119; *Relaciones Diplomaticas Entre España y los Estados Unidos Segun los Documentos del Archivo Historico Nacional*, ed. Miguel Gómez del Campillo (2 vols., Madrid, Spain: Instituto Gonzalo Fernandez de Oviedo, 1944), 1: xli–xlii; Michael A. Otero, "The American Mission of Diego de Gardoqui" (Ph.D. diss., University of California, Los Angeles, 1948), 64–65.

to bolster its position in North America, Spain closed the river to navigation by Americans.[2]

Westerners, who depended on access to the Gulf of Mexico to export their products, were alarmed. If a distant Congress could not secure access for them, maybe a foreign power could. As George Washington put it, Westerners stood "upon a pivot—the touch of a feather, would turn them any way."[3]

Gardoqui arrived with a four-part mission: negotiate the disputed boundaries between the two nations, increase US commerce to Spain, prevent US commerce to Spain's American dominions, and halt US demands for access to the lower Mississippi.[4]

Ever cagey, Gardoqui launched a two-pronged strategy to convince Americans to fold on the Mississippi question. First, he flattered and bribed influential leaders to his side. "There are many needy in the government body," he smirked. Some fancy dinners, "good wines," and effective bribes masquerading as loans, he hoped, would cajole influential leaders to his side. John Jay, Congress's secretary of foreign affairs in the Confederation government, and his wife, Sarah, were the main targets. Eventually John received a fine horse as a gift with Congress's permission. Virginia delegate to Congress Henry Lee received at least two loans of 5,000 pesos. "He is very much mine," bragged Gardoqui.[5]

2. Larrie D. Ferreiro, *Brothers at Arms: American Independence and the Men of France and Spain Who Saved It* (New York: Knopf, 2016), 161–162, 253–254, 288–290; Jonathan R. Dull, "Diplomacy and Independence," in *The Routledge History of U.S. Foreign Relations*, ed. Tyson Reeder (New York: Routledge, 2022), 117; David J. Weber, *The Spanish Frontier in North America* (New Haven: Yale University Press 2009), 204–206; Otero, "American Mission," 60–61; David Narrett, *Adventurism and Empire: The Struggle for Mastery in the Louisiana–Florida Borderlands, 1762–1803* (Chapel Hill: University of North Carolina Press, 2015), 126–127, 210–211; Providence (RI) *Gazette*, August 14, 1784; Arthur Preston Whitaker, *The Spanish-American Frontier, 1783–1795: The Westward Movement and the Spanish Retreat in the Mississippi Valley* (New York: Houghton Mifflin Company, 1927), 65.
3. Drew R. McCoy, *The Elusive Republic: Political Economy in Jeffersonian America* (Chapel Hill: University of North Carolina Press, 1980), 123–124; George William Van Cleve, *We Have Not a Government: The Articles of Confederation and the Road to the Constitution* (Chicago: University of Chicago Press, 2017), 142.
4. Campillo, *Relaciones Diplomaticas*, 1: xxxvi–xxxvii; James G. Lydon, *Fish and Flour for Gold, 1600–1800: Southern Europe in the Colonial Balance of Payments* (Philadelphia: Library Company of Philadelphia, 2008), 239; Otero, "American Mission," 187.
5. Van Cleve, *We Have Not a Government*, 165; Gardoqui to Floridablanca, August 27, 1784, and May 12, 1787, both in Campillo, *Relaciones Diplomaticas*, 1: xxxv, 518 ; John Jay to Gardoqui, October 4, 1785, and March 1, 1786 and Jay to Charles Thomson, March 3, 1786, all in *The Selected Papers of John Jay Digital Edition*, ed. Elizabeth M. Nuxoll (Charlottesville: University of Virginia Press, 2014–); Garoqui to Floridablanca, December 6, 1787, Estado, Legajo 3893, Archivo Historico Nacional–Madrid.

For the second part of his strategy, Gardoqui depended on the northern commercial community. He knew Northerners cared more about Atlantic trade than access to the Mississippi. He offered Jay the chance to reassert North American trade in Spain (though not in Spain's American colonies) if he would abandon the Mississippi for some three decades. If Jay refused, Gardoqui threatened to close the valuable markets to Americans.[6]

The treaty Gardoqui proposed outraged Southerners and Westerners, who complained that Jay was abandoning them to the whims of a foreign power.[7]

Gardoqui was intrigued by the discontent of Westerners. They clamored for statehood for their new settlements in the Tennessee River Valley, such as the future state of Kentucky and the would-be states of Franklin and Cumberland. Congress had ignored their pleas, making them an inviting target for Spain. As a North Carolina Congressman told Gardoqui, if Spain granted independent Westerners access to the Mississippi, the empire could "win them forever."[8]

On March 13, 1787, Congressmen James Madison of Virginia and William Bingham of Pennsylvania met Gardoqui in his home, in hopes of negotiating United States access to the lower Mississippi. "Spain never would give up" its exclusive control of river, Gardoqui told his visitors. But, he added, "the people of Kentucky would make good Spanish subjects." He said it as a lighthearted gibe, but it caught Madison's attention.[9]

Just over two weeks later, on March 29, Madison again called on Gardoqui, this time with others of Virginia's congressional delegation by his side.[10]

6. Lydon, *Fish and Flour*, 238–240; Gardoqui to Floridablanca, June 30, 1785, Estado, Legajo 3884bis, Archivo Historico Nacional; Campillo, *Relaciones Diplomaticas*, 1: xlv–xlvi; Lydon, *Fish and Flour*, 240.

7. James Monroe to Madison, May 31, 1786, https://founders.archives.gov/documents/Madison/01-09-02-0014; Campillo, *Relaciones Diplomaticas*, 1:li–liii, esp. liii; Lydon, *Fish and Flour*, 240.

8. Kevin T. Barksdale, *The Lost State of Franklin: America's First Secession* (Lexington: University Press of Kentucky, 2008), 3–4, 146–148, esp. 147; Solano, José Navarro Latorre y Fernando Solano Costa, *Conspiración Española? 1787–1789: Contribución al Estudio de las Primeras Relaciones Históricas Entre España y los Estados Unidos de Norteamérica* (Zaragoza, Spain, 1949), 45, 57; Kathleen DuVal, *Independence Lost: Lives on the Edge of the American Revolution* (New York: Random House, 2015), 310–311, 315–316; Gardoqui to Floridablanca, May 12, 1787, in Campillo, *Relaciones Diplomaticas*, 376.

9. Madison, "Notes on Debates," March 13, 1787, https://founders.archives.gov/documents/Madison/01-09-02-0164.

10. Madison, "Notes on Debates," March 29, 1787, https://founders.archives.gov/documents/Madison/01-09-02-0184.

Toward the end of the conversation, Gardoqui returned to his joke from a week earlier that Westerners might become Spanish subjects. This time, however, Gardoqui sobered his tone and told the Virginians that "some person connected with the Western Country" had suggested such a plan. Carlos III's "dignity & Character" would never allow him to adopt such a scheme, Gardoqui reassured the delegates. Maybe not, but they wanted more assurance than the "dignity & Character" of a monarch.[11]

In the quarrel over the Mississippi, Madison thought he spied the elements that had destroyed confederations throughout history. A year earlier, he had undertaken an arduous study of past confederations, and he noticed a common pattern. Internal discord divided members of the confederation. The quarrelling regions allied or colluded with stronger foreign powers. Foreign powers asserted gradual power over the confederation until they stole its sovereignty or the confederation dissolved.[12]

As the Constitutional Convention approached, Madison labored to devise a system that could accommodate America's political diversity while withstanding foreign meddling and foreign collusion. When William Paterson presented his so-called "New Jersey Plan" to counter the "Virginia Plan," Madison questioned whether the proposal could "secure the Union agst. the influence of foreign powers." Madison pushed hard for a Constitution capable of uniting the young states with each other—and against the machinations of foreign intriguers.

Ultimately, Madison's constitution thwarted Gardoqui's plotting. When New Hampshire ratified the Constitution in June 1788, it became operative and dampened disunionist spirits. The United States won back the loyalty of Westerners. That December, Gardoqui learned that Kentuckians would gamble on the United States rather than on Spain. Likewise, Spanish support for the breakaway territory of Franklin collapsed.[13] In February 1789, Franklin's leadership swore allegiance to North Carolina.[14]

11. Madison, "Notes on Debates," March 13 and 29, 1787, https://founders.archives.gov/documents/Madison/01-09-02-0164 and https://founders.archives.gov/documents/Madison/01-09-02-0184.

12. Madison, "Notes on Ancient and Modern Confederacies," April–June 1786, https://founders.archives.gov/documents/Madison/01-09-02-0001.

13. Narrett, *Adventurism*, 165–166; Gardoqui to Floridablanca, July 25, 1787, in John Mason Brown, *The Political Beginnings of Kentucky*, (Louisville, 1889), 146–148; Brown to Gardoqui, September 15, 1788, Dec. 17, 1788 [misdated by Gardoqui in his translation as 1789], and January 15, 1789, all in Estado, Legajo 3894, Archivo Historico Nacional—Madrid; Gardoqui to Floridablanca, November 22, 1788, Estado, Legajo 3894, Archivo Historico Nacional—Madrid.

14. Barksdale, *Lost State*, 153–161; Narrett, *Adventurism*, 167, 169; Solano, *Conspiración Española*, 79, 144n28, 323–325; DuVal, *Independence Lost*, 320.

Faced with the inevitable, Gardoqui publicly celebrated the new government in April 1789. He put on a fireworks show for George Washington's inauguration, with the explosions illuminating a brilliant display of transparent paintings on the façade of Gardoqui's house. The Castile and León coat of arms ornamented the doorway just above the crossed flags of the United States and Spain emblazoning the motto "Natural Union."[15]

The display belied the tension that had prevailed for years between the two powers. The festivities accompanied the new Constitution, which stipulated that the two-thirds Senate approval requirement for treaties became active. Gardoqui might find a few supportive states, but he knew he would never get to nine. He would not get his treaty.[16]

His mission a failure, in fall 1789, Gardoqui boarded the *San Nicolás* and departed the United States, having become the face of an acrimonious struggle for continental power that was only beginning.

This essay is drawn from the author's contribution to *A Republic of Scoundrels: The Schemers, Intriguers, and Adventurers Who Created a New American Nation* (Pegasus Books, 2023), ed. by David Head and Timothy Hemmis.

15. "Relación de las ceremonias y funciones que se celebraron el día de la proclamación del President General de lost Estados Unidos, Ilustre Jorge Wáshington," May 1, 1789, in Campillo, *Relaciones Diplomaticas*, 1: 546–547.
16. Otero, "American Mission," 279–280.

Rediscovering Charles Thomson's Forgotten Service to Early American Historiography

DANIEL L. WRIGHT

George Washington's perseverance kept the American army in the field long enough to win negotiated independence, and later saw him through the first presidency under the Constitution. Benjamin Franklin's ingenuity and sagacity guided the formation of the young nation before it yet realized it could be a country of its own. Thomas Jefferson's eloquence gave expression to the fundamental principles of equality and liberty in America's Declaration of Independence. Their places in the popular memory are secure, even as they have and will continue to change.

Yet, the man who stood at the center of those vital years between 1774 and 1789 as the lone Secretary of the Congress, Charles Thomson, is quite often forgotten. It must be considered why this is so. It seems remiss that one whose zeal for patriotic resistance and formal separation from Britain earned him the moniker, "Sam Adams of Philadelphia," should be shut out from the leading figures in the Founding pantheon. Since he is not included there, it must be wondered why and what has disqualified him. As historian James M. Smith notes, "There are many, many founding fathers in the story of America's Revolution and unfortunately only a few are really known to the general public. Yet without those who are less known, there would have been no revolution. One of those men was the official secretary of the Continental Congress, Charles Thomson."[1]

1. James M. Smith, "Charles Thomson and the Delaware," *Journal of the American Revolution*, May 23, 2022, https://www.allthingsliberty.com/2022/05/charles-thomson-and-the-delaware/.

Charles Thomson was the lone figure at the center of the Continental Congress through the fifteen crucial years of Revolution up to the adoption of the Federal Constitution, 1774 through 1789. The glaring absence of Thomson's definitive history of the American Revolution has furnished a contentious discussion among scholars focusing on him. Some biographers accept Thomson's reasons for not publishing his history with little editorial comment.[2] Others can only mourn the "irreparable" loss of what never reached completion.[3] Still others find it "doubly difficult to forgive" that he should deprive future generations of the truth when the entire era deserves a thorough demystification, a labor they recognize only Thomson could have accomplished.[4] Some even take the task upon themselves, so driven are they by the loss of it, to reconstruct what that apparently destroyed manuscript ought to have said.[5] The literature is sharply divided between condemnation and exoneration.

Condemnation, as seen in monographs like Schlenther's *A Patriot's Pursuit*, is undeserved. Thomson was not negligent as a record keeper or historian. In fact, he contributed significantly to historiography. He was anything but an inconsequential, passive observer. From removing names out of Ramsey's *History of the American Revolution* to preserving the content of the Congressional Journals, Thomson was a central force behind the collection and preservation of the earliest primary and secondary source materials on the Revolutionary and Confederation eras. The Journals of the Continental Congress and the thousands of related documents would not exist had he failed to preserve and protect them. He is neither a "secondary figure of the Revolution" nor among the "young men of the Revolution" (as Elkins and McKitrick describe the generation who led the 1787 constitution).[6] Rather, as Maier asserts, Thomson, like Samuel Adams, stands among the "primary figures of a distinct and early part of the Revolution . . . for reasons that have little

2. J. Edwin Hendricks, *Charles Thomson and the Making of a New Nation, 1729-1824* (Rutherford, NJ: Associated University Presses, 1979), 188-189.

3. Lewis R. Harley, *The Life of Charles Thomson, Secretary of the Continental Congress and Translator of the Bible from the Greek* (Philadelphia: George W. Jacobs, 1900), 158-160.

4. Boyd Stanley Schlenther, *Charles Thomson, A Patriot's Pursuit* (Newark: University of Delaware Press, 1990), 228.

5. James Mitchell Smith, *Undeceived: A Political History of the American Revolution as Inspired by Charles Thomson, Secretary of the Continental Congress, 1774-1789, Volume 1* (Columbia, SC: Createspace, 2018), 8-10.

6. Pauline Maier, *The Old Revolutionaries: Political Lives in the Age of Samuel Adams* (New York: W. W. Norton), 1990, 280.

to do with their objective historical importance."[7] Without Thomson, there would have been no Revolution.

THE COSTS OF CREATING AMERICA'S PRIME MINISTRY

Thomson kept in the main current of decisions; in fact, he helped form them as America's "Prime Minister."[8] It was his name alongside President John Hancock's which appeared on the first copy of the Declaration of Independence circulated in America. He designed the Great Seal of the United States. He exercised remarkable discretionary authority over the keeping of Congressional Journals, maintained a wide and regular official correspondence, authenticated communiques and dispatches, authorized war documents, served on vital committees, safeguarded secret records, and stood as the link between the nation and the States.[9]

He certainly did not serve for regular pay, which came in unsteady intervals, or (as the First Congress appropriated) in nothing more than a silver bowl at the end of his service in October 1774.[10] He seemed to envision a broader role for the Secretary's office, a department that would have combined powers of a Home Secretary coordinating between the executive departments and legislative committees of the young federal government. He also seemed unaware of the political risk of leaving New York for Mount Vernon just as they the new Congress was to decide its officers, as Thomson confided in his letter to Senator Robert Morris on April 7, 1789:

> I cannot express the anxiety I feel on the determination I had taken to retire to private life while so many of my friends whom I love and esteem express such an earnest desire that I should continue in a public line. I am afraid they rate my abilities too high. Sure I am they rate them much higher than I do myself and more than they deserve. But such as they are to shew that I am not unwilling to devote them to the public service, I will make this proposition: that the keeping of the great seal with the duties thereto annexed and to be annexed, and the custody and care of the papers which belonged to the late Congress be com-

7. Ibid., xxii.
8. Fred S. Rolater, "Charles Thomson, 'Prime Minister' of the United States," *The Pennsylvania Magazine of History and Biography*, Vol. 103, No. 3 (July 1977): 322f.
9. Kenneth R. Bowling, "Good-by 'Charle': The Lee-Adams Interest and The Political Demise of Charles Thomson, Secretary of Congress, 1774-1789," *Pennsylvania Magazine of History and Biography*, Vol. 100, No. 3 (July 1976), 314-335.
10. J. Edwin Hendricks, *Charles Thomson and the Making of a New Nation, 1729-1824*, (Cranbury, NJ: Associated University Presses, 1979), 135.

> mitted to me, this office to be made the depository of the acts laws and archives of Congress; that the same salary be continued to me . . . and my style be Secretary of the Senate and of the United States or Congress . . . If this proposition be approved by the Senate and acceptable I am ready to serve them to the utmost of my power, at least till the present government be organized and begin to take its due tone. If otherwise I must pursue my first determination and retire to the private walk but with an anxious wish and most earnest prayer that the measures of the present government may prove effectual to secure the tranquility and promote the happiness and glory of the United States.[11]

It seems therefore that Thomson left town at the worst time for his personal fortunes, simultaneously the most advantageous for his enemies. He was thus deprived by the unrecorded vote of a narrow margin that conspired to exact recompense for old incidents during the Continental Congress years, sore spots like the Silas Deane and Arthur Lee affair along with old grievances going back to Thomson's clash with John Adams over what the Congressional journals should include, not to mention the Secretary's problems with President Henry Laurens. It seemed these old offenses were finally coming home to roost. This revival of the animus by Lee, Adams, and their friends against Thomson gave them the opportunity to block once and for all his apparent political resilience. Thus, it was not some character deficiency on Thomson's part—aside from what Senator Maclay attributes to Thomson's relative ambivalence—but unpaid grievances by Congressional enemies that denied him a vital role in federal office, relegating him to an undeserved and forgotten place in the shadows.[12]

11. Edmund C. Burnett, ed. *Letters of Members of the Continental Congress*. Vol. 8 (Washington: Carnegie Institute, 1936), 829-830. It appears that Army quartermaster (and James Otis, Jr.'s younger brother) Samuel A. Otis of Massachusetts had been the most eager lobbyist for Senate clerk, though not the first choice, and was positioning to cement the votes by early April, with the active help, it seems, of Thomson's adversaries like incoming Vice President John Adams, Elbridge Gerry and Tristram Dalton, with South Carolinian Ralph Izard and Virginian Richard Henry Lee, who employed their efforts to divert just enough votes in favor of Thomson – in coincidence with the absence of Thomson and his stalwart ally, Senator George Read – to prevent his selection. They moved the day after Thomson was dispatched from New York to escort President-elect Washington from Mount Vernon to his inauguration (Bowling, "Good-by 'Charle'," 319-321).

12. Maclay confided to his diary on April 29, 1789 that Thomson was most certainly "ill used" by the whole glaring oversight that excluded him in the inauguration plans and future involvement. Kenneth R. Bowling and Helen E. Veit, eds., *The Diary of William Maclay and Other Notes on Senate Debates* (Baltimore: Johns Hopkins University, 1988), 10n16.

ONE MORE PUSH TO CRAFT AMERICA'S OFFICE OF THE "HOME SECRETARY"

Nevertheless, Thomson carried out his responsibilities to the end. He steadfastly supported President Washington, remained the reliable protégé of Franklin, and continued the provocative correspondent of Jefferson. He avidly supported the arguments by Alexander Hamilton, James Madison, and John Jay for a strong political alternative to the Confederation, advocating with Jay for the end of slavery, an institution that he reminded Jefferson continued to be "a blot in our character."[13] Yet, when it was in President Washington's power to name him to a cabinet post, he did not. The one who could have been an unshakable asset to the administration—especially as voluntary federal service was at a premium, only to increase with time—was not even given the opportunity to decline an offer to serve in the executive branch, an offer altogether absent in Washington's letter to Thomson of April 14, 1789. It was that same day Thomson, appointed by the newly-seated federal Senate, arrived at Mount Vernon to escort Washington to his inauguration in New York City.[14] The Inauguration was especially humiliating to Thomson, who wrote: "I was struck with surprise at being passed by unnoticed in the arrangement made by the committee . . . To what cause this has been owing I am altogether a stranger."[15] Thomson included this in his resignation to Congress on April 30, which he never sent. Instead, he dispatched his notice of retirement to President Washington in July 1789, only after Thomson's conception of a centralized "Home Office" fell short of passage in Congress on July 23.[16] Washington, sensible to this slight to the Secretary, wrote to him the following day that while Congress had been remiss in gratitude to Thomson,

> The present age does so much justice to the unsullied reputation with which you have always conducted yourself in the execution of the duties of your office, and posterity will find your name so honourably connected with the verification of such a multitude of astonishing facts, that my single suffrage would add little to the illustration of your merits . . . Accept, then, this serious declaration, that your services have been important as your patriotism was distinguished; and enjoy that best of all rewards, the consciousness of having done your duty well.[17]

13. Schlenther, *Charles Thomson: A Patriot's Pursuit*, 201.
14. George Washington, "Reply to Charles Thomson." *Washington Writings* (New York: Library of America, 1997), 729; David S. Heidler and Jeanne T. Heidler, *Washington's Circle: The Creation of the President* (New York: Random House, 2015), 10-13, 436n14.
15. Thomas Patrick Chorlton, *The First American Republic, 1774-1789: The First Fourteen American Presidents Before Washington* (Bloomington: AuthorHouse, 2012), 618.
16. Ibid., 618-619.
17. Ibid., 619.

Skeptically read, this was salt in the wound for an injured public servant, but it gave some explanation of why Washington did not extend an invitation to the Cabinet. Thomson's integrity remained unimpeachable in the estimation of John Jay of New York. "No Person in the World is so perfectly acquainted with the Rise, Conduct, and Conclusion of the American Revolution, as yourself," Jay later wrote to him.[18] Jay wrote again to Thomson after more than two years on the Supreme Court, offering some consolation:

> As we enter this, our new beginning in the history of our nation and have reflected on the fact that you are not part of our new government, I know that you are disappointed in that omission. However, upon reflection I wonder if that may not turn out for the best. My friend, you have been at the very center, the heart of our revolution from the beginning to the end . . . When others have absconded and abandoned their duties, you have remained at your post. During the fifteen years of our government in which the Continental Congress was our government and led us through the revolution and early days of peace and hard times you have never failed your duty.[19]

SAVING THE PAPERS OF THE REVOLUTION: CRAFTING THE STORY

Maybe it was for the best that Thomson, so closely associated with the Continental Congress of the 1780s, avoided close association with the turmoil of the Washington administration. But Jay was not done. There remained a silver lining in Thomson's forced retirement. Even though it offered no guarantee of inclusion in favorable memory for posterity, it gave an opportunity to supply what early historiography of the Revolution was lacking. Jay continued,

> As you know a number of persons, none of which have been as faithful from the beginning to the end, have written histories of our revolution. I have found them all wanting, either in completeness, candor, or truthfulness. They are almost all full of faction and point of view. You, my friend, who have been at the very center of it all, from the beginning to the end, can set the record straight. I am persuaded that heaven in its mysterious ways, have spared you further employ to your country in order that you may perform more great and lasting service. You, my friend, should be the one to tell the story of our struggles as a nation. Only you were there from the beginning to the end, only you have the

18. Elizabeth M. Nuxoll, *The Selected Papers of John Jay*, Vol. 3, *1782-1784* (Charlottesville: University of Virginia Press, 2013), 435.
19. Smith, *Undeceived*, 8-10.

> reputation to tell the story as it really happened without regard to faction or personality. Do this, my friend, do this great service for your country and posterity.[20]

Thomson had not evaded this difficult task. Back in 1785, he admitted, he already had a thousand folio pages underway for his "secret historical memoirs," encompassing what was omitted from the Congressional journals, a manuscript he continued to build upon in retirement. David Ramsey consulted him continuously in his own two-volume *History of the American Revolution*, published in 1789.[21] Thomson actively censored Ramsey's history, excising names that would be compromised by inclusion.[22] In 1786, Thomson even wrote a seventeen-page review of Ramsey's account, the original now lost.[23]

Then something changed his mind in the 1790s. Perhaps it was the solidification of the two political camps around Hamilton and Jefferson. Moreover, the historiographical narratives that began circulating, as inadequate as they were, served a higher good when the Republic needed continuity of a gilded legend over fuel for disillusionment and division. His decision to destroy his manuscript solidified his decision to consistently decline any urge to write a "real" account. "No, no . . . I will not," Thomson went on to declare, giving his reasons to Dr. Benjamin Rush (who also urged him to compose such a history), which Rush reported to John Adams in 1812, adding his own editorial comments to Thomson's reply:

> I could not tell the truth without giving great offense. Let the world admire our patriots and heroes. Their supposed talents and virtues (where they were so) by commanding imitation will serve the cause of patriotism and our country. Perhaps they may adopt the qualities that have been ascribed to them, and thus good may be done. I shall not undeceive future generations.' I concur in this sentiment, and therefore I earnestly request that you will destroy this letter as soon as you read it. I do not even wish it to be known that General W. was deficient in that mark of true greatness . . . *the talent to forgive*.[24]

Perhaps this was less a stubborn refusal to correct falsehoods than a justification that it was not Thomson's place to demolish reputations

20. Smith, *Undeceived*, 8-10.
21. Ibid., 160.
22. Maier, *The Old Revolutionaries*, xiv.
23. Smith, *Undeceived*, 160.
24. Hendricks, *Charles Thomson and the Making of a New Nation*, 189; *The Letters of Benjamin Rush*, Lyman H. Butterfield, ed., 2 vols. (Princeton: Princeton University Press, 1951), 1123.

in so honest a history as he had written. His would be a lone voice crying in the wilderness with few readers inclined to take him favorably let alone seriously.

THOMSON'S CHOICE NOT TO WRITE HIS HISTORY

If, on the other hand, his history had the power to alter impressions, the future could get much darker than it already was. Joanne Freeman has well documented that disturbing turn for American politics.[25] As Thomson noted, it would not necessarily be beneficial to attempt that coup for truth and orchestrate constructive results. It could also circumvent what good may yet be possible despite the deception under which Americans remained. The very careful balance—which some today call "surrender"—worked out because leaders were prepared to sacrifice something for still larger causes, outcomes that were not easily replicable. Washington, not one given to grand hyperbole, considered the work at Philadelphia in the summer of 1787 nothing short of a "miracle."[26]

Such miracles were not waiting in the wings on subsequent attempts. If the "great men" were dismantled, Americans may not have been inclined to continue the constitutional experiment at all while what took its place promised less not more in return. If Providence had wrought success *in spite of*, not because of, leadership by less than wise and able men, Americans might take their chances with another revolution under no greater circumspection, led by lesser characters and baser motives than those of the First Continental Congress of 1774, however imperfect it was. Perfection was hardly more attainable in 1815 than it was forty years prior.

Thomson did not destroy everything he wrote. Two companion manuscripts on Pennsylvania politics during the critical developments in 1774 and 1775 survived destruction. They underscore that the old Secretary "possessed a rare talent for vivid personal characterization and shrewd historical analysis."[27] As James M. Smith has observed, Thomson anticipated the critical historiography of British (and American) attitudes toward the indigenous peoples of the North American con-

25. Joanne B. Freeman, *Affairs of Honor: National Politics in the New Republic* (New Haven: Yale University Press, 2001).

26. Catherine Drinker Bowen, *Miracle at Philadelphia: The Story of the Constitutional Convention, May to September 1787* (New York: The American Past, 1986), xvi, xxiii.

27. Eugene R. Sheridan and John M. Murrin, eds., *Congress at Princeton: Being the Letters of Charles Thomson to Hannah Thomson, June-October 1783* (Princeton: Princeton University Library, 1985), xxi-xxii; Charles Thomson, "Early Days of the Revolution in Philadelphia," *The Pennsylvania Magazine of History and Biography* 2, no. 4 (1878), 411-423.

tinent in his writing, so he offers a welcome voice to the record. It was Thomson who wrote:

> It is a matter of no small consequence to know the ground of complaints made by the Indians, that in case they are false, justice may be done to the characters of those who are injured thereby; and if true, that proper remedies may be applied, and that the Crown of Great Britain may not, by the avarice and wickedness of a few bė deprived of the friendship and alliance of those nations who are capable of being our most useful friends, or most dangerous enemies.
>
> It could be wished, for the sake of truth, that access had been allowed to the minutes of Council, which are the only public records kept of the transactions between the Government of Pennsylvania and the Indians, or the minutes of several conferences with the Indians had been duly taken, and regularly published, or that all the deeds granted by the Indians had been recorded in the Rolls-Office, as they ought to have been: had these been done, the matter might have been set in a fuller and clearer light. However, by perusing the following extracts taken from such treaties as could be met with, from the votes of the assembly, from the deeds as have been recorded, and from other authentic papers and letters, it will be clearly seen whether the complaints of the Indians are only invented to palliate their late conduct; whether they are objects of party; or whether their pretensions are reasonable and their demands consistent with justice.[28]

Thomson reflected further on what differentiated the Anglo-Americans from the French, with astonishing clarity, a pointedness befitting current historiographical debates. Of British North America, he declared:

> In order to get their lands, drive them as far from them as possible, nor seem to care what becomes of them, provided they get them removed out of the way of their permanent settlements; whereas the French, considering that they can never want land in America, who enjoy the friendship of the Indians, use all the means in their power to draw as many into their alliance as possible; and to secure their affection, invite as many as can to come and live near them, and to make their towns as near the French settlements as they can. By this means they have drawn off a great number of Mohawks, and other Six Nation tribes and having settled them in towns along the banks of the river St. Lawrence, have so secured them to their interest, that even these, they

28. James M. Smith, "Charles Thomson and the Delaware."

> can command about six or seven hundred fighting men . . . a purchase of land was made by the proprietors of Pennsylvania which ruined our interest with the Indians and from then, especially those westward of us and drove them entirely into the hands of the French . . . By this the lands where the Shawnese and Ohio Indians lived and the hunting grounds of the Delaware, the Mohicans and the Tuteloes were included and consequently these nations had nothing to expect but to see themselves in in a short time, at the rate the English settled, violently driven from their lands, as the Delaware had formally been, and reduced to leave their country and seek settlement they knew not where. This engaged many of the people to give ear to the French, who declared that they did not come to deprive the Indians of their land but to hinder the English from settling westward of the Alleghany hills.[29]

Perhaps this frankness is why President Washington later decided not to task Thomson with addressing the indigenous tribes on behalf of the Americans after all.[30] It makes the loss of Thomson's "secret historical memoirs" even more painful for historians. Even so, it is not without good reason that Thomson chose to destroy his manuscript. It seems the decisively divided parties threatened to undo the ideals of the Revolution, and so warranted destruction of his pages.

CONSIDERING THE REASONS FOR THOMSON'S NEGLECTED PLACE AMONG THE FOUNDERS

It is remarkable that one so central as Thomson became so utterly unknown in American memory. Why is he forgotten? It may be that his specialized place so central to the early years of Revolution, like the place of Samuel Adams, is now the reason for his marginalization in the shadow of the "young men of the Revolution," as Elkins and McKitrick dub the Framers of the 1787 Constitution.[31] According to Schlenther, Thomson left his revolutionary roots and so crafted a comfortable position over continuing radical politics. This claim is not persuasive to all scholars.[32] By declining to complete his history of the Revolution as his contemporaries advised him to do, he may, it is argued, deserve his obscurity. Still, most of the remembered figures of the founding were not historians of it. It has less to do with his steadfast

29. Ibid.

30. Richard H. Kohn, *Eagle and Sword: The Beginnings of the Military Establishment in America* (New York: The Free Press, 1985), 151.

31. Maier, *The Old Revolutionaries*, 280.

32. Douglas M. Arnold, "Review of *Charles Thomson: A Patriot's Pursuit* by Boyd Stanley Schlenther," *William & Mary Quarterly* 48, no. 3 (July 1991), 501-503.

friends and more to do with how effective, even spiteful, his enemies were. The fact remains that Charles Thomson was abruptly excluded from federal office and unceremoniously retired for his remaining thirty-five years. For friends like John Jay, this was an egregious mistake.

Another possible cause for his being neglected may stem from his association with the weak, and often inept, Congress, especially through the demoralizing 1780s and fractious 1790s. In this light, perhaps Thomson's withdrawal can be seen as a fitting end to a career rife with self-inflicted political wounds. None had quite been where Thomson stood through it all. Presiding officers came and went. So did Congressional delegations. He took no part in the attempts to replace General Washington but also knew the score, had the ability to name names, retained full access to the mountain of documentary records, and had the backing to have it printed. He lacked only the will.

The omission of Thomson's own memoir for posterity disappoints historians, to be sure, who grieve its absence and fault Thomson for preserving the mythic narrative of America's Founding. The one the Delaware knew as *Wegh-wu-law-mo-end* ("the man who tells the truth"),[33] fell prey to a refusal to mercilessly expose his enemies, even when it may have been self-serving. When he had it in his power to correct the record and demystify the era, "the man who tells the truth" stepped back from doing so. This determination of one reputed to be so honest should give us pause.

Thomson's place in America's historical memory deserves closer examination. His alleged disservice to historiography must be weighed against his definitive preservation of some 50,000 pages of materials catalogued in the National Archives, "now inventoried in the five-volume *Papers of the Continental Congress*."[34] It is unfair to claim his role leaves only a deficit in the documentary record. The resentment by John Adams, the Lees, and their allies that traced back to Congressional disputes over diplomatic correspondence seemed to spill over into Thomson's unilateral authority as steward of the official record. The Journals of the Continental Congress exist in the first place primarily *because of* Thomson's efforts.

Thomson's reasons for keeping all the minutiae of Congressional debates out of the written record in favor of what was finally adopted was as much about the legitimacy of decision-making as it was about

33. Bowling, "Good-by 'Charle'," 330: Thomson was arguably "the Founding Father most committed to humane treatment for the Indian."
34. Chorlton, *The First American Republic*, 2012, 591.

the credibility of decision makers, many of whom were vital to the new federal government convening in New York by 1789. A number of those officers, seeking to distance themselves from their previous roles in Congress, found it easier to affiliate Thomson with the error-laden past. Thomson's concerns, grounded in serious anxieties for the young country increasingly rending itself into two deepening party factions, are not insignificant simply because the nation weathered the dangers. His reluctance to publish myth-shattering revelations of the nation's formative years may have prevented greater harm than realized by some historians now. The young republic lived on a fragile thread. Perhaps it has lasted more than two centuries with enough strength to forbear exposure to its mythic beginnings *because* Thomson refrained from the temptations of deconstruction in his time. His self-denying forbearance is what prevailed. It is doubtful whether an unleashed spirit of vengeance would have commended him any higher in the estimate of posterity. Spewing venom on one's contemporaries often backfired then as it does now.

Thomson, through it all, stood by Washington, Franklin, Jefferson, John Dickinson, and even John Adams in spite of *their* shortcomings because, it seems, he understood the republic's need for them, a need rising above the warts very much on display in the last decade of that century. Pointing out flaws in detail would have been an obvious thing to do but detrimental to future Americans, free and enslaved, in the long term. It becomes apparent, then, that without Thomson not only might there have been no American Revolution nor a documentary record preserved of those critical years. His role in preserving thousands of pages of Continental Congress records far outweighs the absence of an expose that could have easily derailed the American experiment in its infancy. Wisdom is not necessarily vindicated by satisfying our intellectual curiosities but by all of widsom's children: actions, motives, and results taken together.[35]

35. A reference to Luke 7:35, ESV.

A Kingly Government? Benjamin Franklin's Great Fear

RAY RAPHAEL

In the beginning, there was Congress. On May 29, 1787, a Tuesday, with delegates to the Federal Convention seated and rules settled, Virginia's governor Edmund Randolph introduced his state's vision for the new nation. Article 1 set the stage: "Resolved that the Articles of Confederation ought to be corrected & enlarged" to provide for "common defence, security of liberty, and general welfare." A "revolution in favour of government," as one writer reported in the *Pennsylvania Gazette*, was under way. Articles 2 through 6 outlined a bicameral legislature, while Article 7 resolved that "a National Executive be instituted, to be chosen by the National Legislature," with the "general authority to execute the National laws." Whether this executive would be a single person or several, one thing was clear: he/they would be derivative of Congress, selected by that body and charged with doing its bidding.[1]

That Friday, with Article 7 on the floor, Pennsylvania's James Wilson moved "that the executive consist of a single person." This brought the convention, which was just reaching its stride, to a sudden standstill. "A considerable pause ensuing"—that's how James Madison, in his notes, denoted the uncomfortable silence.[2] Delegates to the "grand federal convention" had been chosen for their ability to communicate and deliberate, but just this once, communication ceased. Wilson's motion raised a host of contentious issues. Who will choose the chief executive? How long will he serve? What authority will he exercise? Who can check his power? Each question opened a range of possible solutions, and all fields were interconnected. An executive imbued with extensive powers, for instance, might require greater checks or shorter terms.

1. James Madison, *Notes of Debates in the Federal Convention of 1787* (New York: W.W. Norton, 1987), 30-31 (May 29).
2. Ibid., 45. (June 1).

Madison opened the bidding. Wouldn't it be "proper," he asked, "before a choice should be made between a unity and plurality in the Executive, to fix the extent of the Executive authority?" Madison proposed minimal powers: "to carry into execution the national laws" and "to appoint offices in cases not otherwise provided for."[3] With little dissent, state delegations agreed. Executive authority was subservient to legislative demands, save only for some lesser appointments. Most significantly, he/they would not possess the "powers of war and peace."

Next up: length of service. Some delegates favored three years, with the possibility of repeating in office; others argued for one seven-year term. On a hasty vote, seven years prevailed over three by five states to four, with one divided.[4]

Method of appointment? Wilson, stunning his peers, favored popular election. All delegates wanted the new government to be philosophically grounded in the people, yet few wanted to place it directly in their hands. Wilson found only one kindred spirit, George Mason, who liked the idea in theory yet pronounced it "impractical."[5]

That night, Benjamin Franklin stewed over the prospect of a single executive serving for seven years. "Being very sensible of the effect of age on his memory," he told the Convention the next morning, he carefully wrote down his objections. Saddled with a weakened voice and failing eyes, he would find it difficult to read aloud what he had just penned, so James Wilson offered to read it for him:

> It will be said, that we don't propose to establish Kings. I know it. But there is a natural inclination in mankind to Kingly Government. It sometimes relieves them from Aristocratic domination. They had rather have one tyrant than five hundred. It gives more of the appearance of equality among Citizens, and that they like. I am apprehensive therefore, perhaps too apprehensive, that the Government of these States, may in future times, end in a Monarchy.

To counter this "natural inclination," Franklin preferred multiple executives:

> And shall we doubt finding three or four men in all the U. States, with public spirit enough to bear sitting in peaceful Council . . . merely to preside over our civil concerns, and see that our laws are duly executed. Sir, I have a better opinion of our Country. I think we shall never

3. Ibid., 47. (June 1).
4. Ibid., 49. (June 1).
5. Ibid., 49. (June 1).

> be without a sufficient number of wise and good men to undertake and execute well and faithfully the office in question.[6]

Madison reported the soft response: "No debate ensued, and the proposition was postponed for consideration of its members. It was treated with great respect, but rather for the author of it, than from any apparent conviction of its expediency or practicability."[7]

Franklin did have allies. Edmund Randolph, the previous day, had warned: that "unity in the Executive" was "the fetus of monarchy," and "the permanent temper of the people was adverse to the very semblance of Monarchy."[8]

George Mason agreed. "We are not indeed constituting a British government, but a more dangerous monarchy, an elective one . . . Notwithstanding the oppressions & injustice experienced among us from democracy, the genius of the people is in favor of it, and the genius of the people must be consulted." The people, he predicted, "never could agree to give up all the rights of the people to a single Magistrate." Like Franklin, Mason favored an executive council. If the framers opted for more than one executive, the office could not appear too "kingly."[9]

Despite such concerns, on June 4 the convention opted for a single executive—seven states in favor, three opposed, and one divided.[10] There was one critical safeguard against overreach: the executive would be "removable on impeachment & conviction of mal-practice or neglect of duty."[11]

Over the next two months, the office took shape. On August 6, the Committee of Detail tabulated the convention's interim findings. A "president," chosen by Congress, could "recommend" legislation but neither push for it nor vote on it. He could commission officers and receive ambassadors, but the authority to appoint ambassadors and judges lay with the Senate, as did the power to make treaties with foreign nations. He could command military forces but not raise them. He could neither declare war nor negotiate peace. He could write letters to governors, but he was not empowered to force their hands, supersede their authority, or, on his own authority, suppress insurrections within their states. He could be removed from office through "impeachment by the House of Representatives, and conviction in the supreme Court,

6. James Madison, *Notes*, 51-3. (June 2).
7. Ibid., 55. (June 2).
8. Ibid., 46. (June 1).
9. Ibid., 64. (June 4).
10. Ibid., 60. (June 4).
11. Ibid., 58. (June 2).

of treason, bribery, or corruption." His authority, in short, was tightly circumscribed. Only once, to check the judiciary, did the committee use the word "power": "He shall have power to grant reprieves and pardons; but his pardon shall not be pleadable in bar of an impeachment."[12]

Four weeks later, on September 4, the "Committee of Eleven" rewrote the script:[13]

- The president would be chosen by special electors, not a joint session of Congress. If electors failed to produce a winner, the Senate would determine the result. At the insistence of small states, the deciding body was later changed to the House of Representatives, with each state delegation having one vote.[14]

- Although the president's term was shortened to four years, the restriction against re-eligibility was dropped. Until the mid-twentieth century, a president could remain in office indefinitely. Might this open a door to "kingly government"?

- With the "advice and consent" of the Senate, the president could appoint ambassadors, Supreme Court justices, and "other public ministers"—authorities previously granted to the Senate alone.

- The president could make treaties, pending approval of two-thirds of the Senate.

The first of these alterations, establishing what we now call the Electoral College, fundamentally altered presidential politics, while the others significantly increased presidential powers. Had such consequential changes been suggested in June, July, or early August, they might have stirred opposition and been discussed at length, but at this late date, they did not receive full scrutiny. Yet James Madison, ever astute, noted potential danger in the treaty-making provision. "The President would necessarily derive so much power and importance from a state of war that he might be tempted, if authorised, to impede a treaty of peace." To counter this, Madison moved that two-thirds of the Senate could "make treaties of peace, without the concurrence of the President."[15]

Pierce Butler "was strenuous for the motion, as a necessary security against ambitious & corrupt Presidents. He mentioned the late perfid-

12. Ibid., 392-3. (August 6).
13. Ibid., 573-5. (September 4).
14. For a detailed account of this dramatic and consequential reversal, engineered in large measure by Gouverneur Morris, see Ray Raphael, *Mr. President: How and Why the Framers Created a Chief Executive* (New York: Alfred A. Knopf, 2012), 93-109.
15. Madison, *Notes of Debates*, 599. (September 7).

ious policy of the Statholder in Holland; and the artifices of the Duke of Marlboro to prolong the war of which he had management."[16] Nobody else came to Madison's defense. His motion was defeated, three states in favor and seven opposed, yet his concern was apt. By placing political gain above the needs of a nation, might a president exemplify "kingly government," what all framers except Hamilton hoped to avoid?

We know that Franklin and Mason opposed a single executive, fearing the extent of his powers. They had sounded the alarm at the outset of the convention, and Mason's opposition to ratification would highlight the dangers of a single executive as well as the absence of a bill of rights. But Madison's concern has received scant attention. A chief architect of the Constitution's checks and balances, he failed to gain traction for this protection against an executive who put himself over country. Convention fatigue might well have played a role.

Franklin, famously, moved on:

> I confess that there are several parts of this constitution which I do not at present approve, but I am not sure I shall never approve them . . . The older I grow, the more apt I am to doubt my own judgment, and to pay more respect to the judgment of others . . . Thus I consent, Sir, to this Constitution because I expect no better, and because I am not sure, that it is not the best. The opinions I have had of its errors, I sacrifice to the public good.[17]

Yet he still worried. We've all heard the story. On September 17, 1787, the closing day of the Federal Convention, as delegates exited Independence Hall, a lady asked Franklin, "Well, Doctor, what have we got, a republic or a monarchy?" "A republic," replied the Doctor, "If you can keep it."[18]

The informant, James McHenry of Maryland, is quoted in Max Farrand's *Records of the Federal Convention*, and the "lady" was allegedly Philadelphia's Elizabeth Willing Powell. The tale is legendary, and it

16. Ibid., 600. (September 7).
17. Ibid., 653. (September 17).
18. McHenry's chronicle of the Convention has been eclipsed by Madison's *Notes*. The quote here is from his entry for September 18, the day following adjournment, in "Papers of Dr. James McHenry of the Federal Convention of 1787," Avalon Project, Yale Law School: https://avalon.law.yale.edu/18th_century/mchenry.asp. McHenry later added a footnote: "The lady here aluded to was Mrs. Powel [presumably Elizabeth Willing Powell] of Philada." J.L. Bell adds in an email: "During the early 1800s, McHenry used the anecdote (misquoting his own notes) in an early version of the 'a republic, not a democracy' argument. He even dropped Powell's name publicly. She responded privately that she didn't remember the exchange, but it would have happened in her salon. (Many modern writers set the scene on the street instead, something she would have deplored.)"

endures for a reason. One person who "rules" or "governs" a nation might indeed present a risk. "There is a natural inclination in mankind to Kingly Government"—Madison, a trusted source, took these words directly from "a literal copy" of the paper Franklin wrote on the night of June 1, 1787. Madison, Franklin, and their peers, with the exception of Hamilton, kept this "inclination" in mind and provided multiple checks to thwart it. But their handiwork is not foolproof. There will always be an "*if.*"

Guilty as Charged: Convicting Vermont's First Governor

GARY G. SHATTUCK

Transitioning from a complicated war footing to an organized civil society at the close of the Revolution proved every bit as difficult as the nation's early leaders feared. Thirteen proud colonies surrendering aspects of their hard-fought independence in exchange for a new form of federal government generated significant hesitancy after the guns silenced. The placeholder Articles of Confederation (1781-1789) provided some assurance of order at first, but hardly as well as the Constitution did when it took center stage.

As a result, the entire rule of law practiced throughout the newfound states changed virtually overnight, including the state admitted into the fold in 1791, Vermont. In the rush to accommodate the demands made by fledgling federalism in this historically tumultuous region, one of its first leaders, Gov. Thomas Chittenden (1730-1797), soon fell victim to the changed legal landscape. Upon suffering the indignity of being compelled to appear in a newly created federal courtroom in 1797 to go before a jury of his peers, charged with committing a federal offense, he faced immediate imprisonment upon their finding of guilt, only to escape that fate by dying soon after; the only governor among eighty-two others in state history to experience such an ignoble end.[1] His offense? Selling alcohol without a license and allowing its consumption in an unlicensed establishment.

1. The author thanks former Governor James Douglas and Vermont historian Kevin Graffagnino for noting the prosecutions brought by state prosecutors against governors Horace F. Graham (1920) and Charles M. Smith (1937). While similar to Chittenden's case because of their shared position, neither of them involved offenses determined to have been committed during their terms as governor. Only Chittenden bears that distinction.

That Chittenden ran afoul of the law in such a seemingly innocent way could not have surprised anyone who knew him. Greatly admired, his solid, pragmatic political reputation preceded him for more than two decades of public service, including as governor overseeing the region's coalescence and admission into the Union as the fourteenth state. At the same time, Chittenden was also well-known among his peers for his hail-fellow-well-met, bon vivant bearing. A surviving document titled "Wine Account for the General Assembly of 1787" provides ample evidence of the copious amounts of alcohol "His Excellency Gov. Chittenden" and other politicos consumed in their work environment.[2] Now, in the physically weakened autumn of his life, instead of basking in the glow of his accomplishments among friends, he faced the conviction for a federal crime for his alcohol-infused gregariousness, penalized for doing what so many others did.

The question for modern students of those times is why has this information of Chittenden's stumble not been revealed until now? Why did those in positions of power and a probing press at the time, each knowing full well of his problem, fail to publicly acknowledge or report it? For answers, it is necessary to inquire into not only the context of these turbulent times, but also the extant Vermont federal court records housed at the National Archives and Records Administration in Boston pertaining to Chittenden and some of his constituency receiving similar convictions.[3]

In the process, it is worth remembering that "history records what people do, rather than what they are."[4] Reserving judgment on Chittenden's personality, these documents will, with reasonable certainty, allow us to reconstruct what happened to finally reveal a missing part of that long-ago story.

BACKGROUND

Following the end of the Revolutionary War and settling the lingering border dispute with New York, the recognition of Vermont as a state in 1791 meant the sudden introduction of federal laws and accompanying institutions into the Green Mountains, changes embraced by its inhabitants with varying degrees of enthusiasm. Foremost were those

2. Wine Account, Johnson Family Papers, Doc 574, Vermont Historical Society.

3. *United States vs. Thomas Chittenden,* RG 21.48.1, Vermont U.S. District Court, 1792-1797, Box 1, National Archives and Records Administration, Waltham, MA., *passim.*

4. *Saint Ansgar,* Franciscan Media, https://www.franciscanmedia.org/saint-of-the-day/saint-ansgar/.

provisions surrounding the collection of revenues to fund the new nation's infrastructure, assure its operations, and retire its significant debt incurred fighting the war. Accordingly, customs laws and a supervising collector and his deputies gathering fees and operating customs houses suddenly appeared across the landscape. They worked zealously to bring malefactors before newly created federal judges presiding in district and circuit courthouses in Burlington, Rutland, and Windsor. They were backed up by a US marshal and his deputies, alongside bailiffs and clerks, solidifying an all-too-real federal presence in the state.

The will of strong-minded advocates of a national government, called Federalists, overlaying this new legal system across the existing, domestic one that independent Vermonters, including Chittenden, had already become familiar with, presented its own unique challenges. Unaware of the disruptive changes awaiting them, some gathered on the eve of statehood in Rutland to celebrate. Their revels were attended by esteemed legal illuminati, including: "judges of the supreme federal court, the attorney general and other officers of the court." Then, to the sound of booming cannon, the assemblage raised their glasses in recognition of a new dawn. Making a series of rousing "federal toasts," they praised "his excellency governor Chittenden," prayed that "federal officers . . . act with integrity and merit the confidence of the people," and wished that "may we never experience a less happy moment than the present under the federal government."[5]

The timing of these events coincided precisely with those taking place only a few hundred miles away in Pennsylvania. There, violent opposition rose up against the same federal government that Vermonters welcomed. Indigent frontier settlers deeply resented the government's recent imposition of the Tariff of 1791 imposing an excise tax on the large quantities of spirits they distilled, with great difficulty, from their abundant grain crops. Their steady opposition soon escalated into the Whiskey Rebellion (1791–1794) that President George Washington was forced to send thousands of troops to quell. The response further prompted the government's prosecution of dozens of farmers for treason; an effort many viewed as heavy-handed overstepping, a trampling of the downtrodden by the powerful.

How national leaders handled the Pennsylvania problem generated significant interest in Vermont. Increasingly, after the arrival of federal personnel in 1791, the laws they enforced seemed to appear overnight. In addition to their courts, in May 1793 revenue officials established

5. *Vermont Gazette* (Bennington), February 28, 1791.

offices in each of Vermont's counties. They required their inhabitants to license every still producing spirits they operated, and assessed unwelcomed fees on each, with fines for violators.[6] These early, unpopular efforts to support the young federal government with its intrusive laws soon tested Vermonters' tolerance for them and provide an important backdrop to Governor Chittenden's own impending legal problems.

REVENUE WOES

Nobody likes to pay taxes. Vermont, of course, is endowed with an international border separating the United States from Canada, then also known as British North America. The onus of paying the customs duties for goods crossing south from Canada fell principally on local Vermont importers. While the law initially imposed only modest duties on their shipments of alcohol (i.e., five cents for a gallon of beer, ten cents for Jamaica proof spirits, eighteen cents for Madeira wine, etc.), they became more burdensome, doubling on the heels of Pennsylvania's rebellion.[7] Only days before Chittenden's breach of the law in March 1796, the Democratic Society of Rutland expressed concern about the effects these duties imposed on those living in the northwest part of the state, including in Williston where Chittenden lived. The duties were onerous, the society said, forcing honest merchant-retailers to shoulder an unfair monetary burden passed on to them by their suppliers, but which their smuggling neighbors could avoid. As a result, it placed the honest retailer in an untenable position of having to "constantly account to his customers for a higher price of his goods."[8]

Honest retailers were also required to purchase licenses from customs officials, costing $5 a year. In the government's eagerness to ease the flow of alcohol to generate needed income, the law made generous provision allowing virtually anyone to obtain a pre-signed license from Vermont's supervising collector of revenue or any of his five auxiliary officers. Then, after receiving alcohol in bulk casks from their importers or wholesalers, the licensed retailers could sell it in smaller quart and pint quantities from their licensed taverns and inns. It could be consumed either on the premises or taken away as the customer desired. Those failing to obtain the necessary license to sell faced a $50 fine and paying the costs of prosecution.

The first revenue officers in the Green Mountains did not face serious challenges to their authority in the months following statehood.

6. Ibid., May 10, 1793.
7. *Vermont Journal* (Windsor), July 29, 1789.
8. Ibid., February 29, 1796.

But on December 17, 1792, at "Bason Harbor" on the east shore of Lake Champlain, where officials stored seized casks of illegally imported spirits, the first recorded, coordinated attack against federal authorities took place. Perhaps because of its remoteness and insufficient number of officers guarding the casks, the assault marked Vermont as an outlier among its New England neighbors. None of the records of the federal courts for Connecticut, Massachusetts, New Hampshire, or Rhode Island, where a denser population lived along the Atlantic seaboard and a more robust federal presence existed, reveals a single instance of such violence against revenue officials throughout the 1790s.

In response to the attack, Vermont's new federal district court held its first "special term" convening in Burlington by order of recently-appointed Federalist judge Nathaniel Chipman. The term was commenced in May 1793 with the swearing in of a fourteen-member grand jury. Six men from Vermont and New York were quickly indicted for their roles in the attack. They were charged with violently removing two casks of spirits ("with force and arms"), containing thirty-seven gallons each, valued at $200 out of the custody of two revenue officers, and then "secreting" them from discovery.[9] Thereafter, between 1793 and 1795, the courts' records reflect a period of relative calm. In Washington, Congress passed two new laws (effective June 1794) strengthening the government's grip on alcohol-related issues, outlawing the unlicensed sale of wine and spirits, provisions that came into play in Chittenden's case.[10]

By February 1796 the escalating violence in Pennsylvania, where hundreds of rioters set fire to the regional revenue collector's home, alarmed Vermont's second federal district court judge, Federalist Samuel Hitchcock (soon to oversee Chittenden's prosecution). Hitchcock feared similar conduct in the Green Mountains, possibly even exceeding the violence that had occurred at "Bason Harbor" two years earlier. To ward off such a prospect, in welcoming a newly-empaneled grand jury in Windsor, he told it to vigorously protect the new federal government's interests by enforcing its revenue laws. Initially, he acknowledged that "Hitherto there has been but little business before this Court," attributed, he "hoped," to "the virtuous and orderly disposition

9. *U.S. v. James Fitch; Martin Van Dusen; David Callendar; Jacob Green; Philerus Brush; Joseph Poor,* RG 21.48.1, Box 1, National Archives, Boston.

10. *An Act laying duties on licenses for selling Wines and foreign distilled spiritous liquors by retail; An Act making further provision for securing and collecting Duties on foreign and domestic Spirits, Stills, Wines and Teas,* eff. June 5, 1794, Public Statutes at Large, vol. 1, chaps. XLVIII; XLIX (Boston: Charles C. Little and James Brown), 376-381.

of its citizens." But then he pragmatically acknowledged the inclinations of some of them to use the increased forms of violence seen in Pennsylvania. Wishing that "exemplary punishment" might rain down on such offenders, he urgently instructed the grand jury, with palpable concern, to "Let no character feel himself above the law" in bringing charges against them.[11]

It is not surprising, then, that between 1797 and 1799, prosecutions for the unlicensed sale of alcohol in Vermont escalated dramatically. Authorities brought forty-nine defendants before the district and circuit courts in that short period of time. While the specific number of others operating outside of the law is unknown, the name of "Thomas Chittenden, Esq.," as he is notably identified in the court's papers, ranks among the first snagged by vigilant customs officers headed by Supervising Collector Stephen Keyes (Federalist). Chittenden's alleged transgressions were then brought to the attention of newly-appointed prosecutor District Attorney Charles Marsh (Federalist) in the spring of 1797.

OFFENSES

The heavy drinking that Chittenden and his friends engaged in during the legislative session seems to have continued unabated at his home in Williston. One history describes him (in a coded manner) as someone who "enjoyed the fellowship and love of his friends and neighbors." He was "particularly noted for sociability and hospitality, his house being at all times open to the ever-welcome guest."[12] Other watering holes like the one at Chittenden's home existed throughout the county. They probably operated in the same informal manner, selling alcohol without a license. In 1796, only 49 licenses to sell wine and 187 for spirits were issued statewide, generating a measly $1,180 for the national treasury.[13] In a state notorious for its alcohol consumption, sales of wine and spirits were clearly taking place outside of those few licensed outlets servicing a population of 154,465 in 1800.[14] Records reveal that in 1801, Chittenden County officials identified 34 licensed

11. *Vermont Journal,* February 15, 1796.

12. Hamilton Child, *Gazetteer and Business Directory of Chittenden County for 1882-1883* (Syracuse: Hamilton Child, 1882), 256.

13. *American State Papers. Documents, Legislative and Executive, of the Congress of the United States, Commencing March 3, 1789, and ending March 3, 1815,* vol. 5, (Washington: Gales and Seaton, 1832), 396.

14. Gary G. Shattuck, *Green Mountain Opium Eaters: A History of Early Addiction in Vermont* (Charleston, SC, The History Press, 2017), *passim*; Return of the Whole Number of Persons Within the Several Districts of the United States, 1800, Vermont Historical Society, https://vermonthistory.org/client_media/files/Learn/Census%20Records/1800-Census.pdf.

inns operating within their bounds among the 489 doing so statewide.[15] Some obtained the necessary licenses to sell alcohol, but not all did.

There was always an undercurrent of lawlessness surrounding the enforcement of federal alcohol revenue collection efforts in these years because manpower was spread too thin around the state. Lax enforcement continued after Chittenden's misstep in 1796, leading up to 1808 when two militiamen attempting to enforce the revenue laws were killed by smugglers in an alcohol-infused ambush (the Black Snake Affair) on the Onion River downstream from his home.[16] But in 1796 Chittenden's transgressions would have been commonplace.

According to court papers, on March 1, 1796, Chittenden committed two offenses, one concerning the unlicensed sale of wine and the second involving allowing the consumption of spirits on his unlicensed premises. The quantity involved was sizeable: gen gallons of wine distributed in quart and gallon containers and two gallons each of French Brandy, West India Rum, and Holland Gin dispensed in the same manner, sixteen gallons in total. No one can say today what occasioned this well-lubricated event.

The timing of it coincides with the topsy-turvy Democratic-Republican run-off election cycle taking place between December 1795 and February 1796 for the US House in Vermont's western district that included Chittenden County. The outcome of that election was not known at the time with candidates Matthew Lyon (his son-in-law) and Israel Smith swapping leads. From the opposing political party, Federalist Judge Hitchcock's name was also in the mix, but he ultimately came up short when Lyon won out.[17]

Thereafter, the timing of events surrounding Chittenden's prosecution offers undertones of political payback, possibly related to the election results. His democratic-republican sympathies may have prompted those stern instructions made by the law-and-order Hitchcock in February to the grand jury advocating for rigid enforcement of the liquor revenue laws so that "no character" could "feel themselves above the law." Aside from the prospect of violence presented by increasingly bold smugglers and those intent on disrupting the work of revenue officers, his comments could also have been intended as a shot across the bows of Chittenden and his friends.

15. Innkeepers Licenses, 1791-1849, A123-00001, Vermont State Archives and Records Administration.

16. Gary G. Shattuck, *Insurrection, Corruption and Murder in Early Vermont: Life on the Wild Northern Frontier* (Charleston, SC, The History Press, 2014), *passim.*

17. Elections Division, Vermont Secretary of State, https://electionarchive.vermont.gov/elections/view/83330/.

PROSECUTION, CONVICTION, SENTENCE

Proceeding by "Information" (thereby bypassing the need to present evidence before a grand jury as used in similar prosecutions) and using the same boilerplate language appearing in other violators' paperwork, that pertaining to Chittenden was filed by prosecutor Marsh with Judge Hitchcock, sitting in Rutland, on May 15, 1797, more than a year after Chittenden's alleged missteps. The reason for this delay is uncertain, but we do know that the sixty-seven-year-old governor's health was already in decline at the time. In February 1797, Chittenden either wrote, or dictated, a one-page letter to his lieutenant governor, Paul Brigham, to advise that he had been confined to his home for the preceding fortnight making him unable to attend the approaching legislative session. He was suffering, he explained, from the effects of "an extraordinary cold."[18]

Perhaps acting with speed because of Chittenden's health, Judge Hitchcock immediately accepted Marsh's allegations. Just days later, on May 20, he summoned Chittenden to appear in his Windsor court "on the first Monday of August next" to attend trial. However, Deputy US Marshal Samuel Fitch did not serve the summons on Chittenden until July 21. As Fitch noted on its reverse, he did so by leaving a copy of it at "the dwelling house of the within named Thomas Chittenden, Esq." in Williston.

Despite Fitch's delay, Chittenden must have been aware of the summons beforehand. Subpoenas issued by Hitchcock on July 1 and 20 commanding the presence of several noteworthy witnesses at trial to provide testimony "in behalf of the United States" could not have escaped his knowledge. They were Chittenden's associates and friends and included: Federalist Solomon Miller, Esq. (Chittenden County justice of the peace appointed by Chittenden and probate court judge); Jonathan Spafford (Williston representative); Joshua Stanton, Jr. (attorney, Colchester town clerk and assistant county judge); and Amos Brownson (Richmond justice of the peace and former Williston representative). But did they actually appear? Did any of them testify? If so, did their testimony concern witnessing Chittenden's transgressions or were they willing participants themselves? Could politics have in-

18. Thomas Chittenden to Paul Brigham, February 13, 1797, Paul Brigham Papers, mss-940, Silver Special Collections, University of Vermont. Thanks, again, to Kevin Graffagnino for referring the author to this resource.

fluenced their testimony in any way? Were there additional witnesses whose names did not survive in the court's paperwork? There are no transcripts of the proceedings, so we do not know.

In an undated entry, and with Hitchcock's approval, attorney Daniel Buck (Federalist) made his appearance on Chittenden's behalf, entered not guilty pleas to the two counts and placed his client's fate in the hands of a jury (or, in the period vernacular, "puts himself on the country"). The experienced Buck was a Revolutionary War veteran who saw action at Bennington in 1777, where he lost an arm. The injury did not hold him back from advancement. He was involved in several pivotal moments in the state's formation, served as its second attorney general (succeeding Hitchcock) and, just two months before assuming Chittenden's representation, on March 3 ended a two-year term as Vermont's representative to the U.S. House of Representatives.

In July 1797, facing mounting pressure from his prosecution and health, Chittenden penned his only public statement about his plans not to seek continued public office. While many in Vermont's power structure at the time were aware of the charges he was facing in Hitchcock's court, they remained silent. Neither was there any press coverage of them, while Chittenden was similarly silent. As an unfortunate result, *in toto,* they allowed the letter's representations to stand alone, lacking context omitting the trial's importance thereby leaving a gaping hole in the historical record.

Despite its open-ended date of "July 1797," Chittenden's de facto resignation letter first appeared on August 4, three days before the trial commenced, in *Spooner's Vermont Journal*, published in Windsor where the trial unfolded. The letter omitted any mention of the impending trial. Neither did the newspaper's editor mention it, thereby allowing him to graciously end his many years of public service without further comment.[19] No doubt "Impaired as I am, as to my health," he wrote, it was the sole reason he identified "to decline being considered as a candidate" at the next election. Thanking his constituency for their past support, he asked them to choose someone other than himself.

Chittenden's court papers provide no direct information about the conduct of the trial itself, relating only that it occurred over the course of a single day, on August 7. A brief entry regarding the jury's verdict, signed by local storekeeper foreman Allen Hayes, states simply that it found Chittenden "guilty of the first count [selling ten gallons of wine] and not guilty of the second count [selling six gallons of spirits]."

19. *Vermont Journal,* August 4, 1797.

Whereupon, in accord with the applicable statute, Judge Hitchcock sentenced Chittenden "to pay a fine to the Treasury of the United States of Fifty Dollars and the costs of prosecution taxed at sixty one dollars and seventy nine cents."

No doubt shaken by the jury's verdict and sentence, as well as his health, Chittenden sought to excuse himself from attending any further proceedings. Accordingly, the following day Buck requested of the court that his client's "personal appearance . . . be dispensed with & he be allowed to proceed by attorney." Hitchcock granted the request. Buck then moved for a "new tryal" arguing that the jury's verdict was wrongfully imposed because it believed the law allowed the Secretary of the Treasury to remit, or negate, the finding of guilt and/or the fine. Correcting that misinformation, he explained that no such provision existed and that "the jury have mistaken the law in this case," rendering its verdict invalid. Motion denied.

Four days later, on August 12 Hitchcock ordered US Marshal Jabez Fitch to seize $111.79 of Chittenden's property to pay the fine and costs. Should Fitch be unable to find such assets, he was further "commanded to take the body of the said Thomas and him commit to the keeper of the gaol in the City of Vergennes . . . who is hereby commanded to receive the said Thomas within the said gaol and him safely keep until he pay [the penalty] with your fees, or otherwise be discharged by order of Law."

It soon became impossible for Fitch to fulfill the order because Chittenden died quietly in his sleep on August 24 or 25 (inconsistent dates are cited).[20] Marking the document "wholle unsatisfied" on September 13, Fitch wrote that "before I had time . . . [to execute it] Thomas Chittenden departed this life."

CONCLUSION

Thomas Chittenden is the only governor in Vermont's history to be convicted of a crime committed while in office. Those unsettled first years of statehood brought myriad newfound challenges for many: new federal laws, new federal institutions, and uncertain enforcement mechanisms creating a legal landscape difficult to navigate. The changes affected even those with the best intentions, regardless of rank or position, including himself. It may be that Chittenden was specially targeted for prosecution by those with federalist intentions (i.e., Judge Hitchcock, Collector Keyes, and District Attorney Marsh) because of

20. Ibid., September 22, 1797.

his democratic-republican leanings. Were they fearful that if he went unpunished, violence against revenue officials would increase as it had in Pennsylvania? If he was meant to serve as an example to other licensing scoff-laws, then why was information about his offense suppressed? Could the federalists have realized, too late, that they had overplayed their hand against an accommodating elder statesman held in high regard and in a weakened state commanding sympathy instead? Or was Chittenden simply caught up, like his neighbors, in their frenzy committing seemingly inconsequential violations of the revenue laws marking this important man as undeserving of public condemnation? The current evidence is silent on all points.

When he was housebound with illness in February 1797, unable to attend the upcoming legislative session, Chittenden temporarily passed the baton to Lieutenant Governor Brigham: "You will therefore of course," he counseled, "take my place, put on the fortitude of a man and conduct the business to the best advantage in your body."[21] He recovered only briefly after that, turning to face his tormentors in his last days. Then, after experiencing the indignity of having his reputation besmirched by a jury of his peers, his body quietly gave out. Choosing to ignore the circumstances of that last, sad chapter in his life, the press respectfully announced his passing, ending with praise: "Superior to a PRINCE—A GREAT MAN here has fallen."[22]

21. Chittenden to Brigham, February 13, 1797.
22. *Vermont Journal,* September 22, 1797.

The Great Pillars of John Adams

GEOFF SMOCK

It is in those first frenzied moments of war fever when declarations of patriotism are their most ardent. So it was for the "Young Men of the City of Philadelphia" in the spring of 1798, when the United States stood within a hair's breadth of war with France.

These young Americans, "anxious to preserve the honor & independence of their Country," begged leave to assure President John Adams that "filled with a spirt of friendship towards the whole world" as he was, he could rest assured that he had employed "every just & honorable means of conciliating the friendship of the French Republic," who in the opposite spirit had responded to his entreaties with a "determined hostility and contempt."

Adams could also be confident that "The Youth of the American Nation" would eagerly share in the "danger difficulty and glory of its defence," acting on "every occasion" with all they were capable of, to which they pledged themselves to their president, "to our country, and to the World."[1]

"Nothing of the kind could be more welcome to me than this address," Adams wrote in reply. "For a long course of years, I was called to act with your fathers in concerting measures the most disagreeable and dangerous," all for the sole purpose of preserving "the honor of our country" and to "vindicate the immemorial liberties of our ancestors."

Deeply grateful and, at the same time, loathe to lecture young men as noble and learned as they, Adams nevertheless begged leave to be "indulged the privilege of a father" in recommending to their "serious and constant consideration, that science and morals are the great pillars on which this country has been raised to its present population, opu-

1. Young Men of Philadelphia to John Adams, May 7, 1798, https://founders.archives.gov/documents/Adams/99-02-02-2449.

lence, and prosperity, and that these alone can advance, support, and preserve it."[2]

Just over fifteen years later, Adams made this address and his reply the main subject of one of his letters to Thomas Jefferson in their renewed correspondence.

Beneath the joy he felt at its resumption, and in spite of the enduring feelings of tenderness and affection he felt towards his former colleague, the second president still seethed at the treatment he had received from his successor and allies. Adams was determined to defend himself—to assure Jefferson that he was as much a proponent and believer in American liberty as he had been since those heady days when they had worked together to declare American independence.

He also knew that he and Jefferson were writing not just to each other, but to future generations, and he was just as interested in defending himself to them as he was to the proprietor of Monticello. To that audience, Adams expressed the hope that they would first "hunt up" that Address from the Young Men of Philadelphia, read it in its entirety, and return to the present epistle.

"Who composed that Army of fine young Fellows that was then before my Eyes?" Adams asked. They all had come from different religious sects, he answered, some of them Roman Catholics, some "Anababtists," some "Priestleyans," still others "Horse Protestants and House Protestants," and so forth. Very few of them adhered to the same sect, yet all of them were "Educated in the *general principles* of Christianity: and the general Principles of English and American Liberty." It was these "*general principles*" upon which Adams, Jefferson, and the rest had achieved independence, and they "were the only Principles in which that beautiful Assembly of young Gentlemen could Unite."

Adams then avowed that he long believed, "and now believe, that those general Principles of Christianity, are as eternal and immutable, as the Existence and Attributes of God; and that those Principles of Liberty, are as unalterable as human Nature and our terrestrial, mundane System."

Adams declined the opportunity to expand on what, in his own mind, these general principles of Christianity and English-American liberty were. Perhaps he was wary of boring his audience: "This letter is already too long."[3]

2. Adams to Young Men of Philadelphia, May 7, 1798, https://founders.archives.gov/documents/Adams/99-02-02-2450.
3. Adams to Thomas Jefferson; June 28 1813, in Gordon S. Wood, ed., *John Adams: Writings from the New Nation, 1784-1826* (New York: The Library of America, 2016), 554-555.

Or perhaps, in his seventy-eighth year, he was tired of repeating himself, for these "great pillars" of the "general principles" of Christianity and English and American Liberty were among the very first topics he had speculated upon through his pen—topics he had discussed, with others and with himself, decades before in letters, his diary, and public pamphlets.

It had been in his early twenties while working as a schoolmaster in Worcester, Massachusetts—bored, lonely, and unsettled—that he first set out against sectarian Christianity in favor of the general principles thereof. "The Church of Rome has made it an Article of Faith," he declared, "that no man can be saved out of their Church, and all other religious Sects approach to this dreadfull opinion in proportion to their Ignorance, and the Influence of ignorant or wicked priests."

Two days later he returned to this idea:

> Where do we find a praecept in the Gospell, requiring Ecclesiastical Synods, Convocations, Councils, Decrees, Creeds, Conffessions, Oaths, Subscriptions and whole Cartloads of other trumpery, that we find Religion incumbered with in these days?

Having summarily dismissed the pretensions of any one denomination's claims to doctrinal truth, four days later he enunciated the essence of Christianity he adhered to and that would constitute the general principles he believed served as the pillar to American independence and prosperity:

> Suppos a nation in some distant Region, should take the Bible for their only law Book, and every member should regulate his conduct by the precepts there exhibited. Every member would be obliged in Concience to temperance and frugality and industry, to justice and kindness and Charity towards his fellow men, and to piety and Love, and reverence towards almighty God.

In this idealized "commonwealth," the common human vices—"gluttony, drunkenness, or lust," card games and other "trifling and mean" amusements—would be absent; and the citizens thereof would "live in peace and goodwill with all men."

"What a Utopia; what a Paradise would this region be!"[4]

Adams, even in the flower of his youth, was far too much the skeptic of human nature to believe such a heavenly idyll was remotely possible here on earth. Yet it was the pursuit of a near-enough facsimile, in

4. John Adams, "Diary and Autobiography," in John Patrick Diggins, ed., *The Portable John Adams* (New York, NY: Penguin Books, 2004), 2-3.

Adams' somewhat mythologized understanding at least, upon which the peopling of America by European colonists had taken place over a century before. Then "a few people came over into this new world for Concience sake."[5]

Edified by a growing knowledge of the universe those first Pilgrims had lived in, Adams would write, but laboring still under the "canon and feudal laws" that had shackled Europeans for centuries, "a struggle between the people and the confederacy . . . of temporal and spiritual tyranny" had become "formidable, violent and bloody."

This "great struggle" had peopled America. "It was not religion *alone*, as is commonly supposed, but it was a love of *universal Liberty*" that had, at long last, resolved Adams' Puritan forebearers to "fly to the wilderness for refuge."[6]

Though Adams had no love to lose for the theological pretensions or zealotry of his Puritan forebearers ("Religious to some degree of enthusiasm it may be admitted they were"), it was not upon this ground that they should be deplored by his generation, if for no other reason than "because it was at that time almost the universal character, not only of England, but of Christendom."

Instead they should be honored, for the principles they had risked their lives venturing into an unknown wilderness for were the ones Adams' generation of Americans were defending in their disputes with Parliament:

> Their greatest concern seems to have been to establish a government of the church more consistent with the scriptures, and a government of the state more agreable to the dignity of humane nature, than any they had seen in Europe: and to transmit such a government down to their posterity, with the means of securing and preserving it, for ever.[7]

Not only an exegesis of the Puritans' mission over a century before, it was one of the first expressions of the "great pillars" Adams mentioned in his letter to the Young Men of Philadelphia over thirty years later—and then expanded upon further fifteen years after that in his letter to Jefferson.

The search for, and establishment of, religious and political liberty centered around a fundamental agreement on the basic principles thereof, regardless of differences in doctrines and creed, was the essence of America. As historian John Ferling writes:

5. "To Nathan Webb," in Wood, ed., *Writings from the New Nation*, 3.
6. "A Dissertation on the Canon and the Feudal Law No. I," ibid., 117.
7. "A Dissertation on the Canon and the Fedual Law No. II," ibid., 118-119.

> A native-born American whose Massachusetts ancestry went back nearly a century, Adams looked upon his America as a revolutionary enterprise. Here, his Puritan ancestors had gained religious freedom. Here, government based on the consent of the governed had achieved a status unimaginable in England. Here, not only his ancestors but he too had enjoyed the opportunity to rise above his birthright. This was the American Revolution of which he spoke.[8]

In his later years, Adams would routinely tackle the question, "But what do we mean by the American Revolution?" In his mind, the "Revolution was in the Minds and Hearts of the People," beginning with a change "in their religious Sentiments of their Duties and Obligations." From there the "habitual Affection for England as their Mother Country" was altered in their finding Great Britain to be "a cruel Bedlam willing, like Lady MacBeth, to 'dash their Brains out.'" Having so found, "it is no wonder their filial Affections ceased and were changed into Indignation and horror."

From there, one of the most amazing feats in world history had been achieved by his generation:

> The Colonies had grown up under Constitutions of Government so different, there was so great a Variety of Religions, they were composed of so many different Nations, their Customs, Manners and Habits had so little resemblance, and their Intercourse had been so rare and their Knowledge of each other so imperfect, that to unite them in the same Principles in Theory and the same System of Action was certainly a very difficult Enterprise. The compleat Accomplishment of it, in so short a time and by such simple means, was perhaps a singular Example in the History of Mankind. Thirteen Clocks were made to strike together; a perfection of Mechanism which no Artist had ever before effected.[9]

As he had told the Young Men of Philadelphia as president, and then Jefferson and posterity as retired statesman, those thirteen clocks had been made to strike as one because, at the risk of cruelly mangling metaphors, they had all stood upon the "Great Pillars" of the "*general principles* of Christianity: and the general Principles of English and American Liberty."

To John Adams, these "Great Pillars" were what put the *unum* in the United States' *e pluribus*.

And what made the United States indivisible.

8. John Ferling, *John Adams: A Life* (New York: Oxford University Press, 2010), 154.
9. "To Hezekiah Niles," in Wood, ed., *Writings from the New Nation*, 629-630.

Constitutions and the Rule of Law: Ten American Voices from the Founding Period

JETT B. CONNER

The idea that no one is above the law is a long-held and repeated precept of American constitutionalism. Its roots go back to the philosophical and historical foundations of western political thought. Holding a prominent place in this history is the thirteenth-century English Magna Carta. Although it does not explicitly use the phrase, the document—a 1297 copy of which is on display in the Rotunda for the Charters of Freedom at the National Archives Museum in Washington, D.C.—is often cited for codifying limits to a king's exercise of powers. As the following ten quotes show, Americans were keenly aware of the principle and the necessity of enshrining it in republican charters. Original spelling and grammar as cited have been retained.

1. John Adams
"There is no good government but what is Republican . . . the very definition of a Republic, is an Empire of Laws, and not of men."[1]

2. George Mason
"All power of suspending laws, or the execution of laws, by any authority, without consent of the representatives of the people, is injurious to their rights and ought not to be exercised."[2]

1. Jett B. Conner, *John Adams vs Thomas Paine: Rival Plans for the Early Republic* (Yardley, PA: Westholme, 2018), 32.
2. George Mason, *Virginia Declaration of Rights*, Article 7, 1776, https://constitutioncenter.org/education/classroom-resource-library/classroom/5.3-primary-source-and-activity-guide-virginia-declaration-of-rights-and-the-bill-of-rights.

3. James Madison

"If men were angels, no government would be necessary. In framing a government which is to be administered by men over men, the great difficulty lies in this: you must first enable the government to control the governed; and in the next place oblige it to control itself. A dependence on the people is no doubt the primary control of the government; but experience has taught the necessity of auxiliary precautions."[3]

4. Benjamin Franklin

"I agree to this Constitution with all its faults, if they are such; because I think a general Government necessary for us, and there is no form of Government but what may be a blessing to the people if well administered, and believe farther that this is likely to be well administered for a course of years, and can only end in Despotism, as other forms have done before it, when the people shall become so corrupted as to need despotic Government, being incapable of any other. I doubt too whether any other Convention we can obtain, may be able to make a better Constitution."[4]

5. Thomas Paine

"But where, say some, is the king of America? I'll tell you, friend, he reigns above, and doth not make havoc of mankind like the royal brute of Great Britain. Yet that we may not appear to be defective even in earthly honors, let a day be solemnly set apart for proclaiming the charter; let it be brought forth placed on the divine law, the Word of God; let a crown be placed thereon, by which the world may know, that so far as we approve of monarchy, that in America the law is king."[5]

6. Abigail Adams

"I long to hear that you have declared an independency—and by the way in the new Code of Laws which I suppose it will be necessary for you to make I desire you would Remember the Ladies, and be more generous and favourable to them than your ancestors. Do not put such unlimited power into the hands of the Husbands. Remember all Men would be tyrants if they could. If perticuliar care and attention is not paid to the Laidies we are determined to foment a Rebelion, and will

3. Garry Wills, ed., *The Federalist Papers by Alexander Hamilton, James Madison and John Jay* (New York: Bantam Books, 1982), 262.

4. Rob Crotty, "What Franklin Thought of the Constitution," https://prologue.blogs.archives.gov/2010/09/17/what-franklin-thought-of-the-constitution/.

5. Thomas Paine, *The Complete Writings of Thomas Paine*, 2 vols., ed. Philip S. Foner (New York: Citadel Press, 1969), 1:29.

not hold ourselves bound by any Laws in which we have no voice, or Representation."[6]

7. Alexander Hamilton

"A constitution is in fact, and must be, regarded by the judges as a fundamental law. It therefore belongs to them to ascertain its meaning as well as the meaning of any particular act proceeding from the legislative body. If there should happen to be an irreconcilable variance between the two, that which has the superior obligation and validity ought of course to be preferred; or, in other words, the constitution ought to be preferred to the statute, the intention of the people to the intention of their agents."[7]

8. William Lenoir (Antifederalist)

"The president may be as good a man as any in existence, but he is but a man. He may be corrupt. He has an opportunity of forming plans dangerous to the community at large. I shall not enter into the minutiae of this system [the Constitution], but I conceive that whatever may have been the intention of its framers, that it leads to the most dangerous aristocracy."[8]

9. Thomas Jefferson

"The executive in our governments is not the sole, it is scarcely the principal object of my jealousy. The tyranny of the legislatures is the most formidable dread at present, and will be for long years. That of the executive will come in it's turn, but it will be at a remote period. I know there are some among us who would now establish a monarchy. But they are inconsiderable in number and weight of character. The rising race are all republicans. We were educated in royalism: no wonder if some of us retain that idolatry still. Our young people are educated in republicanism. An apostacy from that to royalism is unprecedented and impossible. I am much pleased with the prospect that a declaration of rights [Bill of Rights] will be added [to the Constitution]: and hope it will be done in that way which will not endanger the whole frame of the government, or any essential part of it."[9]

6. Abigail Adams to John Adams, March 31 - April 5, 1776, *Adams Family Papers: An Electronic Archive*, Massachusetts Historical Society, https://www.masshist.org/digitaladams/.
7. Wills, *The Federalist* Papers, 395.
8. Alpheus Thomas Mason and Gordon E. Baker, *Free Government in the Making, 4th ed.* (New York: Oxford University Press, 1985), 244.
9. Ibid., 290.

10. George Washington

"The basis of our political systems is the right of the people to make and to alter their constitutions of government. But the Constitution which at any time exists, till changed by an explicit and authentic act of the whole people, is sacredly obligatory upon all. The very idea of the power and the right of the people to establish government presupposes the duty of every individual to obey the established government. All obstructions to the execution of the laws, all combinations and associations, under whatever plausible character, with the real design to direct, control, counteract, or awe the regular deliberation and action of the constituted authorities, are destructive of this fundamental principle, and of fatal tendency."[10]

10. George Washington, "Farewell Address, 1796," https://constitutioncenter.org/the-constitution/historic-document-library/detail/george-washington-farewell-address-1796.

AUTHOR BIOGRAPHIES

Tim Abbott has presented his research at the Shays Rebellion Symposium in Springfield, Massachusetts, and before numerous historical societies. His paper documenting the route and encampments of the Convention Army in Connecticut is housed in the collections of the David Center of the American Revolution at the American Philosophical Society in Philadelphia. His first book, *Additionals: Spencer's Regiment and the American Revolution*, has been accepted for peer review with an academic press. He lives in North Canaan, Connecticut.

Salina B. Baker is a multiple award-winning historical fiction author, presenter, and historian of the American Revolution. Her latest published work is a biographical novel about Major General Nathanael Greene titled *The Line of Splendor, A Novel of Nathanael Greene and the American Revolution.* She has done presentations about General Greene at events such as History Camp Boston and Valley Forge, Washington Crossing State Historical Park, the General Nathanael Greene Homestead, Cowpens National Battlefield, Camden Revolutionary War Visitor Center, and chapters of the Sons of the American Revolution/Daughters of the American Revolution. She has also been interviewed on podcasts including Revolution 250, American Revolution Podcast, and Emerging Revolutionary War. In addition, she is currently writing a biographical novel about Dr. Joseph Warren titled *Act Worthy of Yourselves.* Salina lives in Austin, Texas, with her husband, John.

J. L. Bell is the author of *The Road to Concord: How Four Stolen Cannon Ignited the Revolutionary War* (Westholme, 2016). He maintains the Boston1775.net website, dedicated to history, analysis, and unabashed gossip about the start of the American Revolution in New England.

His other historical writing includes *Gen. George Washington's Home and Headquarters—Cambridge, Massachusetts*, a comprehensive study for the National Park Service, and contributions to *Reporting the Revolutionary War* (Sourcebooks, 2012), James Marten's *Children in Colonial America* (New York University Press, 2007), and many journals and magazines. He has been elected a fellow of the Massachusetts Historical Society, a member of the American Antiquarian Society, a member of the Colonial Society of Massachusetts, and a trustee of the Dublin Seminar for New England Folklife.

Todd Braisted is an author and researcher of Loyalist military studies. His primary focus is on Loyalist military personnel, infrastructure and campaigns throughout North America. Since 1979, Braisted has amassed and transcribed over 45,000 pages of Loyalist and related material from archives and private collections around the world. He is author of *Grand Forage: The Battleground Around New York City, 1778* (Westholme, 2016), as well as numerous journal articles and other publications. He has also been a guest historian on episodes of "Who Do You Think You Are?" and "History Detectives." He is the creator of royalprovincial.com, the largest website dedicated to Loyalist military studies. Braisted is a Fellow in the Company of Military Historians and serves on the RevolutionNJ Advisory Council.

William Caldwell is an American Revolution historian based in the western Carolinas. His focus is the second half of the eighteenth century in the western districts of the southern American colonies. He is a graduate of North Greenville University and Clemson University, and has worked with various agencies to share history, including the National Park Service.

Jack Campbell has a degree in history from Manhattan College. He is a native of New York State, and has a lifelong interest in history, especially the American Revolution. Particularly enjoying biography, Jack also enjoys Presidential history, U.S. military history, including World War II, baseball history, and some Irish history. In his free time, he enjoys baseball, specifically his New York Mets, watching movies, reading, and doing historical research.

Jett B. Conner is a retired political science professor, college administrator, and academic policy officer for the Colorado Department of Higher Education. He studied the political thought of the American founding period during a National Endowment for the Humanities summer fellowship at Princeton University, and is author of *John Adams vs Thomas Paine: Rival Plans for the Early Republic* (Westholme, 2018). He lives in Denver where he pursues numerous interests, including travel, wildlife watching, and reading and writing about the history and political thought of the American Revolution.

Douglas R. Dorney, Jr. is a licensed architect specializing in Higher Education, Science, and Technology projects. When not designing buildings, he is researching the Revolutionary War in the Carolinas. He lives in Chapel Hill, North Carolina. For links to his other publications and research interests visit revwarcarolinas.blogspot.com.

Katie Turner Getty is a Revolutionary War researcher, writer, and speaker who explores exciting aspects of the American Revolution and posts her historical action-adventures on YouTube. She also writes for various history publications. Katie is based in historic Boston and loves sharing her passion for history with audiences. For more about Katie, visit www.katieturnergetty.com.

Don N. Hagist, managing editor of *Journal of the American Revolution*, is an independent researcher specializing in the demographics and material culture of the British Army in the American Revolution. He was a consultant on the PBS *American Revolution* series and has published a number of articles in academic journals. His books include *The Revolution's Last Men: the Soldiers Behind the Photographs* (Westholme, 2015), *Noble Volunteers: the British Soldiers who Fought the American Revolution* (Westholme, 2020), and *These Distinguished Corps: British Grenadier and Light Infantry Battalions in the American Revolution* (Helion, 2022). Don works as an engineer in Rhode Island, and also writes for several well-known syndicated and freelance cartoonists.

Phillip Hamilton is the author of a number of books and journal articles dealing with America's founding era, including *The Making and Unmaking of a Revolutionary Family: The Tuckers of Virginia, 1752–1830* (University of Virginia Press, 2003) and *The Revolutionary War Lives and Letters of Lucy and Henry Knox* (Johns Hopkins University Press, 2017). He is a professor of history at Christopher Newport University in Newport News, Virginia, where he teaches courses on the American Revolution, the Early Republic, and the Age of Jackson. He is currently writing a biography of General Henry Knox.

Derrick E. Lapp, a former US Army officer, holds a BA in history from the Virginia Military Institute and an MA in historical studies from the University of Maryland, Baltimore County. His work has been published in *Journal of Military History* and *U.S. Military History Review.*

Jane Lancaster earned a PhD in history from Brown University. In an eclectic publishing career she wrote *Making Time*, a prizewinning biography of efficiency engineer Lillian Moller Gilbreth, subtitled *Wasn't She the Mother in Cheaper by the Dozen?*, followed by a history of the Providence Athenaeum, *Inquire Within*, one on Emily Post's 1916 cross-country journey, *By Motor to the Golden Gate*, and then co-authored a book on the Providence Marine Corps of Artillery. Her current work involves Black Loyalists and their role in American, British, and colonial history. She was born in England and has lived in Providence, Rhode Island, since the 1980s.

Joseph Manca received his PhD from Columbia University, and since 1989 has taught at Rice University, where he is the Nina J. Cullinan Professor of Art and Art History. His teaching and research focus on American art and architecture and on European art from 1300 to 1900. His book *George Washington's Eye: Landscape, Architecture, and Design at Mount Vernon* (Johns Hopkins University Press, 2012) was awarded the John Brinckerhoff Jackson Book Prize for 2014, which is given out by the Foundation for Landscape Studies. He is also author of *Shaker Vision: Seeing Beauty in Early America* (University of Massachusetts Press, 2019) and the forthcoming *Virtue in the Garden: Writing about Designed Landscape in Britain* (Harvey Miller Publishers).

Shawn David McGhee (PhD, Temple University) is author of *No Longer Subjects of the British King: The Political Transformation of Royal Subjects to Republican Citizens, 1774-1776*. (Westholme, 2024). His main areas of interest include the politics of eighteenth-century British North America, the Early National Period, and political identity formation. He is an educator in the Philadelphia metropolitan area and adjunct professor of history at Moore College of Art and Design. He lives in New Jersey with his wife and children.

David Otersen is a history enthusiast with a particular interest in Constitutional Law. He studied at the University of Maryland, where he majored in Government and Politics and earned Dean's List distinctions.

Jim Piecuch earned his BA and MA degrees in history at the University of New Hampshire and his PhD at the College of William and Mary. He is a former history professor and has written many articles on colonial and Revolutionary history. He is also the author of a number of books, including *The Battle of Camden: A Documentary History* (History Press, 2006), *Three Peoples, One King: Loyalists, Indians, and Slaves in the Revolutionary South* (University of South Carolina Press, 2008), *Cavalry of the American Revolution* (Westholme, 2012), *General Nathanael Greene and the American Revolution in the South*, co-authored with Gregory Massey (University of South Carolina Press, 2012), and *South Carolina Provincials: Loyalists in British Service During the American Revolution* (Westholme, 2023).

Gene Procknow earned a masters in American history from Norwich University. His research includes interpreting "the politics of command" among the Continental Army major generals and Ethan Allen and the creation of Vermont. He is the author of *William Hunter, Finding Free Speech: The Son of a British Soldier Who Became an Early American* (Sunbury Press, 2022) and the *Mad River Gazetteer*, which traces the naming of prominent Vermont place names after Revolutionary War patriots. Procknow's website, Researching the American Revolution, aids students and researchers. He is married with two historian sons and lives in Washington, DC.

Ray Raphael has authored many books on the Founding Era, including *A People's History of the American Revolution* (Harper Perennial, 2002), *The First American Revolution: Before Lexington and Concord* (New Press, 2002), *Founding Myths* (New Press, 2004), *Founders: The People Who Brought You a Nation* (New Press, 2009), *The Complete Idiot's Guide to the Founding Fathers and the Birth of Our Nation* (Alpha Books/Penguin, 2011), *Revolutionary Founders: Rebels, Radicals, and Reformers in the Making of the Nation* (co-edited with Alfred F. Young and Gary B. Nash, Alfred A. Knopf, 2011), *Mr. President: How and Why the Founders Created a Chief Executive* (Alfred A. Knopf, 2012), *Constitutional Myths* (New Press, 2013), *The Spirit of '74: How the American Revolution Began* (co-authored with Marie Raphael, New Press, 2015), *Hamilton: Founding Father* (co-authored with Marie Raphael, Fall River Press, 2017), *U.S. Constitution: Explained—Clause-by-Clause—for Every American Today* (Knopf-Doubleday, 2017). A complete list of his books and articles, as well as some key historical documents not published elsewhere, can be found at rayraphael.com.

Tyson Reeder is assistant professor of history at Brigham Young University. He is the author of *Smugglers, Pirates, and Patriots: Free Trade in the Age of Revolution* (University of Pennsylvania Press, 2019) and *Serpent in Eden: Foreign Meddling and Partisan Politics in James Madison's America* (Oxford University Press, 2024).

Anthony Roney II is a master's graduate from the Paris Lodron University of Salzburg in Austria, where he studied political science with a focus on international relations and comparative politics. He received his bachelor's degree in history and political science from the University of Alabama at Birmingham. His research interests include interstate conflict, Eastern European and Balkan affairs, insurgencies, and military history. Anthony is also passionate about the American Revolutionary era, particularly the Southern and Gulf Coast theaters, Native American relations, and international relations of the burgeoning United States. He has been published in the *Journal of Advanced Military Studies*.

Gary G. Shattuck is a New Hampshire native who graduated from the University of Colorado, the Vermont Law School, and the American Military University. He served more than three decades in law enforcement as a deputy sheriff in Boulder, Colorado, a patrol commander with the Vermont State Police, and as an assistant Attorney General prosecuting Vermont Drug Task Force cases. Gary went on to become an assistant United States attorney with the U. S. Department of Justice where he served as an organized crime prosecutor, as Vermont's antiterrorism coordinator, and then overseas as a legal advisor to governments in Kosovo and Iraq. He has received many awards for his work, including from U.S. Attorney General Alberto Gonzales for his efforts in Iraq standing up that country's legal system after the invasion of 2003. Since leaving government service, Gary has written six books and many articles on early Vermont history.

Geoff Smock is a native of Western Washington and is a lifelong student of the American Revolution. He received a degree in history from Pacific Lutheran University and a M.Ed from the University of Washington. He currently teaches middle school social studies outside of Seattle.

Scott Syfert is a corporate attorney at Moore & Van Allen in Charlotte, North Carolina. He is a graduate of the University of North Carolina, the London School of Economics, and the University of Virginia. He is also co-founder of the May 20th Society, a non-profit dedicated to commemorating the Mecklenburg Declaration of Independence. He writes frequently on local North Carolina history and politics. He is author of *The First Declaration of Independence? The Disputed History of the Mecklenburg Declaration of Independence of May 20, 1775* (McFarland & Co, 2013).

Philip D. Weaver is an author, presenter, independent researcher, and renowned tailor, and has been an active living historian for fifty years. Phil's articles on the colonial period and living history were first published nationally in 1979. An original member of the West Point Chapter, Company of Military Historians, he was elected a Fellow of the Company in 2004. His most recent book *The 3rd New Jersey in New-York: Stories from "The Jersey Greys" of 1776* was published in 2020.

Selden West is a retired US history teacher. She lives with her husband, dogs, and assorted livestock on a farm in the High Peaks of the Adirondacks. Her special interest is the Revolutionary War in southwestern Connecticut and Long Island Sound.

Colin J. Wood earned a BA from Liberty University and is currently a graduate history student at the University of Chicago. He is the co-founder and lead intern of the Redbank Valley Historical Research Project (RVHRP), an annual summer research internship for students of history to gain valuable experience in the historical process by looking at the town of New Bethlehem, Pennsylvania. His area of interests, broadly construed, are in American history, giving special attention to the interactions between economic, social, and religious history.

Michael M. Wood inherited a group of eighteenth-century family letters in 1987 and has been actively researching, writing, and sharing family history ever since. His works include the two volume *Legacy, a Family History and Genealogical Record* (2001), *Fifteen Generations of the Wood Family* (2008), *Jonathan Wood (1747–1820) of Little Compton, Rhode Island and Dutchess County, New York* (NEHGS, 2009), *The Farrow Family of Virginia* (2010), and *Colonel William L. Farrow—Pioneer, Soldier, Statesman* (2011). Michael currently lives with his wife and two children in Munich, Germany.

Daniel L. Wright is a graduate student in the Gettysburg College, Gilder Lehrman MA in American History Program. He has recently published an anthology on 1920s America entitled, "Salient Cal's

America: Reappraising the Harding & Coolidge Era." He is also working on a full-length biography of Judge Genevieve Cline, the first woman in the federal judiciary. He has maintained a blog called The Importance of the Obvious since 2013. A full-time 6th grade teacher at a classical academy in Florida and an avid enthusiast for teaching in historic garb, Mr. Wright's passion to impart a love for history is evident to all his students.

INDEX